Deformed Discourse
The Function of the Monster in Mediaeval Thought
and Literature

In *Deformed Discourse*, David Williams explores the concept of the monster in the Middle Ages, examining its philosophical and theological roots and analysing its symbolic function in mediaeval literature and art.

Part I traces the poetics of teratology, or the study of monsters, to Christian neoplatonic theology and philosophy, particularly Pseudo-Dionysius's negative theology and his central idea that God cannot be known except by knowing what he is not. Williams argues that the principles of negative theology concerning epistemology and language made possible a symbolism of negation and paradox whose chief sign was the monster. Part II provides a taxonomy of monstrous forms with a gloss on each, and Part III examines the monstrous and the deformed in three heroic sagas – the mediaeval *Oedipus*, *The Romance of Alexander*, and *Sir Gawain and the Green Knight* – and three saint's lives – Saint Denis, Saint Christopher, and Saint Wilgeforte. The book is beautifully illustrated with mediaeval representations of monsters.

The most comprehensive study of the grotesque in mediaeval aesthetic expression, *Deformed Discourse* successfully brings together mediaeval research and modern criticism.

DAVID WILLIAMS is professor of English, McGill University.

Seraph with two Ophanim. Bronze mirror

Deformed Discourse

The Function of the Monster in Mediaeval Thought and Literature

DAVID WILLIAMS

UNIVERSITY
of
EXETER
PRESS

First published in Great Britain in 1996 by
University of Exeter Press
Reed Hall, Streatham Drive,
Exeter, Devon, EX4 4QR, UK

© 1996 McGill-Queen's University Press

British Library Cataloguing in Publication Data
A catalogue record of this book is available from the British Library

ISBN 0 85989 541 6

Published as a co-publication between
McGill-Queen's University Press and
University of Exeter Press

Printed in the United States

Pour Adèle

Contents

Figures

Acknowledgments

I wish to thank the many colleagues who have given advice and criticism of the present work over several years, particularly Professor Antonio D'Andrea, who suggested valuable perspectives on the "allegory of the poets" and made useful suggestions about the structure of the book; I wish to thank Professor Robert Myles who, early on as my research assistant, did important scholarly investigations and read numerous versions of the manuscript. I am grateful for the expert assistance I have received throughout this work from my librarian-colleagues at McGill, especially those at McLennan, Blackader-Lauterman, and Blacker-Wood libraries. Most of all I wish to thank Christine Jolliffe who, originally as my research assistant and then as "volunteer labour," contributed enormously to this work. A special thanks to M.sa Crispolti-Parisi for her endless hospitality, which made possible my research in the Vatican Library.

Despite all this generous help, whatever errors and infelicities remain, they are my own.

The research for this book has been generously supported by grants from the Faculty of Graduate Studies and the Faculty of Arts of McGill University.

Abbreviations

Deformed Discourse

Grunewald, The temptation of St Anthony. Retable, Isenheim (Colmar)

Introduction

"But since Substance is one, why are Forms so various?" asks the hermit in Flaubert's *Temptation of Saint Anthony* and continues, "There must be, somewhere, primordial figures whose bodies are nothing but their image. If one could see them one would discover the link between matter and thought, what Being consists of!"[1]

In this, the last episode of the work, Saint Anthony's desire is answered by the appearance of the monsters. The question of the relation between monstrosity and being and its representation constitute the subject of the present discussion, which concentrates, as did Flaubert, on the mediaeval origins of this relationship. The nineteenth-century French author, inspired by Breughel's painting of the temptation of Saint Anthony, prepared himself for the writing of his novel through meticulous research into mediaeval teratological treatises and seems to have arrived at a genuine comprehension of the mediaeval concept of the monstrous as a deformation necessary for human understanding.[2]

Although some mediaeval uses of the monstrous amount to little more than decorative or rhetorical excercises and sometimes serve a rather arid didacticism, the deformed functioned more often as a complementary, sometimes alternative, vehicle for philosophical and spiritual inquiry during this most intellectually speculative period of Western civilization. Unlike an earlier period in which the monster was conceived as omen and magical sign, the Middle Ages made deformity into a symbolic tool with which it probed the secrets of substance, existence, and form incompletely revealed by the more orthodox rational approach through dialectics.

For the present purpose of delineating the significance of monstrosity in mediaeval thought, the philosophical corpus of Pseudo-Dionysius assumes a primary and distinct importance. The deformed discourse, as I have called it, finds its original conceptual basis in the pre-Christian tradition of philosophical negation which, in turn, finds its mediaeval expression in Dionysian negative theology, an intellectual system of vast influence throughout Christian history, but especially influential in the period from the eighth through the fourteenth century. The Neoplatonic roots of this tradition are evident throughout the Middle Ages, nowhere more obviously than in the theories of symbolism and representation articulated within Christian Neoplatonism, which valorized the grotesque and monstrous. The more unwonted and bizarre the sign, it was thought, the less likely was the beholder to equate it with the reality it represented. In the highest representative operation of all, that of signifying God, a purification of the naturally anthropomorphic human mind was necessary and could be accomplished through the negation of every possible affirmation about God. After this process of affirming and negating, the mind, encountering a reality beyond affirmation and negation, a reality which *is-not*, finally knows God as paradox: the One who is source of the many, beyond being yet cause of being, present everywhere within the world while totally transcendent. The most suitable representation of such a being is likewise that which is-not, achieved, according to Pseudo-Dionysius, by resorting to the most inordinate, absurd, and monstrous images. Thus the grotesque enables the "divinization" of human intelligence by initiating a negation of all affirmative names: "The radical critique and rejection by the intelligence of each of the names that are more or less accessible to it indicate definite steps forward of this same intelligence in the direction of its own divinization. Paradoxically, then, the divinization of the intelligence is dependent on this same intelligence renouncing its own output, its order of thought, and, more radically, its own self."[3]

This perception, while primarily theological, found expression in various contexts. Concepts such as paradox, negation, contrariety, nonlimitation, and related ideas were as attractive and useful in aesthetic speculation as they were in metaphysics, and the basic concept of nonbeing found symbolic representation in the monsters and misshapen fantasies of mediaeval art and poetry. Like the deformations used in the philosophical and theological discourses, aesthetic deformations also propose a fundamental critique of rational discourse.

Such a critique is created through a certain dismantling of rational and logical concepts in which conventional signs of these concepts are deformed in ways intolerable to logic so as to "show forth" (*monstrare*, as distinguished from *(re)praesentare*). Thus the etymological origin of the monster contains within it its intellectual kinship to heuristic understanding. Whereas the rational concept of time insists upon the separate and discrete realities of past, present, and future, the monstrous Cerberus with his three heads, each representing one of the modes of time, united in the body of a single being, transcends these exclusionary categories imposed by logic. Geoffrey Galt Harpham, emphasizing the connection between the deformation of time and the deformation of being, shows that to create the grotesque, one need only "attach a creature to another phase of its own being, with the intervening temporal gap so great that it appears that species boundaries, and not mere time, has been overleaped."[4] While strict analogies between grotesque configurations and topical intellectual concerns cannot and, perhaps, should not be drawn, monstrous significations in the Middle Ages are often clearly enough related to philosophical and theoretical objects that the contextualization of these signs in the intellectual currents of the culture may be profitable.

The present study attempts to explain the conceptual function of the monster in mediaeval culture as the symbolic expression of a philosophical tradition most fully articulated in the negative theology of Pseudo-Dionysius, the Areopagite. The centre of that theory, that God transcends human knowledge utterly and can be known only by what He is not, eventually becomes a more generalized mediaeval habit of thought that conceives of the human intellect as remaking in its own image, at least partially, all of the objects of knowledge it seeks to understand. The corrective to this process of "misrepresenting" the intelligible was borrowed from the originally theological method of Pseudo-Dionysius and involved the progressive negation of logical affirmations about the world and the real.

In the aesthetic production of the Middle Ages a favoured way of achieving this negation was to deform the representation of the thing described in such a way as to call into question the adequacy of the intellectual concept of the thing in relation to its ontological reality. Thus the monstrosity of a human figure with three heads or a tree with the power of speech functions to upset the mental expectations about the relation of the sign to what it is supposed to signify and to underscore the element of the arbitrary in the relation of the two. Pseudo-Dionysius had warned of the dangers of anthropomorphism in intellection and in representation:

Just as the senses can neither grasp nor perceive the things of the mind, just as a representation and shape cannot take in the simple and the shapeless, just as corporeal form cannot lay hold of the intangible and incorporeal, by the same standard of truth beings are surpassed by the infinity beyond being, intelligences by that oneness which is beyond intelligence. Indeed, the inscrutable One is out of the reach of every rational process. Nor can any words come up to the inexpressible Good, this One, this Source of all unity, this supra-existent Being. Mind beyond mind, word beyond speech, it is gathered up by no discourse, by no intuition, by no name. (*DN* 588B)[5]

Here Pseudo-Dionysius draws an analogy between the relations of the various pairs (senses/mind, representation/concept, form/essence) and the fundamental relation of beings to Being. That is, we can understand something about the relation of our existence to its incomprehensible source by examining the comprehensible and more accessible relations of body/mind, sign/signified, form/content – and vice versa. In a complicated play of analogies to analogies, the Areopagite suggests that as we learn more about the incomprehensible Being, we can transfer that understanding to the other side of the analogies: to our understanding of the nature of the senses and mind, representation and concept, appearance and reality. What is fundamental in this deeper understanding is negative: we learn that the senses *fail* to adequate the mind, the sign is *incommensurable* with the signified, form *cannot contain* being.

Focusing on the relation of representation and the represented, shape and the shapeless, the first part of this study explores how the Middle Ages, extending Pseudo-Dionysius' theological principles into poetics, developed the tradition of the monster into a symbolic language that, like its more formal theological-philosophical parent, expressed the inadequacy of human cognition in containing the limitlessness of the real. The first half of part I, "The Context of the Monstrous," examines the thought of Pseudo-Dionysius and his Neoplatonic followers in order to discover how that thought contributed to the development of the grotesque. This chapter focuses on Dionysian symbolism, especially the Areopagite's insistence on the superiority of the deformed image over the natural (see, for example, *CH* 145B), as the matrix of monstrous conceptualization for the later Middle Ages. During the long period we call the Middle Ages, the Neoplatonism of Pseudo-Dionysius waned, and the more rational methods of logic and dialectics as represented by scholasticism came to prevail.[6] Paralleling this development, it is suggested, is a migration of deformed imagery to the culturally more marginal discourse of mediaeval mysticism. While the discussion here concentrates on and contrasts two thinkers and their times crucial to the development of mediaeval philosophical thought, the fifth-century Pseudo-Dionysius and the thirteenth-century Thomas Aquinas, it does not attempt an exhaustive historical description of the complicated intellectual and cultural developments characteristic of this epoch. Rather, it juxtaposes two ways of conceiving and approaching the intelligible and its representation and tries to relate the grotesque to them. While juxtaposed as points of view, Dionysian Neoplatonism and Thomistic scholasticism are not seen as binary opposites; in the space between the two, it is suggested, looms the monster, a product of paradox, functioning to critique the overconfident constructs of rational analysis.

Just as Christian Neoplatonism asserted the superiority of negation in theology and philosophy, so, too, in its epistemology it followed the *via negativa*, and once again the sign of this superior form of unknowing was the deformed. Indeed, the process of true understanding described by Pseudo-Dionysius and his many followers is one consisting of building up propositions and assertions about a subject and then dismantling them through progressive negation, so as to free the object of knowledge from all characteristics not inherent to it but imposed by the human mind in the process of knowing and representing: "We therefore approach that which is beyond all as far as our capacities allow us, and we pass by way of denial and the transcendence of all things and by way of the cause of all things. God is therefore known in all things and as distinct from all things. He is known through knowledge and through unknowing" (*DN* 869D–872A).

In the Middle Ages all signifying involved language operations in which a sign was attached to a concept of a thing known, and this sign carried with it properties of both the mind that created it as well as the thing known. The best guarantee of escaping the otherwise inevitable error of taking the sign for the thing was to construct signs so deformed and so transgressive of the process of signification itself that confusion of the real with its language construct was impossible, even scandalous: "Since the way of negation seems to be more suitable to the realm of the divine and since positive assertions are always unfitting to the hiddenness of the inexpressible, a manifestation through dissimilar shapes is more correctly to be applied to the invisible" (*CH* 141A).

Related to this emphasis on the relation of knowing and unknowing are the questions, more pertinent here, of representing and unrepresenting and of form and nonform. For the Middle Ages, there are two types of signifying, just as there are two descriptions of knowing, and these traditions provide the "Context of the Monstrous."[7] One tradition, pursuing logic and trusting in the power of discourse to reveal the world, emphasized affirmation and the constructs of intellect. We will call it the "cataphatic" tradition, since it followed what the Middle Ages termed the *via positiva*. It tended to conceive of art as mimetic, producing an accurate representation of a wholly positive world of things, made present by the power of the mind and the verbal sign. The other tradition embraced rhetoric and considered allegory as the primary vehicle for human knowing. This tradition taught that the mind must rise progressively from cumulative affirmations about reality to the purgative negations of them until it transcends the limitations of its own discourse and comes to know in silence. It views art as heuristic and self-reflexive, pointing always to its own process of representation, and it regards all languages as striving ultimately toward the revelation of that which is-not. Unlike simple mimesis and the realistic representation it entails, this highly symbolic mode represents wholly new creations arising from its own discourse. The mimesis of this originally Platonic tradition is of a wholly different kind from that derived from the Aristotelian tradition, since it attempts to communicate representations, not of the particulars of a material world, but rather of an absent world of Forms. Joseph Mazzeo, in a discussion of Augustine's theory of signs and his theory of Christian rhetoric, expresses the difference concisely:

It is important for us at this point to clarify the sense in which Augustine uses the mimetic dialectic. It is, exactly as in Plato, the making of images of an eternal and intelligible reality. The images are more or less accurate, closer or farther from the realities they imitate, but they are always merely images of an absolute reality made up of pure forms. This is to be carefully distinguished from the Aristotelian concept of *mimesis*. Such imitation is always of a particular thing, of a substance in the primary sense, and it is the essence of all artistic activity, of all making.[8]

The mediaeval tradition of Christian rhetoric is preeminent within the tradition associated with apophasis and is discussed in the second half of part I, entitled "The Language of the Monstrous." Somewhat ironically, Christian rhetoric is also the science that most emphatically underscores the limitations of human discourse as a means to understanding and representing the true nature of reality. Saint Augustine, the founder and principal exponent of Christian rhetoric, recognizes throughout his writings that it is ultimately impossible for language to describe fully that which it is meant to express, but at the same time Augustine and those who followed him declare verbal signification to be the most effective tool for the transcendence of that very limitation. In a monumental work on mediaeval cognitive theories, Marcia Colish has described this paradox:

They [mediaeval commentators] had been called, they believed, not only to attain a knowledge of God themselves but also to convey the knowledge of God to the world. To this task they bent at once the resources of their Divine commission and the various techniques of thought and communication that human nature and their historical situation had imposed upon them and placed at their disposal. The acutely paradoxical implications of their mission did not fail to inspire in them mingled feelings of enthusiasm and unworthiness. God had commanded them to express the inexpressible, in terms accessible to the speaker and the audience alike. These very terms, however, would remain permanently inadequate to the assignment. Neither their logical rigor nor their verbal precision or eloquence could compass the mystery of the Godhead.[9]

Christian rhetoric admits the failure of discourse in order to explicate the very model of discourse; that is, it encourages us to "step outside" language so as to observe more fully the process of human cognition. Precisely because language is not fully adequate for complete understanding, the Christian missionary felt it necessary to convert the heart of the hearer, not only the mind, because as Plotinus and other early Neoplatonists had pointed out, the nature of reality is such that the comprehension of it may be attained only through the conversion of the "whole man." For Christian rhetoricians such as Augustine this meant openness to divine grace, an openness that began with humbleness of heart. But, as Marcia Colish has demonstrated in her discussion of Augustine's own conversion, this change of heart is brought about by words – not primarily by the intellectual signification of words, which, in the case of Augustine, the hearer already possessed, but rather by their "sweetness." This idea, that there is something in language beyond the sign's signification of a concept, a kind of natural relation between the human intellect and the real, is the basis of the mediaeval concept of metalanguage, again largely to be ascribed to Augustine. Stepping outside language in the direction of metalanguage is made possible partially through the poetic and rhetorical constructions of the paradoxes, ambiguities, grotesqueries, and monstrosities of mediaeval art and legend, which sufficiently deform the normal process of signification so as to urge the mind beyond the restrictions of language and logic.

The incarnational character of Augustine's sign theory also introduced another paradox into the idea of language by providing as a model for signification the concept of God-made-man. Christian theology conceived of the second person of the Trinity as the divine Being who had taken on human form and nature in order to reestablish the communication between God and his creatures, which had been interrupted in the Fall when we chose carnal, discursive knowledge over the earlier angelic, nondiscursive understanding. "The Language of the Monstrous" undertakes a more detailed exploration of the metaphor of Christ as "Word of God," redeeming in the trinity of "speaker-concept-word" human language that had fragmented into sign and signified through the disunity brought about by the preference for the material over the spiritual. Such a redemption of the natural relations of things is possible only through a figure who "unnaturally" resolves within the monstrous paradox of his own double nature, man and God, the opposition of spirit and matter. This rhetorical model and its epistemological implications are clearly set out in Augustine's description of the paradoxes of knowing and speaking:

Before you perceived God, you believed that thought could express God. Now you are beginning to perceive Him, and you think that you cannot express what you perceive. But, having found that you cannot express what you perceive, will you be silent, will you not praise God? ... "How," you ask, "shall I praise Him?" I cannot now explain the small amount which I can perceive in part, through a glass darkly (*in aenigmate per speculum*) ... All other things may be expressed in some way; He alone is ineffable, Who spoke, and all things were made. He spoke, and we were made; but we are unable to speak of Him. His Word, by Whom we were spoken, is His Son! [10]

Just as the Word-made-flesh was conceived as a kind of supreme marvel, so language, the science derived from Him, retained something of the same monstrous dimensions in its own double nature, which consisted of immaterial meaning incarnated in sensuous sound. This highly symbolic quality of language, cherished by the rhetorician, was regarded with suspicion and sometimes regret by thinkers who gave priority to the clarity and precision of rational analysis. Against the logicians and dialecticians, the rhetorician defended the symbolic and rhetorical features of discourse by describing the nature of the real that language was meant to describe as itself similarly symbolic. Because the world and the cosmos that surrounded it were ultimately an allegory revealing a transcendent reality, so too, it followed, must be the discourse about it. While mediaeval logic and scholastic dialectic succeeded in describing with greater accuracy empirical reality and human knowledge of it, Christian rhetoric emphasized the ineffability of the real and the negative ability of the human mind to approach it.

The operation of the deformed as a symbolic language within the cultural and intellectual context of the Middle Ages is discussed in this second half of part I in such a way that the term "language" functions to indicate generally an extended system of signs conveying a range of meanings. Although the language of the monstrous does not achieve, even in the Middle Ages, the cognitive status of religion, art, myth, and language – what Ernst Cassirer called symbolic forms – it seems, nevertheless, to approach Cassirer's symbolic forms and to constitute a type of disquisition within and about these forms: standing partially outside each of the particular symbolic languages, the monstrous is able to act as an exegesis on them.[11] However, this exegetical power of the monstrous serves not only to "lead out" the truths buried in the texts of these conventional forms, but, as well, to underscore the limits of their cognitive powers. "The Language of the Monstrous" discusses the function of the monstrous language specifically as developed by John Scotus Eriugena from the fundamentals that he inherited from Pseudo-Dionysius, whose thought John made available to the West. It was, in fact, in the act of translating the Areopagite that Eriugena was able to develop far more than had his source a theory of teratological imagery, thereby transforming Dionysius' dyadic system of representation, based on similar and dissimilar images, into a more typically Neoplatonic triadic system based on the similar, dissimilar, and *monstrous*. In addition, in his own exegesis Eriugena demonstrates the utility of the concept of the monstrous through his development of two kinds of allegory: allegory *facti et dicti* and allegory *dicti non (autem) facti*. The first is a discourse that derives its images from nature and history; the second, a purely spiritual discourse, contradicts, deforms, and transcends nature and mundane reality so as to reveal an extralogical, extraempirical truth.

The language of the monstrous is parasitic, depending on the existence of conventional languages; it feeds, so to speak, at their margins, upon their limits, so as to gain the power to transcend these analytic discourses and, true to its etymology (*monstrare*: to show), it points to utterances that lie beyond logic. It is argued here that this difference between constructing the object to be known through the logical analysis that language makes possible and showing, pointing to that object as it is in itself, is crucial to understanding the function of the monstrous in mediaeval thought. The Middle Ages understood that our knowledge of a thing is obscured by the fact that our representation becomes confused with the thing itself, and our knowing merges with the known to form a subjective knowledge of the object. It is by emphasizing the subjective aspect of this kind of cognition that modern relativists call into question the possibility of objective knowledge. But ostensive demonstration, what I have called "showing the object," incapable though it is of logical analysis, eschews the confusion of the thing with its sign, albeit by appeal to transcendence. The epistemological problems involved in the relation of language to thing, of the sign to the signified, arise because language tends to involve itself in the nature of the thing by "imposing" its own form upon the world that it seeks to know and calls the world thus formed the real. Monstrous discourse, by its very definition a deformity, possesses no form that it can impose and is constituted only by signs that signify nothing in the affirmative sense; they stand for no thing and no reality other than themselves. They are, as Flaubert suspected, "primordial figures whose bodies are nothing but their image."[12]

It should be clarified at this point, however, that there are at least two major manifestations of the monster in the Middle Ages: the symbolic and the literal. Although the present discussion emphasizes the symbolic, it is not to be supposed that mediaeval people conceived of the monster only in abstract terms, nor should it be supposed that what has been called the "symbolic universe" of the mediaeval mind excluded the literal and the concrete. On the contrary, the mediaeval manipulation of the grotesque would seem to indicate a process in which the metaphorical and figurative is steadily concretized to produce the idea of living races of monsters populating various remote corners of the world.

There is ample evidence that the Middle Ages believed fully in the physical existence of the monstrous beings that they represented in manuscripts and church architecture. It is probable, as well, that the relation between monster and symbol was seen to be one in which the prior physical existence of the monster produced and made possible its symbolic representation. However, as is often the case in the relation of art to life, the opposite is true. It is clear from the geographical tradition (including the "eyewitness" accounts) that the description of the races of monsters and their habitats are copied directly from literary sources. But mediaeval literalism does not exclude the symbolic; rather it guarantees it. Just as the allegorical function of the figure of Cain, connoting archetypal violence and dissension, was grounded in the original historical existence of Cain, so too, monstrous semiology is authorized by the physical existence of the monsters, despite the fact that this existence is invented. The fiction of an historical existence authorizes a symbolic program that in turn produces signs that can be applied metaphorically to other "things" so as to reveal their grotesque absurdity: "The sheer crassness of the signs is a goad so that even the materially inclined cannot accept that it could be permitted or true that the celestial and divine sights could be conveyed by such shameful things" (*CH* 141B–141C).

The relation of the monster as "sign" to the monster as "thing" is partially explained by Augustine's famous distinction between the literal sign and the figurative.[13] As an example of a literal, or natural, sign, Augustine uses the word *bos* (ox), which indicates the actual, existing animal. Transferred to something other than the "thing" it literally represents, the sign becomes a figurative sign. Such signs are characterized by degrees of ambiguity. Thus "ox" as a figurative sign stands for an evangelist in Scripture and throughout sacred art. At the level of praxis there can be an analogy between this example and the sign of the monster: as "literal" sign the monster refers to the geographical-teratological tradition and indicates a member of those races inhabiting far-off regions of the earth, flesh and blood creatures understood to exist physically.[14] As figurative sign, or metaphor, used outside the geographical tradition, the monster carries with it an ambiguity more extreme than other *figura* because, in fact, it refers to nothing phenomenally real, nothing that physical nature confirms or authorizes. In a reversal of the normal semiological process in which the form of a real ox is used to create a sign, that of Saint Matthew, the monstrous sign is used to create a physical form, one that, as all mediaeval commentators insist, the natural world never condoned. Instead, the monstrous sign, whether literal or figurative, has the effect of expanding the human concept of nature so as to begin the elevation of the mind to the level of the divine. Furthermore, the very idea of the monster as "thing" functioning as monster as "sign" confirms its relation to the sacred, for as far as the Middle Ages is concerned, only the Divine can use things as signs. Mazzeo explains: "In the strict sense, a thing (*res*) is never employed as a sign of any other such as wood, stone, cattle, etc. However, in the case of Scripture this does not apply. The wood which Moses cast into the bitter waters to make them sweet, the stone which Jacob used as a pillow, the ram which Abraham offered up instead of his son are all, to be sure, things. But they are also signs of other things. Now words are also realities; otherwise they would not exist at all, but they are never employed except as signs of something else."[15]

It is, then, in the sense of figurative sign that there is, paradoxically, no difference between the monstrous sign and what it stands for, since the sign, signifying "nothing," stands only for itself; and yet in another sense there is no similarity between the monstrous sign and that concept it stands for either, because the absolute deformity of this kind of sign excludes it from standing for any real signified. The deformed simultaneously exposes the gap between sign and signified and bridges it. In this way grotesque language not only eschews the epistemological problems of conventional language, it functions as a point outside language from which we may observe the very form of language itself.

To paraphrase Isidore of Seville's declaration concerning "real" monsters, the monstrous is not a contradiction of nature but of human epistemological categories: "Varro says that portents are things which seem to have been born contrary to nature, but in truth, they are not born contrary to nature, because they exist by the divine will, since the Creator's will is the nature of everything created … A portent, therefore, does not arise contrary to nature, but contrary to what nature is understood to be. Portents are also called 'signs,' 'monstrosities,' and 'prodigies' because they seem to portend and to point out, to demonstrate, and to predict future happenings."[16]

It would be difficult to exaggerate the importance of this definition of the monster, not only because it was universally accepted in the Middle Ages and not only because by its acceptance and celebration of the monster, it sets this period apart from the periods that preceded and succeeded it but also because this definition elevates the monster in all its various manifestations – as the deformity and as the grotesque that arise from negation – to the level of conceptual sign. Isidore's understanding of nature, a nature which, as we see, includes the monster, is as "the power of making and begetting."[17] This creative force, originating in God, extends to the human ability to know and to signify what it knows. The monster is part of this semiotic aspect of nature in that, unlike other signs that "re-present" the intelligible, it "portends," "points to," and "de*monstrates*," to use Isidore's terms.

The monstrous races, deformed beings who had wandered the world since the time of Cain, were a continuous source of enrichment of the vocabulary of the deformed discourse. The most important sources of this lore were the Greek geographers, figures like Megasthenes, who, according to his own testimony, had travelled as ambassador to India and observed these fantastic creatures first hand.[18] From the Greek writers the tradition of races of monsters passed to Roman writers such as Solinus and Pliny,[19] who were to have an enormous influence on the mediaeval idea of the dimensions of monstrous existence.

When the locus of these fantastic beings was not specified as India, Ethiopia was identified as their place of origin. The confusion between India and Ethiopia in teratological lore is significant and its development has been fully described by Rudolf Wittkower.[20] Also, John Block Friedman has suggested that the very imprecision of spatial site and the unfamiliarity of the matrix of the misshapen may have been a requirement of the dynamics of the marvellous.[21] Just as the Middle Ages had transformed the classical view of the monster's metaphysical reality from one *contra naturam* to one *extra naturam*, so, too, it seems, it needed an extrageographical and supraspatial locus for the phenomenon. The India-Ethiopia complex is an example of mediaeval sign-making at work in the field of teratological geography, where spatial semiotics expresses the idea of the monster as simultaneously participating in the material and spiritual worlds and thus forming a bridge between the two. It is in this sense that the Middle Ages conceived of the monster as a being that really existed, but whose existence was highly contingent: the monster existed, but *far away, not here*. This displacement of the physical reality to remote and unreachable locations secured the theory of the real existence of the monster by guaranteeing that it could not be empirically authenticated, while at the same time securing the symbolic reality as one corresponding to nothing that *is*. The monster both affirms the discourses that describe the physical world by grounding the teratological phenomenon in geography, history, and science, and then negates these discourses by transcending their limitations in order to raise the signifying power of the deformed to an anagogical level, raising nature from the physical to the divine, as Isidore stated.

Both the geographical races of monsters and their purely symbolic siblings meet in part 2, "Taxonomy," which confronts the paradox of an ordering of disorder by trying to suggest a taxonomy of the monstrous. Attempts at classifications of the monstrous abound, beginning with Isidore's,[22] continuing into the present, and ranging from the relatively simple to systems so complex as to be useless. The principles of these various classifications reveal, not surprisingly, the philosophical assumptions of the classifier, and the general similarity from one system to another reveals how constant these assumptions have remained in Western thought from the early Middle Ages to the present. The taxonomy established in chapter 3 is not structurally very different from many others that have been created in order to understand the concept of the monster, except that it attempts to articulate the philosophical principles that it is built on, to show how the monster's proper function is to negate the very order of which the monster is a part, and to critique the philosophical principles that sustain order itself.

Clearly one of the most compelling features of the concept of the deformed, and one often commented upon, is that the monster engages at a fundamental level the very principle of order developed in Western thought. This engagement involves, as well, a series of primordial concepts related to order that were the first to be contemplated by nascent philosophy and in some ways remain its principal subjects: such related concepts as being, essence, causality, universals, and the like impinge upon our concept of order. When, for instance, Isidore of Seville in the seventh century, Ambroise Paré in the sixteenth, and Claude Kappler in the twentieth[23] create in their taxonomies a class of monsters based on unnatural combinations of physical forms, they not only make a convenient habitation for the siren – a composite of fish and human – and the dragon – a fusion of serpent, bird, and fish – but they reaffirm, as well, a sense of the natural order in which such combinations are prohibited, while other combinations such as wings, talons, and beak are considered possible and "right."

To a degree the teratological order is a manipulation and commentary on the natural order, which it both affirms and negates; by making the natural order the subject of its exegesis and thus its very raison d'être, the teratological discourse demonstrates the indispensibility of the natural, affirmative order and confesses its reliance upon it. But its commentary is aimed directly at exposing the cognitive limitations of this order as well as its arbitrary origins in human logic and language. For instance, an entire category of deformity is constituted by the sole monstrosity of lack of a coherent language, a taxonomic principle behind which one may glimpse the importance attributed to language and the metaphysical role it plays in distinguishing normal human beings from all other creatures.[24] The speculative consideration of such ideas as simplicity and multiplicity, unity and individuation, similitude and difference, permanence and mutability, appears to have been carried out at various moments and to various degrees through a discourse characterized by a certain discursive deformation modelled on the inversion and reversal of the logical principles of conventional discourses. Thus the possible relation of the one to the many, explored with the tools of philosophy and theology, may also be suggested by the grotesque figure of the single body with three heads; the distinction between male and female, mediated by philosophical metaphors of unity, may be utterly dissolved in the sign of the monstrous hermaphrodite. The taxonomy of part 2 of this study attempts to build on these philosophical principles and their contradictions.

The realm in which the monster is given pride of place is the aesthetic text. Part 3 of this study examines two types of literary narratives in which the monstrous and the deformed seem particularly prominent, the heroic saga and the saint's life. The choice of these two genres is dictated not by the conspicuousness of monstrous negation within them, nor by its absence in other genres, but by the range of literary discourse they represent. The secular reality of the martial hero, conqueror of the material world and ruler of its peoples and riches is the subject of deformation and negation in the first; the spiritual and mystical principles of the saint and the encoded language of the holy are the subject of the second.

The particular emphasis given in Christian Neoplatonism to language in its rhetorical and symbolic modes provided rich ground for the growth of fabulous expression, since these modes provided greater access to the paradoxical understanding of language as both the principal tool of human understanding and its greatest barrier. Where mediaeval dialectics sought ever-increasing clarity in presenting its subject, poetic language sought obscurity through a deeper encodement as a way of helping the mind to go beyond logic and the literal. It is through the presence of the monstrous signs in the text, it is argued here, that the reader sees through the assertions of the discourse to its contradiction, and by the same grotesque mockeries that the reader hears the silence of the text and understands its meaning as what is not said. Thus in the mediaeval accounts of Oedipus, Alexander the Great, and Camelot's Sir Gawain a monstrous presence introduces into each text a deforming principle that progressively deflates the heroic figure and the self-constructed image of his society and contradicts the conventional meaning of these heroic traditions. In the other set of texts, the fabulous elements of the stories, images, and cults of Saint Christopher, Saint Denis, and Saint Wilgeforte work to undermine the apparent meaning of the saint's biography so as to begin a decoding of its narrative that leads to an understanding beyond the historical, literary, and devotional.

Theoretical interest in the monster has been chiefly directed to its recusative function. Signifying either the demonic or the morally reprehensible, this use of monstrous signification seems to be the easiest to comprehend and to describe. The exclusive emphasis on this aspect of monstrosity found in many studies tends to present the grotesque as primarily a vehicle for irony.[25] Thus gargoyles, we are told, perched on the most extended architectural points of mediaeval cathedrals, are there to preach about the exile from sanctity caused by sin; through fear, repulsion, or ridicule various deformities represent the satanic and its triumph through sin. In this discussion I do not consider the monster's role in demonology;[26] I concentrate instead on the positive, even sacred, signification of the monster. However, given the importance of the negative in the theoretical foundations of this study, I have used the term "recusative" rather than "negative" to describe the approach that focuses on demonology, so as to avoid confusion with the more specifically philosophico-theological term "negative." In the sense of Pseudo-Dionysius, a sense that informs this discussion throughout, all monsters are negations whose apophatic function is to raise the mind to a higher level of perception of the real.

Although the historical period treated here ranges from the eighth century to the end of the fourteenth, I refer to premediaeval and postmediaeval periods as well, in order to contextualize and contrast the mediaeval concepts and uses of the deformed with the concepts and uses in the ages that preceded and succeeded the Middle Ages. I make no attempt here, however, to provide an exhaustive description of the historical development of the concept of the grotesque and the monstrous, nor do I trace, one by one, the cultural and intellectual steps that lead from Pseudo-Dionysius to Eriugena and to (for instance) the Pearl Poet. Rather, the contrasts in this study are more broadly between the ways in which the cataphatic and the apophatic are distinguished, and between Pseudo-Dionysius and Saint Thomas Aquinas, the symbolic and the analytic, similitude and dissimilitude.

The terms "monster," "grotesque," and "fantastic" are generally used more or less interchangeably but, it is hoped, not uncritically. While I am aware that the grotesque must be distinguished from the fantastic and that the monstrous is neither a genre nor a style, I am nevertheless faced with a generally admitted poverty of definitions for these phenomena. However, since no attempt is made here specifically to amplify these definitions, the problem is

considerably simpler: although in some fantastic literature and in some grotesque figures as well, the deformed as such is completely absent, the monster
is equally comfortable in each genre and frequently found in both.

The ubiquity of the monster dictates that its analysis will draw upon a
wide variety of subject areas, and critical studies of the monstrous reflect this
range. Particularly useful to the present discussion have been the work of art
historian Jurgis Baltrusaitis, especially, but not exclusively, his *Le Moyen age
fantastique: Antiquités et exotismes dans l'art gothique*, and the seminal study
of historian Rudolf Wittkower, "Marvels of the East: A Study in the History
of Monsters." Both employ an historical method which, backed by each
man's massive scholarship, succeeds in raising many of the right questions
about the use of the monster in mediaeval thought and art. Many of the questions concerning the *how* of mediaeval monsters are abundantly answered by
this method – how the monstrous is represented, how the grotesque functions
within different aesthetic modes, how monstrous characteristics are passed
from one culture to another and from one historical period to another – but
the question as to *why* there is resort to the monster and to the deformed sign
is rarely, if ever, extensively addressed. While it is essential to know when
and how the Western dragon acquired his wings, it is clear that this imported
figure did not retain the symbolic charge that it had had in the East, and we
are left to wonder why the Middle Ages continued to elaborate the monstrous figure of the dragon and why, in an age that grounded the essence of
things in form, deformity was so frequently the preferred aesthetic expression.

If the "superstitious" Middle Ages gave a place of prominence in the
world to the monster, while the "enlightened" Renaissance exiled the disordered and imperfect from its world,[27] does this contrast reveal to us something about the nature of the two periods? Why are the monstrous races
placed at the edges of the world in mediaeval maps when, while branding
them as exiles, such a location identifies the monsters as God's only neigh-
bors and suggests their proximity to the Divine? It is insufficient to interpret
locus in this case as merely indicating a place outside the world of order. A
consideration of symbolic dimension reveals that "edge" is not the outside so
much as it is the threshold and conductor between outside and inside. Particularly in maps and other visual representations of monstrous lands, this edge
may be regarded more informatively as a frame, functioning, as frames do, to
contain and structure what is within and to orient the viewer to beginning,
end, and continuity. In this light the threshold position of the races suggests,
perhaps, a greater importance for their locus than does the simple historical
explanation that it is a sign of exile.

A different methodology is found in the more recent study of Gilbert Lascault, *Le monstre dans l'art occidental*, which investigates the monster as
critique of rationality, as gloss on the nature of language, as philosphical

symbol, and under several other rubrics. Although, from our point of view, Lascault asks the right questions about the conceptual basis of the monster and the origin of the grotesque, an overly psychological method leads him to define the grotesque as an aesthetic artifact that produces fear and disgust, a definition that few are likely to find adequate or even original.

In one way or another the psychological approach to the concept of the monster locates the analysis of the subject in the reader or viewer and concludes, not surprisingly, with a theory of the grotesque as a subjective, psychological reality.[28] Tzvetan Todorov's approach is shared by many contemporary critics and, indeed, has widely influenced the concept of fantasy. His *Introduction à la littérature fantastique* provides a more theoretical and nuanced discussion of the subject than others, but despite its denunciation of the "sentimental" definition propounded by H.P. Lovecraft and others, which situates the reality of the genre in the sentiments that it provokes in the reader, the emphasis given by Todorov to the role of *lecteur* leads him ultimately to a similarly restricted definition based in the psychological and subjective. His further prohibition against allegorical or "poetic" readings of the fantastic causes a historical distortion by excluding the aesthetic sensibilities of the longest period of Western civilization and privileging Romantic and post-Romantic aesthetic preferences. Todorov finds himself required to dismiss allegory as a component of fantasy, partially because his model for the fantastic is drawn from an age that has already dismissed allegory: "If what we read describes a supernatural event, while the words themselves must be taken, not in a literal sense, but in another sense which does not refer directly to the supernatural, then there is no place left for the fantastic."[29]

Far more satisfactory is the study of the grotesque by Geoffrey Galt Harpham, which examines the phenomenon under such conceptual rubrics as formation/deformation/reformation, marginality and centrality, and the grotesque and the divine.[30] While Harpham's study is not principally concerned with the Middle Ages, it is sensitive to the kind of philosophical concerns that had their origin and early development in that period.

Eschewing the excesses of both historicism and psychologism, Claude Kappler's admirable study, *Monstres, démons, et merveilles à la fin du moyen age*, remains the generally most satisfactory analysis of the monster in mediaeval art. Grounding her study principally in the voyage literature from the thirteenth to the fourteenth century, complemented by theoretical and didactic texts from the same period and earlier, Kappler structures the discussion along the pertinent conceptual categories of the monstrous: the theory of form, the intellectual interests of the period, and the dominant myths and legends, constitute the first three chapters and lead in the fourth to a helpful typology based on conceptual dimensions of the monstrous. While by no means neglecting the historical and the psychological, Kappler strikes a balance by governing the whole with a structural and conceptual methodology.

While her study informs the discussion throughout this book, Kappler does not base her analysis of the monster in the concept of the deformed as it was developed from the tradition of Pseudo-Dionysius. Unlike the present study, Kappler does not give particular prominence to the influence of mediaeval Neoplatonism or theological considerations generally. Yet Claude Kappler's work has been a valuable point of departure for this study, and it is therefore appropriate, perhaps, to begin our discussion of the context of the monster with Kappler's concluding image of it as one of the possible responses to the fundamental and eternal questions of humankind: "In such a fantastic universe the monster does not get the last word despite his ability to endure through the centuries; the monster is a flash of light, as fugitive as it is fulgurant, to which respond a myriad of other flashes in a storm of lightning that has no end, just as it has no beginning."[31]

PART ONE

Theory

The Tower of Babel. Kircher, *Turris Babel*, 41. McGill University, Osler Library

1 The Context of the Monstrous

A fine grotesque is the expression in a moment, by a series of symbols
thrown together in bold and fearless connection, of truths which it
would have taken a long time to express in any verbal way.

John Ruskin, *Modern Painters*

PSEUDO-DIONYSIUS AND THE NEGATIVE TRADITION

The cosmos of Pseudo-Dionysius is thoroughly realist and Neoplatonic, as it
was in varying degrees for most of his mediaeval followers.[1] The Areopagite's explanation of God, the world, being, and human knowledge became
the singularly most influential conception in Western thought until it was
superseded by the philosophy it had rejected totally, the rationalism and reliance on logic that begins to emerge in the thirteenth century and soon
becomes the dominant characteristic of Western thought, presupposed as
fundamental to intellectual inquiry. Denys' works were the subject of study
and formal commentary by virtually every major mediaeval thinker from
John of Scythopolis (sixth century) in the Byzantine tradition and John Scotus Eriugena, Denys' translator in the West, as well as Thomas Aquinas eight
hundred years later, throughout whose work he is cited, after Aristotle, more
than any other authority.

Curiously, however, one cannot point to any complete and lasting Dionysian "tradition" in the West, partly because Dionysianism is not a theology in
the Thomistic sense,[2] much less a philosophy in the Greek sense. It is closer
to a mystical program centered on the idea of personal conversion triggered
by a profound metalinguistic understanding of the world and of God. Nevertheless, Denys' theoretical writings were a mine of ideas and perceptions for
the Christian thinkers of the Middle Ages, and none abstained from employing them in his own writings. However, each thinker who used Denys' ideas
modified them in some way to suit another – not always congenial – system.

Even Eriugena, who would seem the closest and most faithful follower, could not accept without condition the radical implications of what may be called the antimetaphysics of the Pseudo-Dionysius, and in his translation of the works that became the authoritative Latin version for the Middle Ages, John seems to have deliberately "mistranslated" certain passages in a way that made crucial philosophical differences. The eminent French scholar, René Roques, who has been aptly called "the Nestor of modern Pseudo-Dionysian studies,"[3] has described in detail the adaptations by Scotus Eriugena of the master's work and their importance,[4] and following Roques, we will see in the next chapter that Eriugena's translation of the Areopagite, far from being a faithful Latin version of the original Greek, manipulates its source in such a way as to fulfill a promise inherent in it. As Roques has shown, translation for the Scot was the occasion for laying the foundations for a whole symbolic theory.

Others, however, "corrected" the thinking of Denys through interpretation, reshaping and redirecting his ideas in their commentaries. The thrust of these modifications (other than those of Eriugena) may be summarized as the forming of analytic cognitive systems from what was intended as an extra-analytic "revealing," the rational containment of elements that discouraged exclusive reliance on reason, linguistic affirmation in place of the original insistence on the value of negation and the silence appropriate to it. At the very beginning of his *Divine Names* Pseudo-Dionysius sounds a warning against overreliance on logic and language when, citing Paul, he describes the cognitive ability granted by the Spirit as "a power by which, in a manner surpassing speech and knowledge, we reach a union superior to anything available to us by way of our own abilities or activities in the realm of discourse or of intellect. This is why we must not dare to resort to words or conceptions concerning that hidden divinity which transcends being, apart from what the sacred scriptures have divinely revealed" (*DN* 585B–588A).

Because Being itself is beyond cognition, beyond human representations and concepts, it cannot be approached through intellectual demonstration. Rather, the knower must approach it through a gradual perception beginning with the affirmations about what is revealed (both in Scripture and in creation), proceding through the *via negativa* to the negation of all affirmations, and arriving at a transcendent understanding beyond all affirmations and negations: "Since it is the Cause of all beings, we should posit and ascribe to it all the affirmations that we make in regard to beings, and, more appropriately, we should negate all these affirmations, since it surpasses all being. Now we should not conclude that the negations are simply the opposites of the affirmations, but rather that the cause of all is considerably prior to this, beyond privations, beyond every denial, beyond every assertion" (*MT* 1000B). Thus this process of understanding involves a complete transcendence of all naming, all analysis, and all discourse as it moves toward a final transformation of these "affirmative" procedures; through this transformation, the knower and the known become one.

Rational, analytic thought has, of course, a place of importance in Pseudo-Dionysius' method, but it is, at it were, a starting point rather than a terminus. Over and over again the Areopagite recommends the use of reason to achieve an understanding of God and creation[5] and even claims to have written an entire treatise on the subject: "In my *Theological Representations*, I have praised the notions which are most appropriate to affirmative theology" (*MT* 1032D; the treatise referred to either never existed or is lost). Nevertheless, Pseudo-Dionysius is far from privileging rational analysis as a tool for understanding. Indeed, by fitting rational analysis into the most elementary level of the cognitive process, Dionysius privileges the extra-rational, mystical comprehension which, however, depends upon the rational. It was probably the promotion of extra-rational discourse in the ranks of intellection that caused a certain uneasiness about Dionysianism in the West and provoked such typically mixed reaction to his work as that cited by Jean Leclercq in his informative and aptly titled "Influence and Noninfluence of Dionysius in the Western Middle Ages": "He [Dionysius] is cited by Helinand of Froidmont (d. 1229), but with the comment that 'his words evoke amazement and astonishment rather than knowledge' ... [And] Adam of Dryburgh, known as the Scot, observed that the words of Dionysius were 'profound but unclear (*perplexa*).'"[6]

No western reader of Dionysius, whether of the Middle Ages or of today, can be completely unsympathetic to the difficulties of Adam and Helinand, and it is, of course, this same underlying unease that they express about going beyond the rational that doomed Dionysius' worldview to failure in the West. Yet Denys himself never dismissed affirmative thought. He recognized the reality and value of two distinct modes of understanding and emphasized their mutual dependence: "the theological tradition has a dual aspect, the ineffable and mysterious on the one hand, the open and more evident on the other. The one resorts to symbolism and involves initiation. The other is philosophic and employs the method of demonstration" (*Letter Nine* 1105D). That the lifeline between the two would eventually be broken, Dionysius could neither anticipate nor prevent.

While all mediaeval commentators of Dionysius recognized the importance of his thought and approached it with the sincere intention of faithful dissemination, they also seem to have felt the powerful threat it posed to the development of rational systems aimed at the explication of the world and its causes and the control and governance of the world through such explication. The Christian Middle Ages frankly declared the ultimate unknowability of the Supreme Cause, who remained, and would remain forever, a mystery beyond human intellection. But mediaeval thinkers were vigorous in their pursuit of whatever could be known – of causes, beings, concepts – even if they could not know Being, Cause, or *Nous*. After the Middle Ages, however, the balance between the rational and the suprarational, or mystical, approaches to understanding was disturbed, and we witness the rapid development of the rationalism that characterizes the Renaissance. Nevertheless, this later development was initiated and made possible in the Middle Ages by the very thinkers who repeatedly rejected its implications.

The thesis that the conceptual basis of the monstrous in mediaeval thought has its origin in the vision of Pseudo-Dionysius gains its strongest support from the Areopagite's theory of representation and symbolism. Especially helpful in delineating this symbolic theory are Paul Rorem's exhaustive study of the subject and René Roque's brilliant examination of Scotus Eriugena's extension of Dionysius' symbolic system[7].

The Areopagite's theory of cognition and his theory of symbolism are tightly integrated, so much so that it is often difficult to distinguish one from the other. Both depend on the dynamic of what Dionysius calls affirmation and negation in the cognitive mode and what he designates as similitude and dissimilitude in the process of representation. Symbolism and representation are the very centre of Dionysius' thought, just as they were for Proclus and other Neoplatonic predecessors, for they are divine in origin and only in a derivative sense constitute a human science. In one sense the entire goal of the Dionysian system is nothing more than the proper interpretation of sacred symbols, although, as is suggested here, Dionysius' description of the structure and function of sacred symbolism made possible the extension of his theory to include symbols and images of all kinds.

Just as for Proclus the source of the most noble images was mythology, so in the Areopagite's discussion of representation is found his biblical exegesis, and it is Scripture that provides for him the wealth of symbols that he interprets. In several instances Pseudo-Dionysius warns us that only those images and signs provided by sacred Scripture may be entertained as rightly representing the "hidden" divinity (for example *DN* 588C), but even these images and signs, because they are affimative, must in a further act of purifying exegesis be negated and replaced with "incongruous" symbols (for example, *CH* 145A).

It may with some justification be said that Pseudo-Dionysius' is a pessimistic semiology, given that the author takes every opportunity to insist upon the inadequacy of sign, upon the ultimate failure of the sign to present really the thing that it signifies: "For they call it nameless when they speak of how the supreme Deity, during a mysterious revelation of the symbolical appearance of God, rebuked the man who asked, 'What is your name?' and led him away from any knowledge of the divine name by countering, 'Why do you ask my name, seeing it is wonderful?' This surely is the wonderful 'name which is above every name' and is therefore without a name" (*DN* 596A).[8]

However, like other principles in Neoplatonic thought, this seeming pessimism is, paradoxically, optimistic, since what it discourages is merely an overreliance on the rational and what it warns against is facile anthropomorphism. In recompense it guarantees that through a proper approach to the image, a real and fulfilling comprehension of the intelligible may be had. Indeed, in Pseudo-Dionysius' epistemology as well as in his symbolism, cognition of a thing through its image leads to the *experience* of the thing, a becoming one with, through the transcendence of the image: "The truth we have to understand is that we use letters, syllables, phrases, written terms and words because of the senses. But when our souls are moved by intelligent energies in the direction of the things of the intellect then our senses and all that go with them are no longer needed. And the same happens with our intelligent powers which, when the soul becomes divinized, concentrate sightlessly and through an unknowing union on the rays of 'unapproachable light' " (*DN* 708D).

This "movement" of the soul is, in fact, the source of images, since image-making is a dynamic relation between divine and human cognition. The Dionysian theory strongly echoes the Neoplatonism of thinkers like Proclus, whose symbology involves the theory of a hierarchy or descending "series" of beings, beginning "above" and going down to the lowest creature. Each being in the hierarchy carries within it an image of the being just above it and becomes a figure of that higher power. Every being is an image, and every image "represents" the divine origin of the series. Images and signs are created through a dynamic described by Jean Trouillard: "Progressing circularly, the [divine] power spreads itself out into signification, and the signification becomes a symbol divinely infused."9 It is thus the activity of the human soul in communication with the divine that produces symbols: "Far from being a lifeless trace or a simple object, the concrete sign condenses a long, uninterrupted progression and is charged with a power of conversion toward the serial principle. But the sign does not deliver this power unless we enter into the dynamic with it, rather than receive it in a passive way."10

In Proclus there is a divine inspiring of the soul to "move toward," or "tend toward" knowledge of the One as simultaneously the One "proceeds" out toward the soul; the proceeding is one and the same with the inspiring. This motion is given form by the imagination (*morphotikos*: μορφωτιχῶς) according to the nature of the knower, and the image is born. It is worth noting, perhaps, that several "forms" of the Ineffable are possible in Proclus: the spirit participates in the divine in an ecstatic mode; reason participates in a discursive mode; imagination in an imagistic mode; the senses in a passive mode.11

Thus the image is a stepping stone to the imageless. In the process of imaging, as in the process of perceiving the intelligible, one moves from the affirmative to the negative. In terms of biblical symbols Pseudo-Dionysius continues to use this double concept (affirmative/negative), but in the exegetical context describes it as, on the one hand, open, on the other, mysterious. Paul Rorem explains: "The doubleness of the scriptural tradition does not refer to two 'senses' of the same passage, but rather to two types of scriptural text. The one is explicit and didactic, and receives little attention in the entire Pseudo-Dionysian corpus. The other type of passage is symbolic and contains within itself a duality of external absurdity and internal meaning. This type of biblical material receives our author's sustained attention."[12]

The idea of "external absurdity" is crucial to the theory of imagery in Pseudo-Dionysius, and it is what links his thought directly to a theory of a mediaeval metadiscourse constituted by monstrous metaphor. In *Letter Nine*, which Rorem and others take as central to the Areopagite's image theory, the author explains that divine mysteries can only be approached through perceptible symbols. Having made this approach, it is then necessary, he urges, to uncover them through contemplation so as to perceive their inner truth. Their outer "veil" is accessible by intellect; their inner truth is, however, attained only by becoming one with it. The greatest symbols possess an "outside" (that is, what is perceptible to the mind) constituted of "incredible and contrived fantasy" (*Letter Nine* 1104C), and it is this very fantastic, physical layer of the image that draws the mind beyond and through it to a perception of its signified, "so that what is hidden may be brought out into the open and multiplied, what is unique and undivided may be divided up, and multiple shapes and forms be given to what has neither shape nor form" (*Letter Nine* 1105C).

Once again in his specification of his image theory in the direction of the grotesque, the Christian Areopagite echoes the pagan Neoplatonist. Proclus' extensive theory of the semiotics of myth and monster also gives precedence to the deformed. Trouillard sees the relation of the two in Proclus as religious: "Between myth and prodigy there is a mutually formative exchange. Myth gives to prodigy its meaning and its horizon, while prodigy actualizes myth. The bond between the two is the *sacred rite*, which is the symbol enacted."[13]

Proclus expresses his teratography in terms of contraries that he further describes as perfect images of each other:

The original authors of the myths having understood that nature, which elaborates images of immaterial and intelligible ideas and fills the visible world with their various imitations, figures forth the indivisible by the divided, eternal beings by temporal processes and the intelligible by the sensual, that she represents in a material way the immaterial, as continuous with what is unitary ... [These authors] signify by what is contrary to nature that which surpasses nature in the realm of the divine, by what is contrary to reason they signify that which is more divine than all reason, and by images of the ugly that which surpasses in simplicity all partial beauty.[14]

Trouillard generally explains Proclus' theory of representation by pointing to his juxtaposition of discursive communication and figurative communication; both are symbolic: "In each case there is no common measure between sign and signified. There is, nevertheless, a power of evocation and a signifying mediation during the process of conversion and assimilation. If the symbol pretended to possess within its 'veiled showing' that which it mediates, it would be a failure and an illusion. But if it acts as a deviation and a detour so as to rediscover what has already been communicated above and beyond all senses, then it exercises a necessary function of awakening."[15]

The Areopagite's insistence on the anagogical goal of all symbols is what provides for his mediaeval followers the possibility of a teratology, both as *episteme* and as symbology. Images of the immaterial are inspired by God; a motion of the soul inclines the human spirit toward the divine; the image-making faculty (imagination) then incarnates this inspiration in order to represent the immaterial. Although the image is anthropomorphic in expression, it originates conceptually as a theophany. Such a "condescension" is, of course, a movement downward of the Eternal One into the souls of the created many. The human response is a movement upward, an anagogy, just as is the ontological "return" of the soul to God following the path of the *vita Christi*. Furthermore, just as the soul descends – is incarnated in the body at the moment of conception – and immediately begins its return to its origin, so the images descend from the Formless, are incarnated in figures, and begin a return to the signified. Just as the soul must eventually leave the body behind in its *reditus*, so too, the image, as it becomes intelligible, casts off its outer frame. The images least weighed down by the dross of similitude are those that help the mind to rise most easily and quickly to pure understanding. Thus the monster, the prodigy, and other contradictions of nature and reason are preferred because they automatically inspire an anagogical motion of the mind.

As Paul Rorem has convincingly argued, Dionysius' idea that we must rise above all symbols to pure contemplation is not a devaluation of the symbolic. Dionysius makes clear that images and symbols are the remaining traces of the presence of what they signify: "And we must certainly not disdain them, for they are the descendants and bear the mark of the divine stamps" (*Letter Nine* 1108C). Rorem comments: "The Dionysian argument for the importance of the symbolic is pushed even further. The realm of the symbols is not merely an optional means through which one may be elevated: it is the only means. The uplifting of those not yet angelically free from sense perception is impossible without the use of symbolic representations."[16]

Notwithstanding the Areopagite's preference for the grotesque, his division of all signs into two categories, similar and dissimilar, is provisional. Ultimately all images of the spiritual are inadequate, and they are, therefore, deformations of their signified. Some are more obviously inadequate and therefore preferable. As we shall see in the following section, Eriugena transformed this view into a rather more optimistic one in which monstrous symbolism becomes a category in and of itself, the apogee of a tripartite system of representation capable of guiding the mind to the threshold of truth.

The cosmos of Pseudo-Dionysius is produced by the "procession" of the Divine Cause in the act of creation "ex nihilo." All that is created participates in a "return" to the One from which it comes. This process of procession and return, "*editus-reditus*," is the chief dynamic of Denys' thought, but the thought is completed by the addition of the concept of "remaining," creating the triad of "remaining-procession-return" which is the source of all the many other triads in his system. The One proceeds (and continually proceeds) into the triad of the Trinity while remaining (and continually remaining) One. In the hypostatic union of the Trinity,[17] the monad always proceeds into the triad, which always returns into the monad, each of the "Persons" always remaining in the One[18]; thus the Trinity is the essence and paradigm of "remaining-proceeding-returning." The Deity proceeds "outward" from Itself in an overflowing of love to create all that is and all that is-not, but while proceeding outward the Divine cause remains totally within Itself as one, unified, and simple.[19] Thus Being comes into existence as multiple beings; the One is the source of the many. The created beings are not of the same nature as the Creator; the cause is not the effects. Nor is the One as source of beings Being itself, for as Denys tells us repeatedly, the One is beyond Being; the One is the source of that which It is not: "He is the being immanent in and underlying the things which are, however they are. For God is not some kind of being. No. But in a way that is simple and indefinable he gathers into himself and anticipates every existence. So he is called 'King of the ages,' for in him and around him all being is and subsists. He was not. He will not be. He did not come to be. He is not in the midst of becoming. He will not come to be. No. He is not" (*DN* 817C–817D).

In this way, the way of paradox, the Deity both proceeds and remains simultaneously. This is the concept that Pseudo-Dionysius adopts from Plato and the pagan Neoplatonists, but as a Christian he adapts it in such a way that the inherent paradox is deepened. John Marenbon analyzes the adaptation:

In commentaries on Plato's *Parmenides*, it had become the practice to apply the series of negations found in Plato's dialogue to the One (whose absolute transcendence had been stressed ever since Plotinus), and the series of positive statements to the hypostases which emanated from the One ... Consequently, he [Pseudo-Dionysius] applied both series of statements, positive and negative, to God himself. God is at once describable by every name, but only metaphorically, by reference to his manifestation of himself in his creation; and he can be described by no name – every attribute may be more truly negated of him than applied to him positively.

And further:

Despite his adoption of the Neoplatonic scheme of hierarchies, the Pseudo-Dionysius was a Christian, who had to accept both that God was immutable and transcendent, and yet that it was he, directly, who created and who administers the universe. He could not therefore equate God with the positively indescribable One; nor could he directly transfer every description of God to some lower emanation.[20]

The continuation of this process is found in the Incarnation, where the Divine proceeded from One to Trinity, "then" proceeded into Creation, completely entering into time and space and mundane plurality, and "now" enters the world and history as man. This movement, from One to Trinity, to Creation, to Incarnation constitutes, as it were, a first cycle, albeit one totally enacted within the Trinity.[21] For human reality the next cycle is return, and this is both a metaphysical and cognitive event. Metaphysically, the plurality of creation returns to the simplicity and unity of the One: "This is what unites everything, begetting and producing the harmonies and the agreement of all things. All things therefore long for it, and the manifold and the divided are returned by it into a total unity" (*DN* 948D). The paradigm for the metaphysical return is contained in the quite distinct events of the crucifixion and the resurrection in which Christ, who is God proceeded from God, returns (to Himself) under the figure of sacrifice. In a somewhat parallel way, all beings proceed from Him and return to Him from their existential plurality to their essential simplicity.

Cognitively, the human mind works in a way similar to the metaphysical reality it seeks to know: it also exhibits the paradigm of remaining-proceeding-returning. All cognitive activity is return: "And so it [the Good] assembles into a union everything possessed of reason and of mind. For just as it is ignorance which scatters those in error, so it is the presence of the light of the mind which gathers and unites together those receiving illumination. It perfects them. It returns them toward the truly real. It returns them from their numerous false notions and, filling them with the one unifying light, it gathers their clashing fancies into a single, pure, coherent, and true knowledge" (*DN* 701B).

In his discussion of theological tradition, Dionysius economically describes human cognition as a double process, one the intuitive and mystical understanding, the other discursive and analytic: "The one resorts to symbolism and involves initiation. The other is philosophic and employs the method of demonstration. (Further, the inexpressible is bound up with what can be articulated.) The one uses persuasion and imposes the truthfulness of what is asserted. The other acts and, by means of a mystery which cannot be taught, it puts souls firmly in the presence of God" (*Letter Nine* 1105D).

Cognition is an intellectual retracing of the process of creation from its present complexity and materiality to its original simplicity in first principles. In this sense all understanding ultimately requires a process that dismantles and disorders the cognitive constructs that the mind has imposed on the real. However, within the triadic system of knowledge an ascending motion is also implied: parallel to the descent of being from the Deity into the material world, from simplicity to multiplicity, from identity to difference, discursive and analytic knowledge "descends" from the articulation of names for the larger and more comprehensive principles to ever more specific affirmations concerning the subject. This is the *via positiva* – the affirmative, or cataphatic, phase of knowing, in which one begins by asserting such broad statements as "God is life," "God is the good," and proceeds to more particular descriptions of God, such as "still, small voice" (1 Kings 19:12).

While Denys' science is theology and his subject is always God, the epistemology he describes is applicable in general to the way the human mind works in relation to all objects of knowledge. Paradigmatic of the descent of Being into beings, affirmative discourse multiplies the names of God as well as the names of all other things, and in so doing, adds more and more qualities to the subject. Denys recognizes the value of affirmative thought – indeed, its inevitability – but also provides a critique of it:

The fact is that the more we take flight upward, the more our words are confined to the ideas we are capable of forming ... In the earlier books my argument traveled downward from the most exalted to the humblest categories, taking in on this downward path an ever-increasing number of ideas which multiplied with every stage of the descent. But my argument now rises from what is below up to the transcendent, and the more it climbs, the more language falters, and when it has passed up and beyond the ascent, it will turn silent completely, since it will finally be at one with him who is indescribable. (*MT* 1033B–1033C)

Affirmative discourse is, again, necessary but limiting. Every affirmation about a subject imposes a limitation on it, because affirmation functions through differentiation. To call the dog brown, or to name it Spot, is to limit it to its name and its colour, or whatever other quality is noted. While this is clearly useful for logical understanding and discrimination between things of the same kind, what becomes clear through a negative critique of affirmation is the inability of language to present the wholeness of its subject. This appears particularly acute when the subject is one of the "transcendentals," or is related to one of them, such as God, Being, One. What the Pseudo-Dionysius has made the core of his theology is the perception that all affirmation has within it a negative priority: every affirmation tells us what a thing is not. To name someone is to differentiate, to put aside during the description his or her unity with other beings and with other things, and so, to call him John is to say and to know what he is not: not an animal, but human; not female, but male; not Peter, James, or any other man, but this one defined, contained, isolated individual. He is named. The Areopagite, who fictionalized himself (or herself) through the adoption of a pseudonym, suggests that the real nature of affirmation is, somewhat ironically, similar to fiction and that it is a mask or veil for the more fundamental reality of negation that lurks always just behind it.

Therefore, Denys regards negative or apophatic theology as a crucial second step: "This second way of talking about him seems to me much more appropriate, for, as the secret and sacred tradition has instructed, God is in no way like the things that have being and we have no knowledge at all of his incomprehensible and ineffable transcendence and invisibility" (*CH* 140D–141A). Negation is the way up and corresponds epistemologically to the metaphysical "return." Its trope, that is, the intellectual procedure it employs, is anagogy. It begins by denying the lowest and most specific descriptions and proceeds up to the most comprehensive, negating every possible affirmation. Thus the journey that begins with "God is not a worm" (*CH* 145A) will end with "God is not" (*DN* 817D). The force of Dionysian negation is, however, not one of privation, but of liberation from the limitations of predication, and in this sense we see that just as affirmation is a mask for a negative truth fuller than itself, so, too, negation contains within it a superior form of the positive. To assert that a subject "is-not" any of its qualities is not to eliminate that quality but to open the subject's "is-ness" indefinitely: in this kind of negation, a thing is what it is and is-not (merely) what it is, but instead is more than what it is and more than what it is named.

Apophatic thought is the return of the mind out of its own logico-linguistic assertions toward an unmediated encounter with the object of its search. In the *via negativa*, as in the ontological "return," each differentiation of dialectical philosophy is stripped away, its multiplicity reduced, and its presence replaced by absence. However, if Denys prefers the negative and the dissimilar, it is because of the exaggerated human predilection for the affirmative, not because of any real and inherent superiority of one in relation to the other.[22]

Affirmation and negation are not opposites in the Dionysian world because that world is not conceived in binary terms. All contraries and the hierarchies built upon them are resolved through the triadic process of which they are parts; the third member of the triad functions as the bond between the other two and the resolution of any opposition between the parts. The ultimate Christian model for such a resolution is the Trinity, wherein the apparent distinction between persons is resolved mysteriously into union by the very nature of the Trinitarian relationship. So, too, may such contraries as "speaker/spoken," "signified/sign," "reason/appetite" be resolved by a third term that creates a relationship between the two oppositions. In these examples the third terms each create basic triads: "intention" yields the triad speaker-intention-spoken, "concept" produces signified-concept-sign, and "will" gives reason-will-appetite. Resolved, too, through the triad is the ambiguity of the affirmative as proto-negation and negation as proto-affirmation. The third term in this case is transcendence, the mode in which all potential contraries are harmonized into a simple and complete understanding of the object. Opposition and hierarchy are the product of human logic, tools used within the boundaries of human understanding so as to give access to the real. But in the system of Denys, once the mind has travelled the apparently opposite roads of affirmation and negation, it perceives that the one is the other, and both can be left behind in favour of a "meta-understanding" that dissolves method, opposition, and discourse.[23]

Procession, return, remaining; affirmation, negation, transcendence. The human journey of understanding repeats the very process of God's self-manifestation from One to Trinity, to Pancreator, to Messiah, and back to One. Having climbed the ladder of knowing, the mind looks back to discover that there is no ladder. Hierarchy gives way to triad. But triad, too, in its turn gives way to the still more perfect and simple form of circle. And circle gives way to the greatest perfection of all – formlessness. Thus Denys' final description of the Deity is appropriately a non-description, one that leaves the inquirer with the challenge of understanding that which is superessential: "The Cause of all is not inexistent, lifeless, speechless, mindless ... It does not live nor is it life. It is not a substance, nor is it eternity or time ... It falls neither within the predicate of non-being nor of being ... It is beyond assertion and denial" (*MT* 1040D–1048B).

Denys insists that the rejection of the positive is not the proper corrective to self-deluding discourse. Nihilism is merely the arbitrary privileging of one term over another, which leads to hierarchies as limiting as the hierarchies that it seeks to replace. There is no possibility of negation without affirmation; there can be no meaning of absence without the reality of presence. Thus Pseudo-Dionysian philosophy rejects all forms of relativism, agnosticism, and nihilism, and, unlike some forms of Platonism, it valorizes the material world and intellectual activity as the very bases of possible understanding of the truth: "I am convinced in my mind that one may not disregard the received knowledge of divine things. I believe this not merely because one's spirit naturally yearns for and seeks whatever contemplation of the supernatural may be attainable but also because the splendid arrangement of divine laws commands it. We are told not to busy ourselves with what is beyond us, since they are beyond what we deserve and are unattainable. But the law tells us to learn everything granted to us and to share these treasures generously with others" (*DN* 684B–C).

The measured celebration of the created, material world by Denys and other Neoplatonists, Christian and non-Christian alike, is described by Hilary Armstrong: "All which comes down from him [God], down to the lowest level of the sense-world, is real and permanent. No Neoplatonist ever maintains that the material universe is a mere illusion, still less that the soul or self and whatever higher spiritual realities are recognized are only inadequate ways of thinking about the One. And even in the culmination of the return ... nothing at any level is done away with or disappears ... Things become more, not less, real if they are seen as theophanies."[24]

The basic division in Dionysian theory between affirmation and negation extends itself into all the structures of reality. For our purposes, three related subjects will be looked at through the paradigm of cataphasis/apophasis: the epistemological, the rhetorical, and the textual. As examples of the affimative we discover Pseudo-Dionysius singling out analogy as the appropriate epistemological tool, metonymy and synecdoche as the typical rhetorical figures, and the concept of the "text" as the corresponding literary phenomenon. In the *via negativa*, on the other hand, we discover in anagogy the successor to analogy in human understanding, metaphor as the proper rhetorical device, and interpretation as the corresponding literary activity.[25] Thus we have sets of terms arranged within the cataphatic and apophatic modes: analogy/anagogy; metonymy/metaphor; text/interpretation.

In metaphysical speculation, affirmative theology principally employs knowledge of cause through effects. The *via causalitatis* fashions all sorts of analogies between the qualities of dependent beings and produced things and the nature of the cause of these; this kind of analogy seeks out the direct relation of one thing to another. In theology it takes beings and things as effects, the analysis of which leads to an understanding of God as their cause. Like all theologians, Denys claims that God can be known partially as First Cause through His effects – that is to say, through creation. Although true, this knowledge is only partial because the cause is never found completely present within the effect. Just as the complete nature of fire is not discovered through the analysis of a warm object, still less is the First Cause of all contained within the aggregate of His effects. Nevertheless, the analogy of proportion does furnish a certain correct, if limited, understanding and is essential to analogy.

In logical or dialectical speculation, then, proportional analogy discovers similarities among differences and uses these similarities as the basis of understanding. While varieties of analogy were distinguished and carefully set out by mediaeval thinkers – particularly the scholastics – what is basic to analogy is the production of knowledge through degrees of similitude, and Dionysius regularly identifies analogy this way.[26] For analogy to work there must be evident similarities between distinct things being compared; from the evident similarities other similarities are inferred. In Dionysius' thought analogy is akin to affirmation and shares its characteristics, moving downward as mental process from higher things to lower things and discovering more and more qualities about its subject:

In my *Symbolic Theology* I have discussed analogies of God drawn from what we perceive. I have spoken of the images we have of him, of the forms, figures, and instruments proper to him, of the places in which he lives and of the ornaments he wears ... In the earlier books my argument traveled downward from the most exalted to the humblest categories, taking in on this downward path an ever-increasing number of ideas which multiplied with every stage of the descent ... When we assert what is beyond every assertion, we must then proceed from what is most akin to it, and as we do so we make the affirmation on which everything else depends. (*MT* 1033A, 1033C)

Just as causality and analogy are respectively the metaphysical and logical devices proper to affirmative thought, so in rhetoric certain devices suggest themselves as appropriate to cataphasis. Metonymy and synecdoche as figures of speech that seek out similarities between names in order to transfer meaning are found to be more suitable for affirmation than other devices that tend to emphasize difference. In metonymy, where one word is used for another, the possibility of making this exchange rests upon the natural and obvious likeness of the two terms. When, for instance, Denys, referring to the Trinity, speaks of "the font of life" (*EH* 373C), he is resorting to metonymy, or "substitute naming," behind which similitude lies the concept of causality. Synecdoche, which uses a part to stand for the whole, is also a natural ally of affirmation and is used often by Denys: "They praise its eyes, ears, hair, face, and hands, back, wings, and arms, a posterior, and feet" (*DN* 597A–B). Yet with his habitual uneasiness about affirmation, Denys even warns us concerning the possible deception of synecdoche when applied to the Deity who has no parts: "I have shown how in scripture all the names appropriate to God are praised regarding the whole, entire, full, and complete divinity rather than any part of it"(*DN* 636C).

The relationship of metonymy and synecdoche to affirmation, as opposed to negative analysis, is economically expressed in Earl MacCormac's recent study of metaphor: "Metonymy employs an attribute as an expression of the entity, and synecdoche takes a part and lets it stand for the whole or takes the whole and lets it stand for a part. These two figures of speech do not often juxtapose referents with contradictory semantic markers."[27] Indeed, in the system of Pseudo-Dionysius and the mediaeval Neoplatonists, the very utility of such figures is that they permit the contradictory to be held in abeyance until the completion of the affirmative process. The necessary "correction" of such figures and the discourse they produce is the work of another, superior figure of speech: metaphor.

Just as the world has been created by the exuberance of divine love causing the *editus* of the One out of itself (while remaining) into matter and multiplicity, so too in the vision of the Areopagite, the Word goes out from the
Speaker to create the text, in one mode as the second person of the Trinity,
the *Verbum Dei*, and in another as Scripture, the written intention of the divine author about his creation. In this sense the *via affirmativa* is akin to the
concept of text. The completed concept of "procession" in Denys is constituted not only by Trinity, Creation, and Incarnation but also by Revelation,
the proceeding of the One into the material world in the form of the written
word in Scripture and the unwritten word in liturgy. This is the view and the
central thesis concerning Dionysian procession of Paul Rorem's study of
Pseudo-Dionysius' symbolism: "In the Pseudo-Dionysian corpus, the scriptures and the liturgy are viewed as the divine procession into the world of the
senses; their spiritual interpretation, correspondingly, is part of the divine return which uplifts the faithful."[28]

Denys' view of the nature of the sacred text may be extended to secular
texts, as well, just as all of creation and everything within it appears as an
extended text of God's authorship. Every text proceeds from the mind of its
author, beginning in the unity and simplicity of an idea or intuition and developing, according to the necessities of communication, into discursive expression, multiplying words, sentences, paragraphs. Sign is piled upon sign,
one concept gives rise to another, and meaning – although having its origin
in the simplicity of mental concept – is reconstructed through the multiplicity of words. In this way the authoring of a text is seen as comparable to the
creation of the world, an *editus* of the author, betokening the *editus* of God in
creation; the complement of this image, found so frequently in the Middle
Ages, is the representation of God's creation as a book: "Every creature in
the world is, for us, a book, a picture, and a mirror, as well."[29]

In this thoroughly textual metaphor for creation, God is seen as a writer
inscribing His words upon an empty parchment as He brings into existence
the heaven and the earth, light, water and land, and the living beings. The increasing multiplicity of God's creation – from the relatively unified phenomena of heaven and earth to the "manyness" of animals, plants, insects and the
innumerable individuals of the world – is paralleled by the writer's opening
words of his discourse, followed by the cumulative stream of signs that
makes a fuller and fuller communication of the writer's thought. Just as the
material creation of Genesis ("In the beginning God created the heaven and
the earth") is paralleled by the verbal creation of the Gospel of St John ("In
the beginning was the Word"), so the Christian Middle Ages found in the
scriptive metaphor a far-reaching sign. Just as God's *editus* did not stop with
the single act of creation but continued through time to the Incarnation in
which he "came out of himself," as Jesus, so the *Verbum Dei* is regularly
conceived in terms of God's textuality: "For Christ is a sort of book written

into the skin of the virgin ... That book was spoken in the disposition of the Father, written in the conception of the mother, exposited in the clarification of the nativity, corrected in the passion, erased in the flagellation, punctuated in the imprint of the wounds."[30]

While all texts are, then, constitutive of the affirmative stage of understanding, they contain within themselves, like the created world, the possibility of their own transcendence. Denys, like other Christian Neoplatonists, saw the ultimate task of intellect to be, not the understanding of the physical world, but the "reading" of the physical world in order to understand its referent. Again Professor Roques expresses best Denys' sense: "For him the most important thing is not to explain the material world as such, already attempted by all the ancient philosophers and by Basil, as well. Rather, the material universe is conceived of as a field of symbols which can and must lead human understanding to a perception of the intelligible world."[31]

Thus on the side of cataphasis we may group "text," synecdoche and metonymy, and analogy. In contrast, we may now look at the apophatic side of the paradigm, where we will discover the parallel phenomena of anagogy, metaphor, and interpretation, in one sense contradictory because they negate, in another, complementary because they complete.

While affirmation is associated with the concept of text, no text of any worth can be taken literally at the level of its rhetorical surface, and, even more important for the Neoplatonist, it must never be conceived as a simple mimesis of the material world; rather, these layers must be peeled away and their limitations transcended in order that the reader may rise above the *integumentum*, the disguise, to an understanding of the meaning of the text. This is achieved through a process of negation. In this way no text is fully created through authorship alone, but requires the reader's intelligent interpretation for its completion, and the dynamic into which composition and interpretation enter parallels the process of *editus-reditus*: the mind of the reader, transcending the affirmative surface of the text, rises and returns to the source of meaning, joining the intellect of the author. The ascent of the reader's mind to authorial intention and meaning suggests a form of anagogy.

Anagogical thought is said to be "mystical." Its mystery (from the Greek μυστήριου, root of μυειυ: "to close" [the eyes and lips]) arises from its proclivity for using paradox in order to transcend discourse and arrive at a blind and silent knowing. Dionysius opens his treatise on *Mystical Theology* with a poem describing anagogy:

> Lead us up beyond unknowing and light,
> up to the farthest, highest peak
> of mystic scripture,
> where the mysteries of God's Word

lie simple, absolute and unchangeable
in the brilliant darkness of a hidden silence.

(*MT* 997A–997B)

The need to transcend analogy arises out of the relation of analogy to causality: understanding a thing by its effects entails the process of drawing the elevated, unique cause down to the lower, derived effects. Causality is not a helpful concept in the *via negativa*, because negation seeks to rid concepts of inference and to arrive at the essence of the thing through elimination of everything nonessential to it. Apophasis simply denies the efficacy of understanding through cause and effect by negating the copula between them: God is not being; or, better still, God ⅓ being. The inadequacy of causality is shared by analogy. Since God is above being and is-not, He does not share the perfections found in beings in the same mode as they exist in beings, and therefore none of these perfections can be attributed to the Deity. There is nothing proportionate to the One. Recognizing that analogy can bring the human mind only so far, Dionysianism employs anagogy as the appropriate tool for negation and "return." The "uplifting" that anagogy causes occurs with the stripping away of all attributes of the intelligible, including being, through progressive negation of similarity and proportionality. Thus there is a parallel between the One's descent into the many, seen as a divine "condescension," and the mind's uplifting, the matching anagogical process: by its own power the intellect draws the One down, so to speak, making it commensurate with itself; but it is by the power of the One that the human intellect is inversely drawn upward to meet the downward motion of God. The first motion is achieved by analogy, affirmation, and similitude; the other, by anagogy, negation, and dissimilitude. Professor Roques delineates the relation between these three dimensions:

To bring symbolism and negative theology within the only perspective which can clarify them and into the center of their own power, we must understand them as the encounter of two exstases, recognizing this term in its broadest, Dionysian sense of a "departure out of self." The first of these leads God out of himself (ἐξίστημι) and carries him to the outer limits of multiplicity: it corresponds to the immense theophany of all symbols. The second, in an opposite sense, "draws the intelligences outside of themselves," snatches them out of the multiplicity that divides them … makes them abandon everything and even abandon themselves, in order to rediscover the One. Thus it is at the junction of these two exstases brought about by the One that occurs the anagogical work of intelligence upon symbol.[32]

Paul Rorem shows us another aspect of the relationship in the process of intellectual transference from the idea of *reditus*, or the metaphysical dimension of the system, to the idea of anagogy, or the literary-epistemological dimension: "Thus 'return' and 'uplifting' are one and the same ascent toward an identical goal. When expressed in terms of 'return' this elevating movement receives a stark metaphysical expression, such as 'from the many to the one', or 'toward that which truly is' ... When the terminology of 'uplift' is used, this same ascending movement is described in more detail and is tied to the interpretation of symbols."[33]

Denys asserts that the fullest kind of understanding is symbolic knowledge, which he distinguishes from analytic, logical knowledge. What can be known is the degree of dissimilitude and difference between the sign and that which it signifies. Thus there is a preference for symbolism because it calls attention to its relationship with its referent, unlike logic, which encourages certitude about the bond between the object of knowledge and the discourse about it. Further, Denys encourages us to use incongruent, deforming symbols: "A manifestation through dissimilar shapes is more correctly to be applied to the invisible ... I doubt that anyone would refuse to acknowledge that incongruities are more suitable for lifting our minds up to the domain of the spiritual than similarities are" (*CH* 141A). Denys goes on to call for "appropriate adjustments" of similar signs into dissimilar ones so as to avoid "one-to-one correspondences" that would be unacceptable because of the great distance "between the intelligible and the perceptible" (*CH* 144C). Dionysian aesthetics, then, suggest a clear preference for a style in which the most inappropriate and unnatural relation between sign and signified will be employed, because the deforming of the bond between like and like reveals the true but hidden process of meaning. What Denys is describing is the theoretical basis of the grotesque.

Denys' symbolism reflects the same ambiguity of sense as do the cognitive ways of affirmation and negation. Certain symbols preferred by Denys contain within their affirmative representation a negative charge, and while they figure forth their subject, they also conceal a more fundamental negation of it. This representation Denys calls the symbolism of dissimilitude, and it is anchored in incongruity. Such symbolism grapples with the limitations of representation by showing what is not, by sundering the sign and the signified, and by deforming the very form that contains the subject. In a passage important for his theory of the deformed, Denys uses the Biblical examples of descriptions of God as a worm: "Add to this what seems the lowliest and most incongruous [image] of all, for the experts in things divine gave him the form of a worm" (*CH* 145A); and as a drunkard: "He is represented as someone drinking, as inebriated, as sleeping, as someone hung over (*Letter Nine* 1105B); "He is said to be drunk and hung over" (*MT* 1033B). Denys explains that he is attracted to such figures precisely because they are sufficiently transgressive as to automatically negate their content:

High-flown shapes could well mislead someone into thinking that the heavenly beings are golden or gleaming men, glamorous, wearing lustrous clothing, giving off flames which cause no harm, or that they have other similar beauties with which the word of God has fashioned the heavenly minds. It was to avoid this kind of misunderstanding among those incapable of rising above visible beauty that the pious theologians so wisely and upliftingly stooped to incongruous dissimilarities, for by doing this they took account of our inherent tendency toward the material and our willingness to be lazily satisfied by base images. At the same time they enabled that part of the soul which longs for the things above actually to rise up. Indeed the sheer crassness of the signs is a goad so that even the materially inclined cannot accept that it could be permitted or true that the celestial and divine sights could be conveyed by such shameful things. And remember too that there is nothing that lacks its own share of beauty, for as scripture rightly says, "Everything is good." (*CH* 141B-141C)

Negation and return eschew such figures of speech as metonymy and synecdoche. Extended metaphor is seen as a more useful figure, the contemplation of which may lead to a perception of absence and an understanding "from within." While Aristotle included metaphor within analogy and was echoed in this by his mediaeval followers, a certain awkwardness has always been recognized in the accomodation. In any case, in the thought of the Areopagite the superiority of one rhetorical figure over another rests in its dissimilitude, incongruity, and obscurity.

The comparisons created by metaphor acquire their power by relating things that are radically different and even incongruous. The force of the comparison is not directed toward diminishing difference or making the subject present through similarity to the figure. Rather, what metaphor does is to make us aware in a dramatic way that the signified is *not* as its sign presents it, and by this negative realization, metaphor draws us through the sign to an awareness of transcendent absence and a certain obscurity. Metaphor jars the mind by disordering our expectations about comparison and signification. At the same time, we enjoy it and often characterize good metaphors as "fresh," "brilliant," "daring," and even "outrageous," evidently because while it disturbs, metaphor also frees the mind from its habitual course. Denys' sense of the value of the sign and his linking of the aesthetics of negation with the grotesque seems to be echoed in MacCormac's definition of metaphor as "a combination of referents that produces semantic conceptual anomaly."[34]

"Conceptual anomaly" describes well the poetic dynamics of Andrew Marvell's famous lines, "The grave's a fine and private place, / But none, I think, do there embrace."[35]

The comparison between the bridal bed and the grave suggests a rhetorical similarity between the two objects being compared. But the deeper metaphoricity of the figure renders habitual comparisons and similarities related to beds (sleep, sickness, sex) and graves (death, corruption, coldness) inadequate and forces us to negate them in favour of the more transgressive comparison of dissimilitudes.

Metaphor as the preferred rhetorical figure of the *via negativa* leads directly to the third sense of return, "interpretation." All of the signs that fill a text, like all those that fill the world, betoken original concepts and, beyond these concepts, a removed and hidden author. For the Neoplatonist the whole purpose of signs is to allow the intellect to pass through them to become one with that which they represent. This "passing through" is what Pseudo-Dionysius means by apophasis, the negating of the similitudes of signs so as to discover, first, their superior dissimilitude and, finally, the need for the transcendence of both likeness and difference. This is also the goal of interpretation.

The multilayered interpenetration of Dionysian models is seen again in the phenomenon of interpretation. Just as human history is always incomplete, always in the process of returning to the Source, the possibility of that return is already signified and a model for it provided in the life of Christ who, as the narrative of Scripture details, enters the world of signs and then returns to the Source. In a similar way, every text is always incomplete, always in the process of interpretation as each reader encounters it, but the pattern of its completion is already at hand, even before its composition, and it is the same as the model for the completion of history. While for the Neoplatonic reader the intention of the author is important, the ultimate goal of interpretation is beyond authorial intention. Proclus, whom Dionysius clearly echoes, describes interpretation as going beyond what the author sets before the reader, a task greatly facilitated by the grotesque style: "It seems to me that the grim, monstrous and unnatural character of poetic fictions moves the listener in every way to a search for truth, and draws him toward the secret knowledge; it does not allow him, as would be the case with something that possessed a surface probability, to remain with the thoughts placed before him. It compels him, instead, to enter into the interior of the myths."[36]

In a sense all human authors are scribes, partial copiers of the truth established by God in His Word. In the multitude of texts that human inspiration produces, authorial intentions, like the signs used to express them, are to be comprehended and then "passed through" to the ultimate Author's intention, the one Author who is the same as His intention, the same as His sign.[37] Christ, the *Verbum Dei,* functions ideally as both word and meaning, sign and signified, text and interpretation. Just as Christ is both Father and Son in the hypostasis of the Trinity, so He is both speaker and word; just as God-Pancreator is the "author" of the text of the world, so that text is completed by an "audience" represented by God-Jesus, and in His life author and audience merge. Thus there appears a series of models for the transcendence of the separations: speaker and word, knower and known, text and exegesis. In his brilliant study of sixteenth-century poetics, Justus George Lawler explains the paradoxical role of Jesus as the arch-exegete: "That is the meaning of the following from the prologue to John's Gospel, where one reads: 'No one has ever seen God; it is God the only Son, ever at the Father's side, who has revealed him.' The verb 'revealed' here is in French translated 'expliqué'; the Greek is 'exēgeisthai.' The Son is thus the exegete of the Father; he is the first literary critic; he explicates God and is the model for all literary criticism in which ideally the Explicator is the Text and the Text is the Explicator, while the Commentary which joins the two is the Spirit."[38]

This idea of text and interpretation in Denys' theory is of the utmost importance in clarifying the literary dimension of mediaeval Neoplatonism as well as the function of the monstrous within it. The Neoplatonic disparagement of mimetic art has much to do with this interdependency of intention, interpretation, and text, for, unlike the Aristotelians and their scholastic successors in the Middle Ages, the Neoplatonists conceived of aesthetic constructs as noetic, at least potentially. This ability of art to lead to an understanding of the real was made possible by the function of symbol, conceived of as a special type of sign free of many of the limitations of other components of discourse. The chief of these limitations, according to the Neoplatonist, is found in the mimetic character of most figures of speech and thus in ordinary discourse itself. The imitation of the world, itself a composition of signs, limits the mind to the reality of the mundane, creating a closed circuit of the sign of a sign, the imitation of an imitation. Worse still, mimesis tempts the intellect into believing that what is copied is the extent of the real. James Coulter, in an invaluable study of the aesthetic extension of Neoplatonism, describes the literary vision of this school by commenting on Proclus' distinction between *eiconic* representation (simple mimesis) and *symbolon* (symbolic representation):

The most important matter to note for the present is Proclus' assertion that in symbolic poetry there is no question of a "relationship of model to copy," a characteristic, apparently, of eiconic representation and paideutic myth. Rather, there is a mysterious and much more complex relationship between the symbols of mythic narrative, on the face of it often bizarre and monstrous, and that divine world these symbols were thought to evoke. It is a *mysterious* relationship because of the seeming unlikeness of the symbol to that at the existence of which it secretly hints."[39]

Perhaps the single most important element of Neoplatonist interpretation is found in the assertion that every text is constituted *in the first instance* by its author's intention. In this view, art is an intellectual phenomenon possessing great philosophical value; it raises the mind above the surface of the text itself to an encounter with the mind of the artist and in so doing repeats the same fundamental movement of divine condescension matched by intellectual anagogy. It is not difficult to perceive in such an aesthetic theory the importance of exegesis, for once the function of authorial intention is made central, the discovery of that intention emerges as equally central. Secular texts created by human authors labour under the problems of the separation of author and audience on the one hand, and the separation of sign and signified in language on the other. Just as it is necessary to understand the sign in order to "pass through" it to the signified, so, too, the intention of the author must be grasped before it can be transcended. Interpretation is here not a separate act subsequent to the act of creation; it is the second phase of the act of creation that completes the text: "For with the Neoplatonists it is above all the *conscious intention* of the artist, what they call the *skopos*, which imparts to the various elements of his work the quality of being necessary or of belonging. In the same way, it is only a correct understanding of this intention on the part of the exegete which allows him to settle the question of unity."[40]

Pseudo-Dionysius and his followers make clear that this process of exegesis is a negative one complementing the cataphatic process of authorial creation. In a motion complementary to an outgoing *editus* from the unified intellectual intention of the author's mind to the multiple signs of his expression, an uprising *reditus* of the interpreter's mind from the surface level of textual signs leads to an encounter with the author's intention during the exegetical process and results in the unification of text and interpretation. This anagogy is achieved because of the mind's capacity to "see through" the signs employed to their reality, and this achievement is possible only because of the inherent dissimilitude between sign and signified. The measure of a great artist is not only the loftiness of his intention, but his skill in fashioning incongruous representations; the success of the exegete depends on his ability to perceive these incongruities and discover in them the key to deconstructing the discourse.

Deconstruction here is not antagonistic to the author but rather a harmonizing *amitié* between author and exegete. In a passage discussing the figures appropriate for the representation of the divine, Denys provides us with one of the several examples of how the intelligent reader should read to correct the text by making "appropriate adjustments":

So, then, forms, even those drawn from the lowliest matter, can be used, not unfittingly, with regard to heavenly beings. Matter, after all, owes its subsistence to absolute beauty and keeps, throughout its earthly ranks, some echo of intelligible beauty. Using matter, one may be lifted up to the immaterial archetypes. Of course one must be careful to use the similarities as dissimilarities, as discussed, to avoid one-to-one correspondences, to make the appropriate adjustments as one remembers the great divide between the intelligible and the perceptible". (*CH* 144B–C)

To summarize, the vision of Pseudo-Dionysius is presented as a triad constituted by divine procession, return, and remaining. The triad is a paradigm of the relation of God to himself in the Trinity, and, further, the Trinity is a model of human cognition. Correlative to procession is affirmation, the discursive naming and predicating of being. Affirmation is based on the logic of causality supported by analogy, and its rhetorical expression is through metonymy and synecdoche. In the activity we call art, procession and affirmation find a correspondence in the concept of text and provide a paradigm for it. As in Creation, the text is brought into being by the intention of its author and is constituted by the many figures of speech that language uses. Among them, metaphor provides the possibility of interpretation because within it is concealed the apophatic quality that makes possible a certain liberation from the limits of language. Such a liberation occurs in the process of interpretation, a motion of intellect paralleled by the *reditus* of Christian metaphysics. Like it, too, interpretation is in a certain way apophatic, since interpretation requires the audiences to negate the illusions of language and penetrate the signs to arrive at meaning.[41] Just as the process of metaphysical *reditus* is achieved by a cognitive "uplifting," so, too, the ultimate interpretive act is seen as anagogic, as an upward intellectual analysis that progresses by negating all the affirmations of discourse, from the lowest to the highest.

Whereas *editus*, or procession, is conceived principally as an act of the Father, return is associated with the Son and is understood theologically through Christ. His incarnation, while in an obvious way a form of procession of the One into the many, is actually a pivotal event in the process, since within it is contained both procession and return. The earthly life of Jesus is humanity's model for its return, and this *reditus* trope begins at the moment of the Incarnation, continues to the Crucifixion, and is completed in the Resurrection.[42] While procession is always a descent, returning is always a going upward, understood either as Jesus' Resurrection or as the ascent of the human intellect in knowledge toward union with the One. Return requires negation, and the ascent of the mind is conceived of as an apophatic process. Thus the *via negativa* and the *via positiva* cover the same terrain but in different directions.

Such a system, both as metaphysics and as poetics, is grounded in paradox, and it is paradox that is the central feature of Denys' entire worldview. Deity as Trinity is the essence of paradox; the triadic One, origin of the many; He who is and is-not, all motion and perfect stasis. The pervasiveness of paradox in the highest descriptions of God suggests paradox itself as inhabiting the core of truth. Nicholas of Cusa expressed the concept of God that was to become the foundation of Christian mysticism and its perfect trope, and it is one that frankly expresses the essential paradox of the divine as "that Simplicity where contradictories coincide."[43]

Throughout Christian thought two attitudes toward paradox are discernible: the scholastics tended to treat it as a phenomenon of language and thus a logical problem; the Neoplatonists tended to see paradox as ontological and thus as a subject appropriate to metaphysics. As manifested in ambiguity, paradox may be treated as a purely linguistic problem, and so it was by

Aristotle,[44] and for the scholastics, as heirs to Aristotle, these ambiguities were considered fallacies. But as Rosalie L. Colie's classic work on paradox has shown, an entirely different attitude prevailed among the heirs to negative theology. According to Colie, paradox is a thing crafted to deny and destroy "systems," and she identifies three basic types: the rhetorical, the logical, and the epistemological.[45] Colie takes the famous paradox of the liar as the primary example of the epistemological type and describes it in terms that strongly echo Pseudo-Dionysius and the sense of transcendental value that the Neoplatonists saw in paradox: "The problem it presents is a special case of all 'speculative,' or self-referential operations – a special case, then, of what I call the epistemological paradox, in which the mind, by its own operation, attempts to say something about its operation." [46]

Better, perhaps, than anyone else, Colie shows that all self-reflexive thinking leads to paradox. The choice then is either to deny paradox, labelling it as fallacy or "solving" it logically, or to enter into paradox by accepting it as the terminus of understanding. The latter choice creates a situation in which the process of thought and the content of thought become indistinguishable, forming a kind of paradigm for the union of knower and known. Colie first describes the acceptance of paradox in her explanation of Zeno's paradox of the arrow, motionless at every point of its trajectory, yet always moving: "Beneath the paradoxes of motion lies Zeno's real point: motion is merely relative and apparent. By his logic, both relativity and appearance can be demonstrated, in their own terms, not to exist; thereby an absolute monism can be demonstrated to be the only truth in existence. In these paradoxes, relativity is (paradoxically) necessary to the proof of Zeno's absolute. As the paradoxes are at once rationalist and antirationalist, so are they at once relativist and absolute, equivocally and irrevocably."[47]

She describes paradox again in the Christian context:

Christian paradoxes, in an ultimate oxymoron, are always orthodox, not only in the propriety of their doctrine but also in the fact that they appear to describe accurately feelings deeply rooted in human nature. When God, man, and all things are seen under the aspect of *concordia discors*, then everything in human experience, however materially distant from abstract divinity, is nonetheless immediately – without mediation – metaphysical also. Each thing contains or implies its opposite; each thing refers to transcendence. Both by correspondence (all things "match" as aspect of *logos*) and by contradiction (all things coincide in deity), anything in human experience can be perceived at once in its metaphysical as well as in its experiential aspect.[48]

God's theophanies are always paradoxical, and they are many: the paradox of the Trinity is followed by that of the production of the many by the One in Creation, and both are followed by the paradox of the Incarnation. Alanus de Insulis in his hymn on the Incarnation expresses at once the fun-

damentally linguistic nature both of the paradoxical Incarnation and of paradox itself, as well as the ability of paradox to transcend the limitations of
language:

> New is the metaphor!
> New the rhetorical bond!
> All new the syntax!
> In this verb TO BE,
> All the rules are silenced!
> (Nova fit translatio
> Novus color in junctura
> Nova fit constructio
> In hac Verbi copula
> Stupet omnis regula).[49]

In Alan's splendid grammatical conceit, it is the prodigy of the Word
Made Flesh that stupifies the grammatical rules of human discourse, and it is
in this enigmatic figure of the Incarnation that the mediaeval connection between paradox and monstrosity is best seen. As late as the seventeenth century the Spanish theologian Balthasar Gracian (1601–55) states the concept
bluntly: "Paradoxes are the monsters of truth"![50]

Colie traces the development of the concept of paradox from its origin in
Parmenides to the writings of Saint Paul and Pseudo-Dionysius and through
them to the Middle Ages and Renaissance. Following the seminal work of
Raymond Klibansky on the Platonic tradition in the Middle Ages and Renaissance, Colie points to Nicholas of Cusa as the main exponent of Dionysian paradox for this later period. She identifies paradox as intrinsic to
negative theology and, further, views the theological context of the development of mediaeval and Renaissance paradox as the origin of its triadic structure as seen in the rhetorical, logical, and ontological categories of paradox.
While being, on the one hand, and non-being, on the other, are conceived in
negative theology as two ontological modes, a third concept, "being-and-
not-being," is introduced as a mediating and transcending factor that simultaneously creates the triad and the paradox. It is in this way that paradox
exists in an ontological mode.[51]

The negation of negations, the dissimilitude of all likeness, and the coincidence of opposites are the mainstays of the Dionysian universe, where the
deepest foundations of reality are set in paradox. So, too, in cognition, intellectual "ascent" describes metaphysical "descent"; metaphysical "assent"
is achieved through intellectual "dissent." Juxtaposed to the logic of analogy
is the mystery of anagogy. Denys' particular concept of negation, as we have
said, involves, not privation, not the limiting of the thing by its reduction,
but the liberation and increase of the thing by the overcoming of limiting

affirmative definitions. Paradox, by its very nature, refuses closure both intellectually and ontologically, and this limitless openness of Being is found
preeminently in the One. Denys' apophatic description of the Supreme
Cause identifies it in a striking way with paradox: "It [the Supreme Cause]
cannot be grasped by the understanding, since it is neither knowledge nor
truth. It is not kingship. It is not wisdom. It is neither one nor oneness, divinity nor goodness. Nor is it a spirit, in the sense in which we understand that
term. It is not sonship or fatherhood and it is nothing known to us or to any
other being. *It falls neither within the predicate of nonbeing nor of being*"
(*MT* 1048A, emphasis added).

It is here that we encounter Denys' most telling description of the One,
and it is a deeply paradoxical description expressing simultaeously all three
modes of paradox: the Supreme Cause is, to our understanding a logical impossibility – a proposition and a non-proposition. We express this impossibility rhetorically in paradoxical figures; ontologically we contemplate the
nature of the Supreme Cause as being and non-being. Thus the Supreme
Cause is itself paradox.[52] Again, Colie summarizes: "Unavailable to human
experience and to human speculation, the transcendent deity deals in *impos-
sibilia*, is itself an *impossibilium*."[53]

The mediaeval development of Pseudo-Dionysius' epistemological theory
of negation and his related theory of dissimilitude in symbolism provided a
conceptual foundation for the extra-philosophical, poetic construct of what is
called here a deformed discourse. This discourse involved a vocabulary of
monstrous forms drawn from both the tradition of the monstrous races and
the iconographic traditions that figuratively expressed much of the original
sense of the Dionysian philosophical critique of rationality. As poetic figure,
the monster functions to negate the similitudes of mimesis; it denies the
commensuration of sign and signified, widening the gulf between them. It
undermines the adequacy of symbol to symbolized so as to force the mind
through the symbol and beyond it. Itself a paradox, the monster locates paradox at the hidden center of all discourse by inverting margin and text. This
perspective is not, of course, universal in the Middle Ages. Although the grotesque style is widespread in visual arts and poetry, it is not dominant, any
more than the Neoplatonic dialectic of negation predominates in philosophy
and theology. By the thirteenth century, the dominant philosophical discourse is one that emphasizes the affirmative, rational way of understanding,
and it is in this context that the concept of the monster undergoes its final
mediaeval development.

ST THOMAS AND THE SCHOLASTIC AFFIRMATIVE TRADITION

The foundation of Aristotle's metaphysics may be said to be the laws of noncontradiction and the excluded middle. These conceptions not only describe

how the mind defines being but are considered inherent to being itself. The minimum character of that which has being must be that it "is" and cannot also simultaneously be "is-not." Following his master, St Thomas puts it succinctly: "Only that is excluded from the divine omnipotence which contradicts the reason or essence of being, that is, that something at the same time be and not be" (*ST* 1.25.2). For Aristotle and his mediaeval followers being must be able to take either the predicate *X* or not-*X* and may never take both at the same time. Also, between two contradictories, *X* and not-*X*, no third term is possible: either the one exists or the other exists.

It is the emphasis on this basic law that most clearly distinguishes Aristotelian metaphysics from the thought of Pseudo-Dionysius and his followers, for where Aristotle grounds the nature of being in a clear logical principle, Denys envisions it as supralogical and residing in paradox, and where the Aristotelians construct a metaphysics on binary opposition, Denys builds his on a triadic coincidence of opposites.[54] From this basic distinction flow the numerous differences between the two systems of thought, including, preeminently, the subtle difference of emphasis each places on affirmation and negation, the priority given in cognition to the existent or to the *neant*. In the Middle Ages the distinction accounts not only for the great variety of solutions to particular philosophical problems but also for whole differences of perspective and styles in art. The monster as the embodiment of paradox presents a challenge to the validity of the law of noncontradiction and the idea of being based in binary opposition, for what the metaphysician would keep apart as the very guarantee of existence, the monster combines in a representation of being which "is" and "is-not."

In his commentaries on the works of Dionysius, St Thomas exhibits, along with a reverent attentiveness to the texts, a certain anxiety about their content. As Marie-Dominique Chenu suggests, what Thomas was seeking in the works of the Areopagite was a reinforcement of the views of Aristotle, and he was ultimately disappointed: "It would seem, on the strength of a few external resemblances, that Saint Thomas thought for a time that Dionysius, whose symbolism promotes the value of the sensible as regards the life of the mind, approximated the views of Aristotle. Very soon, however, he perceived that the Dionysian contemplation of the sensible world had nothing to do with the Philosopher's almost sensualistic experimentalism, and he recognized that Dionysius lived in another universe."[55]

Nevertheless, Thomas pursued his commentaries on the neoplatonic Denys, and some of what he found unsympathetic, he simply changed: "Herein as in the case of Aristotle, by declaring himself in agreement with Dionysius, St Thomas is sometimes consciously drawing him to his own meaning, as for example when he has the metaphysics of the good concurring with the metaphysics of being."[56] Chenu goes on to specify the goal of Thomistic correction of Dionysius: "to reduce to homogenous mental categories the mystico-metaphysical attire of the Oriental doctor."[57]

In certain cases, St Thomas' resistance leads him to state as Dionysian thought what is, in fact, its contrary. Commenting on a passage in the *Divine Names*, a text crucial to Dionysianism, Thomas inverts the ideas of his author so that he says the opposite of what he meant. Dionysius states his theory of cognition as a process consisting of negation, transcendence, and affirmation, giving to negation and transcendence their usual priority: "We pass by way of the denial and transcendence of all things and by way of the cause of all things" (*DN* 872A). Thomas attributes to Denys the reverse order: "[Dionysius] says that from creatures we arrive at God in three ways, namely: by way of causality, of removal, of eminence."[58] Such reversals of Dionysian thought allow Thomas to claim elsewhere what could not be further from the truth: "Almost everywhere Dionysius follows Aristotle, as appears evident to one inspecting his books with care."[59]

In the fundamental and ongoing tension in mediaeval Christianity between knowledge of God as subject of logical discourse on the one hand, and union with God through transcendence of cognition on the other, Thomas and his followers opted to develop the former. What is at stake here, as elsewhere when the Aristotelian encounters the Neoplatonist, is the precedence of affirmation or of negation, the precedence of particulars or of universals, and the precedence of logic or of rhetoric.[60] Thomas and the scholastics, while scrupulously noting the idea of God's unknowability and the ineffability of being, consistently pursue an affirmative metaphysics bolstered by analytical reasoning and logical discourse. The symbolic language and paradoxical mode of Denys and his followers are suspect to Thomas and to the scholastics, who followed Aristotle and Thomas in search of a precise and logical analysis of being and a language capable of presenting the transcendent as knowable and immanent. An important step in that process was Thomas' transformation of Augustine's theory of signs into rigorous logical form. The pursuit of the logical nature of language and the increasing identification of understanding with language itself is what characterizes scholasticism and contrasts it most dramatically with the apophatic tradition. The resistance of logic to the cognitive value of the transdiscursive and of negation and the gradual restriction of the investigation of the real to the scope of logical principles sealed the fate of universals that was already betokened in the views of Roscelin (1050–1120) and Peter Abelard (1079–1142).

The Angelic Doctor, in agreement with Aristotle, had taken the philosophical position of moderate realism which, simply put, asserts that universals exist in and through the existence of particulars, or individuals. This position, dominant in early Scholasticism, contradicted the view of Platonism and Neoplatonism, which held universals to be independent of and prior to particulars. For the Platonist, Justice, Humanity, the Good, and so forth, possess real existence either in the realm of Ideas or as the ideas in the mind of God or in some unspecified mode, and they are the matrix of individual acts of justice, of the human nature in which mankind participates, and the individual acts of goodness, or expressions of order, that we experience. While Platonism proffered this concept as the basis of its metaphysics and conceived of universals ontologically, Aristotle helped to shift the grounds of the discourse from metaphysics to logic by revealing the fallacies inherent in realism when considered from a purely logical perspective.[61]

The role of analogy in the construction of affirmative philosophy in general and in the concept of the ontological basis of language specifically is given unprecedented importance by the scholastics, and one of the major contributions of St Thomas has long been recognized as his development of the analogy of being. The classic view of the use of analogy in St Thomas and the scholastics regards it as divided into three categories: analogy of attribution, analogy of inequality, and analogy of proportionality; this last was further divided into proper and improper analogies of proportionality. Professor Colish warns that to label one kind of analogy rather than another as typically Thomist is to misrepresent his thought,[62] and the warning is too well-founded to permit the simple assertion that Thomas favours the analogy producing the greatest affirmation. However, the further claim that he uses analogy of attribution to reveal similarities between God and creatures and analogy of proportionality to counteract these similarities with the dissimilarities produced by this latter analogy gives the impression, on the one hand, that St Thomas strikes a balance between apophatic and cataphatic thought, and, on the other, that the analogy of proportionality itself is apophatic in direction. Such an impression would be incorrect on both counts.

Although it is true that the understanding gained through analogy of proportionality may be expressed as the difference between the analogates, the more basic concept of this analogy and all others is similitude. In the example Professor Colish uses – man's being is to man as God's being is to God – the nature of being in each case may be diverse and only relatively one, but the idea of being itself remains intrinsic to both and diversity is suppressed through the proportionality created between them through analogy. James F. Anderson in his study of the analogy of being makes the point clearly that analogy means "likeness in difference" and that what analogy always shows us is the presence of being through proportional similarity. Further, he describes the analogy of proportionality not only as the most effective in producing knowledge of being but as inherent in the nature of the concept of being itself. Speaking of the theological description of God as Supreme Analogate and all contingent beings as Secondary Analogates, Anderson says that after the knowledge gained through the analogy of attribution, "we proceed to see that in actual fact there exists between the Supreme Analogate and the Secondary Analogates an actual community of relations, notwithstanding the essential diversity in mode of being proper to them. We are then regarding not the relation itself between the terms of this Analogy but the *proportional likeness* within the very being of the related terms: the interior harmony of relations in which they stand vis-à-vis their respective acts of existing."[63]

This likeness within the "very being" of related terms is produced by the analogy of proportionality. Contrary to the claim that the analogy of proportionality reveals difference and distance between analogates, this analogy, like all others, operates on the principle of degrees of ontological likeness and, through sameness, overcomes the inherent difference and absence of the prime analogate.

What all analogies appear to strive for is a rendering of "being" as present and intelligible, but it is the analogy of proportionality that is most successful in this project: "If this is so, then the metaphysical idea of being, properly so called, is analogical, originally and in its very essence; it is not a univocal notion afterwards employed analogically, as in both Analogy of Attribution and Analogy of Metaphor."[64] The Thomistic employment of the various kinds of analogy would seem not so much an effort to preserve and to balance the cataphatic and apophatic understandings of the real as a gradual establishment of the adequacy of affirmation.

The moderate realism of the Philosopher and of St Thomas made it possible to give priority to material phenomena and their empirical investigation, since the locus of the real was seen as the individual phenomenon; beings were the origin of essences. Platonism, both classical and Christian, with its thorough-going realism, had viewed the ultimate nature of reality as transcendental and thus incompletely accessible to human understanding and, more particularly, unconfinable within logical discourse. Its rejection of the adequation of the real to human knowledge gave a place of importance in the Platonic worldview to negation and dissimilitude. Moderate realism, shifting the locus of the real to that which is, brought with it further confidence in the ability of intellect to circumscribe the object of its activity. The greater intelligibility of beings and the certainty of that which may be predicated about them fuelled the process of constructing affirmative systems of thought based on the empirical method.

The modist logicians of the thirteenth century who provided inspiration to St Thomas, held a view of language that made it a tool for full, accurate, sufficient knowledge about beings. This logic conceives of cognition as a process of initially assigning names to known properties of things; such names then acquire the status of signs in their function of signifying the real properties of realities. Because these signs may function in different ways – when, for instance, more than one sign expresses the same nature – we use *modus significandi*, or modes of signification, to distinguish their function. Thus the name of the school, modists. When signs acquire modes of signification, they become parts of speech with fixed meanings signifying real beings together with grammatical meaning. In respect of the Aristotelian principle that the essences of real things as well as the rules of grammar are changeless and absolute, the modists assert that this signification of them is likewise absolute, complete, and thoroughly analyzable. Language and its logical structure are equivalent to the real.

The scholastics' logical reconstruction of St Augustine's theory of signs presented all knowledge as beginning in sensual experience for which the intellect supplies an intelligible sign, called a mental word or concept. This concept, the primary sign for Thomas, reflects the sensual sign of the sense impressions exactly and, except for the possibility of accidental confusions at one stage or another, the concept-sign represents completely and truly the thing it signifies. In the employment of active reason, the knower analyzes the accuracy of the sign possessed in the mind by verifying the similarity between the sign and the thing signified. Because the mind takes the object itself as its criterion of judgement – the *significatum* and not the *signum* – intellectual knowledge of what is can be accurate. This knowledge is possible because it is inherent in what exists to be knowable to the human mind. The structure of reality is logical, and demonstrative logic is the means to knowledge and the possession of it. The dialectics of negation has little place in St Thomas.

Colish describes the attraction of modist theory for the thirteenth century thinkers: "Modism was a way of asserting the primacy of concepts and words as authentic signs of real beings. Modism was consistent with the Aristotelian notion that real beings are fixed essences whose intelligible components can be appropriated by the human mind through empirical observation and mental abstraction. Further, the modist approach made it possible to apply a rigorous logic to universals and causes, to metaphysical and theological realities that are not empirical, experienced not in themselves but through their effects."[65]

This approach to the real through empiricism and the logic of causality leads the scholastics toward a thoroughly affirmative metaphysics and to the progressive marginalization of an original Christian philosophy that involved a negative approach to the transcendent through metaphor. The latter approach will be gradually diminished in philosophy until it is excluded altogether, placed in a separate and inferior category called "mysticism."

Nevertheless, for Denys and for Thomas the quest was the same: the fullest possible penetration of the real and union with it. Their different methods posed diverse obstacles and implied quite different consequences for the future of philosophy. Discussing Thomas' method for the discovery of true signs of God, Professor Colish not only exposes the inherent difficulties in Thomas' insistence on affirmative theology and logical demonstration but in so doing gives us a clear sense of the difference between the two principal ways of Christian understanding:

One of the tasks of the theologian, Thomas states, is to provide likely similitudes about God, for the purpose of clarifying the divine truths which he teaches. These similitudes must bear a resemblance to God; otherwise, they are useless. They cannot be anything but probable, because they are to be dealt with under the heading of *sacra doctrina* rather than natural theology. The problem of locating signs such as these was one that both Augustine and Anselm had to face. For Thomas, the quest was even more difficult because he was obstructed by his logical habits of mind and by the scholastic method of his theology from finding the easiest solution to it. Where Augustine and Anselm respond with apt figures of speech and are able to specify the paradox posed by the assignment of discussing the known yet unknown God in the programmatic arrangement of their works, Thomas is blocked by the impersonality and argumentativeness of the *quaestio* style and by the fact that his stylistic predilections incline him to replace figurative language with literal and discursive speech wherever possible.[66]

Thomas' "stylistic predilections" are dictated directly by his philosophical options, and the argumentativeness of the scholastic method to which Professor Colish points arises out of its insistence on affirming the presence and intelligibility of Being. This privileging of the affirmative through similitude is signalled especially by the eschewing of metaphor and its replacement with analogy, as, again, Professor Colish so clearly perceives: "Given the problem of dealing with transferred meanings, Thomas's response was analogy. Analogy is his attempt to make logic do what can be done much more easily by metaphor, in speaking about God from the limited vocabulary provided by human ways of knowing."[67]

There can be little doubt, however, that the Angelic Doctor and his brilliant followers understood what they were doing when they chose analogy and rejected metaphor and that they realized from the beginning the difficulties involved in the construction of a logical discourse about the transcendent. Thomas and the scholastics had, after all, ample testimony to the effectiveness of metaphor for this task in the works of Pseudo-Dionysius, Augustine, and Scripture itself. But the route of metaphor, as Thomas had learned in his study of Pseudo-Dionysius, leads away from similitude and affirmation and, through its foundation in difference, toward the recognition of the priority of dissimilitude and negation. St Thomas perceived, perhaps better than his master, the danger of metaphor (and the more remote danger of "nothingness"), and he bluntly condemns Plato's method of exposition as being more aesthetic than scientific, due precisely to his employment of metaphors and symbols.[68] Nor should the risks of the *via negativa* be underestimated, for if negation provides a corrective to anthropomorphic illusions, it is also in another direction the threshold of anti-intellectualism, nihilism, and despair. As Professor Colie has pointed out, there has always been in Western thought a certain uneasiness about Nothingness: "The major philosophers of Greece were chary of 'nothing,' denying its validity as fact and as concept. Platonic plenism and Aristotelian *horror vacui* denied existence to 'nothing'; Christian orthodoxy followed them in this respect, canonizing a single, divine *creatio ex nihilo* at which *nihil* was transformed, for good, by the blast of God's mouth into *omnis*, the cosmos, the universe, total being."[69]

Thomas perceived that analogy seeks to resolve paradox by presenting its contradictions logically, while metaphor leads to a perception of paradox as the very foundation of meaning. The latter was not, as Chenu points out, the most promising route for an integration of Aristotle into Christian thought. However, St Thomas' decision to follow the path of analogy can hardly be regarded as unfortunate, for it is largely thanks to him that the most limiting excesses of Platonism – its crippling gnosticism, anti-intellectualism, and spiritually debilitating pantheism – were overcome in the West.[70]

Thomas Aquinas was not a rationalist; nevertheless, it is apparent, at least with hindsight, that the direction he moved in determined the future character of Western thought in certain ways and led, both through the challenges to his views as well as their defence, to the rationalism that has come to characterize occidental philosophy. It was precisely because of his brilliant success in the categorical analysis of the intelligible that Thomas, along with other mediaeval scholastics, could set a direction for future debate. But the same success also focused the discourse in such a way as to begin to limit the representation of being and the real to the narrower scope of dialectics, to be succeeded, in a future unimaginable to the mediaeval scholastics, by the discourse of science.

The note of caution sounded by Professor Colish in regard to Thomas' actual reliance on analogy must, however, be kept in mind; it is probably equally applicable to other scholastic thinkers. Colish has rightly criticised the scholarly position that describes Thomas as a protorationalist bent on developing a philosophical system to prove the total intelligibility of the real. She is, again, undoubtedly correct and more complete in her description of Thomas' reliance on analogy when she portrays it as a useful but limited tool in the hands of a thinker who was himself keenly aware of the ultimate unintelligibility of his subject: "Analogies are never intended by Thomas to bring anyone to a knowledge that he does not already have. Rather, they are a means of showing forth the relationships between things that are already known by faith, and are hence a species of *intellectus fidei*."[71]

Let us, then, recall here that after years of labour Thomas abandoned his greatest systematic work, leaving the *Summa Theologiae* unfinished, and resisted all efforts to have him resume what was recognized, even in his own time, as the greatest monument of human intellection. Thomas, the master of demonstrative logic, perceiving, perhaps, the gulf between signification and the real, declared: "All that I have written seems like straw!"[72]

To succeeding generations, however, it was with such straw that the bricks of the edifice of scholasticism were made. From this structure begins the progression of the affirmative, empirical, and rationalist strains of Western philosophy. The greater intelligibility and analytic understanding of the real that made possible the moderate realism of Aristotle and the scholastics was self-propagating, and the dialectics of affirmative philosophy was applied by the scholastics to wider and wider areas of thought.

Showing what analogy could do for the logical, systematic understanding of reality, scholasticism opened the door to more exclusively affirmative systems which, while they often overcame various philosophical problems of earlier scholasticism, eventually undermined the ground on which scholasticism had stood. Thomas' separation of reason and faith distinguished so as to unite; its purpose was to demonstrate that reason and faith each lead by different roads to the same terminus of divine and human rapprochement, but such a distinction not only increased traffic on the road of reason but also encouraged the creation of major detours from it. His predilection for analogy may have been based on a desire to keep in balance the transcendent and the immanent, the ineffable and the intelligible, since analogy was theoretically capable of striking a balance between the univocal and the equivocal through its revelation of similarity in difference. But the logical pursuit of analogy in an increasingly nominalist framework soon rendered analogy itself superfluous.

The general perspective here is that the rise of logic and the accompanying decline of rhetoric in the thirteenth century, followed by the challenges of nominalism in the fourteenth century and the affirmations of Cartesianism and early modern science, culminates in the scepticism of the modern period. To a certain degree the process is made possible and characterized by the increasing exclusion of the concept of negation and the apophatic from Western speculative thought. A similar perspective is articulated by the Orthodox theologian Christos Yannaras:

Descartes is the characteristic expression of the historical temptation of the West: consolidate the reality of God through metaphysics and philosophy. In the classic chapter IV of the *Discours de la Methode* (1637), the existence of God is proved by giving exclusive weight to the power of thought of the subject. The power of thought, through abstract demonstration, leads to the universal idea of being and, through the same process, to the existence of God. We are assured of the absolute by conceiving the relative and the finite. And, since the only means of proving a truth is through its rational conception, we demonstrate the existence of God by conceiving the idea of him, because the existence of God is contained within the idea of God, just as within the idea of the triangle is contained the truth that the sum of the angles is equal to two right angles.[73]

Yannaras is, perhaps, too severe in his judgement of scholasticism and its contributions to what he considers the most unfortunate characteristics of contemporary Western thought. Neither Thomas nor his followers set out to sow the seeds of relativist worldviews, but rather attempted to fortify and make unassailable faith in God by making all being contingent. Nevertheless, as Yannaras shows, there is more to a philosophical system than its internal structure and consistency, and the history of Western philosophy exhibits a certain movement toward total affirmation and the scepticism that inevitably succeeds it. Beginning with Anselm and Thomas Aquinas, who at least acknowledge the value of the *via negativa* while abandoning it, mediaeval philosophy leans further and further in the direction of positivistic rationalism: "These two founders of the analogical understanding of God simultaneously preach the apophatic character of this knowledge, the essential unknowability of God and the impossibility for human intelligence to approach and to define divine truth. Other scholastic masters, like Peter Abelard (d. 1142), Albertus Magnus (d. 1280), Duns Scotus (d. 1308), the great mystic Master Eckhart (d. 1327), and Nicholas of Cusa (d. 1464) also follow the apophatic tradition in theology. But their theology in no way interrupts the historical course of Western atheism. It is an organic part of it."[74]

If there was a tension in mediaeval thought, it was due not so much to attempts to privilege the cataphatic at the expense of the apophatic, nor vice versa, but to the original error of separating the two. From this first misstep grew the occidental dichotomy of a rational tradition and a mystical tradition, neither one erroneous, but each the poorer for their separation. Mediaeval thinkers, while cultivating affirmative cognitive systems, attempted to ensure the inclusion of negation and dissimilitude as a basis of metaphysics and epistemology. The Church even attempted to legislate its survival, as the formula of the Fourth Lateran Council shows: "Between Creator and creatures it is not possible to distinguish similitude without [first] distinguishing the priority of their dissimilitude."[75]

What for Pseudo-Dionysius was a tripartite mode of understanding that reflected the nature of the real itself – the successive yet simultaneous ways of affirmation, negation, and transcendence – became in the logico-metaphysics of the Middle Ages an opposition. The *via negativa* became the methodological contrary of the *via affirmativa,* leading, not to complementary understandings of the same reality, but to categorically different knowledge of different and even unrelated subjects. With the rise of logic in the thirteenth century and the triumph of the *via moderna* and nominalism in the fourteenth, negation was successively exiled to metaphysics, then to theology, and finally to mysticism and poetry, while the "real work" of logic continued its process of constructing a fully anthropocentric perspective for Western philosophy and an aggressive secular-humanist perspective for Western culture.

The eventual predominance of affirmative discourse in Western philosophy was not achieved without a certain resistance. Mediaeval Neoplatonism had established through the works of Augustine, Boethius, Scotus Eriugena, and others a thoroughly literary style of discourse as the appropriate one for intellectual inquiry. The suitability of literary language is seen to lie in the very inexactness of its description of its subject and in its peculiar ability to make evident the difference between itself as discourse and its subject as an independently existing thing; the self-reflexive character of literary discourse continually underscores the ontological transcendence of the subject all the while that it is presenting that subject. It is, in other words, the sheer rhetoricalness of literary expression that reveals discourse as being about truth, not constituting truth itself. This is St Anselm's sense when he declares: "No signification is right by virtue of any other rightness than that which remains when the signification perishes ... [T]he signification is made in accordance with a rightness which always exists."[76] This is the outstanding feature of the dialogue as the form of inquiry originally adopted by Plato and continued by the later Neoplatonists. Within the extensive discussion of the nature and significance of the Platonic dialogue form, David Burrell perceives its self-negation as fundamental to the Platonic discourse concerning understanding of the transcendent:

Plato has recourse to the dramatic and literary form of the dialogues to construct this special style of account which exhibits its own inadequacy. It is particularly in evidence when he deals with analogous expressions like order, good, and unity. For among other logical idiosyncrasies, these notions behave in so obviously self-reflexive and "recursive" a manner that we can expect to find them operative everywhere ... But ... statements containing these terms easily tend to paradox. Hence Plato had to control the context of the statement, so as to show what could be said only clumsily, if at all. The tendency to reversal and paradox is translated into the dramatic setting.[77]

Inadequacy, paradox, and reversal are the hallmark of the poetics of deformation, a poetics that has its conceptual beginnings in the negative methodology of Pseudo-Dionysius and the Neoplatonists and its continuation in the art and thought of mediaeval poets and mystics. Examples of this aesthetic are found early in the mediaeval period: the eighth century *Book of Kells* and other early Celtic manuscripts feature monstrous forms in their illuminations; the ninth century Winchester Psalter reveals capitals constructed of grotesque grylles; Rabanus Maurus' *Encyclopedia* created at Montecassino in the early eleventh century pictures the monstrous races in striking illustrations. These and many more examples attest to the lively presence of monstrous form in the thought and expression of the early Middle Ages.

The continuation and even excrescence of monstrous forms in literary and artistic texts during the centuries of growth of scholastic logic suggests the monstrous as a kind of response to the increasingly affirmative discourse concerning the nature of the real and human knowledge of it. If, as the embodiment of paradox, the monster functions as the ideal sign of the *via nega-tiva* in both the philosophic and poetic discourses of early mediaeval culture, by the fourteenth century, and with the triumph of Aristotelian logic, it may perhaps be seen as the very "excluded middle" exiled by that logic. By its impossible form, the monster bridges the gap between contraries in an aes-thetic defiance of logical rule; it provides the third term, the copula, the me-diation, between all those entities doomed, by logic and language, never to be joined. Such a union remains illogical, indeed absurd, but it is an absur-dity that raises paradox out of its purely logical function and places it at the centre of ontology.

For example, the hermaphrodite sculpted in cathedral decorations, painted in liturgical illuminations, and reported in the *Book of the Monsters* and other texts is a contradiction of more than gender distinctions within biology, and it denies more than logical principles: the hermaphrodite is the third term reaching out to join contraries and bringing nonbeing side by side with being, showing through its deforming combination the meaning of that which is and is-not.

The grotesque and the monstrous express unities that are basic both to metaphysics and to psychology. The reunion of male and female evokes not only the urge represented in myth for the discovery of the original, whole psyche but also the metaphysical inclination toward the union of all beings into common, simple Being; the dragon in its monstrous combination of ser-pent, bird, and fish points not only to the transgression of natural categories separating species but also to the dissolution of individuality into original oneness. The taxonomy of the monstrous is constituted not only through in-ordinate combinations but also through other types of deformation; the prin-ciples of excrescence, deprivation, and displacement of parts also function to contradict the physical and conceptual limits of being and its forms. Each de-forming transgresses the law of the excluded middle, replacing its gover-nance with the law of paradox. Monstrosity makes metaphysics possible at the same time that it undermines it by keeping present the ineffable nature of Being and refusing the adequation of the real with intellect. By its symbolic representation of being as grounded in nonbeing and its origination of mean-ing in negation, the deformed makes possible understanding at the same time that it critiques it.

Within whatever discourse it finds itself, the deformed challenges the epis-temological authority of form, structure, and identity and leads the mind to-ward a different perspective of how things are. In this perspective, order must be related to disorder; distinctive forms have their origin in shapeless and un-individualized chaos; and the proportionality of analogy finds its beginning and end in the equivocity of being and the univocity of nonbeing. The confi-dent affirmations of mediaeval logic about the powers of human cognition and the ultimate intelligbility of the world are reproduced in the literary discourses of the Middle Ages in monstrous forms that tend to critique their absoluteness. The function of the monstrous and the deformed is, however, not merely to parody the affirmative – and certainly not to destroy it – but rather to elevate understanding beyond anthropocentric affirmations to teratomorphic negations and ultimately, in an anagogical leap, to a transcendence of both cataphatic and apophatic intellection.

2   The Language of the Monstrous

> From the universal cataclysm and confusion after the tower of Babel
> were born such beings as fauns, satyrs, androgyni, "sciapodes"
> (i.e. skiapodes), cyclopes, centaurs, pygmies, giants, headless men,
> dog-headed men and cannibals.
>
> Cornelius Gemma, *De Naturae Divinis*[1]

The association of monsters with language is a profound, longstanding one that simultaneously reveals something of our historical conception of monstrosity as well as an ambivalence toward language itself. Several ancient teratological legends trace the appearance of the monster in the world to the moment of the collapse of the Tower of Babel and suggest a causal relation between the two events. The story of the Tower of Babel constitutes a pivotal moment in human symbolic history, containing as it does the mythic explanation of the origin of human discursive activity and the beginning of diversity and division in human society. Language existed before the Babylonian cataclysm, but it was of a different nature: "And the whole earth was of one language and of one speech" (Genesis 11:1).

This single, unified language betokening not only harmony in human society but, as well, a kind of remnant of an original unity of being, is confounded when it is used to assert arrogantly the autonomy of human cognition from the divine One as signified in the Babylonians' efforts to penetrate Heaven and "create a name": "And they said, Go to, let us build us a city and a tower whose top may reach unto heaven; and let us make us a name, lest we be scattered abroad upon the face of the whole earth" (Genesis 11:4).

This story, like other biblical episodes, establishes the contradictory tendencies in human desire, the one toward individuation of the self, the valorization of the particular and the material, and the establishment of hegemony through naming; the other a longing for unity with the other, for universality, and for simple "being" in the place of knowing, the transcendence of the gulf between knower and known. The tower builders strive to name themselves and thus become distinct from the generality of existence around them, and

to do so they choose, as the legend makes clear, basic matter of sand and "slime," out of which to make bricks and mortar, with which to make material structures. Through an inversion characteristic of such legendary narratives, these means are devoted to the achievement of a primal unity (lest we be scattered) and the continuation of an integrity of language.

Roger Caillois, who employs the Babel metaphor to organize a discussion of art and literature, follows the traditional exegesis and interprets the building of the tower as a monument to human pride. In an interesting turn, however, he reads the offense of the arrogant builders as one not only against God, but against their own society as well. Rejecting, in particular, all the sciences of the past as contemptible, they refuse all instruments invented by their predecessors. Because they themselves did not invent geometry and physics, they will not accept the truths of these sciences, and eventually all work on the tower is abandoned. In an ultimate act of *superbia*, they reject all objective meaning of words and signs, whimsically preferring the endless play of signifiers; it is, suggests Caillois, this intellectual relativism, rather than divine intervention, that causes the confusion of tongues:

Construction on the tower stopped. Little by little, the monument of arrogance, having become one of confusion (believed to have been the meaning of the word Babel), fell to ruin. This was not because of divine intervention which, all of a sudden seized by a caprice for diversity, prevented everyone from understanding his neighbor! This is a superstitious tradition likely based on the fact that, along with all their other excesses, the builders of the tower decided to renounce the use of words in their conventional meaning, and instead began assigning whatever meaning happened to please them at the moment. Faithful to their principles, they refused to accept that words had any meaning at all![2]

Echoing the encounter in the Garden of Eden with another temptation to a certain kind of knowledge, the story of the tower of Babel provides a kind of postlude to the drama of original sin, constituting a second Fall in which, like the first, the essential lapse is figured as a linguistic one. The serpent's subtle offer in Paradise economically expresses the fundamental paradox of language: it is both gain and loss. It is gain in the sense that Adam and Eve do, indeed, have their eyes opened and are able to distinguish not only good and evil as promised by the Enemy but each other and the difference between themselves and all those things they now know objectively. And it is loss in the sense that they are no longer one with that which they know, nor with each other, signified by their immediate sexual self-consciousness: "and they knew that they were naked" (Genesis 3:7).

The theme of loss of cognitive and linguistic unity is continued and made more specific in the legend of the Tower of Babel where the simultaneity of the origins of discourse and monstrosity suggests that the mythic structure conceived of them as born of the same matrix and, like warring twins, both similar and opposed. Like language, the monster is a sign of a unity now lost, the unity of Being dispersed in the multiplicity of forms and the plenitude of creation, and like language, the monster is the possibility of the reconstruction of the very thing that it, itself, has deconstructed. As complementary opposites, language and the monster signify contrast and counterpoint, in which the grotesque union of disparate forms functions as a negation and a corrective to the rational ordering of discursive analysis. In this perspective the relation of language to the monstrous in the story of Babel is in harmony with the standard mediaeval method of Scriptural allegory in which the idea and its opposite are always present together – where, for instance, Christ the Word restores the unity lost in the Babylonian attempt to create a "name."

The entire story of Babel in Genesis is one of fabricating and building, and two kinds of structure are specified: bricks, mortar, tower, and city, alongside of words, names, languages, and verbal constructs. The goal of all this fabricating is to produce a single, integral thing – a tower, a common name. The irony contained in the legendary version of the story of language is the same as the paradox of human understanding – that in the presumptuous attempt to establish its own hegemony and exclude the One, humanity loses authentic unity of knowledge and of idenity and being, and is condemned to reconstruct it through discourse, the very means it first misused. Thus the climax of the story is the divine destruction and confounding of such fabrications expressed through the exceedingly simple literary formula of juxtaposition: building up and breaking down. The sons of Noah have learned to make bricks and to pile them up one upon the other to erect the famous tower, just as they pile word upon word, sign upon sign, and discourse upon discourse in their growing confidence that such constructs can enclose and control history and reality. But just as such fashioning reaches its highest point, another process, inaugurated by the divine, begins the negating and dismantling of both tower and speech ("Go to, let us go down, and there confound their language" [Genesis 11:7]). In the iconic function of the monster, which in its own way oversees the breaking down of impertinent structures, we may glimpse a parallel between the very structure of the biblical story and the teratological.

DISCOURSE AND ITS FORMS

The narrative of the Tower of Babel legend expresses in symbolic language the idea of a prelapsarian state in which knowing and being are one. It is the same state that allows Adam to "name" the animals (Genesis 2: 19–20), not in any arbitrary or conventional way (there are no conventions in solitude), but by intuiting the sign that is connatural with the individual being. It is only after the Tower of Babel that these unique Adamic signs, inherent in being, become multiplied relative to various groups of speakers. In other words, before the construction and destruction of the Tower, man knows as the angels know; the legend of Babel signifies the loss of unity between being and knowing, precisely the unity possessed by angels.

It is within this general perspective that John Scotus Eriugena describes the kinds of knowing and their communication: human knowledge as "knowledge of sensible things through the phantasies of bodies," and angelic knowledge whereby angels "do not receive the knowledge of sensible things through the phantasies of their bodies, but perceive every corporeal creature spiritually in its spiritual causes ... The angels lack corporeal sense because they are above it" (*Periphyseon* 3.733C).[3] This is to say that, like the pre-Babylonian characters of Genesis, angels require no mediation between the knowledge of the thing and the thing itself. Interestingly, Scotus seems to indicate that human knowledge is, if not better, at least more expansive than angelic knowledge;[4] nevertheless, human knowing in its ultimate, redeemed state will return to an angelic level in which the "phantasy," or sign, will be altogether superfluous, and we will, like Adam, be able to perceive in the thing itself its very nature. Such unmediated understanding begins, however, in present efforts of comprehension that attempt to transcend binary semiotics by seeking out discourses more, rather than less, transparent in their mediating function.

Discourse, then, takes on several forms according to various forms of human understanding and according to the nature of the object to be understood. In *The Philosophy of Symbolic Forms,* Ernst Cassirer describes the relationship of basic modes of human understanding according to different structures for organizing reality, emphasizing as the basis of his system the identical function of each mode:

Essentially, cognition is always oriented toward this essential aim, the articulation of the particular into a universal law and order. But beside this intellectual synthesis, which operates and expresses itself within a system of scientific concepts, the life of the human spirit as a whole knows other forms ... Each of these functions creates its own symbolic forms which, if not similar to the intellectual symbols, enjoy equal rank as products of the human spirit. None of these forms can simply be reduced to, or derived from, the others; each of them designates a particular approach, in which and through which it constitutes its own aspect of "reality."[5]

The particular means that each form adopts to achieve its goal and the ways in which each succeeds and fails provide the space in which a kind of antidiscourse of the monstrous and deformed may inscribe itself. Cassirer identifies these fundamental cultural forms as language, art, science (with which we may include logical discourse), and myth (with which we may include religion). Each is characterized by a relentless striving toward the discovery and representation of the unity of reality and each, by the very nature of its structure, is limited in the attainment of that goal. In this Cassirer reminds us somewhat of Eriugena who conceived of cognition and discourse as structured according to four divisions of life: the intellectual (angelic), the rational (human), the sensitive (animal and matter), and the insensitive (plants and matter) (*Periphyseon* 3.733A).[6] Cassirer's four basic cultural cognitive forms are often hostile to each other, while Eriugena's may be confused by human error. Thus the scientific, or logical mode – what Scotus calls the rational – claims to go beyond language to create a "logos" more precise and more thorough than linguistic principles permit. Science investigates natural forms and their necessary connections. Intellectual constructs made possible by logical form permit the investigation of the phenomenal and cognitive world and provide a means of relation between knower and known, between mankind and the objects of intellect.

Although art uses language in the formation of its particular discourse, its goal is not to represent the world as it is, but rather, through an imaginative manipulation of natural signs and figures of speech, to depict the representational power of the human spirit. Myth and religion employ language, logical form, and art, too, in a discourse that attempts to transcend human symbolizing as such in order to achieve an ontic, supra-symbolic relation of the human and the divine.

Whether they be the signifiers of language, mathematical signs, or the iconographs of art, all cognitive forms and their discourses involve symbols with which they formulate ordered structures so as to reveal universals in particulars. In this sense the ultimate goal of all symbolic systems is apparent; it is what Cassirer calls "unity of being," echoing a term more precisely developed by Thomas Aquinas and expressed as *unum et ens convertuntur* (*ST* I.II.I):

The One Being, to which thought holds fast and which it seems unable to relinquish without destroying its own form, eludes cognition. The more its metaphysical unity as a "thing-in-itself" is asserted, the more it evades all possibility of knowledge, until at last it is relegated entirely to the sphere of the unknowable and becomes a mere "X." And to this rigid metaphysical absolute is juxtaposed the realm of phenomena, the true sphere of the knowable, with its enduring multiplicity, finiteness and relativity. But upon closer scrutiny the fundamental postulate of unity is not discredited by this irreducible diversity of the methods and objects of knowledge; it merely assumes a new form.[7]

In an extensive study of Eriugena's theory of *phantasia*, Jean-Claude Foussard reveals not only a symbolic system based on this concept of unity of being but a full-fledged epistemology. Given the considerable influence of Eriugena's thought on mediaeval philosophy and art generally, it is easy to understand the particular importance that his theory of *phantasia* may have had upon the grotesque; through the distinction articulated by Scotus between "visible and invisible forms" a theoretical basis for the genre is made possible. Foussard explains *phantasia*: "John Scotus begins with the principle that in his present state, man cannot know any 'nature' by direct intuition (*per seipsam*). It is thus necessary that some intermediary relate man and thing. This mediation between that which is outside and that which is inside has as its purpose to make the thing appear by providing it with an image. Such is the *phantasia*: 'imago quaedam et apparitio.' "[8]

The double sense of *phantasia* and of understanding in Scotus' theory has to do both with the nature of the thing represented and with the process of perception within the knower. As Foussard explains, the exterior thing impresses its form on the sense organs, which relay an image of this form to the soul. The "first" phantasy, then, is purely physical, arising out of a physical object that impresses itself upon a physical sense (as word, image, smell, touch upon the ear, the eye, the nose). From this is formed a "second" phantasy that is an intellectual image received into the soul and preserved in memory. What John calls the *sensus exterior,* as well as the truth of its two-step process, is, as Foussard says, "guaranteed by the real object which is its starting point: this phantasy is *naturalium rerum imaginatio*, and nothing which does not appear in reality can possibly appear."[9] Thus the *phantasia* of the *sensus exterior* connects (*conjunctio*) the body and the soul, as well as connecting the outside (the world) to the inside (the intellect). John envisions this process of representation to be not unlike the process of incarnation: "In fact, it is the soul which senses fully (*tota in sensibus sentit*), the soul which gives itself a body and organs of sensation."[10]

There is, however, another *sensus* that is superior to the first and in which the *phantasia* is an image of the "invisible" (*apparitio de invisibili specie*). In this *sensus interior*, phantasies are not based on physical things really in the world, nor do they have their origin in physical sense impressions. Through a "descent" from intellect to reason, evocative of the descent of the One into the many, imageless understanding appropriates, from that part of reason called memory, *phantasiae* which it uses to make itself manifest and to show forth those forms that illuminate it (*Periphyseon* 3.658C). However, the signified itself is purely intellectual, having no material reality. It is this that John calls "that which is-not."

What is noteworthy here, among other things, is the fact that for Eriugena there are two kinds of image: one has its origin and nature in the natural, physical form of the thing represented, modified by the mind; the other has its origin and nature in an existence that has no form and to which one is loaned by intellect. As epistemological process, the first is a gradual spiritualization (or abstraction) of the material; the second is a gradual incarnation of the spiritual.

Through an operation proceeding from sensing to naming to conceptualizing and symbolizing, the human mind progresses from sensation to ideas, and herein lies the foundation for intellectual analysis, logical form, and imagination. But, like the story of Babel, human history attests to the persistence of the sense that involved in this progress there is a fundamental loss: the transformation to knower and known, while permitting "relationship" and intellection, is also indelibly marked by separation and difference, a loss of a former unity that, while mindless, was real.

In this epistemological evolution certain characteristics are salient. The naming process first requires distinction – the ability to identify differences between one thing and another. Distinction leads to separation and association, which makes possible further reduction and isolation of phenomena through analysis. Language achieves the crucial distinction and separation when the "I" is discovered as independent of what it names.

The movement toward "unity of being" appears to be filled with contradiction, beginning as it does with all that is opposite to unity. But cognition is apparently circular or, better still, spiral in form; it disjoins and ruptures to reconnect and synthesize in relations of greater richness and complexity. Its circularity is always incomplete, and the perfect union of knower and known is never fully achieved in any of the cognitive forms. Nevertheless, the human spirit strives constantly for the identity and union between speaker and spoken, between the signified and the sign, seemingly trying to outwit language, as if the linguistic dynamic of perfect expression betokened the metaphysical goal of unity of being. In striving to transcend rather than accept its own limits, language exhibits a cognitive characteristic superior to logic, particularly in its poetic discourse and symbolic manifestations. This, as we have seen, is the reason that the Neoplatonists, in their search for an adequate expression of the ineffable, favoured metaphor and symbol, because in poetry, unlike nonaesthetic uses of language, structure is not merely in service to content but is itself the content.

In Eriugena's system there is a double dynamic described variously as outside/inside, ascending/descending, visible/invisible; and each of these can serve as paradigms for the process of understanding and representing. Just as the *phantasia* of *sensus exterior* bring the outer world into the mind, purifying the physical into the abstract and raising the material to the intellectual, so by a simultaneous, reverse motion the *phantasia* of *sensus interior* bring the inner reality of intellect into the world, embodying it with images found in the lower level of the imagination. There is for John, however, a third motion in cognition and representation, making it, like all other realities, a triad. That third motion is "transcendence"; it allows the mind, having passed through the symbols of things that are (*visibili*) and through the symbols of things that are-not (*invisibili*), to achieve a union with what it knows, unmediated by any discourse at all. There are many descriptions of transcendence in Scotus' writings, but the clearest in terms of the identification of transcendence with union is, perhaps, the description at the end of his *Periphyseon* depicting the seven steps of "Return":

The first will be the transformation of the earthly body into vital motion; the second of vital motion into sensation; the third of sensation into reason; then of reason into mind, wherein lies the end of every rational creature; then this fivefold unification of the parts of our nature, in which body, vital motion, sensation, reason, and mind are no longer five but one, in each case the lower nature becoming absorbed in the higher not so as to lose its existence but to become with that higher nature one, shall be followed by three more stages of the ascent: first the transformation of mind into the knowledge of all things which come after God; secondly, of that knowledge into wisdom, that is into the innermost contemplation of the Truth, in so far as that is possible to a creature; thirdly, and lastly, the supernatural merging of the perfectly purified souls into God Himself, and their entry into the darkness of the incomprehensible and inaccesible Light which conceals the Causes of all things. (4.1020C–1021A)

Allegory and various linguistic models provided the principal methods for the explication of cognition in the Middle Ages, although their possible transcendence was always reiterated. The object of intellect is not grasped in its essence but in its expression: the speaker is known in his words. The necessary incompleteness of identity between the sign and the signified indicates the imperfectness of cognition itself. In his discussion of the Gospel according to St John, Scotus Eriugena broaches this problem while reflecting on the various scriptural passages that refer to the identical nature of the Father and the Son: "No man has seen God at any time; the only begotten Son, which is in the bosom of the Father, he hath declared him" (John 1:18); "he that hath seen me hath seen the Father" (John 14:9); and "no man knoweth the Son, but the Father; neither knoweth any man the Father, save the Son, and he to whomsoever the Son will reveal him" (Matthew 11:27). Eriugena comments: "All this applies not only to men but to angels as well, for even angels are unable to know, in His very nature, God who transcends all intelligence for he is the invisible and the unknown. But with the Incarnation of the Word, they knew their Lord, the Son of God: in Him and through Him they knew the inscrutable Trinity."[11]

Scotus reveals here the mediaeval model for fullest possible cognition, the Word of God, God in his Word, in which the sign is the perfect representation of the signified – in which, indeed, we have the only instance where the sign and the signified are one. All derivative discourses aspire to the perfect intelligibility that is itself a paradox – unity in triad – depicted in the Christian Middle Ages as a linguistic version of the prodigious unity of the Trinity – the Speaker, the Word, and their relationship. Each mundane discourse is limited by the necessary distinction between its signs and their signifieds, but each somehow strives toward an integration of the two, toward a perfect representation by the sign of its object, which is never achieved. In the Middle Ages the enigma of this impossible union is met with not only in the religious paradoxes of the Trinity and the Incarnation; the extension of the linguistic paradigm to explicate the divine also attaches to that paradigm the paradox that is inherent in that which it seeks to explicate. In a second extension, a return of the paradigm back to its linguistic-literary sense, the paradox is carried over into the secular realm. Thus, the legions of monsters that inhabit mediaeval art connote through their deformations all kinds of enigma, originally religious, that defy the limitations of form and test the thresholds of intelligibility.

The model of the divine triad serves the mind's continual effort to unite opposites and reduce multiplicity in the various intellectual discourses about opposites and multiplicity. While language attempts to bring about the integration of the "I" and the world, the integration accomplished is always less perfect than that of the model; thus the ability of language to integrate the "I" and the transcendent reality appears all the more inadequate.

The philosophical and theological truths described so painstakingly by the mediaeval thinker had a purpose beyond their own brilliant existence that was the description and revelation of the One to the human intellect. Philosophy and theology as rational sciences address the realm of matter and intellect as a necessary point of departure on the journey toward unity. But religion as discourse is directed beyond this starting point toward the realm of the ineffable, and thus it enjoins more than the human cognitive faculties in its demands for the activation of will and desire – the conversion of the "whole person" – and has as its ultimate goal, not merely the imparting of the content of its science, but the creation of a real relationship and identity between that content and the knower. The "relationship" that religion makes possible is the gateway to the realm of the ineffable. This relationship the Middle Ages called love. In this mediaeval sense love is ultimately a way of knowing, built up from logical structures but superior to all discursive modes of knowledge. While central to Christianity, the concept is not exclusive to it and was a salient feature of Neoplatonic thought: "Thus love characterizes the ascent of intellects to their objects, truth signifies the highest point to which rational thought can attain and therefore constitutes a kind of medium between the rational and the ineffable, and belief characterizes that activity which transcends cognition as such and can only be described as mystical union."[12]

St Bonaventure put it economically when he described love as the terminus of knowledge, and the anonymous author of the great mystical text *Cloud of Unknowing* develops the Christian connection between cognition and love more richly: "He cannot be comprehended by our intellect or any man's – or any angel's for that matter. For both we and they are created beings. But only to our intellect is he incomprehensible: not to our love. All rational beings, angels and men, possess two faculties, the power of knowing and the power of loving. To the first, to the intellect, God who made them is forever unknowable, but to the second, to love, he is completely knowable, and that by every separate individual."[13]

The various forms of discourse are related to and superseded by another discourse designed to lift us out of the realm of intellectual analysis toward the unity we seek, a unity that is seen to reside in the realm of the ineffable. The author of the *Cloud of Unknowing* implies that if other discourses are limited, having arrived at their boundaries, we are enabled by means of "love" to escape them and to continue the journey toward the ineffable. Such an escape, as we have seen, is triggered by the negation of the previous discourse by means that were delineated by Pseudo-Dionysius and his followers. The passage from the mundane to the ineffable is, then, one facilitated by a discourse that is, properly speaking, not a discourse at all insofar as the discursive is eliminated, but an antidiscourse and a transcendence of form that can be identified in mediaeval aesthetics with the monstrous and the grotesque and that in turn identifies the monster with the divine, as both are described in terms of their deforming power: "Given that the Good transcends everything, as indeed it does, its nature, *unconfined by form,* is the creator of all form. In it is nonbeing really an excess of being. It is not *a* life, but is, rather, superabundant Life. It is not *a* mind, but is superabundant Wisdom. Whatever partakes of the Good partakes of what preeminently gives form to the formless. And one might even say that nonbeing itself longs for the Good which is above all being. Repelling being, it struggles to find rest in the Good which transcends all being, in the sense of a denial of all things" (*DN* 697A, emphasis added).

However, prior to this "uplifting" beyond all discourse, the intellect masters a whole series of signifying processes characterized by the increasingly successful unification of the usual binary oppositions of cognition: knower/known, subject/object, self/other. In this semiotic hierarchy, symbolism and allegory are penultimate steps.

SYMBOL AND ALLEGORY

It is the desire for synthesis of the "I" and what it knows and loves that maturates the transformation of rational knowledge to spiritual intuition through the use of symbolic systems. Cassirer effectively communicates the power of symbolism in human consciousness: "Another indication that the creation of the various systems of sensuous symbols is indeed a pure activity of the mind is that from the outset all these symbols lay claim to objective value. They go beyond the mere phenomena of the individual consciousness, claiming to confront them with something that is universally valid. This claim may possibly prove unwarranted in the light of subsequent critical inquiry with its more highly developed concept of truth; but the mere fact that it is made belongs to the essence and character of the particular cultural forms themselves."[14]

While the symbols of language, logic, and art are adequate to the forms they serve, they cannot normally, by themselves, fully represent the ineffable realities they strive toward, for the constitutions of their very structures create the limit. It is particularly the simple sense of the "standing for" of signs that is inadequate, for while it facilitates a cognition of the signified by its substitute, it only deludes the knower into believing that a union with the known has been achieved. This is the danger of the mimesis of simple representation. For this reason all symbols must finally be negated and mimesis eschewed, an insight that the Neoplatonists bequeathed to the West: "The pagan Neoplatonists, from Plotinus onwards, as is well known, detested the anthropomorphic, artisan view of creation, in which God makes up his mind to create, and proceeds to design and bring into being a universe with all its diverse contents quite external to and other than himself ... And Christian theologians consciously or unconciously influenced by Neoplatonism ... incline to do their best to exclude the 'artisan' way of looking at creation."[15]

Thus, early on the "negative way" addressed itself not only to the purification of concepts and propositions but in a first instance to the correction of symbolic representations. For the Christian thinker the main source of transcendent symbolism, of signs less fettered by the limitations of human understanding, was Holy Scripture, which had its origin "above" and had been handed down so that human intelligence might rise with the comprehension of these symbols up to their very source. As we have seen, Pseudo-Dionysius and the schools of Christian Neoplatonism that came after him make much of the transcendent character of scriptural symbolism, as well as the need to eliminate mundane reference when attempting to understand it. In speaking of how scripture reveals its sacred subject, René Roques makes it clear that the system according to Dionysius is one of detaching symbols from their "normal" context: "Scripture imposes (upon its object, i.e., God) signs that do not belong to it and, conversely, eliminates those that are proper to it, those which no human discourse can ever express."[16]

To understand scripture, the human intellect must work to free the signs it encounters from significations of its own creation. The usual signs of language and logic will be found insufficient and exegesis must employ a method capable of dissociating these signs from their natural *significata* so as to reattach them to what the mediaeval thinker would regard as their authentic referent. Since, as Scotus Eriugena would have it, all texts are created through a double source of symbolism, one drawing signs from the outside world, the other from the inner reality of intellect, interpretation consists precisely in reversing the authorial motion: where the author has abstracted physical things into signs, the exegete must separate sign from original thing so as to restore

the materiality of the thing by designifying it; where the author has concretized concepts by giving them material signs, again the exegete must separate
sign and signified so as to restore the spiritual nature of the signified. While it
is true that Christian exegesis aims at transcendence, it is inaccurate to assert,
as some contemporary discussion does, that its search for meaning is satisfied
by the discovery of authorial intention, for even the intention of the author
must be transcended.[17] These dissociations of the sensible sign from mundane signification, of speaker from spoken, of author from text, are, for the
Neoplatonist, paradoxically not a dissociation at all, but a restitution of true
relations through the surpassing of all relations. Lazy satisfaction with the
easiness of cataphatic symbolism, however, prevents this restitution, as
Roques reminds us: "Thus the truth of the symbol is no longer sought in its
authentic signification which is necessarily 'above': through laziness, ignorance, or perversity, intelligence dissociates symbol from its connatural and
sacred signification in order to highlight the materiality of its sensual elements, even adding to them, perhaps, pseudo-signification of purely human
fabrication."[18]

The principal method employed by exegesis to achieve the elevation of the
mind beyond the binary relation of sign and signified, text and author, meaning and interpretation, is that of allegory, a symbolic system thought capable
of transcending many of the restrictions of cognitive forms by "saying one
thing to mean another." Meditating on the indirectness of allegorical expression, St Augustine wonders, "But why is it, I ask, if anyone says this [as a direct statement], he delights his hearers less than if he has said the same thing
in expounding that place in the Canticle of Canticles where it is said of the
Church, as she is being praised as a beautiful woman, 'thy teeth are as flocks
of sheep, that are shorn, which come up from the washing, all with twins,
and there is none barren among them'?" His answer reveals that the power of
allegory over logical discourse has much to do with an obscurity of expression that plays on the relation between the idea and its representation, rather
than on "plain words": "No one doubts that things are perceived more
readily through similitude and that what is sought with difficulty is discovered with more pleasure."[19]

For scriptural allegory as well as for most mediaeval literary allegory the
natural order is a matrix of symbols refering in the first instance to phenomena in nature but having a higher meaning in the supernatural, divine order.
By the same process that anagogy, as the ultimate step of allegory, moves the
mind from the sign to the natural concept and thence toward the intellection
of sacred truths, it also represents through a certain self-reflexivity the relation of the natural order to the supernatural. That is, the relation of the literal
level to the allegorical, the relation of authorial intention to meaning, and the
relation of the text to the interpretation are each analogous to the relation of
the material to the spiritual, the relation of intellect to its object, and the rela-

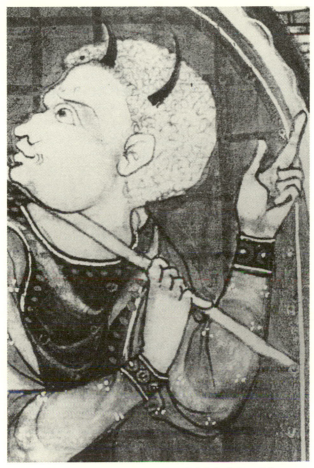

Horned Cain. Thirteenth-century psalter, St John's College Library, Cambridge, MS K26, fol. 17b

tion of the world to its divine exemplar. Thus the literary structure that is allegory is also a paradigm of metaphysical and epistemological structures. Beginning in the literal-historical phenomena of nature and existence, allegory was meant to reveal the transcendent and permanent realities within such mutable phenomena, without in any way negating their particular truth. More simply, the integrity of the literal level is seen as the guarantee of the meaningfulness of the more abstract levels of allegory that are "above."

The signs that allegory employs, therefore, are drawn from nature, history, and human conceptualization (it employs, as well, the purely sacred signs revealed by Scripture and independent of mundane sources). In the relations that allegory creates between these various phenomena and the various "levels" of reality, it habitually defies the normal logical and linguistic categories of cause and effect, universal and particular, temporal sequence, and contrariety, along with the limitations these categories impose. So, for instance, the literal understanding of the introduction of death into the world viewed the murder of Abel by his brother Cain as an historical event that occurred at a particular time and in a particular locus; the meaning of the event begins as a fundamentally historical fact. The crucifixion of Christ was also an event in time and space, historically unique, and having the status of historical fact. However, the allegorical understanding of each event required the recognition of a series of analogies between the two temporally and narratively distinct events. Just as temporality and individuation function in all cognitive forms to render objects and propositions intelligible, so too, on the primary level of allegory they act to present the subject. But the dynamic of allegory immediately calls for a further motion that transcends this level while in no way distorting the literal, historical "fact." This scruple is important because it shows the difference between allegory and those cognitive and interpretive methods that bring their own meaning to their objects, rather than revealing inherent significance. For the Middle Ages, it was important to discover, not to fabricate, the analogies inherent in temporally discrete occasions that united them in their ontological status and revealed their higher meaning.

Thus, as Abel is killed by his brother and becomes the first martyr, so Christ is killed by his brothers and becomes the prototype – although historically later – of that martyrdom and all others. Abel's acceptable sacrifice of a lamb makes of him the first priest, while Christ Himself, the Agnus Dei, in self-sacrifice again provides the prototype. Through a whole series of such analogies the historical event of Cain's fratricide becomes a temporal prefiguration of the crucifixion; the posterior event becomes the paradigm for the earlier occurrence and the possibility of its fullest interpretation.

Like all other allegorical texts, this allegory defies the narrative and historical logic of temporal succession. It makes the Crucifixion a prototype of Cain's fratricide and Christ the archetype of Abel's priesthood and martyrdom; it negates in a figurative way the individuality of the characters by uniting them as signs of each other, and supersedes causality by inverting beginning (Genesis) and end (Redemption). Through the suggestion of such amalgamations, allegory as a symbolic process suggests the outlines of a language of reconstructed unity.

The basic narrative of such an allegory is grounded in history and its symbols in nature. Its symbolic meaning depends on relations between these separate realities of the events in question. From the relations between them, the tropological or moral significance of each event emerges, and, last of all, through contemplation of the cognitive structure of the relation of the narrative events and their meanings – that is, through an understanding of the allegorical analogies – the anagogical sense is made manifest as the transcendent and ineffable reality that informs all symbols. While allegorical understanding is linear and hierarchical, guiding the mind, step by step, to higher meanings, its ultimate nature is circular, since the intellect, arriving at the anagogical understanding, immediately reinterprets the "lower" levels, discovering the inhering presence of the divine even at the literal-historical level. The intellectual unity of the symbols at all levels is finally seen as constituted by their anagogical origin and terminus.

While scriptural allegory is always rooted in history and its symbols in nature, secular allegory, or the allegory of the poets, as it was called in the Middle Ages, is similarly founded in the integrity of an initial sense, the narrative or plot of the story. Antonio D'Andrea has described in detail the difference between the allegory of the poets and scriptural allegory in Dante's *Convivio*: "For 'allegoria dei teologi,' which presupposes the historical truth of the persons of the Old Testament resulting from the literal interpretation and reveals in them the prefiguration, *in facto* but not *in verbis* (De Trinitate XV, ix, 1) of Christ, his coming and his works, is substituted the quite different 'allegoria dei poeti.' "[20] This difference is essential to an understanding of the grotesque. Both scriptural and secular allegory, however, aimed ultimately at uncovering a level of meaning that was extrahistorical, extranarrational, and extranatural.

DISCOURSE AND THE NEGATION OF ITS FORMS

The symbolic function of the monstrous is clearly akin to allegory and much of the marvellous in the Middle Ages has allegorical characteristics. Like allegory, the monster depends heavily on the process of analogy and the transfer and combination of intellectual significations that analogy permits, even if, in this case, the transfer distorts normal expectations. While allegory itself may be seen to transcend the normal structures of logical analogy, it nevertheless possesses a form and is limited by that form. Indeed the allegorical process may be seen as the ideal Neoplatonic paradigm for human cognition itself, beginning in material symbols, ascending to conceptual relations, and arriving at the ineffable source and full meaning of those symbols first perceived materially.[21] Secular allegory is, however, always linked to the historical or to the narrative level, and whatever cognitive illumination takes place in allegory, it is always grounded in and meshed with history and nature. It is, in fact, the historical-literal level of allegory that gives its meaning "authenticity," providing for conceptual ideas an origin in existence, a basis in "fact."

Just as allegory is limited by its origins in time and nature, so, too, the various forms of discourse that precede it are limited by the elements that constitute them. Language, science and logic, art, and myth and religion as cognitive forms express themselves as grammar and syntax, propositions and logical relations, mimesis and representation, and self-identity and alterity. All of these structures must, in a final step of understanding, be negated. These are the same categories that the monster plays havoc with. Every taxonomy of the monstrous reveals its structure to be founded in the contradiction of the same rational categories that made posssible the affirmative discourses of the culture, and in the Middle Ages it is this common apophasis that provides the connection between the grotesque and the theological.

In language, grammar, word order, and syntax permit communication with others and the shaping and ordering of reality in both speech and writing. The form of logical conception depends on the recognition and description of order in nature, of time, growth and decay, cause and effect, and the opposition already established by language, and makes possible, based on these principles, the fashioning of propositions and concepts. As it affects personal identity, the psychological dimension of form requires diversity and difference in order to establish the autonomy of self, as well as similarity to allow the recognition of self in relation to all the various forms of non-self. Once again, the conundrum encountered in the search for unity is that all the available means for achieving it are themselves sources of distinction. It was in the context of their philosophy of form that early thinkers attempted to solve this conundrum by developing theories of deformation and deconstruction.

If allegory, while liberated by the fiction of metaphor, is limited by the concreteness of its natural and historical referents and possesses strict requirements of form, the fantastic and the grotesque, in their employment of the monstrous figure, are free both of logical constraint and of nature and history. The multicephalic monster of mediaeval legend begins by defying nature, for neither is it a sign of anything in nature, nor is history its matrix. Regardless of the pseudo-historical and pseudo-geographical context in which it is presented, the multicephalic grotesque, like other monstrous figures, does not function symbolically in the same way as a Cain, revealing meaningful relations grounded in historical acts. This is not to say, however, that monsters are not "real," or that the Middle Ages did not "believe" in their existence. Monsters are, indeed, very real, but they are supranatural, having what Scotus Eriugena would call the existence of that which is-not and what the scholastics termed *esse in sola intellecta*. The representation of such beings naturally required literal narratives anchoring them in time and space, and thus we have the highly developed tradition of the monstrous races, in which considerable effort is expended in injecting verisimilitude into the accounts. While such efforts do, indeed, create a certain credibility for the narrative, they seem always to be accompanied by an undermining contradiction, as if to assure the fictional dimension of the monstrous. Thus, in most pseudo-geographical accounts, the monsters are, as we have noted, located in parts of the earth that, while quite well understood to exist, were nevertheless physically inaccessible. Such a situation rendered the reality of the monster theoretically true but experientially unverifiable, if not specious. A stunning example of the erosion of narrative is seen in the interruption by the anonymous author of the *Book of the Monsters*, who asserts his disbelief in the narrative that he, himself, is recounting.[22] That the mediaevals did not have difficulty assenting to the truth of the immaterial and unempirical is confirmed throughout their rich intellectual history.

The Platonists and Neoplatonists understood the relation of substance to form as one in which being arises out of the imposition of form on substance: "Universal nature ... is the natural recipient of all impressions, and is stirred and informed by them, and appears different from time to time by reason of them. But the forms that enter into and go out of her are the likenesses of eternal realities modeled after their patterns in a wonderful and mysterious manner" (*Timaeus* 50b–c).[23]

Substance, or matter, is the vehicle by which form is fulfilled in existence, and form is the principle and force by which substance grows, takes shape, and becomes what it is. Pure form is free of substance, and substance, prior to the imposition of form, is identified as chaos. These opposites, form and matter, are nevertheless similar in an important sense: they are both unlimited and unrestricted until form "informs" matter and the now-inherent form responds. Again we are faced with the concept of order and the limitations it requires to individuate beings; to be is to lose – or, as the Platonists would say, to forget.

Logical Form

Loss of form entails two contrary attitudes: attraction and repulsion. On the one hand, disorder and formlessness deprive the mind of a habitual structure necessary for understanding and acting and, ultimately, for being. On the other, disorder frees the mind in certain circumstances from the restrictions of order and reason. Loss of what we have called logical, or scientific, form demolishes reason and its categories so that the mind is initially confronted with absurdity. The introduction into a logical context of an idea or event negating logic is usually met with derision and rejection, and this is, perhaps, what accounts for the famous reaction of St Bernard to the grotesque deformations of mediaeval ecclesiastical art as "ridiculous monstrosities, a kind of deformed form, and form of deformity."[24] Much later, in post-Reformation days, the grumbling of St Bernard would become the more formal condemnation by the Church of grotesque representations of the divine: "Struck with grief that in the sanctuary of God there should be foolish pictures, and what are rather misshapen monstrosities than ornaments, I wished if possible to occupy the minds and eyes of the faithful in a more comely and useful fashion."[25]

The multiplication of logical negations, extensive enough to transform the context itself from logical to illogical, can create a world of multiple absurdities so overwhelming that the very principle of existence appears to be disorder and chaos. Such is the world of St Anthony or Guthlac, crowded with deformities, nonbeings, and "illusions." The loss of logical form to this degree produces a kind of delirium, a state in which the normal cognitive and psychological workings of the mind are distorted or nullified.

The readjustment of perspective demanded by the loss of form also makes possible, however, a state beyond absurdity and delirium that may permit a new and greater understanding of the very subjects normally revealed by logic, but free of logical constraint. The attraction felt for this state of mental formlessness is explained by the hint that it gives of the longed-for unity of being that is spoken of by thinkers and mystics of all times. Such a perspective is what the mystics called ecstasy, and it is in descriptions of their experiences in treatises such as *The Ascent of Mount Carmel* by St John of the Cross that it is best described:

> To reach satisfaction in all
> desire its possession in nothing.
> To come to possess all
> desire the possession of nothing.
> To arrive at being all
> desire to be nothing.
> To come to the knowledge of all
> desire the knowledge of nothing.[26]

Aesthetic Form

The aesthetic repulsion, even horror, experienced by the audience of a deformed text is well known to the modern spectator, for texts of this sort and commentary about them are numerous. Ranging from the seeming deformations of Joyce, where "stream of consciousness" invites the audience to imitate speech and reconstruct the logic missing in random thought,[27] to the genuine incoherence of Dali and Beckett, modern art displays an affinity for assaulting its own form. Its predecessors, Chaucer, Bosch, and the anonymous sculptors of Gothic cathedrals, also produced texts that could confuse and even repulse their audiences through similar, if more culturally integrated, rhetorical games and aesthetic distortions. The incoherence inspired in the audience by such self-deforming texts is explained by Aristotle: "It does not matter if a word has several meanings, if only they are limited in number; for a separate word might be assigned to each meaning. If the meanings are unlimited, no account can be given of the thing. Not to mean one thing is to mean nothing, and if words mean nothing rational, intercourse with others is destroyed, and even with oneself, for if we do not think one thing we do not think at all."[28]

This annihilation of the relation with the other and the self brought about through the excrescence of the word's signification is the negation of limits that causes the abhorrence of the deformed in aesthetics and in all its other manifestations.

Aesthetic deformation produces styles and genres such as the grotesque, the monstrous, the absurd, and the fantastic. The factor common to all aesthetic expressions of deformity appears to be that they take mimesis as their target; rather than presenting the mundane as the real, the deformed artifact negates the ontological status of "copy," eliminating the "world" and its differentiations in order to create a space for unions that are at once apophatic and grotesque. René Girard provides a striking analysis of how such grotesque syntheses function in tragedy; recognizing that the structure of tragedy begins in a certain difference and opposition between protagonist and antagonist, hero and villain, force of good, force of evil, Girard shows in text after text how the deformation of this surface structure progressively reveals the convergence of the identity of hero and villain. For Girard, the very core of tragedy is the monstrous mutual absorption of the protagonists, one into the other:

The symmetry of the tragic dialogue is perfectly mirrored by the stichomythia, in which the two protagonists address one another in alternating lines. In tragic dialogue hot words are substituted for cold steel. But whether the violence is physical or verbal, the suspense remains the same. The adversaries match blow for blow, and they seem so evenly matched that it is impossible to predict the outcome of the battle. The structural similarity between the two forms of violence is illustrated by the description of the duel between the brothers Eteocles and Polyneices in Euripedes' *Phoenician Women*. There is nothing in this account that does not apply equally to both brothers: their parries, thrusts, and feints, their gestures and postures, are identical.[29]

Psychological Form

Like loss of logical form, loss of psychological form also provokes a double reaction of repulsion and attraction. The loss of identity of the self is met with abhorrence, for it betokens an assault not only upon the individual being that is the self but on the very possibility of Being. The question of the deformation of the form of self is at once psychological and religious, since it is an experience that extends beyond the dimensions of psyche to encounter those of metaphysics. Just as personal form structures the understanding of the self and makes possible the various rapports between self and other, it is also that form that permits and limits the relation of the self and God.

The deformation of being is an annihilation more extensive than death, for it is a negation of the principles of existence, diversity, autonomy, and

separation. While death marks an end to the sentient, experiential, and temporal existence of the individual, it does nothing to undermine being itself. The
death of the individual reaffirms life in the sense that endings make possible
beginnings; indeed, for Aristotle death is merely one of the poles of the process of being. But deformation proffers the living witness of the arbitrariness
of the individuality of being or, in the case of certain sacrilegious offenses to
the dead such as cannibalism and zombiism, the possiblity of an annihilation
more extensive and more profound than mere physical expiration.[30]

Loss of psychological form may be caused by an actual deformation of
being, as in the case of metempsychosis, or by the mere deformation of the
appearance of being, as in lycomorphosis. In both cases loss of form awak-
ens a fundamental anxiety and reveals the human obsession with the very
idea of distinction. Again, René Girard provides the seminal analysis of this
phenomenon, which has its original and its clearest expression in art and
myth. Girard has shown us how mythic structure leads unremittingly toward
a confrontation with the vulnerability of the identity of the self; through a rit-
ualized negation of all differentiation, we are led to a destruction of form and
individuality. Culture itself, Girard shows, is based on this fragile system of
distinction: "The sacrificial crisis can be defined, therefore, as a crisis of distinctions – that is, a crisis affecting the cultural order. This cultural order is
nothing more than a regulated system of distinctions in which the differences
among individuals are used to establish their 'identity' and their mutual relationships."[31]

From another perspective, however, loss of self is desirable as a positive
state of liberation. Prominent in Neoplatonic thought is the idea that all being
strives to return to its origin in the One, or *Nous*, which is correlative with
Being, the matrix of forms, from which it came. In that bosom the self is re-
united with all other forms of being as it joins Being itself. Since, in fact, the
individual is the product of multiplicity produced from unity, complexity
arising from simplicity, difference out of sameness, the original and pure
state of existence inheres in sameness, simplicity, and unity. Return, as ontological desire, is a recognition of the paradox of self-sacrifice as self-fulfill-
ment. Such a return, however, is not accomplished without violence,
negation, or regret, but in the balance between repulsion and attraction, the
desire for union, seen from the perspective of spiritual integrity, eventually
prevails. The anxiety of the individual self and the resolution of that anxiety
through the arduous struggle of negation is a central concern of the mediaeval Christian discourse of the return to God through the transcendence of
self: "A soul that is truly united to God is not conscious of itself; it neither
sees nor loves itself, nor anyone else, but keeps its thoughts on God alone,
not on any creature."[32]

While Christian theological speculation spoke of the retention of personal
identity in beatitude, the language of the mediaeval mystics, distinguished by

ideas of absorption into God, permeation by God, and divine ravishing, emphasizes the disappearance of the self into the Godhead, not in the pantheistic sense of diluting God into the forces of nature, but rather in the erotic sense of union in which lovers become as one. Again, the fourteenth-century mystic, St Catherine of Siena best expresses this sometimes convoluted idea: "Being united in love in this way – a love which increases day by day – the soul becomes as it were changed into our Lord."[33]

The relationship of self to God is not univocal. Religion in its affirmative mode paves the rational way for the seeker operating within the limits of self and logic to come to the One: in the roles of penitent, petitioner, and seeker, the devout are provided with discourses in which God is cast as the ultimate Other: the Just God who punishes, the Merciful God who answers our prayers, the Hidden God who is object of a life-long search. This is, indeed, a complex but necessary experience in the development of the relationship, and one which, as mediaeval Christianity understood, demanded its own negation for its completion. Such a negation occurs through a transcendence of self in which the self ceases to be all of the persona demanded by its discourses and in which God ceases to be a chief protagonist as ultimate Other. This is the sense of the merging of self and God taught to St Catherine by the Lord: "Daughter, do you not know who you are and who I am? If you know these two things, you are blessed and will continue to be so. You are she that is not, and I am he who is."[34] The reemergence of the negated self in God presents in still another way the paradox of being. On the one hand, in the return to the One the many dissolve and yet acquire their true identity; on the other, the self is attained by fleeing itself, and its identity is discovered to inhere in the "other": "A soul in this state sees that in itself it is nothing, that all its virtue and all its strength belongs to God, its maker, alone. So it abandons itself and all other creatures completely and takes refuge in its Creator, our Lord Jesus Christ, to such an extent that it casts all its spiritual and physical actions wholly onto him, in whom it sees that it will find every blessing and the fulness of goodness. This means that it has no desire to look for anything outside this intimate knowledge of him, for any reason whatsoever."[35]

Loss of self is related to loss of form and to loss of order. As the monster deforms to "show forth" the reality of Form, so too it disorders to reveal the full nature of Order itself. The constituent elements of the ideas of form and order are similar: categorization, hierarchy, differentiation, and similarity. The monstrous is constituted by the same characteristics inverted and denied: the confusion of categories, the levelling of hierarchy, the synthesis of differentiated phenomena, and dissimilitude. Disorder, like the deformed, seems to have its own dynamic – one would like to say its own "order," its own "form" – and it plays a crucial role in the structure of reality. Paul G. Kuntz distinguishes between disorder and chaos, the latter being, however, the matrix of the former: "Disorder is the uncoordinated which we can coordinate, whereas chaos is the undifferentiated which we cannot differentiate."[36]

Differentiation and coordination are equally essential to form and to order; the monster's kinship to disorder and chaos lies in its function of deforming. In the monster of combination, for example, the absolute differentiation between forms of existence is denied. Similarly, in the monster of deprivation the coordination of pairs is negated, as we see in the one-eyed Cyclops or the single-footed sciapode. More extended annulments of the objective coordination in order are seen in the hermaphrodite's cancellation of sexual pairs and in the discoordination of temporal sequence represented in the multicephalic monster. Order and disorder are fundamental to the structure of the monstrous and are parallel in a way to the concepts of similitude and dissimilitude. The conceptual importance of disorder and the interrelation of disorder and order is described by James Feibleman in his essay on the subject: "Order, then, can be identified with similarity and disorder with differences. Is this an acceptable definition of order: similarity among differences? If so, then order has the limitation that it cannot be total. The distribution of the terms is crucial. For total order would be order among all the elements and not merely among some, as required by the definition. But if order is not total then disorder is required in any total account, and so disorder becomes as important as order. Disorder from this description would seem to be a larger domain."[37]

Indeed, from Feibleman's perspective, disorder is the basis and support of all systems of order, while simultaneously the contrary of order itself. Such a concept seems to echo Plato's theory of being and nonbeing: "It must, then, be possible for 'that which is not' [i.e. is different from existence] to be [to exist], not only in the case of motion but of all the other kinds. For in the case of them all, the nature of difference makes each one of them different from existence and so makes it a thing that 'is not,' and hence we shall be right to speak of them all on the same principle as things that in this sense 'are not,' and again, because they partake of existence, to say that they 'are' [exist] and call them things that have being [existence]."[38]

The often-noted function of the monster as contradicting and undermining human categorizations of nature and reality, its role as "exception to the rule," is given a new and more formal significance in the light of Feibleman's description of the concept of disorder. While the taxonomy of the entire range of monstrous forms may be viewed, as indeed it always has been, as the contradiction of our effort to order and categorize our experience of the world, in the larger perspective it must also be seen in the first instance as providing the very possibility of that ordering function, and in the second, as providing the possibility of transcending it to understand "order" itself. Feibleman again specifies this superior function: "The point is that disorder accounts for existence. Existence depends upon movement and opposition; but with order completed there would be no such activity. This state will never occur, however, for chaos is primeval and eternal, the matrix of permanent possibilities of order."[39]

Thus the identification of the monster with disorder makes it also the potential for order. As the appropriate sign for disorder, the monstrous reveals disorder as the precondition for being, since being depends on process/ differentiation/opposition; the monster, itself nonbeing in the sense of Eriugena's "that which is-not," stands as a sign of the nature of being. It reminds us of the fragility and incompleteness of ontological and cognitive orders and provides the perspective from which the essence of order itself is revealed. Paisley Livingston, in his introduction to an important collection of essays on order and disorder, reflects on the involvement of the concept of order in hierarchy and notes both the need for hierarchical order and the fundamental opposition between hierarchy and paradox: "In logic, hierarchy has been perceived as the means of forestalling paradox, and in epistemology, the affirmation of hierarchies between subject and object has provided two traditional manners of attempting to resolve the paradoxes of dualism. Hierarchy, finally, is central to our conceptions of artistic form insofar as we speak of the orderly levels within a work and of its final 'unity in multiplicity.' "[40]

While such a perception clearly associates order with hierarchy and rightly understands hierarchy as inimical to paradox, it thereby implies the even more telling identification between disorder and paradox, which itself is the key to the Christian Neoplatonic metaphysics. In this view, disorder provides a proper description of the ineffable, both in its basic negativity and in its unlimited potential, because the divine One is also properly described as the 'matrix of permanent possibilities of order' – above all order, source of existence beyond existence, origin of movement without movement. The sign of this disorder is the monster, a sign that also evokes what Nicholas of Cusa called the least imperfect definition of God: the *coincidentia oppositorum*.[41] Feibleman's connection between disorder and chaos evokes the same idea: "It is not a far step from the conception of disorder to the original conception of chaos from which order emerges. Chaos is the sum of all orders, the matrix from which particular orders are derived. That it must remain a chaos and not become itself a kind of super order is required by Gödel's theorem. Chaos cannot therefore be defined as order in the sense of 'all orders,' for if it contains all orders it cannot itself be an order."[42]

Transported into the discourse of negative theology, Feibleman's description would identify chaos and disorder as metaphors for God. In Neoplatonic terms, the total simplicity of the One is understood as the source of multiplicity; the total nondifferentiation of the Divine, which cannot be ordered, is the origin of all differentiation. But while in modern logic simplicity and multiplicity are unresolved opposites, they do not remain so in Neoplatonic metaphysics, as Stephen Gersh explains in discussing the nature of forms: "Each form also represents a number in the sense that its nature is both single and multiple. This concept is a very important one in later Neoplatonism, and great pains are taken in demonstrating how the combination of unity and plurality in the Forms differs from the nature of sensible compound objects. Proclus remarks that 'each Form is both one and many, not as a result of some composition in which the many produce a unity but because the one causes the many particular characteristics contained in it.' "[43]

Nondifferentiation and disorder, since they are proper to the divine, have precedence over order and differentiation, and in the aesthetic expression of the idea, the monster functions to signify this fundamental reality. The monstrous construct in its dissemblant and negative character is, as the Neoplatonists and Christian mystics stated, a more appropriate (or, at least, less inappropriate) sign of God; but it is not itself a perfect sign, because, like any other sign, the monster also suggests a kind of structure, one correlated to order. The monster requires the dispersion of limited orders into disorder of the kind described here, in which disorder is the liberation from the limitations of order. When elements of a limited order are related to elements of another different, limited order, the result is disorder vis-à-vis the principles of organization of each of the limited orders. So the monstrous centaur disperses elements of human anatomy and those of animal, to recombine them in the figure that confounds the very principle of differentiation and of order. The integrity of the human genus and the integrity of the genus horse are both negated in the centaur. But this is only the beginning of the apophatic function of such a creature, for beyond its relation to each of the categories that it combines, it provides, like other grotesque combinations, a commentary on the very origins of form and order and suggests the common matrix of all differences in unity. While not the perfect expression of chaos, the monster lies somewhere between the Divine, All-Saying Silence and the endless multiplication of human discourses, functioning as a real sign of their relationship, a symbol of the process of emanation of the many from the One, of words from the Word, and of the return. It suggests to the human spirit its origin in simplicity, unity, nondifferentiation, stillness and silence, and such a reminder, achieved through the negation of cognition's discursive monuments, both lures and repulses.

The language of the monstrous expresses the spirit's desire to reattain its source in unity and simplicity. Unlike discursive language, monstrous language exhibits the nature of that reality toward which it guides the mind, the state before distinction, before language, before the fall of human cognition. Contraries and opposites play a decisive role in the hermeneutics of both languages, although in discursive systems, meaning is discovered through logic's multiplication of opposites and its production of ever-more precise categories of distinction. In the language of the monster precisely the reverse occurs, so that contraries and opposites are joined and mixed, while categories and differences are steadily reduced and confused to replace, on the conceptual level, logic with enigma and on the aesthetic level, to substitute the iconic for the narrative.

While the monstrous has frequently been defined as enigma, the sense of enigma with which it has been identified has usually been the vague, impressionistic sense of post-Romantic thought, rather than the more formal, philosophical definition supplied by the Middle Ages. Originally as a division of allegory, enigma possessed the special power of stimulating intellection of the most obscure realities and of "the inscrutable Language which man is not permitted to utter" (2 Cor. 12:4). Throughout the Middle Ages enigma was revered as the most suitable expression of divine mysteries precisely because its obscurity suited the extradiscusive nature of its subject. St Augustine was alert to the advantage of enigma, and, as Marcia Colish has shown, his own analytic method was to construct analogies between the human and the divine and then to deconstruct them to achieve enigma: "Having built up the foregoing analogies with great care and profundity, Augustine occupies himself with breaking them down in the final book of the *De trinitate*. His aim here is to restate the point that God is ineffable and that He towers infinitely over anything men can say about Him. Our knowledge of God in this life, reaffirms Augustine, is partial and shadowy. It is the knowledge of faith, 'per speculum in aenigmate.' "[44]

The theological enigma rejects logic by going beyond it to communicate what it would "resolve." The monstrous enigma deforms the fundamentals of signification to communicate what otherwise could not be communicated. While in normal discourse the similarity and appropriateness of the sign to its signified are the criteria for effectiveness and right representation, in deformed discourse similitude is not intended but rather rejected in favour of the jarring and unsettling inaccuracy and impropriety on which enigmatic understanding is based. The intellectual disturbance effected by the monstrous is due not only to the inappropriateness of the particular sign for what is signified, but also to its inherent negation of the mind's confidence in similitude and mimesis as criteria of language and cognition.

In the Middle Ages and other periods and cultures in which the monster flourished, the existence of a transcendent, ineffable reality superior to and paradigmatic of mundane reality was undoubted. The representation of this essentially unrepresentable reality was the goal of both philosophy and art. The limitations of discursive language seem to have been recognized almost from the beginning of philosophical thought, and the general nature of those limitations identified as language's need for a sign to represent a truth, which sign, by its nature, remains different and distinct from what it signifies. In modern thought, the most influential insight is that of Saussure, who enunciated the

principle of the arbitrary nature of the sign, but this general perception existed
long before Saussure's formulation. Frequent are the warnings in the theology
of the Middle Ages of the dangers of confusing the sign with the reality of the
signified, but the warnings are accompanied by the admission of the paradox
that it is exactly this separation that both constitutes language and prevents it
from leading the mind to an understanding of the ineffable reality that it seeks:
"The soul runs over all truths, and all the same shuns the truths we know if
someone tries to express them in words and discursive thought; for discursive
thought, in order to express anything in words, has to consider one thing after
another: this is the method of description; but how can one describe the absolutely simple?"[45]

The conundrum of the Neoplatonist, then, is the need for a form of language that captures the formless, a discourse capable of denying itself. But is
it possible for the human mind, dependent as it is for its functions on form,
and itself a form-creating tool, to liberate itself from form? The possibility is
prepared for by the early Neoplatonists who, providing for the existence of
formless being, allowed for the greater elaboration of its concept in the later
Middle Ages. Although Syrianus was defending the Platonic theory of metaphysical Form when he answered the objection that all common principles
cannot have corresponding Forms, his enumeration of particulars lacking
form furnishes a basis for the later mediaeval description of the transcendence of form. There are, Syrianus tells us, particulars which derive from no
form whatsoever:

(i) ... "Bad or ugly things," since these signify rather a lack of form. (ii) ... "Nega-
tives." These constitute the removal of the limit and definition which are concomitant
with form. (iii) ... "Transitory things" which have their sources in moving causes
rather than in the stable nature of the Forms. (iv) ... "Parts." Forms are only causes of
things as a whole. (v) ... "Accidents." These can be explained adequately with recourse to physical logoi. (vi) ... "Composites." Forms are simple principles and are
therefore only the source of other simple things. (vii) ... "Things which come to be
from heterogenous combinations" ... These are not simply the result of physical
causes but require the invention of human art. (viii) ... "Acts dependent upon human
will or resulting from concatenation of many causes."[46]

The ugly, the negative, the ephemeral, the incomplete, the accidental, the
composite, the absurd, and the created artefact – to summarize and extend
Syrianus – constitute the formless realities. The transformation of these categories into a system of signs appropriate to the expression of their ontological significance had to await the later mediaeval Christian thinkers, and if the
more thoroughly Platonic Pseudo-Dionysius stopped short of developing a
full-fledged monstrous symbolism, his mediaeval translator and interpreter,
John Scotus Eriugena, did not. As Roques has amply shown, the Irishman

who made Dionysius available to Latin Christianity was not averse to adapting the Areopagite's thinking by creative translation to the thinking of ninth-century Europe. Where, for instance, the Areopagite eschewed the elaboration of a teratological symbolism, Scotus Eriugena went at the task with enthusiasm, on the one hand, in order to make Dionysian theology more acceptable to contemporary orthodoxy and, on the other, to create a symbolic system harmonious with his own philosophical and theological speculations, which were based, in turn, on his own liberal interpretation of Pseudo-Dionysius.

Eriugena and the Form of What Is-Not

The reception in the mediaeval West of the Dionysian system of negative theology had enormous influence not only on mediaeval Christian philosophy but on aesthetics as well, and, it is suggested here, it is the basis for the particular development of grotesque art from the Romanesque period onward. In this period the monster becomes the fullest aesthetic expression of the dominant conceptual system known as the *via negativa*. But this is made possible not merely through the wide reading that the Areopagite's writings received but also by the subtle reworking and expansion they underwent at the hands of Scotus Eriugena. Where Pseudo-Dionysius provided an apophatic metaphysics, Scotus adds an apophatic natural philosophy, and beyond Denys' double system of resemblant and dissemblant symbolism, Eriugena establishes a triadic system of resemblant, dissemblant, and teratological signification; in place of the Areopagite's unarticulated method of exegesis, John Scotus offers a fully developed system of literary analysis based on the apophatic vision of his master.

Where Denys is frankly contemptuous of efforts to understand the world, Scotus Eriugena, perceiving the gap in what he may have wished had been a complete philosophy of Dionysianism, filled it with his own *Periphyseon*. This, the longest of Scotus' works, is a restatement of Dionysian apophasis and Neoplatonic metaphysics with greater attention paid to the human and to human intimacy with God. In the first few lines of the dialogue between Nutritor and Alumnus, a variation on the teacher/student personae of other dialogues, Eriugena articulates the structure of nature as one divided into four modes of "difference": "N[Nutritor]. It is my opinion that the division of Nature by means of four differences results in four species, (being divided) first into that which creates and is not created, secondly into that which is created and also creates, thirdly into that which is created and does not create, while the fourth neither creates nor is created (*Periphyseon* I.441B).

While the structure of the universe is fourfold and this fourfold structure is the basis of the structure of the *Periphyseon*, it is secondary to a more basic binary division between *that which is* and *that which is-not*. This concept is sufficiently important to cite at length John O'Meara's explanation of it:

The primary division of nature, however, is into being and non being. These are to be considered according to five different modes. The first mode is according to *percepti-bility*: that which can be perceived by intellect or sense is said to be; that which is not so perceptible is said not to be. God, for example, is not so perceptible and so is said not to be. The second mode of being and nonbeing is according to *order* or place on the descending and ascending scale from the Creator to the lowliest creature and back again; if being is predicated of man, then an angel has not being, and *vice versa*. The third mode is according to *actualization*: a thing is, if it is actualized; it is not, if it remains merely possible. The fourth mode is according to the *faculty of perception*: that which the intellect perceives, is: that which is perceived by sense, is not. The fifth mode is according to the *realization of God's image* and is applicable to man only: if man is in sin, he is not; if he is restored to God's image through grace, he is.[47]

These divisions provide the paradigm for the understanding of God, man, and the universe, for the stages of life and death, and for the relationship between language and the world. It is clear that the concept of nonbeing is used in both the Dionysian sense of *greater-than-being* ("God ... is said not to be") and in the purely privative sense ("If man is in sin, he is not"). However, the four differences are related to each other through a dynamic of similarity and contrariety that is progressively deconstructed by the intellect into a full paradox in which all four are perfectly distinct and at the same time exactly the same. John is quite conscious of the relations of the oppositions that he is constructing and specifies the primary analogies he will use: "But within these four there are two pairs of opposites. For the third is the opposite of the first, the fourth of the second" (*Periphyseon* 1.442A).

That which creates and is not created, we discover in book 1, is God as source, and Scotus elaborates this idea in the highly familiar terms of Christian Neoplatonism: God is one, simple, and undivided, while the source of the many, diverse, and distinct beings; He is utterly unlike all that He has created, which creation is nevertheless his image; He is perfect harmony and the source of all contraries. Book 2 describes *that which is created and also creates* as the procession of beings from the Creator through the "causes." This corresponds more or less to the Platonic realm of Ideas. In Scotus' Christian context, however, it may be more accurate to describe this division as the logical procession of beings from universals to particulars. O'Meara describes the created-and-creating division as divine ideas, essences, examples, definitions, and predestinations, and it is clear that book 2 describes God-created principles more generally, principles that themselves create further specifications and individuations in being, dividing angel from man, intelligible from sensible, prelapsarian nature from fallen nature, and even male from female.[48]

The third division, *that which is created and does not create,* concentrates on the phenomenal universe and all the beings contained within it. The hierarchy of beings and their participation in Being are considered here, and much importance is given in this book to the concept of "nothing." In the last two books, the mysterious division of *that which is not created and does not create* is presented as a reality earlier described by John as "classed among the impossibles, for it is of its essence that it cannot be" (*Periphyseon* I.442A). In the first instance it is God as end, the terminus of the process of being, the *reditus* of Pseudo-Dionysius. It is uncreated in that it is the Eternal One; it is uncreating in that the mode in which we understand it is eschatological. While this division is formally about God as end, the focus of the discussion in these two books is on man, human nature, and destiny. What emerges in a salient manner through the discussion of these four differences is the paradoxical sense in which each division, while clearly distinct, is really about the same subject as all the others; in this way division and difference themselves dissolve as the intellect works its way through the contraries.

In John's fourth division we discover the metaphysical possibility of the existence of nonbeing, a possibility not provided for as forcefully by earlier thinkers and one that effects his entire concept of reality. For Eriugena goes beyond merely making room for such existence: he identifies it as the foundation of being itself. Scotus describes the fourth division as "terrifying" (*terroris nobis incutit*)[49] precisely because it presents that which is-not as real. Sensitive to the difficulty of communicating the nature of that which is-not, John warns his readers that the voyage ahead will be intellectually terrifying precisely because it goes against the rational grain. In this epic vision of metaphysics, the fourth division constitutes the return of all that is and all that is-not to the source of being itself, and thus we see that existence has its origin in the same matrix as the nonexistent, the unseen, the unknown, and all that is beyond reason and therefore epistemologically nonexistent. This includes the potential, what could-be, because "it is-not-yet"; it includes negations because "it is-what-has-been." Myra Uhlfelder summarizes John's sense of the reality of what is-not: "But reason is created and its competence is limited: what lies beyond it can be said not to be. God transcends all knowing whatever, whether it be human or even angelic, and in this sense He can be said not to be. The essences of all things are grounded in Him and hidden from our view, and they too must be said not to be. Both what is and what is not are found within the hierarchical order of created things, for to affirm the lower is to negate the higher, and to affirm the higher is to negate the lower."[50]

The ontological principle of the *Periphyseon,* then, is double: that which is comprehensible, which can be contained by the human mind – everything that fits into the multiple cognitive schemes of man – these are said to exist in a positive, affirmative way. Beyond this existence lies an entire dimension of being that eludes the limitations of reason and is said to be "is-not." These beings exist through the mode of negation and dissimilitude. The double modes of this ontology are in constant interaction, making possible the gradual theophany of the real and the return of being into Being.

It is in relation to the second, negatory mode that the deformed and the monstrous play their part. Having provided a metaphysical ground for the existence of what is-not, Eriugena then is able to account for the representation of that reality in a system of symbolism that is overtly teratological. Eriugena's system as presented in the *Periphyseon* makes possible a single paradigm for cosmic, metaphysical, logical, linguistic, and aesthetic realities.

The concept that Scotus creates as the structure of universal nature suggests a series of analogies about metaphysics that makes prominent the role of the monstrous and the grotesque in the hierarchy of being. In the great Neoplatonic scheme of creation the return of being into Being is, as John describes it, "terrifying" because it is the experience of negation (not unlike what Heidegger termed the encounter with *Dasein*). It is terrifying because it is exactly that loss of form that both beckons and repulses: it is death. But the return to the not-created-not-creating is much more than privation. It is the locus of encounter between the human spirit and that which is-not, for as John explains, everything that is beyond human intellect can be said to be that which "is-not." It is in this fourth dimension that the unity of all being is at last attained. It is clear that division 1, creating-not-created, and division 4, not-created-not-creating, are the same: each is God in two different modes, as Source and as End. Further, division 1 and division 2, created-and-creating, are also the same, for in the personification of the divisions, the second is identified as God the Son: "And therefore they (the primordial Causes of the second division) were appropriately named by the wise men of the Greeks πρωτότυπα, that is, the principal exemplars which the Father made in the Son ... They are also customarily called by the philosophers θελήματα, that is, divine volitions, because everything that God wished to make he made in them primordially and causally" (*Periphyseon* 2.616A).

In the logical terms of contrariety and analogy, divisions 1 and 3 are opposites, just as are divisions 2 and 4: "The third conflicts with the first, for they confront each other as it were from diametrically opposed positions ... Similarly the second form is opposed to the fourth" (*Periphyseon* 2.525B). This, however, makes pairs once again of divisions 1 and 4, as well as implying similitude between divisions 2 and 3. This latter analogy between divisions 2 and 3 is significant in all of the phenomena that each of these divisions contains. Universal (2) and particular (3) exist in strict relation to each other; causes (2) and effects (3) have a similar analagous relation; Jesus (2) and humankind (3) share human nature. The author himself summarizes the similarities by pointing to the commonality in the names of the divisions: "The third takes on a likeness of the second in that it is created ... Furthermore the fourth is similar to the first because it is not created" (2.525C–525D).

As a paradigm for cognition, the Eriugenian scheme begins, naturally, in division 3, the locus of humanity and the world and the sole region of epistemology. Intellect encounters effects and experiences particulars, the intelligibles of the physical universe. From them it comes to know causes and universals, the denizens of division 2. Thus mind is led in an anagogical movement up to the realm of the transcendent and, passing through these causes, arrives at an understanding of the Creator, understanding Him in His affirmative creation. In a still further step, the one called by both Eriugena and his master, "apophatic," the mind perceives God as End, the *Deus absconditus*, nowhere contained in any aspect of what-is. In an ultimate event that is beyond the epistemological, God is known as beyond *Creator mundi* and beyond *Deus absconditus*, and beyond every name.

Taking the four-part scheme as a paradigm for linguistic and aesthetic activity, we see that it imitates the dynamic of *editus/reditus*. The speaker, in conceiving the concept, engages in a mental act. As a way of expressing that concept, the speaker fashions a sign for it, a representation of the concept outside of mind and in the world. Here, the fourth division is the understanding of the receptor, which suggests the listener into whose mind the sign goes in the process of communication. Thus this last division as paradigm of language resembles the last division in other paradigms; it is the mental terminus of the word that had its origin in mind; that is, it is *end* in relation to the speaker as Creator. The receptor is called uncreated and uncreating in that he is not created in the process of the communication but exists before, and this he shares as a similitude with the speaker, who is also uncreated, existing before the communication. In division 2 is the concept, which is, like all other inhabitants of the second division, created-and-creating, since it is created by intellect and in turn creates its own sign. The third division can accurately be called created-and-uncreating, because it is produced by the concept and represents it, but the third division can never create the signified. The unity of the entire fourfold scheme is strikingly described by Scotus as he, himself, applies the model to the act of utterance: "[Intellect] becomes embodied at will in sounds and letters, and while it is being embodied it subsists bodiless in itself; and when it makes for itself out of airy matter or out of sensible figures certain vehicles, as it were, by means of which it can convey itself to the senses of others so that it may quickly reach *their* external senses, it then abandons these vehicles and penetrates by itself absolutely alone into the heart's core and mingles itself with other intellects and becomes one with those to whom it is joined" (*Periphyseon* 3.633C–D).

The application of John's system to the aesthetic text is a subject that will be developed more fully below, but it seems useful here to suggest the way in which the *Periphyseon* 's structure is paradigmatic of the imagination and its products. In this paradigm the author, like the speaker, occupies the place of the creator in division 1. He produces the imaginative concept that in the Middle Ages, as we have seen, was usually referred to as "phantasia," but sometimes also called a *fictio* (from the verb *fingo*, meaning a fashioning, a forming, a conception, what Sydney would later call a "conceit"). In John's scheme the concept is found in the same position as the *Verbum Dei* who is the source of Scripture; thus concept and text are seen as analogous to *Verbum Dei* and Scripture. This analogy between language and the Divine is widespread in mediaeval Christianity, but expressed nowhere more compellingly, perhaps, than throughout the writings of Augustine: "How did He come except that 'the Word was made flesh and dwelt among us'? It is as when we speak. In order that what we are thinking may reach the mind of the listener through the fleshly ears, that which we have in mind is expressed in words and called speech."[51]

This concept adheres to the formula for division 2 since it is created-and-creating, evoking as it does the symbols or words that create the text in which it comes into being and is made manifest. In the paradigm of nature, division 3 is occupied by the created world; in the paradigm for aesthetic creation, division 3 is occupied by the text. Here individual texts participate in the universal text of the division of causes and ideas. It is created-not-creating, for its meaning (we may say its "being") originates in the author and the author's imagination, and the words and signs themselves create no further meaning of their own. Similarly, the audience inhabits division 4 in this scheme; it is not-created-not-creating and is the terminus for the creative act of the author. In this sense the audience completes the text by acting as its *end*, but the audience itself creates nothing within the text.

In the *Periphyseon* the nature of the fourth division is delineated as God-as-End, apophasis, *Deus absconditus,* and nonbeing. Its name, not-created-not-creating, emphasizes its negative aspect. As the contrary of the division of Forms, Ideas, and Causes, it suggests itself as non-Form, non-Idea, non-Cause. It is, as John says, the realm of the "impossible." Thus one of the manifestations of this division is the monster, that being which is-not, the effect for which no cause exists, the deformity which bespeaks the fragility of form. The monster as paradox is one of the denizens of division 4, for just as the movement from division 2 to division 3 is the divine *editus*, expressed in formation, intelligibility, and individuation, the movement from division 3 into division 4 arrives at an undoing of all this: "*For* everything that is understood and sensed is nothing else but the apparition of what is not apparent, the manifestation of the hidden, the affirmation of the negated, the comprehension of the incomprehensible [the utterance of the unutterable, the access to the inaccessible] … *the form of the formless*" (3.633A–B, final emphasis added).

This is tantamount to the metaphoric representation of God as monster, an identity already well established in the Pseudo-Dionysian tradition and one carried on throughout the Middle Ages. In Scotus not only is God-as-end identified with the deformed as inhabiting the fourth division of universal nature, but through the analogy between division 4 and division 1 already established, God the Creator is also seen as monster.

In a move that is typically Eriugenian, the author completes the square of relationships by linking the previously unrelated divisions 1 and 2 with divisions 3 and 4, and in so doing, negates the oppositions that he has earlier established. In this way Eriugena begins the deconstruction of the entire apparatus. In his lengthy discussion of the Trinity and his even lengthier discussion of the second person of the Trinity, it is clear that as Jesus is division 2, so that division is identical with division 1, God the Creator. Furthermore, in his development of the idea of the creature as the image of God, John establishes a direct link between humanity (division 3) and God. Thus the creature exists in the image of God, but, as we see in the similarities between division 2 (Jesus) and division 3 (the creature), God also exists in the image of the creature. This is initially understood as a similitude between the creature and God the Creator, that is, the God of division 1: "It follows that we ought not to understand God and the creature as two things distinct from one another, but as one and the same. For both the creature, by subsisting, is in God; and God, by manifesting Himself, in a marvellous and ineffable manner, creates Himself in the creature" (*Periphyseon* 3.678C).

Radical as this identification between Creator and creature may appear, Scotus Eriugena does not shy away from the even more "outrageous" assertion of a certain homogeneity between the *Deus absconditus* of division 4 and the unfathomable *humanitas* of divison 3. Relying again upon the idea of the creature as made in the image of God, Eriugena pushes the apophatism of his theology toward its conclusions, beyond theology, into the human sciences: if the creature is made in the image of God, he is similarly mysterious, unknowable, uncontainable, limitless, and formless. The creature, as the image of God, *is-not,* for there is no image of God, because God is beyond representation. Most strikingly, John says that man's substance is his concept of himself in himself, a radical identification of man and God and one that has its basis in the apophatic nature of God and of the human mind:

So it is that what is one and the same thing can be thought of as twofold because there are two ways of looking at it, yet everywhere it preserves its incomprehensibility, in the effects as in the causes, and whether it is endowed with accidents or abides in its naked simplicity: under neither set of circumstances is it subject to created sense or intellect nor even the knowledge of itself as to what it is ... For the human mind does know itself, and again does not know itself. For it knows that it is, but does not know what it is. And as we have taught in the earlier books it is this which reveals most clearly the Image of God to be in man. (*Periphyseon* 4.771A–B)

In a discussion of apophatic anthropology based on Eriugena's development of the negative tradition, John Saward persuasively argues exactly this view, that Eriugena identified man and God as the Unknowable. Saward also enlists the theories of Gregory of Nyssa (*De hominis opificio*) who describes man as like the unknowable God. Gregory points to the innumerable paradoxes that are posed concerning the human and comments that man himself *is* the paradox and, in so being, is the image of God. Saward summarizes Gregory: "Made in the image of God, man reproduces the unspeakable mystery of the Trinity. In this sense 'it is easier to know the heavens than oneself' (*De hom op* 257C). Corresponding to *Deus absconditus* there is *homo absconditus*, to apophatic theology there is apophatic anthropology."[52] Saward's most striking proof of the identification of the human with the God who is-not is taken, however, not from the mystics, but from Augustine: "For what is deeper than this depth? ... I do not think it absurd to understand by this depth man of whom it is said elsewhere: man shall come to a deep heart and God shall be exalted ... For every man, whether holy, or just, or proficient in many virtues, is an abyss, and 'calls to an abyss,' whenever he preaches to a man about some matter of faith or truth concerning eternal life."[53]

Through the identification of the human with the negative theophany, man himself finds his link to the monster of division 4, the "intellectually terrifying" phenomenon of which John writes, for like the God who is-*not* in the apophatic tradition, man contains at the core of his very being the superabundant nothing that is his source. We understand now that the terror of which John warns arises from the ultimate confrontation with a mysterious truth: we are the monster we fear. Like the monster, humanity is paradox, both angel and beast, and like the monster humanity contains all the forms of creation; he is the microcosm containing an amalgam of being that goes beyond mundane nature: "And so not unreasonably we are told to believe and understand that every visible and invisible creature is created in man alone. For no substance has been created which is not understood to subsist in him, no species or difference or property or natural accident is found in nature which either is not naturally in him or of which he cannot have knowledge" (*Periphyseon* 4.773D–774A).

Of course, the similitude between divisions 1 and 3 utterly contradicts the previously established opposition between them, and this is characteristic of John's strategy as he imitates the Dionysian process of creating similitude, dissimilitude, and, finally, transcending both. This ultimate step of transcendence is referred to often in the *Periphyseon*, and it is correlative with the deconstruction of the entire model that is the structure of the real and the structure of the text. Having reduced the first and the fourth divisions, or "differences" as they are also called, to a single reality and having subjected the second and the third to the same reduction, Nutritor is left with two differences, Creator and creature which, as he gets Alumnus to admit, may be further condensed into a single reality: "N. So the four become two. A. I do not deny it. N. But suppose you join the creature to the Creator so as to understand that there is nothing in the former save Him who alone truly is ... will you deny that Creator and creature are one? A. It would not be easy for me to deny it. For it seems to me ridiculous to resist this reduction. N. So the universe, comprising God and creature, which was first divided as it were into four forms, is reduced again to an *indivisible One*, being Principle as well as Cause and End" (*Periphyseon* 2.528A–B, emphasis added).

This final reduction of all reality to the simple unity of One is the ultimate expression of negative theology, for in the one there is neither similarity nor difference, neither affirmation nor negation: all opposition is transcended.

Having provided an ontological space for the monster in the abstract structure of universal nature, Scotus Eriugena went on later to develop a literary symbolism appropriate for the expression of this worldview.[54]

Eriugena's Teratological Symbolism

John Scotus will emphasize one of these characteristics [of Dionysius' second category of symbols], or, more precisely, he will highlight those expressions that most forcefully justify his designation of dissemblant symbolism by most clearly exhibiting that symbolism's "cathartic" and "anagogical" powers. These are specifically the "monstrous" representations which "confuse" and destroy in some way the symbolizing natures (*formarum confusio*), by "blocking" [*miscetur*] in a single image (*in eademque imagine*) elements borrowed from several natures, indeed, integrating many natures which are, in and of themselves, distinct, complete, and independent (*absolutis*).[55]

In Pseudo-Denys the question of symbolism receives considerable development, and what he designates as unnatural, absurd, and outrageous are grouped under his designation of *dissemblant* symbolism. As Roques has pointed out, however, Denys' theory of symbolism does not go much further than his perception that there is an inherent separation between the sign and the signified, which renders the symbol anomalous. Denys makes the important distinction between those signs that attempt to obscure their distance from the reality signified and those that highlight it; the former, he states, operate through similitude, the latter through dissimilitude, or "dissemblance." Ultimately, however, all symbols and signs of every kind are "monstrous" for the Areopagite in the recusative sense that all representations are deformations of their signifieds and doomed to failure. Speaking of Denys' exegesis of the monstrous representation of angels in Isaiah (6:6), Roques states: "For him this disconcerting assemblage of feet, wings, and faces should be interpreted according to the same criteria as pure images, even those that are also 'dissemblant,' such as the lion, the horse, burning wheels, passions, absence of reason or feeling, drunkenness or sleep. In each of these cases spiritual exegesis will apply a standard method, emphasizing the radical alterity that separates the symbolized realities from their banal, crude, or deformed symbols. Thus 'monstrous' symbolism is in this way reduced to 'dissemblant' symbolism."[56]

It is, however, this critique of representation in Denys that inspires the richer development of the specific concept of monstrous symbolism to be found in John Scotus. Perceiving the great theoretical possibilities of the master's undeveloped suggestions about the nature of representation and language itself, and detecting as well a certain "pessimism" about the created world, considered inappropriate for Christianity, Eriugena set about correcting the religiously unacceptable and recuperating the intellectually useful. He accomplished this, as Roques has clearly demonstrated, through creative mistranslation, or as Roques more charitably would have it, through "correction" of the original. Roques contrasts the original passages of Denys' *Celestial Hierarchy* (2.2–3) with John's translation of them and, further, with the translator's commentary on the passages in his *Expositiones in ierarchiam coelestem*, and through this contrast he reveals John's development of Denys' double system of similar and dissimilar symbolism into a typically tripartite system consisting of similar, dissimilar, and monstrous symbolic modes. This Eriugena accomplishes by subdividing Denys' second mode into two parts so that one of the functions of dissemblant symbolism is sufficiently emphasized so as to form a third type; this is found in those dissemblant signs that produce the effects of *catharsis* and *transcendence*, as seen in the earlier citation from Roques.

In the adaptation that the mediaeval translator makes of the earlier theories of Pseudo-Dionysius, it is the transcendent quality of this symbolism that constitutes it as a distinct discourse and that creates a genuine theory of the monstrous and grotesque. What Roques terms "cathartic" and "anagogic" are two aspects of negation: the cathartic negation of the self through the aesthetic artifact that raises the audience above its emotional self-referentiality, and the anagogic negation of the phenomenal that liberates the knower from the habit of limiting the real to the material. In this way Eriugena identifies the monster as the greatest of all heuristic signs and accords to the grotesque the highest place among aesthetic modes.

The metaphysical idea of that which is-not, developed by John in the *Periphyseon*, is introduced into the discussion of symbolism in his commentary on the *Celestial Hierarchy* in such a way as to provide a certain ontology for the grotesque artifact. Again Roques has pointed to the anomaly created, perhaps deliberately, by Scotus in his designation of resemblant symbolism as constituted by images based on simple, unmixed natures (*absolutis*), since the examples of dissemblant symbolism that he gives are themselves ones of simple, unmixed natures wholly contained within the natural realm and the realm of that which is: lions, horses, bears, and worms.[57] While these may be, as Eriugena would have it, ferocious or ugly (*ferocium, turpium*), they are still natural (*absolutis*). The effect of this confusion is double. First, by diluting the difference between certain resemblant and dissemblant symbols, the author highlights the difference between all these symbols and those few that are truly not *simple and natural* and that negate the absoluteness of nature, or that which is; to accomodate this now-separated group of symbols, a third category is needed. Second, this move exposes, without showing any disrespect, the limitations of Pseudo-Dionysius' theory of symbolism, which ultimately offers what Roques seems to suggest is a "subjective teratology": "So we see that what appears to be monstrous or absurd imagery in Scripture is really the result of the ineptitude of the interpreter and the inability of the more or less profane intellect to perceive the inner, hidden meaning of these signs ... The concept of monstrosity and absurdity that Denys uses in no way affects the material or ontological nature of the symbol; what is really monstrous and absurd is the illusion of being able to find reality, or divine significance, in any representational sign of whatever kind they may be."[58]

Most important is the creation by Scotus of the distinction between kinds of symbols, for by exposing the need for an apophatic category of signification, he solves the problem of Denys' "subjective teratology" and provides a basis for the grotesque exploration of the epistemological and ontological status of the work of art. Whereas Denys' indifference toward human intellectual activity leaves largely unsolved the problem of the relationship between sign and signified, Eriugena's third way of teratological symbolism addresses the issue effectively enough that it becomes the paradigm for artists and thinkers throughout the Middle Ages. Whereas resemblant or cataphatic symbolism is based on and proclaims the union of sign and signified and entails all of the epistemological problems associated with such an idea (both in the Middle Ages and today), dissemblant or negative symbolism is founded upon the very separation of symbol and symbolized, admitting the inadequacy of the attempt to represent the real. Although it is an improvement over the illusion of affirmative signification, the dissemblant nevertheless perpetuates the dichotomies it exposes and maintains the existence of the hierarchies that it would seem to level. While preferable because it comments openly on its own referentiality, dissemblant symbolism itself does not solve the problem of the abyss and stops short of the union desired by the mind. In his creation of a theory of monstrous symbolism, John the Scot addresses exactly these problems.

Races of monsters. Rabanus Maurus, *De universo*.
Vatican, Pal. Lat. 291, 75v

Community of monsters. *Livre des merveilles*, pl. 189. McGill University, Blackader Library

John carried out the crucial demonstration of his theory through an exposition of the first chapter of the Prophecy of Ezechiel in which there appear to the prophet beings with animal, human, and angelic characteristics: they are winged and have four faces, those of a man, a lion, an ox, and an eagle; their hands are human, but they have the feet of a calf, and they glow! As monstrous as is their appearance, the creatures' means of motion is even more so: "They turned not when they went; they went every one straight forward ... wither the spirit was to go, they went; and they turned not when they went ... And the living creatures ran and returned as the appearance of a flash of lightning" (Ez 1:9, 12, 14).

The "living creatures" move without motion in space; they are simultaneously where they are going and where they have come from, a characteristic of pure intelligences and a monstrous contradiction of human logic. Eriugena compares the figure to the mythical Daedalus and declares it monstrous on the basis of its mixed nature – angelic, human, and animal, a being *supra naturam* that, in the Eriugenian sense, is-not: "In nature a human being, covered with feathers and able to fly, has never been seen, discovered, or reported."[59] Thus John, having established that no authority, neither experience (*nec vidi*), nor science (*nec legi*), nor tradition (*nec audivi*) permits us to associate such a representation with a natural being, identifies the monstrous as that which is-not: "It is monstrous and entirely alien to human nature."[60] Eriugena makes clear that the real value of this figure and of all monstrous forms resides in the fact that it is completely unintelligible within the sciences of the natural order and therefore must be referred to another order and other sciences. It is specifically the deforming power of "poetic figments" that creates the effect of this kind of symbolism:

For poetic figments such as that of the fictional fable of Daedalus do not at all contrive a body with feathers and wings as a natural sign of the human body; this is, rather, a deformity and an absurdity. Thus such symbolism leads me more readily to deny the limiting effect that such representation has to contain God or divine virtues within a form which is deformed – because everything that is contrary to nature is unseemly and deformed – rather than to affirm that such figures correspond to the natures of celestial beings. And at that point, without stopping to analyze, I perceive that these images of Holy Scripture are signs of natural realities in their full simplicity, stripped of form and of material, limiting representations, but that they are not identical with the very nature of what they signify, for the purgation of our mundane understanding.[61]

Thus the monstrous sign does not, says John, stand for "something," but rather points to the unity of "formless" nature. It is in this sense that the monstrous sign can be understood as standing for nothing, as signifying only itself. Retaining the Areopagite's idea of the value of dissimilitude in representing the divine, Scotus adds to this basically moral and philosophical theory of language an aesthetic dimension and thereby creates a full-fledged system of monstrous symbology. Retaining as well Denys' idea of the anagogic and cathartic function of the symbol and adding it to his own theory of teratological symbolism, John shows us how the process of deformation, in addition to purifying our intellect, also reveals its structure and nature.

Eriugenian monstrous symbology is finally of an entirely different logical kind, indeed of a kind that has nothing to do with logic. While all symbolism, of whatever type, must operate within the play of similitude and dissimilitude to establish its relation to the symbolized, teratological symbolism refuses the relationship altogether and negates both similitude and dissimilitude. Through such eccentric behaviour the monstrous forms a metalevel in the Eriugenian semiotic triad of resemblant, dissemblant, and teratological symbolism. The binary opposition that Pseudo-Denys necessarily creates through his theory of similitude and dissimilitude is resolved by John into a triadic system in which the deformed or monstrous functions as a metasymbolism revealing the very process and nature of symbolic representation and its limitations: it acts as "spirit." In describing the journey of his own mind as it reflected on Ezechiel's monsters ("without stopping to analyse, I perceive [nulla mores interstante]"), Scotus depicts the metasymbolic process of the grotesque by which intellect is brought to a transcendence of the entire system of signs. By its violation of logic the monstrous sign blocks the normal path of mental movement from sign to signified, and it is on this detour that the metasymbolic perspective is gained, revealing the very form of the symbolic through its deformation.

Part of the peculiar power of teratological symbolism arises from the grounding that Scotus gives it in the ontological. Whereas Denys and other

Neoplatonists had usually insisted on this aspect of language and representation, it was to the binarism of affirmative and negative ideas of being that the concept of language was joined. But Eriugena does what no one before him had done in fashioning another paradigm for signification that points to its fulfillment in a mode beyond being and nonbeing. Eriugena's teratological symbolism is, then, the beginning of an analysis of negative discourse rooted in the reality of that which is-not. Again, it is Professor Roques who captures best Scotus' ontological grounding of the monstrous sign:

In the most radical sense of the term, the dissemblance of Eriugena goes much further than Denys'. It penetrates into the very heart of the nature of a thing and there fulfills its mission by causing its rupture, its dislocation, and its amalgamation in a kind of physical and ontological bursting out that dissolves natures; and it fulfills its mission in creating that fantasy that combines different natures according to norms that exist beyond reason. All of which comes down to the fact that such a dissemblant symbolism is constructed upon "teratology": it dissolves the structural integrity of "natures"; it eradicates their distinguishing characteristics by forcing them into combinations in which they lose their essential autonomy; in the metaphysical sense of the term, it attacks nature in its very forms, which it mocks and deforms (*naturales simplicitesque formae naturalibus simplicibusque formis longe dissimiles, deformes imaginationes*).[62]

Eriugena's theory of a monstrous symbolism shows another step in the process of human understanding; while itself not the union of sign and signified, of language and the real, of self and other, it scrambles the hierarchical order that separates them and cancels the linear process of their relationship – understanding in steps of thing/concept/word – and instead of "representing" and "standing for," it "points to" not a signified that exists in reality, but rather to the transcendence of both affirmation and negation and their hierarchical relation, to an understanding that is a *being one with* the known, beyond discourse, beyond sign and concept, an understanding that is not epistemological but ontological. It is not to say that the monstrous *is* this knowledge, but rather that it points to it (*monstrare*);[63] it is the threshold. Monstrous discourse contains within it both resemblant and dissemblant symbolism, but it is neither. It represents nothing, neither that which can be affirmed nor that which can be denied, but instead represents only itself in an extended "demonstration" of how representation works.

Eriugena's Teratological Discourse

Just as John creates a theory of monstrous signification by subdividing already established categories of understanding to form a distinct new type, he also furthers his analysis of language by building on the theory of monstrous symbolism. There are two kinds of allegory, John tell us:

In the New Testament the mystery of baptism, that of the body and blood of the Saviour and sacred anointing are partly accomplished through material means and partly represented and transmitted by words. This type of representing is rightly called by the holy fathers *allegory of the thing and its discourse* (*allegoria facti et dicti*). There exists another type, however, the exact name of which is "symbol," but which is, in fact, called *allegory of the discourse without the thing* (*allegoria dicti, non autem facti*) for it consists entirely in spiritual discourse with no reference to material reality whatsoever."[64]

John Scotus is here commenting on the story in St John's gospel describing the multiplication of the loaves and fishes in which he associates the barley loaves with the discourses of the human intellect; this bread is suitable food for those good people limited in understanding to the phenomenal and the historical truth: "The barley loaves are broken up by the disciples when, in the mysteries of the Law of the letter of grace, historical reality is distinguished from its spiritual signification. The literal-minded are nourished by historical narrative."[65] Significantly, those who have transcended the illusions of discourse are said to feed upon the crumbs left over from the feast (*quasi quaedam fragmenta*),[66] the remnants of the feast that represent complete understanding, the understanding that is able to negate the similitudes that language suggests. Like the barley loaves, the *allegory of the thing and its discourse* can be broken up, divided and multiplied "to feed the faithful." But the *allegory of discourse without the thing* remains whole and without parts, food for the intellect and for the spirit. This type of allegory John associates with the fish of the story: "To the same multitude is brought the two fishes, that is, the purely spiritual understanding which is 'allegory of discourse detached from historical reality.' "[67]

Eriugena insists on the nonreferentiality of this special kind of allegory, describing it more and more clearly as a metadiscourse: "This 'symbol' is read with the eyes and heard with the ears, but it cannot be "broken up" because it does not refer to historic reality; it refers only to itself as a 'discourse' of allegory."[68] This kind of symbolic discourse creates an understanding that is immediate and nonanalytic. Although formed by words, these signs refer to no *thing* – neither material phenomenon nor historical reality – and in so standing alone, *qua sign*, they call attention to the very process of signification. By eliminating the normal, mediating steps of allegory – from historical level to the symbolic, to the moral, and finally to the anagogical – *discourse without the thing* points directly to the anagogic reality, lifting the mind out of the linear process of sign-signified-thing to a perspective permitting reflection upon the process. The sign, operating in the *allegory of the discourse without the thing* and thus freed of any referent in reality, is seized by the mind immediately, without mediation or process in which the mind goes back and forth from word to meaning, from world to sign.

Thus Scotus' metadiscourse is grounded in a theory of antisignification, and when this theory is coupled with his theory of teratological symbolism, it is evident that the ideal form of the *allegory of discourse without the thing* is the grotesque with its fantastic *figura* and monstrous deformations. The discourse that Eriugena depicts is wholly deformed and recalls something akin to the hieroglyphics of the Egyptians in the sense that the latter eliminate the discursive process of language and make the sign a picture standing for a complete meaning. It is precisely this example that John's predecessor, Plotinus, uses to describe a form of understanding without mediation: "The wise men of Egypt, I think, also understood this, either by scientific or innate knowledge, and when they wished to signify something wisely, did not use the forms of letters which follow the order of words and propositions and imitate sounds and the enunciations of philosophical statements, but by drawing images and inscribing in their temples one particular image of each particular thing, they manifested the nondiscursiveness of the intelligible world, that is, that every image is a kind of knowledge and wisdom and is a subject of statements, all together in one, and not discourse or deliberation."[69]

Inspired by the great innovator of negative theology, John Scotus Eriugena adapted the essence of his master's thought to the intellectual milieu of the Middle Ages. In his *Periphyseon*, Scotus combined the apophatic metaphysics of the Areopagite with a *physis* of his own that celebrated the material world as the context and possibility of transcendence. In his *Expositiones*, using Denys' theory of resemblant and dissemblant symbolism, John created a more comprehensive theory of symbolism that revalorizes human language as capable of indicating its own limitations through self-deformation. Finally, in his *Commentary on St John*, Eriugena combines the insights of his other investigations to delineate a science of discourse and its interpretation that, through the self-referentiality of the monster, reveals the possibilities and limits of the process of signification and, more importantly, its very "form."

Monstrous discourse "shows" the sublime form of what Scotus had earlier called that which is-not. While not utterly beyond human cognition, the monster nevertheless remains outside the affirmative, logical discourses used by us to represent things "which are" and so can remind us of the primacy of negation. Once again, we see the monster occupying the threshold between what is and what is-not, beckoning to the mind through its hinting at meaning, but pointing in the opposite direction to a signification deep within the abyss: "By *things that are* I mean all that does not entirely surpass thought, be it human or angelic, in that it is less than God and contained within the limits of the realities created by the one and only Cause of the universe. By *things that are not* I mean everything that transcends absolutely the power of every intelligence. Thus it is that in his flight, St John not only is lifted above what can be contained by intellect and signified by words, but is also transported to the very heart of realities which surpass every intellect and every signification."[70]

PART TWO

Taxonomy

Body as microcosm. Hildegard of Bingen, *Operatione Dei*

3 The Body Monstrous

This passage quotes a "certain Chinese encyclopaedia" in which it is
written that "animals are divided into (a) belonging to the Emperor,
(b) embalmed, (c) tame, (d) sucking pigs, (e) sirens, (f) fabulous,
(g) stray dogs, (h) included in the present classification, (i) frenzied,
(j) innumerable, (k) drawn with a very fine camel hair brush, (l) et
cetera, (m) having just broken the water pitcher, (n) that from a long
way off look like flies." In the wonderment of this taxonomy, the thing
we apprehend in one great leap, the thing that, by means of the fable, is
demonstrated as the exotic charm of another system of thought, is the
limitation of our own, the stark impossibility of thinking that.

Michel Foucault[1]

The attempt to create a system of descriptive categories for that which exists
to resist and confound systematization involves an obvious contradiction, but
in the building of taxonomies of the monster, the contradiction seems not to
have been felt very sharply. Numerous systems have been put forward, either
in ignorance of the absurdity involved, or, in some cases perhaps, with deli-
cate sensitivity to the irony that in attempting to describe the monster that is
itself paradox, the paradox of taxonomy finds its justification. One of the
earliest and most influential mediaeval taxonomies of the monster was that
created by the seventh century encyclopaedist, Isidore of Seville, who, after a
taxonomical exploration of the normal human body, part by part, organ by
organ, provides in rough parallel to it a structural description of all monstrous forms.[2] There are twelve categories in Isidore's taxonomy depending
on how they are counted, and these, by and large, remained the general categories by which the monstrous was conceptually organized throughout the
Middle Ages and even down to our own time.

In Isidore's structure, monstrosity is constituted in one of the following
ways: (1) hypertrophy of the body, (2) atrophy of the body, (3) excrescence of
bodily parts, (4) superfluity of bodily parts, (5) deprivation of parts, (6) mixture of human and animal parts, (7) animal births by human women, (8) mislo-
cation of organs or parts in the body, (9) disturbed growth (being born old),
(10) composite beings, (11) hermaphrodites, (12) monstrous races.[3]

The fact that we cannot describe the monster without violating its essentially apophatic nature further demonstrates a dimension of negation first
seen in Pseudo-Dionysian thought, that of the essential interpenetration of
the negative and the affirmative. The need for a taxonomy of the deformed is

the requirement of an affirmative discourse that attempts to understand the negative; in this sense negation depends on affirmation. But as soon as negation is seized by intellect, the affirmative vehicle of its presentation, now no longer necessary, is dismantled. Thus, a taxonomy of monstrous forms is fundamentally arbitrary and absolutely impermanent; it is the paradoxical morphology of nonforms, a system of categories of nothing, which, however, like the ladder of the mystics, functions to raise the understanding to a point at which its steps, rungs, ranks, and slots and all other affirmative differenti- ations become dispensible. In this chapter a taxonomy of the monstrous and a morphology of the deformed is attempted in light of the necessity for such an apparatus for the sake of description. It is recognized at the outset that a structuring of disorder is a contradiction.

As Isidore perceived, the most useful model for a taxonomy of the mon- ster is the human body. Although physical deformations are by no means the only negations that monstrosity effects, the human body through its symbolic extensions as well as its physical structure, provides the most complete para- digm for order and thus for the disorder that has precedence and priority in the monstrous configuration of reality. As the first construct we experience and as that one with which we remain most intimate – which, indeed, we love and nurture – our bodies provide, not only a model, but an original and continuing symbol of order itself.

The symbolic force of the body is particularly strong in the Middle Ages largely because of Neoplatonism, and it is related to the allegorical concept of microcosm in which the cosmos is contained in the "little cosmos" of the world and both are represented in miniature in the human body: "All things are contained in man, and in him exists the nature of all things."[4] Leonard Barkan, in a brilliant study of the influence of the metaphor of the human body in literary conception, describes the Platonic school's continuous pro- duction of likenesses out of the basic analogy of the human body to the cosmos: " 'Our world must necessarily be a likeness of something,' says Timaeus at the outset. The search for that something gives rise to the notion of an infinite regress of likenesses beginning with man and proceeding all the way to the eternal principle."[5]

Such diverse sources as the classic study of social conceptualization and the organization of dirt and cleanliness by anthropologist Mary Douglas, and the equally classic study of Rabelais by Mikhail Bakhtin are useful for un- derstanding the predilection for the body as metamodel and metasystem. In Douglas' work we see the body as the basic model for the organization of primitive society: "The body is a model which can stand for any bounded system. Its boundaries can represent any boundaries which are threatened or precarious. The body is a complex structure. The functions of its differ- ent parts and their relation afford a source of symbols for other complex structures."[6]

Douglas' specification of the body's distinct physical boundaries as source of its symbolic value also provides a useful insight into the relation of the body and language, the second construct that we experience in growing consciousness. Bakhtin, in his discussion of the grotesque, echoes Douglas' statements about the symbolic function of the body but applies them, not to social systems, but directly to the grotesque as aesthetic system. Bahktin recognizes the crucial oppositions of body function as ingestion and expulsion and identifies those parts of the body playing a key role in one or the other of these functions as the same parts that are generally the indices of the grotesque: "Eating, drinking, defecation, and other elimination (sweating, blowing of the nose, sneezing), as well as copulation, pregnancy, dismemberment, swallowing up by another body – all these acts are performed on the confines of the body and the outer world, or on the confines of the old and new body."[7] Bakhtin's focus on the thresholds between the inner and outer body coincides with a similar focus in the grotesque, since these same thresholds – the mouth, the genitals, limbs, and orifices – are the arenas of deformity in the monstrous discourse.

Bakhtin's suggested typology of the grotesque, despite its insistence on social theory, is useful for an aesthetic analysis of deformity because precisely those parts of the body identified by Bakhtin as "going out to the world" (for example, the penis) or "ingesting the world" (for example, the mouth) were the principal loci of monstrous deformation throughout the Middle Ages. In addition to noting the cosmic and universal signification of the grotesque body, Bakhtin articulates the relation between the figurative and the logical functions of the symbolism of bodily organs: "Thus the artistic logic of the grotesque image ignores the closed, smooth, and impenetrable surface of the body and retains only its excrescences (sprouts, buds) and orifices, only that which leads beyond the body's limited space or into the body's depths."[8]

The transgressions of the body's natural boundaries through disease or deformity constitute not only a threat to the body, but, as well, a kind of denial of the systems modelled on it, rendering vulnerable the principle of order that is the bodily structure and system. In the process of the grotesque, the abnormalization of the body and the negation of order are not coincidental; the one is the habitual method of the grotesque, the other, the conceptual goal at which it aims.

The historian of science, Georges Canguilhem, has developed a theory of biological pathology that illuminates, as well, the aesthetics of deformation. Describing disease and abnormality as evidence for the primacy of negation, he states: "We think that health is life in the silence of the organs, that consequently the biologically normal, as we have already said, is revealed only through infractions of the norm and that concrete or scientific awareness of life exists only through disease."[9] Such a view is reminiscent of the mediaeval sense in which the human body was conceived as a text and its parts and functions seen as a system of signs expressive of its author's intention. In the same way that Canguilhem makes disease a symptomatology indicating the ontological state of the subject, so, too, mediaeval art made the monstrous and grotesque the semiology appropriate to metaphysics. Throughout this fascinating study Canguilhem insists on the priority of the negative over the affirmative by conceiving of disease and deformity as the basis for an understanding of health and normalcy. Important to our purposes is his extension of that idea to the concept of the infraction in which disorder is the matrix and possibility of order: "In order to truly enjoy the value of the rule, the value of regulation, the value of valorization, the rule must be subjected to the test of dispute. It is not just the exception which proves the rule as rule, it is the infraction which provides it with the occasion to be rule by making rules. In this sense the infraction is not the origin of the rule but the origin of regulation. It is in the nature of the normative that its beginning lies in its infraction."[10]

Deforming the symbolic human body produces two effects – the negation of the validity of the correspondence between the human-as-we-know-it and the cosmos-as-we-know-it, and the recognition of the corresponding deformity of the cosmos for which the body is a figure. The first requires that one's confidence in the efficacy of similitude and the *via positiva* be called into question; the second – to which the first leads – calls for a radical adjustment of the view of the cosmos and its laws, one in which nothing and chaos are prior to and constitutive of being and order, and as a sign of which the universe is itself a monstrous construct. Canguilhem, having established the priority of negation in relation to health, then begins an extension of the principle into the imagination and comes up with the originally mediaeval idea that links plenitude with the grotesque:

But as soon as consciousness has begun to suspect life of certain eccentricities and has begun to dissociate the ideas of reproduction and repetition, what's to stop it from imagining life more lively, that is, capable of greater possibility, to imagine it capable, not only of explicable exceptions, but even of spontaneous transgressions natural to it? Faced with a three-legged bird, should we regard it as something with one leg too many or as something with just one more leg? To decide that life is timid or stingy is to feel within oneself the first stirrings of the desire to go further than "life." But what is the origin of this motion that leads the human spirit to juxtapose to life's monstrous productions [art's] multicephalic grylles, perfectly formed humans, teratomorphic emblems? Could it be that life is inscribed, in the geometrical sense of the term, within the curve of poetry's elan in which the imaginary becomes consciousness in revealing it as infinite?[11]

In the Middle Ages, Canguilhem's three-legged bird was understood through a teratological perspective on the theological principle of "plenitude": in His goodness God created everything that could exist. Within the realm of nature, the bird is abnormal, but within the realm of art, particularly of grotesque art, the three-legged creature is an *ens rationis,* a being that Scotus would classify in the superior mode of being as that which is-not. There is also a clear echo in Canguilhem's description of the desire to go further than "life," a clear echo of that mediaeval sense of the limitations of anthropomorphic systems and the contrasting sense of the liberating, expanding, and enriching power of the monstrous. For its expression, that disorder may borrow the systems of order, and that the monster may adopt the model of nature is permitted, not because the deformed is a variation on form or because the abnormal is a failure of the normal, but because disorder in all its manifestations holds an ancient and absolute privilege of authorship. The priority of disorder over order extends into other versions of these opposites: nothing precedes being; negation enables affirmation; dissimilitude validates similitude. The guarantee of this priority, that disorder will never become order, exonerates the attempt to describe a taxonomy of the monstrous.

SIZE

Pygmies

Deformations of the physical body as a whole or of the idea of the body as a whole give rise to several traditional monstrous forms. The most widespread are the pygmy and the giant, who function as physical and conceptual opposites. Their monstrosity consists in contrary violations of the norm for size: the giant exceeds the norm through hypertrophy and becomes a figure of exorbitance; the pygmy, or dwarf, fails to achieve the norm through atrophy and becomes a figure of deprivation.

The most famous account of the pygmies is in the *Iliad* (3.5), where their constant battle with the cranes is described. The legend involves the refusal of the pygmy goddess Gerana to worship the Greek gods and her punitive transformation by Hera into a crane. In this form and with the assistance of other cranes, she attempts to seize her son, Mopsos, whom the pygmies refuse to give up because they do not recognize their former goddess, now deformed. But why a crane?

The transformation of the pygmy goddess into a crane and the neverending battle between the pygmies and the cranes is a way of associating the story of Demeter and the underground with these monsters of diminution. Cranes were the attribute of Demeter, and their presence in the pygmy legends triggers an association with Demeter's campaign to release her daughter Persephone from Hades. The themes of earth's barrenness, the underground, infertility, and the food of the dead, which effects no growth or

Pygmy. Bronze statue, Mahdia

sustenance, are inherent in the story of Demeter and through the figure of the cranes are transferred to the pygmies. As monsters of insufficiency, the pygmies ignore natural requirements and defy the norms of growth and form. Similarly, Hades, by separating the food goddess from her progeny, annuls nature's requirement of a structure of seasons for growth and decay.

Pliny is the other major source of the pygmy legend,[12] and it is from him that much of the mediaeval travel literature receives its accounts of the pygmy. All of the travel literature, purporting to be eye-witness accounts, presents not only the monstrous reduction of the proportions of the human frame in the figure of the pygmy but a reduced reality shrunken in proportion to its inhabitants. Odoric de Pordenone tells us that pygmies are mature and reproduce at six months old; they never live beyond seven years.[13] Mandeville tells us that in the city in which the pygmies live, everything that is engendered is miniature.[14]

In the deforming of bodily size, we see most clearly the way in which the abnormal engenders the normal and transgression precedes limit.The grotesquerie of the minuscule exists only in relation to some norm; how small is small enough to constitute monstrosity? The range of the normal is great, indeed, while there exists no range for the abnormal. The normal is, therefore, relative, the abnormal, absolute. There are many degrees of bigness and smallness within the normal, but only when one has crossed the line out of the range of the normal does one enter the realm of completion: a giant is neither more nor less monstrous than a pygmy, a three-legged bird no more deformed than a four-legged one. The norm of human size is not only imprecise; it is also dependent upon the extreme poles of the spectrum of size. It is not in measuring some suspected deviant against an established, absolute norm that the abnormal is derived from the normal; prior to that measurement there must have occurred a comparison of beings of a range of sizes against extremes of large and small, the maximum and the minimum, for the norm to have come into existence. In this way, the abnormal always precedes the normal, making possible the definition of the normal.

Giants

As the other extreme of size, the giant represents excess, superfluity, and abnormal strength. In the mediaeval tradition of monsters, both symbolic and teratological, the giant is also associated with a number of other concepts of transgression or liberation from the norm. As form, the giant is the uncompleted in the sense of the overcompleted, overfinished; indeed, giganticism suggests a form so complete as to be self-cancelling. The giant is a bodily form moving beyond the limitations of that form toward something else as yet undefined. Whereas the pygmy or dwarf negates the norm of bodily quantity and proportion because it is a form that is too restricted and too contained, the giant denies the norm by violating the concept of containment altogether. The giant shows us what would be possible if the body were not a container and if being were not limited. Canguilhem draws an interesting distinction between giganticism and enormity and finds that what constitutes monstrosity in the giant is the transgressing of limits that constitute both form and essence:

A clarification might be attempted of the relation of enormity to monstrosity. Both the one and the other are that which is outside the norm. The norm which enormity transcends is merely one of measurement. This being the case, why is enormity simply a matter of enlargement? Doubtless because at a certain point of growth quantity

Giant Antaeus carrying Virgil and Dante. *Div. Com.* Budapest University
Library, 33, 25r.

calls into question quality; enormity tends toward monstrosity. The ambiguity of giganticism: is the giant enormous or monstrous? The mythological giant is a prodigy,
that is, his bigness "annihilates the end by which the concept is constituted" (Kant,
Critique of Judgement, 26). If we define man by certain limitations of forces and
functions, the man who transcends by his largeness these limitations is no longer a
man. Yet, to say that he is no longer such is to say in another way that he is still."[15]

The giant is more frequently encountered in mediaeval grotesque art than
the pygmy, and he is given a full historical account and symbology in Hebrew and Christian cultures, as well as considerable place in pagan myth. In
Greek legend the giants are born from the blood shed on the earth by Ouranos at the moment of his castration by his son Cronos.[16] One of the most
frequently employed themes of the classical visual arts, the central story of
the giants is appropriately a war against containment; attempting to avenge
the Titans and to release them from their confinement in Tartarus, the deepest region of Hell, the giants wage battle against the gods. In addition to their

Cronos castrating Ouranos. Boccaccio, French translation of *Genealogia deorum*. Oxford, Bodleian, MS Douce 453, IV.

immensity, the giants of classical myth possess incomparable strength and ferocity; they are always bearded and covered all over by hair, except for their legs, which are often composed of serpents. The repeated symbolic association is with the earth from which they spring and which renews them and with the theme of release from confinements and restrictions, the goal of all their battles.

The Judeo-Christian tradition of the giants is found in Genesis and in exegetical legend and constitutes the historico-philosophical parallel of the

Nimrod designing the Tower of Babel. Athanasius Kircher. *Turris Babel*, frontispiece.
McGill University, Osler Library

Greek myth. With Cain's expulsion from Paradise to Nod and his subsequent
sexual congress with the wild beasts that roamed east of Eden, there arose a
race of beings of mixed natures, human and animal. This story is crucial in
the Western tradition of monstrosity for it identifies the moment and the act
by which monsters come into physical being in the world, making possible

the historical explanation of monsters required by the Judeo-Christian world-view. It is also on this basis that mediaeval travel literature could reasonably include the teratological, since Cain's descendants had been given a place in the world by Scripture. This mixed race contained beautiful women, referred to in exegesis as the "daughters of Cain," who attracted the attention of certain angels so that, falling to earth through their lust, the angels coupled with the daughters of Cain and sired the giants.[17] In light of the mediaeval explanation of monstrosity as produced by the commingling of "natures" that Nature meant to keep apart, the giants are intensely monstrous, for theirs is a nature produced by the forbidden mixture, not of two natures, but of three. The Judeo-Christian giant, then, is a figure whose deformation signifies the breaking of the confines of genus as container of being and the transgression of the separating limits of animal, human, and divine.[18]

In exegetical tradition the giants' appearance is chiefly distinguished by a glowing face and eyes from which shines an eerie light. These are characteristics adopted by other monsters in the development of the grotesque tradition, but they belong originally to the giants, as inherited from their angelic sires. Scripture and exegesis give Nimrod as the first historical giant identified by name, and he is taxed with introducing into the world a number of antisocial activities associated with blood and violence. One of the most important constituents of monstrous nature is established in Nimrod's role as the giant hunter, who, we are told, when game ran short, resorted to cannibalism.[19] In the development of the tradition of the monsters, cannibalism becomes, as we shall see later, an act which in and of itself constitutes the monstrous.

It is Nimrod who, as King of Babel, led his fellow giants to build the tower as a means of waging war on God. Thus, in Nimrod the significance of the giant is extended to the nature of discourse and communication, and the idea of the exaggeration of rational constructs contained in the figure of the Tower attaches to the exaggerated form of the giant. From Nimrod is descended Goliath, perhaps the most famous of Scriptural giants, who is identified in Jewish tradition as "unclean" because uncircumcised (1 Samuel 17). For Goliath the token of giganticism is the foreskin, in that this monster lacks the sign of inclusion, which is, paradoxically, a physical privation, and is therefore an exile, rejected by the clean, humiliated, killed, and beheaded. His story brings us back to Bahktin's insight that monstrosity is encountered only at the threshold, particularly the thresholds of the physical body, at which loci the dramatic and grotesque confrontation of opposites takes place. Circumcision is the eradication of one of the most significant thresholds, an attempt to deny otherness and to "make us a name, lest we be scattered abroad upon the face of the whole earth" (Genesis 11:4). In such a perspective, the giants and all others who are uncircumcised are monsters.

Nimrod, the Tower of Babel, and monsters. *Cité de Dieu*, de Laborde, pl. 122.
Harvard College Library

Hebrew and Christian tradition generally interpreted the giants morally, taking their physical greatness as a sign of the immensity of their sin. However, Christianity typically preserved a positive, even holy, signification for the monstrosity of gigantism, as we see in the legends of the giant St Christopher, whose story will be treated in detail in the last section.

LOCUS AND POSITION

In addition to the deformation of the body through size, the locus of the human body and the total transformation of its form were also means for reducing the normal to the monstrous. Two of the most widespread monstrous beings were created in this manner.

The Antipodes

They say also there is a human genus under the globe which they call Antipodes, and according to the interpretation of the Greek name, they tread the lowest bottom of the earth with straight feet upwards to our footprints.[20]

The Antipodes, first mentioned by Cicero,[21] are humans whose monstrosity is constituted by their inverted repetition of our every move and action in a place, the Antipodes, where inversion is the norm. They are our mirror images functioning only as a kind of pantomime of human existence – exact duplicates of every human body in existence, transported to a realm "below" where, foot to foot, they reenact each human gesture upside down. The monstrosity of the Antipode is that of parody, the location of the human body in a place that is the sphere of travesty itself.

St Augustine, who contributed much to the theory of the monstrous, denies the possibility of the Antipodes on historical and theological grounds. It is impossible, he writes in the *City of God* (16.9) that the human race could be double, since in that case the history of descent from Adam as recorded in Scripture would be incomplete and inaccurate. And yet it is in a fifteenth century manuscript of the *City of God* that we find one of the most remarkable mediaeval illustrations of the Antipodes. Largely through the immense influence of Augustine and for the same reasons that he cites, the Church condemned belief in the Antipodes as early as the eighth century. Nevertheless, interest in them and artistic representation of them continued unabated. They were eventually confused with an originally distinct monster, the retropede, whose feet were turned in the opposite direction to his head. These monsters, described in the *Book of the Monsters*[22] and other early sources as distinct from the Antipodes, are later all conflated, as can be seen, for instance, in the illustration of the Bodleian MS 614, fol. 50r.[23]

Antipodes. *Cité de Dieu*, de Laborde, pl. 102.
Harvard College Library

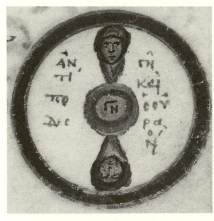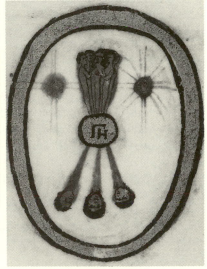

Antipodes. Vatican Library, MS Barberini Greca 372, fol. 172r, 175r

The Antipodes challenge the concept of the individuality of the self and present the monstrosity of self and other as coexistent and identical. The world of the Antipode is a world of pure multiplicity where everything is double and where the very concept of unity is impossible. More devastating to a sense of the real than inversion or antithesis, the Antipode confronts us with the dissolution of meaning through similitude. By the duplication of the self, the distinctiveness provided by the concept of selfhood is undermined in a perverse mimesis of the arch-imitator, humanity.

The Shape-Shifters

Human beings who, by their own power or that of another, change their entire appearance by adopting the body of a foreign creature are "shape-shifters." In most accounts, the human shape-shifter is the victim of a magical curse, and the change of body is experienced as a suffering or punishment. The process may operate in the other direction, so that spirits, both good and evil, take on human form and often human powers as well, most significantly the powers of speech and reproduction.

Lycanthropy, or the transformation of the human to the beast, is named in relation to Apollo Lycaeus, who was the object of a religious cult of the wolf described by Augustine in the *City of God* (17.17) and based on Varro, as associated with ritual cannibalism. Augustine also provides the etymology of the word from the Greek: the lyceum is derived from the name of the temple in which Apollo Lycaeus was worshipped and in which Socrates taught. The magical characteristics of shape-shifting are expressed in the feature of sympathetic wounding, which is present throughout legend. The most common representation of this monster is the werewolf, the human who exchanges his body for that of a beast.[24]

Always male and often the victim of an evil or even demonic wife or stepmother, the werewolf is condemned to live part of his life, usually seven or nine years, in the form of a wolf, but with the special torment of human rationality and human nature retained beneath the bestial form. The mechanism of transformation confirms John Friedman's assertion that the standard indices of monstrosity are speech, diet, abode, and clothing;[25] the changeling becomes a wolf by stripping himself naked, at which point he immediately becomes hirsute and exhibits other lupine features. His restoration to human form usually depends upon the monster's ability to retrieve his clothing. Otherwise, a werewolf may be changed back into human form if killed or wounded while a wolf. In that instance, the human counterpart will be found, usually at home, in bed, bearing the wound on that part of his human body corresponding to the part of his wolf body that actually received it.

The fundamental, even primitive, expression of shape-shifting is in the possession of a man by a god who uses the possessed for his purposes, often leaving him mad or quasi-divinized. Gods also use shape-shifting to become

Retropede. Oxford, Bodleian 614, fol. 50r.
From Wittkower, "Marvels," 47

animals and in that mode more easily relate to humans. Such is the story
of Zeus' enjoyment of Europa and of Leda in the various forms of bull and of
swan. Circe transforms men into beasts, including wolves, as Augustine
reminds us (*City of God* 17.17), and shape-shifting generally seems to be a
monstrosity particularly favoured by the holy and the divine. Numerous folk-
tales exist in which the elderly couple who assist the hero on his journey turns
out to be Mary and Joseph; the child encountered on the beach turns out to be
Christ. Technically speaking, any manifestation of God, like any incarnation
of angels, is a monstrous and unnatural shape-shifting, since God and the angels are thereby appearing in the forms of natures not properly theirs.

Demons wishing to reproduce but lacking material bodies with which to
do so adopt human form, male or female, in order to accomplish this process.
A succubus, having adopted the form of a woman, lies with a human male in
order to steal his sperm. Possessing seed, the demon turns itself into an incu-
bus, a spirit with a human male body, and lies with a woman, implanting
in her the stolen, now-transformed sperm. As can be seen, demons are able
to reproduce only in their male manifestations; that is, they can only sire.
Strangely, the offspring from such an encounter is likely to appear normal.
The attribution of demonic origin to monstrous births was primarily a
Renaissance explanation that had been rejected in the Middle Ages. When

Lycanthrope. Aldrovani, *Monstrorum Historia*, in *Collected Works*, vol. 6. McGill University, Blacker-Wood Library, 163

monstrous births are said to be the result of such intercourse, they are believed to occur so as to warn against the inordinate libido of women.[26]

Because they are pure intellect and lack all material form, angels, like demons, are required to adopt the forms of other natures in order to appear to human beings and to communicate with them. This self-deforming may take animal form, as in the case of Lucifer's appearance in the Garden of Eden as a serpent, or the angel may appear as an ordinary human being, as did the three angels in Sodom (Genesis 18:2). The representations of the Annunciation and other such events usually present the angel as a winged human, or even as a human body part, such as the head, with wings. Still more fantastic, less anthropomorphic, representations of the spiritual beings are found that, although they do not involve the connecting of a foreign bodily form to a nature, echo the same tension between sign and signified. Such are the sixth-century Ophanim, represented as two burning wheels, and the creatures in Ezekiel that are wheels with eyes, wings, and flames.

The monstrosity of the shape-shifter is inherent in the very concept of metamorphosis and transformation. It suggests, terrifyingly, that the

Ophanim. Didron, *Christian Iconography*, 2:91, fig. 152

boundaries of natural form are insecure, that it is somehow possible for a self to slip out of the protective clothing that declares its identity and become trapped in a shape that misidentifies and misrepresents it. For there is no suggestion that in changing appearance the human truly becomes a beast; if that were so, the being itself would be in no way monstrous, but rather simply a beast. Awareness of this double nature is guaranteed by the element of sympathetic wounding found in the shape-shifter stories in which the wound received by the animal form becomes a sign of the continuous humanity of the subject.

The shape-shifter declares the independence of life from the material body. The migrating self is a spiritual reality that, through misadventure, finds itself contained in the wrong container or that, for nobler reasons, chooses the wrong container. This monster is also a warning concerning the power of cognition. How do we know what we know? In the werewolf tales, those who rely on the material sign mistake the werewolf for a ferocious beast; only the wise who look beyond appearances, those who read through the sign, are able to see the true nature concealed beneath the wrong form. Concealing and revealing is part of the process of the body-deforming monstrosity of the shape-shifter, but unlike other rhetorical uses of this device, the concealing-revealing of the monster is paradoxical: stripping naked conceals the self in hairy, lupine form; covering with clothes rids the self of masks and reveals it in its true form. The deforming of the body in this manner creates a monster of signification in which sign and signified are rad-ically divorced and the contingency of their habitual relationship under-scored. But the critique of the relationship between sign and signified is ironic in that it not only parodies the intellectual vulgarity of materialism, which underlies the privileging of the sign over the signified, but also rejects the supposedly spiritual, or ideal, conception of the precedence of the signi-fied over the sign. The contravention that takes place through the monstruous divorce of bodily form from existential nature, when form and nature are seen as paralleled by sign and signified, is the discountenancing of all theo-ries of discourse.

This sense of the shape-shifter merges with the general sense of all mon-strosity by communicating the ultimate inadequacy of human cognition and its tools. The werewolf's return to human form seems to bring with it, both for the werewolf himself and those around him, a new perception that the body, inasmuch as it is a material shape, is a container somehow inadequate to the self, which it confines; the audience, witness and participant in these metamorphoses and transitions, gains the parallel realization that the signify-ing process, in this case, body = being, may be insufficient for the communi-cation of meaning. In one of the most popular English mediaeval tales of werewolves, *The Romance of William of Palerne*, the scene in which Al-phouns is transformed from werewolf back to man emphasizes nonrecogni-tion and misunderstanding as William, who has spent years with his closest companion Alphouns, fails to recognize him even when he has been restored to his "true" form:

"Sir knight, you give me a poor welcome. To keep thee from harm, I have oft risked my life and endured many a blow to keep thee there from. Too little, it seems, you know me and little kinship show." "Certes, Sir, that's so," said William then, "I know not in this world whatever you might be; but I conjure you, by Christ, who on the cross was tortured, that you tell me true who you may be." (4511–19)[27]

The symbolism of the deformed body addresses the significance, deep-rooted in human thought and culture, of the phenomena of the relation of parts to whole, one and many, unity and dispersion. Mary Wakeman, in her study of the function of the monstrous in creation myths, takes the view that through its opposition to fragmentation, and thus multiplicity, the monster looms as a symbol contrary to life, and so, for her, the monster is a univo-cally negative force. But we recall Canguilhem's view that the human spirit strives for something greater than "life" and attempts to fulfill this desire through the imagination.[28] As Wakeman herself points out, the tension in all the myths appears to be between two forms of vitality, what one might de-scribe as the striving to establish one or the other of two polar oppositions as the principle of life: "The conflict is over the control of vital energy. The direction of activity after the victory [of the hero-god over the monster] is toward form: from wet to dry, chaos to order, free to bound energy."[29]

Wakeman's study brings out the crucial character of the involvement of the monster in creation, and it emphasizes the centrality of the body as the figure of creation. A continuous theme in all mythic narrative is the dismemberment and scattering of the monstrous body as the means by which creation as multiple beings comes to be; often joined to this theme is the complementary theme of gathering up the pieces of the whole to create order and civilization. Thus Wakeman cites the story of Cronos' castration of his father, which she interprets as the separation of Mother Earth and Father Sky and the beginning of being. The scattering of Osiris' body parts and their gathering by Isis, the cutting up of Leviathan and the eventual reintegration of his body in the bellies of the Israelites, and numerous myths from various cultures all serve as examples of the differentiation of the roles of god and monster; the former functioning as the principle of order, the latter as the principle of chaos. The movement from chaos to order, Wakeman shows us, is one expressed under the figure of dismemberment and the reassembling and coordinating of parts of the monstrous body. The original state of being is one of prodigious chaos symbolized by a monster defending unified, timeless, undifferentiated being from the limitations of form, order, and the multiplicity of beings that a warrior-god wishes to impose through the dismemberment of the monster.

The use of the body as the locus of deformation introduces into the significance of such monsters as the giant and the shape-shifter considerations not only of physiological, psychological, and cognitive realities but of fundamental metaphysical truths as well. These figures, whose whole body is the arena of monstrosity, remind us that the arch-model of order, the supreme trope of the integration of parts and whole, is brought into existence through the disintegration and mutilation of the deformed, which is prior to it: "The difference between the monster and the god who performs the same acts is the principle of regulation."[30] Thus Wakeman delineates a structure of biblical myth in which god and monster are closely identified, in which, indeed, the "god" is merely the civilized, anthropomorphic metaphor of the monster. In Wakeman's thesis the ur-state of chaos is personified by the monster's grotesque body; the secondary state of civilized society and all forms of organization are personified by the warrior-god who decimates this deformed body (chaos) so as to allow for its restructuring as a body based on order (human organization). Such a structure echoes the Christian concept of divine manifestation as proceeding from apophatic (*Deus absconditus*) to cataphatic (*Verbum Dei*).

THE HEAD

You know that it is to be seen especially by the form of the head if an animal ought to belong to our race. Indeed, if it has a fully formed head, even if in many other parts it be monstrous, it can be said to be one of us.[31]

The head is the most symbolic part of the body for the Middle Ages and for Western culture generally. It is thought that the human head is placed above the rest of the body in order to reflect its superiority as the seat of reason and thus the superiority of the intellectual over the physical; from it emerges speech, the surest sign of humanity. The head is found above because it governs the whole body, just as intellect governs appetite, just as God is above in Heaven, ruler of all Creation. As the locus of intellect, the human head signifies not only mind, but human nature itself, for intellect and soul are closely identified. Similarly, the nature of an animal can be figured by the sign of its head, wherein its soul is thought somehow to reside. It is not surprising, then, that of all the body parts, the head is most often deformed in order to represent monstrous concepts.

The basic deformation of the head takes three general forms: *multiplications* producing the bicephalic, tricephalic, or multicephalic monster; *deprivation* producing the anacephalic monster; *transformation* into the head of another creature of a different genus. Other types of monsters are created by deforming an organ of the head or face.

The Multicephalic

In the iconographic program of the Middle Ages, multicephalic animal forms exist in abundance: the hydra, a quadruped with numerous, serpentine heads, and Cerberus, the three-headed dog, are two of the best known. Because of the designation of the head as an index of identity, being crowned with several heads suggests a plurality of natures or multiple perspectives of some kind.

The hydra of Lyrna, progeny of Echnida, provides Hercules with his second labour. A serpent with nine heads, her breath is poisonous, and she possesses the formidable ability to grow two heads in the place of any that she has lost. Thus Hercules, successfully cutting off head after head of his monstrous opponent, finds himself baffled that his success does not immediately result in a discontinuity that will eliminate her and the threat that she poses.

The object of the twelve labours of Hercules, assigned to him by his cousin Eurystheus, is to rid the world of a number of monsters. Thus the hero's quest is bound up with the fate of the monster, an element, as we have seen, basic to heroic narrative. At a more abstract level of that narrative, we see that the adventures have a function beyond the literal action of the plot, beyond the practical value of ridding the world of inconvenient monsters, a function in which the monsters define the hero. In a symbolic way the hero becomes the monster he destroys or, more accurately perhaps, he discovers progressively in his encounters with the monsters a self free of the limitations of the normal.

Thus in his first labour, Hercules kills the monstrous Lion of Nemea and puts its skin upon himself, even using the monster's head as a helmet. Again in the subsequent confrontation with the many-headed hydra, having cauterized each of the neck wounds that he inflicted to prevent the regrowth of the heads, Hercules defeats the beast, eliminating each and every head. He then uses her poisonous blood to strengthen his arrows for further encounters with other monsters. In doing so, he takes upon himself the power of the hydra by absorbing her blood, just as he did the lion's, by donning his pelt.

This penultimate labour forces Hercules into an encounter in Hell with Cerberus, the multicephalic brother of the Hydra. The hero's success in this adventure is attributed partially to his having been initiated into the Eleusian mysteries, which armed the adept specifically for sallies into the Otherworld. The locus of this encounter, as well as the function of the monster as guardian of the realm of the dead, makes explicit the relation of the monster to death and thus to time. Cerberus is a three-headed dog with the tail of a scorpion and a body covered with numerous serpent heads. He prevents the living from entering into the realm of the dead and the dead from leaving. Hercules is charged with bringing the beast to earth, that is, into the land of the living, which he must do without the aid of weapons. Seeing the monster brought to earth, a terrified Eurystheus hides in a large jar – his usual reaction to the hero's triumphs.

Cerberus is a monster associated with thresholds, specifically the border between the land of the living and the land of the dead; he is a denizen of both and of neither. His three heads are the origin of the three-headed figure for time – each head representing one of its modes: past, present, and future. While the "normal" being, set within the limits of human perception, experiences each of these realities separately and consecutively, only the monster exists, at one and the same moment, in past, present, and future; this abnormality is figured in the three heads that deform him. Besides the monster, only Hercules can travel voluntarily between the realm of the living and the realm of the dead, the threshold having no meaning or limiting force for the "initiated"; this shared characteristic of being denizens of both realms while limited to neither identifies Hercules with the monster that he overcomes.

Transported to Egypt, Cerberus becomes the companion of Serapis, retaining only one of his canine heads: the other two are transformed into leonine and lupine shapes. Here the iconography of the tricephalic representation of time takes shape, revealing the intimate relation of time with death. The three heads – wolf, dragon, and eagle – sported by the monster described by Aldrovandi announce the continuation of the triple theme throughout the rest of the deformed body, which is made up of human breasts, lion's tail, and scaly trunk.[32]

The Bicephalic

The monster with the double head potentially expresses several ideas based on a duality that carries with it a sense of opposition and contrariety. Adam is

Bicephalic Janus. De Laborde, *Cité de Dieu*, pl. 24. Harvard College Library

conceived of as bicephalic in some of the pseudepigraphic accounts of Creation. Hebrew legend frequently represents him through a duality, the usual duality being his two heads: "R. Jeremiah ben Elazar said: Adam the first (man) had a dual face as it is written [Psalms 139:5]: 'Behind and before hast thou hedged me in, and thou placest upon me thy hand.' "[33]

It is through Adam's duality that the creation of Eve is explained: in one Hebrew account the first man is simply divided in two down the middle in order to effect the creation of the first woman.[34] In retrospect, the symbolic force of this bicephalism suggests that in the original Adam both male and female natures coexist, and his two heads figuratively stand for his hermaphroditism. Adamic bicephalism also communicates the priority of the nondistinction and union of opposites by its protohistorical placing of the separation of the sexes in a moment sometime after (and therefore secondary to) the transtemporal act of the creation of the "unified" first being.

The idea and figure of the bicephalic monster has its origin in the mythic representation of opposites and their possible relations. Day and night are expressed in the two faces of the ancient Sumerian sun god, whereas Argus with his two pair of eyes, one behind, one before, is interpreted as signifying sleep and waking. Similarly, the double face of Janus, one of the most wide-spread cephalic monsters, signifies variously, youth and eld, the old year and the new, the past and the future. Composed of a single head bearing a young face – often turned toward a burning fire or depicted in the act of eating, or both – and an old face, turned away from the fire and deprived of food, the Janus monster expresses through bicephalism the essential simultaneity of time. Past and future are presented metaphorically as merely "faces" of the same thing, denying their separate realities and the discrete quality of time by locating their "beings" in the paradoxical figure of a mixed "nature" that presents past, present, and future at once.

It is, however, the discrete nature of time that is essential to logic, and the monstrous relation of past and future in the bicephalic Janus figure seems to identify anti-logic as the goal of this deformation. The concept of time as continuity within succession makes a claim for absoluteness through the fact that this temporal concept underlies and supports virtually all cognitive organization. But the idea of succession is automatically a judgment about the nature of observed events: that they are related, even if discrete; that there is order operating in their movement; that there is a natural course of events and therefore an end and goal. The idea of succession also assumes that each event is distinct, separable, integral, and is therefore capable of relation with another, equally autonomous event. From such an assumption it is possible, further, to conceive of continuity.

Foucault perceives this concept of continuity as the very possibility of the secondary concept of time: "Continuity is not the visible wake of a fundamental history in which one, same living principle struggles with a variable environment. For continuity precedes time. It is its condition."[35] Foucault identifies the monster with difference, the fossil with similarity, and describes the monster as introducing into the affirmations of continuity the necessary negations through dissimiltude: "The monster ensures in time, and for our theoretical knowledge, a continuity that, for our everyday experience, floods, volcanoes, and subsiding continents confuse in space. The other consequence is that the signs of continuity throughout such a history can no longer be of any order other than that of resemblance ... Thus, against the background of the continuum, the monster provides an account, as though in caricature, of the genesis of differences, and the fossil recalls, in the uncertainty of its resemblances, the first buddings of identity."[36]

Janus, although eventually symbolizing time as measured by the unit of the year, first signified coming and going, open and closed, war and peace; one of his faces was placed on the outside of the city gates, the other on the inside. Thus when the city was at peace and the gates were left open for general access, one of his faces was manifest; when the city was at war, the gates closed, and comunication and exchange stopped, the other face of Janus showed.[37] By bringing these two representations together, the two-faced god is created and the bicephalic monster begins its commentary on the nature of opposition.

Janus' role in signifying time originally belonged to Cronos, also a champion of the giants, who, in freeing the progeny of Uranus from the prison of Gaia's womb, introduced generation and degeneration (and thus time) into the world. His name is associated with the concept of chronology, although the etymological identification of Cronos and chronology is incorrect. Janus' two-headed sign also has its counterpart in the Christian representation of God, who was depicted as bicephalic even when He was intended to represent God the Trinity. Two heads, one bearded and white-haired, the other youthful and clean shaven, are attached to a winged body in a fourteenth-century Italian manuscript illustrating Creation. In this representation, as in others, the bicephalic figure is completed by the addition of wings, the symbol of the Holy Ghost, to create an iconograph of the Trinity. The bicephalic God-the-Father and God-the-Son bear a striking resemblance to the Janus figures of the new year and the old.

The Tricephalic

The development of the symbol of the bicephalic monster probably begins in the symbolism of divine decapitation, primordially the beheading of Osiris. And just as the symbolism of two heads grows out of the symbolism applied to one, so the tricephalic figure, according to the great art historian of the grotesque, Jurgis Baltrusaitis, develops out of the two headed figure.[38] It is by combining the concepts of Cronos and Janus that a new concept calling forth a new sign is created, for if Cronos presents the oppositions of past and future, the original Janus relates these oppositions to others, such as open/closed, coming/going, inside/outside. Thus the temporal oppositions of Cronos come together with the conceptual oppositions of Janus. The very concept of opposition is inherent in duality; three cancels opposition and introduces relation. The dyad becomes the triad.

The new head added to the bicephalic form mediates the opposition of the other two, for while the monster of two heads is a combinatory figure, it is not a resolution of the contraries that it expresses but rather a locus for their coexistence. Serapis, companion of Cerberus, strokes a tricephalic monster whose form, a combination of the heads of lion, dog, and wolf attached to a

Tricephalic Jesus in Trinity. Colle Isarco, Museo di Etnografia Italiana

serpentine body, expresses, according to Macrobius, the mystery of time interpreted: "The lion, violent and sudden, expresses the present; the wolf, which ravishes its victims, is the image of the past bringing along its memories; the dog, always fawning, betokens the future wherein hope flatters us without pause."[39]

Without doubt, the tricephalic form most widespread in the Middle Ages is found in the numerous representations of the Trinity, and the concept of trinity, the hypostatic union of three persons in one, is simultaneously one of the most fundamental conceptions in human understanding and one of the most basic structural principles of monstrous representation.[40] It has been suggested that all multicephalism is to be traced to solar worship and is based on the idea of sight: "It may be noted that the solar connection explains polycephaly in its comprehensive sense, as being an iconographical expression of the power of looking in two, three, four, or more directions at a time – that is, ideally, in all directions – and hence of possessing that all-seeing capacity which is attributed to the Sun more properly than to any other divinity."[41]

In the same sense that, according to Pettazzoni, the three-headed figure expresses the idea of "seeing in all directions,"[42] the tricephalic monster, as we have seen, also communicates the sense of "being in every moment." The one sense negates the concept of space – seeing in all directions at once is to eliminate the concept of direction; the other sense negates the concept of time – being in every moment at once makes every moment present and thus every moment one. This reduction of distinction through plurality and the unification of the many in the one is, however, ultimately contradictory, for the opposition of the one (body) and the many (heads) must continue if it is to be transcended through the figure of the polycephalic; the deformed must reinforce form; the monster must be and not be at the same time. This paradox is nowhere more clearly confronted than in the concept of the Christian Trinity which expresses He-Who-Is as simultaneously and "existentially" one individual nature in three differentiated persons. The development of this concept and its representation have the force of locating paradox itself within the bosom of Divinity. God is paradox, paradox is God, and as such, God is the ultimate monster.[43]

Tricephalic representations of the spiritual appeared early in Western history and were widespread throughout Europe from the second century on. In the Balkans, images of a three-headed god known as the "Thracian Rider" were produced by the hundreds.[44] A tree bearing three human heads was found on a slab at Dieburg, Germany, thought to be the "triple Mithras" referred to by Pseudo-Dionysius.[45] Pettazzoni tells us, as well, that in Bulgaria pagan representations of three-headed divinities were venerated as images of Saint George.[46]

The monstrosity of such representations of the sacred is inescapable; a being with three heads too strongly suggests the violation of natural limits to be relieved of its implications by a rational appeal to the idea of divine omnipotence. The seal of Roger, Archbishop of York (A.D. 1154) was made up of a frankly monstrous chimaera with three heads and an inscription: CAPVT NOSTRV. TRINITAS EST (this head is our Trinity) along with a sign of the cross. Similarly, the seal of the Earl of Derby was composed of a human head with three faces identified as an image of the Trinity.[47] The deformation of the mundane to effect the depiction of the transcendent could, however, go too far for more rational sensibilities, and "monstrous" representations of the Trinity were often condemned, officially and unofficially, particularly in the sixteenth century. Molanus, in his seventeenth century *History of Sacred Images and Pictures*, bears witness to the omnipresence of monstrous images of the Trinity, as well as condemning them through the authority of famous theologians. Molanus refers specifically to the highly controversial image

Tricephalic Trinities. *Left*: seal of the Archbishop of York; *right*: seal of the Earl of Derby. British Library

that placed a tricephalic figure in the womb of the Virgin Mary.[48] Several Councils and Papal Bulls condemned and called for the destruction of such monstrous images.

The Acephalic

The most prominent occupant of the category of monsters defined by the lack of a head is the Blemmye or, as he is less frequently called, the Epifuge, whose facial features for want of a head are distributed over his torso. Sometimes the eyes are in the shoulders, the mouth in the stomach; sometimes the eyes are in the place of the nipples with the mouth in the navel. The nose is placed between the eyes, wherever they may be, and above the mouth; the ears are usually dispensed with. It is possible that the origin of this monster is a headless statue of Molus, the decapitated rapist who is always represented with his eyes in his belly and who, according to Baltrusaitis, was also the model for the Egyptian god Bes, patron of music and dancing, who is represented as neckless or headless with facial features on the chest.[49] Bes is usually further deformed through the addition of animal features. In pagan times the image of the headless god was tatooed on the thighs of prostitutes to protect them from venereal disease.

Freud was partial to monsters of the Blemmye type, viewing their decapitation as standing for castration and this sexual symbolism as rejoining the symbolism of food ingestion.[50] Freud refers to the story of Baubo, hostess to Demeter, goddess of harvest, who, mourning the rape of her daughter Persephone, refuses Baubo's food and cheer. Her hostess, throwing her skirts over her head, presents Demeter with a decapitated torso – naked belly with legs – making her laugh. Statues of Baubo in this attitude were apparently common.

The Blemmyes were one of the monstrous races located at one time or another in most of the traditional geographical monster abodes: Ethiopia, India, and central Africa. *The Book of the Monsters* locates them on an island of the Brescian river and adds the feature that they are seven feet tall.[51] They are described in practically every ancient and mediaeval document treating the monsters. Pliny, Martianus Capella, Thomas of Cantimpré, the accounts of Alexander, Mandeville, and Marco Polo are among the many sources mentioning the Blemmyes.[52] Saint Augustine refers to them in a theological consideration as to whether it is possible to believe in such beings as descended from Adam,[53] and in a fifteenth-century French manuscript Augustine himself is pictured as showing the Blemmyes to his companions. Baltrusaitis, describing the resurgence of the acephalic in the visual arts of the Gothic period, attests to the prevalence of the Blemmye: "The Blemmyes that one had already encountered in the Bestiaries and Treatises of the Wonders of the East reemerge in the thirteenth century and later. One discovers them in the Mappamundi (c. 1210), in Gautier de Metz's *L'Image du monde* (c. 1246), in the accounts of Marco Polo and John Mandeville, and in Alexander's Indian wars."[54]

The profound significance of decapitation is also the basis for the inclusion of another candidate among the acephalic monsters, the cephalophore or "head-carrier." These figures, whether or not deformed in any other way, carry their severed heads in their hands and talk and eat at arm's length, so to speak. The chief example of classical myth is Orpheus who, dismembered by the Maenads, continues to sing his beautiful songs from the river Hebrus into which his sundered head has been thrown. Coming to rest in Lesbos, the disembodied head prophesies continually until Apollo, Orpheus' god, requests its silence. Other classical accounts of a detached, speaking head include that of the monstrous progeny of Polycritos, who devours all but his child's head, which became an oracle to the Etolians.

Celtic legend offers other examples of such figures. In one legend the head of Bran goes on talking with his companions after decapitation. The most famous of such monsters, however, appears in *Gawain and the Green Knight*, a Celtic contribution to English culture in which the giant of the poem, having been decapitated at his own request, holds up his head by the hair to announce his defiance of Arthur's court.

The majority of the cephalophoric monsters are, however, found in hagiography, where an entire type of saint's legend is based on this iconography. With St Denis as prototype, a horde of more than 130 head-carrying saints inhabits the sanctuaries of Europe, each of them in some way echoing the monstrous tradition of the cephalophore. It will be recalled that St Denis of Paris

Blemmye with other monsters. *Livre des merveilles*, pl. 35. McGill University, Blackader Library

Group of blemmyes. *Livre des merveilles*, pl. 163. McGill University, Blackader Library

was identified throughout the Middle Ages as Dionysius the Areopagite, and this belief was sacrosanct, especially in France. Indeed, "Abelard narrowly escaped a trial for treason against the crown itself when, as a monk at St-Denis, he dared to suggest that the Apostle of France was not the same person as the Areopagite."[55] In relation to the canonized cephalophores, it might be considered more accurate to refer to this phenomenon as falling within the scope of miracle rather than deformity were it not for the fact that so many hagiographers and historians have themselves singled out the cephalophores as more monsters than saints.[56] A more detailed discussion of cephalophores will be found in later chapters, which analyze at length both the figure of St Denis and that of Sir Gawain's antagonist, Bercilak de Hautdesert.

The Head of the Other

The number of individual monstrous beings composed through attaching a human head to an animal body or through crowning a human body with an animal head is large, indeed. Add to these the sprouting of human heads by plants, and the possibilities for combinations seem almost limitless. The Middle Ages realized a staggering number of these possibilities: *The Book of the Monsters,* for instance, testifies to the great number and types of human-headed animals: "Innumerable monsters are also read about in the boundaries of the Circean land, lions and bears, boars and wolves, who, while in the remainder of their body had the nature of wild animals, had the faces of men."[57] Baltrusaitis records so many examples of these monsters that it is perhaps only necessary here to mention a few that illustrate the nature of the deformation.[58]

In the simplest sense, the exchange of heads with another species is a trespassing of the categories of being established by science and logic and a negation of them. Such a negation of separation is, by the same token, an affirmation of relationship, and this monster presents the concept of identity through differentiation as a relative and fragile one. The element of metempsychosis represented in the grylle plays its part in the meaning communicated by the figure, as it does in all monstrous communication, but the transposition of head and body alludes more to the interpenetration of beings than to the transmigration of the soul of one being into the body of another. The use of the head to achieve this mixture indicates, as well, that the question of rationality is addressed in the composition. The combination of human head and animal body is a deforming that preserves reason; an animal head on a human body gives primacy to bestial nature. In addition, certain preeminent examples of this monster effect an interpenetration not only of the human and the animal but of the divine as well.

In the development of the grylle, the figure is composed not only by interposing a head and body that are foreign to each other but also through the

Groin-head grylles. Ormesby Psalter. Bodleian, MS Douce 366, fol. 131 (*left*) and 119 (*right*)

displacement of the body by the head so as to construe a figure consisting in a head placed between a pair of legs. This monster betrays the long-standing notion that there is a correspondence and a sympathy between various parts of the body; one correspondance that is particularly strong is that between the head and the genitals, and details of this sympathy are often scatologically elaborated in the Middle Ages. The possibilities for allegorical expression are great, and the artistic use of the head-for-body grylle often explores these possibilities in the margins and between the lines of mediaeval manuscripts.

Satan tempting Adam and Eve in the Garden of Eden is often represented in the Middle Ages as a serpent with a human face. Like him, the manticore had an animal body – that of a lion – and a human face, but in addition, he was a cannibal, which the Persian etymology of his name indicates. In the Middle Ages the manticore was used to symbolize the devil. The reversal of the composition through the combination of animal head and human body is seen in the fabulous cynocephali, the race of men with dogs' heads. *The Book of the Monsters* describes these creatures as living in India: "Cynocephali are also said to be born in India, whose heads are canine, and every word which they speak they mar with intermingled barking, and they do not imitate men but the beasts themselves by eating raw meat."[59] Other sources locate the dog-heads in the northern part of the world and add the characteristic of cannibalism.

Since the cynocephali are the subject of our later discussion of Saint Christopher in part 3, a full consideration of them may, therefore, be

Dog-head with lion. *Hortus Sanitatis: De Animalibus*, chap. 37.
McGill University, Blacker-Wood Library

The Dog-heads. *Livre de merveilles*, pl. 92. McGill University, Blackader Library

Manticore devouring a body. *Bestiary.* Oxford, Bodleian, 764 fol. 25

postponed. It should be noted here, however, that the manipulation of the head by its transfer to foreign bodies makes possible a certain metaphoric commentary not only on the subject of rationality and irrationality but, as well, on the phenomenon of combinations of natures, one of the chief iconographic means of achieving the grotesque. The head as seat of rationality and index of the nature of the creature that bears it tends to govern the reading of the given monster, as has already been suggested, so that a monster of mixed natures with the head of a human is taken as a deformed human being, while the monster with a human body and animal head is taken as a deformed animal. This interpenetration of natures reaches its completion with the grotesque representation of the divine as animal-headed or animal-bodied, suggesting the triple interpenetration of animal, human, and divine natures, as well as a monstrous containment of all of these in the Godhead.

The head is also the locus of speech, the sign and proof of rationality. The idea of language and its opposite, speech and its negation, is of such importance that an entire brood of monsters is devoted to its expression, a brood sufficiently large to constitute a type distinct from the monster of the head, although closely related. It is to that type that we now turn.

THE MOUTH

The symbolic significance of the mouth is divided into that organ's two basic functions: admitting and emitting. Strict regulation of what is taken in through the mouth and what is expelled from the mouth contributes to the construction of the concept of the normal, not only in the restricted areas of eating and of speaking but in all forms of behaviour and in the world as a whole. In relation to what may be ingested by the mouth of a human being or what may be expressed by the mouth of a beast, the area of the forbidden is vast, indeed. The mouth consitutes one of the principal thresholds of the body and thus of the self, a border between the inside and the outside, a portal giving access to the recesses of the living organism or, in the other direction, to the phenomenal, physical world. Through the mouth the self deals with the other, and for this reason the rules related to the mouth are crucial. The encounter of the self and that which is not the self is a perilous one, taking place on the ambiguous frontier of the organ of speech and ingestion at which a single misstep may cause the slide of the one toward the other and end in the absorption and annihilation of identity and individuality.

In his study of the artistic expression of the monstrous, Gilbert Lascault perceptively links deformity and language, claiming that it is Plato who identifies language as the monster. Explaining Plato's use of Pan as a monster of language, Lascault states: "Thanks to Plato, language itself becomes the signified of the monstrous, defining itself in a complex metaphor, or rather, that which, by such a metaphor, challenges the universe of definitions. The recourse to a system of mythic relations (son of Hermes), the passage by an etymology more or less fanciful in Plato's eyes (concerning Pan and *tragos*), the description of the monster as the union of contraries – all become applicable to language."[60]

The deforming of the mouth, therefore, produces a series of monsters connoting the dysfunction of speech, abnormal ingestion, and the negation of the separation established by the buccal threshold. The denials contained in the contortions of the mouth address the most fundamental human assumptions and understandings of the nature of reality.

Throughout the Middle Ages, the polyglot is considered a monster because it negates the established distinctions between individual languages and, consequently, between races and nations. From another perspective, however, these divisions, even if historical, are unnatural, since in the primordial time before the tower of Babel such distinctions did not exist; all humans spoke the same language and divisions into tribes had not occurred. While many polyglot monsters use their linguistic gift in harmful ways, there are positive references to a parallel power of speech, for instance, in the account of the Pentecost (Acts 2:1–4) when God the Holy Spirit endows the apostles with the ability to speak all languages, providing in this way a counterpoint to the story of Babel and a suspension of its punishment.

The polyglot monster is an ambiguous sign signifying the division of humans and their languages, as well as their reunification. Employing the numerous tongues that humans speak and that divide them, these monsters lure people to them for the purpose of tearing apart their physical bodies into as many pieces as there are languages. On the other hand, the multiplicity of languages possessed by the apostles signifies the unification of humans and nations in the Word that can be preached because of this gift. The polyglot monster represents both the negative relation of multiplicity to disunity, in that a multiplicity of languages results in less communication between humans, and the positive relation of simplicity to full communication, in that everyone understands one language. The polyglot returns us in symbolic history to the pre-Babel state of linguistic unity and social homogeneity by confounding the distinctions of language and reducing the multiplicity of discourse to maximal comprehension through simplicity; in the mystical sense, it propels us ahead to a state in which discourse is transcended altogether.

That transcendent point to which the monster propels us is where the human and the divine encounter each other. The possession of language is a principal characteristic of both the human and the divine and, as something shared, it unites them. Similarly, language distinguishes the human from the beast, dividing and contrasting the animal and the human. Divine language is ephemeral and simple; it is silence. Human language is sensual – made of sound – and it is discursive. Thus an angel is at one with what it intellectually conceives and communicates instantly and completely to other angels without linguistic process. Humans, however, remain distinct from their thought and thus from their words; they require a multitude of signs and a discursive process for expression. The mediaeval sense of perfect knowledge and discursive knowledge is nowhere more clearly and economically set out than in Kevin Hart's analysis of Dante's encounter with Adam in Purgatory:

Upon meeting Adam in the eighth heaven of Paradise, Dante has no need to voice his questions, for as Adam explains, the poet's intentions are already perfectly reflected in the "veracious Mirror" of God. A redeemed soul, entirely consonant with God's will, Adam knows Dante's thoughts with far more certainty than Dante can know the most elementary truth; his perception of the poet's mind is immediate, unhindered by language; and when he begins to answer, explaining the true cause of the Fall, Adam's hermeneutic mastery is no less complete. He deftly distinguishes between *signum* and *res significata*, informing us that the eating of the fruit merely indicated what was at issue, namely the "trespass of the sign" [*il trapassar del segno*], a failure to observe the proper limits assigned to man by God. In short, Adam offers us a model of perfect understanding, one in which language can be mastered and in which intentions can easily be recovered, whether human or divine.[61]

The ability to speak proclaims a rational nature, and the locus of the origin of speech further enforces the correctness of such signification: speech is produced by a rational nature and emerges from the seat of reason. The deformation of any of these dimensions of the signifying system calls into question all the others, so that a displaced locus of speech suggests the irrational and the subhuman. Such is the case with the *ventriloque*, a human whose speech emerges not from the mouth but from the stomach (*ventre* – stomach; *loquor* – speak). In the Middle Ages ventriloquism was associated with the devil and suggested demonic possession of his victim's reason. The deformation of the ventriloque is, in addition to a displacement of speech, also a monstrous inversion of mouth and anus based on a grotesque analogy between the two orifices, which is capable of extension to the analogy between speech and farting, an extension common in the Middle Ages.[62]

Several monsters cross the imaginary line distinguishing the monstrous mouth of expression and the monstrous mouth of ingestion. One fabulous race of mediaeval monsters, famous for its ability to amaze travellers by speaking their language, has as its purpose only to put them off their guard so that they may be eaten: "There is some race of mixed nature on an island in the Red Sea which, it is attested, is able to speak the language(s) of all nations, and therefore, they make men who come from afar thunderstruck by naming their aquaintances, in order that they might deceive these men from afar and devour them raw."[63]

The ingesting mouth permits nourishment, allows growth, and sustains life itself. Just as the distinctions concerning different languages and different speakers are emblematic of the very ability to organize according to a concept of the norm, so too, distinctions between what is eaten and what is not are fundamental to categorizations aimed at shoring up that fragile concept of the norm. The deformation of this norm produces a monstrosity that negates the boundaries of the self and other while challenging the concept of identity through the figure of the devouring mouth. The most literal and complete denial of the image of the self as an ingesting/digesting dynamic is the monstrous people called Astomori. Described by Pliny as an Indian race, the Astomori have no mouths and neither eat nor drink, but sustain their physical bodies only through vapours inhaled through the nose.[64] Mandeville gives greater detail in describing the nutritional system of the Astomori, stating that they live from the odour of apples and, when obliged to travel, carry with them these special apples, without which they perish.[65]

Far more widespread, however, is the figure of the monstrous hell-mouth, constituted virtually by a disembodied, devouring maw. The moralizing, allegorical use of this figure in the Middle Ages represents the loss of sinners' souls, metaphorically eaten up by Hell or the devil, but the figure goes beyond this didactic message. It conveys the relentlessness of change and

Hellmouth devouring souls. Winchester Psalter, British Museum, Cotton Nero IV

dissolution, the devastating power of time, the inevitability of death. In the hell-mouth figure, humans are God's victim; the inferior species has become food, ingested and digested, disappearing forever down the throat of an insatiable and implacable power. The hell-mouth in its most general sense negates the division between humans and the spirits by presenting humans as physically consumed by the demon and thus becoming part of him.

Although the mediaeval hell-mouth is an overt reference to Satan and the lost souls, as a representation of death it is also an allusion to passage, the emigration from the life of matter and the physical to the state of spiritual existence, albeit damned. The monstrous mouth in this case clearly demarks the threshold between one realm and another over which passes the travelling soul in a movement parallel and equivalent to that of death. The monstrous mouth may be seen as destroying or as purifying, for the act of eating is primarily a reducing of substance to its most fundamental constituents. The symbolic eating of the hell-mouth does the same, distilling humans to their spiritual essence by eating away their physical dross.

In general, one eats one's inferior. In the hierarchy of being, humans are the highest of physical beings, and all of the plants and animals below them are potentially their food. Similarly, cats eat mice and birds, birds eat plants and seeds; mice and birds do not, and must not, eat cats, nor do plants eat birds. Although it happens that, for instance, tigers eat humans, such a reversal of the predatory relation of superior to inferior is always perverse and was so regarded in the Middle Ages.[66] Even more abnormal and horrifying than the reversal of the hierarchy of eaters and eaten is the breakdown of the categories involved in cannibalism, the eating of the equal. While those of our own kind may become enemies – may even, under certain circumstances, be killed – equal may never be eaten.

Not only does the act of cannibalism in and of itself establish monstrosity, it is also a common characteristic among many kinds of monsters. Thus giants, rendered monstrous by their excessive size, are further denatured through their cannibalism. Similarly, dog-heads are often described as cannibals, as are many other monstrous beings. In the monster tradition, cannibalism always refers to the eating of human beings, and therefore helps to clarify the nature of the cannibal. For a giant or dog-head to be condemned as a cannibal, it must, of course, be of the same nature as that which it eats, and what it eats is human. In this way cannibalism is one indication of a monster's participation in human nature.

In a fundamental way, the cannibal, more than other monsters, enjoins the question of the distinction between the self and that which is not the self. In the first instance, cannibalism is, theoretically at least, a response to hunger and, as such, suggests other hungers. The close relationship between cannibalism and eroticism – more generally between sex and eating, more specifically between anthropophagism and incest – has long been noted (for instance, in the story of Cronos and Rhea, mentioned above in the discussion of giants). The monstrosity of cannibalism has to do with the same concept as the taboo of incest; the cannibal confuses the structures that function to establish the identity of self and the identity of other through similarity and difference.

The horror inspired by cannibalism attests to the reluctance of the mind to abandon distinction as the basis of being and identity. From the point of view

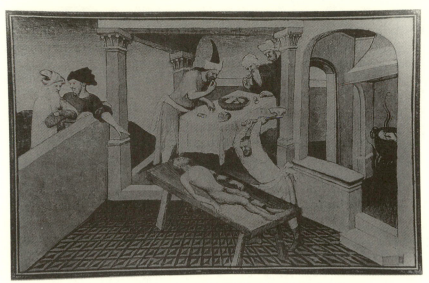

Cannibal meal. *Livre des merveilles*, pl. 94. McGill University, Blackader Library

of the victim, cannibalism threatens a greater and more complete annihilation than death, because it involves a kind of metamorphosis into the other. It reaches further than death, deep into the dread of obliteration and nonbeing, because it attacks the very notion of a natural relation between form, identity, and life. Death, as the liberation of the spirit from the body, requires the cessation and decomposition of the body, the material container so intricately involved with its spiritual content. Through the normal and definitive termination of the body in death, the integrity of self is guaranteed, as it were, by the displacement of the body into the past of the self and the continuation of the spirit in its new present. But the absorption of the body by another suggests a grotesque and perverse postmortem continuation of the self within and as part of another, a monstrosity, not of mixed natures, but of confused existences. Without autonomy, without identity or even consciousness, the formless self continues as an imprisoned particle of the other.

The question of alterity, or "otherness", in this act is not clear-cut. Obviously the other who is eaten is an other within the same species and thus similar to the eater. Indeed, from this perspective, cannibalism is constituted by degrees of similarity to the self, so that, if from one point of view cannibalism is the contradiction of the definition of the other as that which is different from the self, from another point of view it is the extension of the self to the point of inclusion of the other. It is for this reason that much ritual cannibalism has to do with the eating of parents and other close relatives to avoid the loss of a part of the self. Anthropologists tell us that among those peoples who practise cannibalism, there is a sentiment that it is an act of respect to reabsorb that which is part of the self rather than to let it be consumed by worms. Similarly, when enemies from foreign tribes are captured, they are ritually adopted into the eater's tribe before being killed and consumed. Such practices point to cannibalism as a complicated engagement of the concepts of self and other.

In his study of cannibalism, Roland Villeneuve cites a sixteenth-century report of the treatment by the Guaranis of Brazil of prisoners destined to be eaten. After several months of luxurious living, the captured enemy, who has been adopted into the tribe and given a wife and servant, is confronted by his executioner: "Then he who has kept the victim prisoner and who has been absent throughout, arriving with drawn sword, asks the prisoner whether he is not one of the Margaias, thus an enemy. The prisoner responds that he is, indeed, and that he has eaten his tormentor's parents, and that he soon will be avenged. With a blow to the head he is struck dead; his wife and servants, having shed a few tears at his feet, are among the first to carve and eat him."[67]

Such a ceremony seems designed to emphasize, even to the point of insistence, the similarity between the victim and his cannibal killer: in the act of eating the man who has eaten the kin of the devourer, one is consuming a part of one's self. From this perspective, cannibalism is a totalizing of the self. It negates multiplicity by uniting the many in a single, ravenous consumer. As a means to understanding, then, the cannibal abandons similarity and difference by devouring them, leaving the overnourished self as the single, simple, unified principle of reality. If cannibalism is constituted by degrees of similarity of the eaten to the eater, then "perfect" cannibalism is the devouring of the very self. In the final analysis, the monstrosity of cannibalism resides in its symbolic negation of the duality of the objective self – the self as actor, the self as acted on, the self that knows, the self that is known, the self that eats, the self that is eaten. The complete and ideal identity between the subject self and the object self is shown in the figure of self-consumption, an imaginary process at the end of which remains only a disembodied mouth trying to swallow itself.

But only God can "consume" Himself. Because the divine nature is such that God's existence is the same as His essence, God is always at one with Himself. A being who could eat everything would achieve an awareness of self permitted only to God and would become, in a manner analogous to God, a supreme monster. Thus Prajapati, Babylonian Lord of Beings, is sacrificed to himself; Quetzacoatl drinks his own blood; Odin hangs himself as a sacrifice to himself; Jesus is both God and Sacrifice. Humans, through the symbol of the cannibal, imitate God's ultimate transcendence of opposition by His divine self-consumption.

The archetypal cannibal is always God, and the human habit may be seen as derived, as an imitation of the divine and, in that sense, an act retaining something of the holy. As cannibalism is the eating of one's own kind and as gods really have no equals even in polytheism, divine cannibalism is always some form of self-devouring. In the West, Cronos, associated with patricide, castration, and incest, is the great cannibal and thus a monster god. Alone in the universe with his sister-wife Rhea, Cronos eats his own progeny as a way of preserving himself and the undifferentiated cosmos that he governs.[68] When this Olympian cannibalism is ended, the reign of Cronos ends with it, and the rule of Zeus is established. In place of Cronos' single, undifferentiated reality, the ordered universe of Zeus is established in a cosmos filled with multiple gods – all those earlier swallowed by Cronos – with a variey of different ranks and powers, who will begin the complex and entangled adventures that are the narratives of classical myth. The world, and the history to be written about it, now have multiplicity and structure.

The eating of progeny, symbolizing the refusal of order-through-multiplicity, is repaid in the monster tradition by the equally widespread practice of eating parents. Thus Strabo describes the Irish as a nation of cannibals because, as an act of reverence, they eat their fathers' corpses.[69] It is interesting that, according to the rumour that Strabo reports, the Irish also practise incest, another confusion of the boundaries of the self. Herodotus, much earlier (425 B.C.), reports a similar practice among Indians who, he tells us, kill relatives as soon as they fall ill, so as not to let their meat spoil. Those few who, spared all illness, reach old age, are eaten after being sacrificed to the gods.[70] It is also Herodotus who first identifies and locates a race of cannibals known by the general term Anthropophagi, living in the furthest northern reaches of the then-known world, corresponding to present-day central Russia. In the Middle Ages it is Mandeville who reports the sentiment of the cannibals of the Andaman Islands that eating relatives is the ultimate sign of respect.[71]

The mediaeval habit of placing cannibals and all other monsters in the furthest outskirts of the known world corresponds to the symbolic geography of many primitive peoples. Donald Tuzin, inquiring into a patently false explanation by the Arapesh of New Guinea of an incident of cannibalism that befell them, reveals that the Arapesh cosmology involves the existence of another tribe, the Sepik, who are "another kind of man," living at a great distance from the Arapesh and whom, in fact, the Arapesh rarely, if ever, encounter. To these remote, even legendary, people is attributed cannibalism, a thing eschewed by the Arapesh in practice but, as seen in their literature, an idea holding great fascination for them. Tuzin's explanation of this culture's symbolic creation reveals that "the image of 'cannibalism' is, inter alia, a device through which the unthinkable (eating people) gives form to the otherwise inconceivable substance of the relationship to oneself and to the supernatural."[72]

The "unthinkable" is also at play in the monstrous imagery of the more developed culture of mediaeval and Renaissance Europe. The cannibal and other exotic grotesques mediate the encounter between humans and God which, as humans understand, is destined to be a violent and destructive one: "No one has seen God and lived." This obliterating encounter with God is one that is both desired and feared, one that we seek to defer through the mediation of the monsters who, while permitting an anagogical relation with the divine, protect us from its real presence by their own exotic rarity. Thus, mediaeval travellers actually meet up with cannibals, but only in India or Ethiopia, and heroes battle monsters, but only ancient heroes. The monster is there, but only in the farthest reaches of time or space. The parallel in a more intellectual culture is the encounter with paradox, logic's epic battle with the unknown. If paradox really cannot be resolved, the thinking self loses control of what is; its ordering is for naught. Behind paradox, as behind the monster, exists a reality that, when encountered, completely overcomes the limitations of human constructs.

As an image for the unthinkable, the cannibal defers the encounter with the paradox of paradoxes by substituting for it a confrontation with its monstrous image – some deformed figure that encodes the unthinkable, the unsayable, the unknowable, so as to experience it in a mediated way. In Ovid's *Metamorphosis*, a text that supplied the Middle Ages with many of its grotesqueries and monsters, Tereus, who has half finished his cannibalistic meal, asks the whereabouts of his son; beyond the literal level, the answer he receives defines the monstrous meaning of cannibalism and is, significantly, the same as the mystic's response to the search for God: He whom you seek is within you!

The monster tradition of the Middle Ages lends support to Leonard Barkan's view of cannibalism as the trope for the metamorphic world of incest, narcissicism, and homosexuality, not only in Ovid, but in all such "deformed" views of the world: "Cannibalism is the ultimate extension of metamorphosis and its ultimate crime. If transformation bridges organisms and the universe via a corporeal metaphor, then it can all be reduced to a terrible kind of eating. The poem [*Metamorphosis*] is full of cannibals: Lycaon and Tereus, Narcissus ... who cannibalizes himself, the Cyclops and the Lestrygonians, who eat wayfaring sailors. Pythagoras accuses meat-eaters of being cannibals and characterizes all of us as victims of cannibalism: *tempus edax rerum*."[73]

THE EYES

And it is said that there is a certain island in the oriental parts of the globe, on which men are born reasonable in stature, except that their eyes shine like lanterns.[74]

In the monster tradition, shining eyes suggest more than mere strangeness. Their significance arises from the ancient Judeo-Christian idea attributing

Basilisk. *De natura bestiarum*. British Library 3244 fol. 59b

angelic parentage to the monsters. The progeny produced by the angels who copulated with the Daughters of Cain was distinguished by shining eyes, among other things, and so Grendel, in *Beowulf*, is described as having "From his eyes out-shining / A monstrous light" (726–7).[75] As angels were usually represented by the element of fire, fiery or flaming eyes were a predictable inheritance of their descendants, one which denoted the unnatural mixing of angelic and human natures. As Grendel is specifically depicted in the poem as descended from Cain, there can be little doubt that this characteristic is, for him and for other monstrous figures sharing this trait, associated in some general way with the exegetical legend of the fall of the angels.

A different sense of monstrous eyes is found in the description of the basilisk, whose deformity is constituted through a combination of various animal parts and which kills, not with the sting of the serpent that it most resembles, but with a glance of its monstrous eyes. There are also races that share this destructive power of the basilisk, decorating their murderous eyes with gems, according to Mandeville.[76] It would seem that here, in a development of the flaming, angelic eye, we have a variation of the "evil eye" concept, an ancient tradition that Pliny attributes to Greek sources: "Isogonus adds that there are people of the same kind among the Triballi and the Illyrians, who also bewitch with a glance and kill those they stare at for a longer time, especially with a look of anger, and that their evil eye is most felt by adults; and that what is more remarkable is that they have two pupils in each eye."[77] The gorgons, monstrous women of classical myth, become one of the literary versions of this idea, and as we will see in a subsequent section, Alexander the Great, born with eyes each of a different colour, is an example of another.

Argus is the most reknowned example of the monstrosity of multiple eyes. Not surprisingly, such a deformation always carries the symbolic association of exceeding sightfulness, so the legend of Argus asserts that in sleep as many of his eyes remain opened as closed. Nothing can be kept completely hidden from Argus, because he is "ever watchful," and thus his best known task in myth is guarding the cow Io for the jealous Hera. Interestingly, the stories of Argus in mythology attribute to him variously a superfluity of eyes, as well as a deprivation of them, suggesting that the chief function of the characteristic is to establish deformity rather than to specify monocularity or polyocularity and, through deformity, to reveal divinity.

Killed by Hermes in the rescue of Io, Argus is memorialized by the transportation of his innumerable eyes onto the tail of the peacock, the animal consecrated to him. Other associations of eyes and feathers existed, and the *Book of the Monsters* records what appears as an Argus-derived creature of infinite excess: "And they say what is an impiety to be said, that there was a certain nocturnal monster that always used to fly by night through the shade of the sky and of the earth frightening men in cities with a horrible cry. And it had just as many eyes as plumes on its body, and just as many ears as mouths. It is also written that it always existed without rest and without sleep."[78]

The opposite of Argus and the several other monsters of many eyes is the cyclops and related figures possessing only one eye. Although opposites, the monocular and multiocular monsters address the same conceptual difficulties through a symbolism tied to eyes, sight, blindness, and wariness. There are, in tradition, three distinct groups of cyclops: the Uranian cyclops, descended from Uranos; the Sicilian cyclops of the Odyssey; and the builder-cyclops, to whom is attributed the erection of all the prehistoric monuments of the world. The chief chracteristic of all the cyclops and the principal index of their monstrosity is the possession of one gleaming eye in the middle of the forehead. But they share other characteristics: all the cyclops are giants

Cyclops. Ovid, *Metamorphose d'Ovide figurée*, 81

of unequalled strength; they are precivilized in the sense that they are ignorant of the characteristic practices of civilized men; related to this, they are
ignorant of the culture of wine, they do not cook their meat; and the meat
they most delight in is human. From the beginning, the one-eyed, giant cannibals were placed in the underworld. Their later residence in caves and grot-
tos, although attributed to their inability to construct societies, still echoes
this association with Hades and death.[79]

Polyphemus, son of Poseidon, illuminates the relationship between the
monstrous and the *neant* in a particularly striking way. Having devoured several of Odysseus' men, Polyphemus accepts wine to wash down his meal
from the leader who declares his name to be "Oudeis," which in Greek
means "no-man" (οὐδείς). Confused by wine and deceived by the hero's play

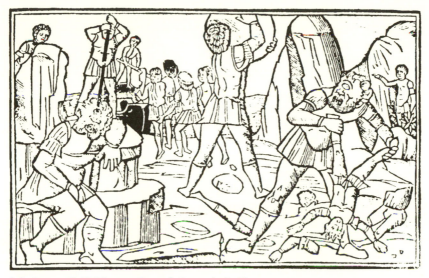

Polyphemus. Ovid, *Metamorphoses*. In Lascault, *Le Monstre*, 353

on words, Polyphemus utters the ironical and paradoxical statement that signifies Odysseus' triumph. The monster intends to say: "I will eat you last,
Oudeis (No-man)," but, caught in the web of language, also says: "At last, I
will eat no man (Oudeis)." Odysseus' victory is one achieved through his being even more adroit at manipulating the deceptive power of language than
Polyphemus, formerly the master of linguistic deceit. As a sign of this semiotic conquest, the hero's destruction of Polyphemus' single eye renders the
cyclops unable to make distinctions; he cannot, for instance, tell the difference between his sheep and his Greek prisoners, between "oudeis" and "odysseus," between no-one and someone.

It is this lack of discrimination in meaning (and thus meaninglessness)
that Michel Serres perceives as the significance of Polyphemus, whose deformity he identifies with the monstrosity of language itself and whom he
identifies as a sign of the excrescence of meaning in language: "Malicious
genius, for whom words bear their every possible meaning, I am called
Polyphemus. I speak, and the thing is present, or absent, here or there, just as
I wish, so that it is quite impossible to escape my cave, enwrapped as one is
in the woven links of my discourse. In this web I place you on a given strand
where all has been foreseen and filled with traps. Death awaits you at the detour, at the intersections of my strategies."[80]

The other half of the monstrous symbol of language appears in Odysseus
who, in the face of the totalizing discourse of the cyclops, invokes the alternate discourse of negation: "To deceive this universally subtle trickster it
takes only a trick, the trick of speaking in such a way that words become

totally deprived of meaning ... 'It is thus essential [says Ulysses] to place me completely outside of all direction, in the negation of place, of locus, of word – indeed, of being itself: my name must be *Nemo*' ... Confronted by the most subtle of tricksters, Ulysses proves cleverer than Descartes. He declares the nothingness of his *I*, not the affirmation of being."[81]

The physical deformation of the singular eye of the cyclops connotes a contradiction of the normal binocular state and the duality for which it metaphorically stands. It is language that is the equivalent of healthy sight. Like vision, which creates the illusion that the two images received by both eyes are one, language simultaneously forces the separation between sign and signified and deludes us into believing that it has not done so. The paradox of the cyclops is that, once blinded, it begins to see things as they really are.

The relentless focus of Polyphemus' eye upon the Greeks who have invaded his grotto robs Odysseus' polite words of all force when he first requests the hospitality that civilization has taught him such language should elicit. Odysseus plays civilization's game of discourse and its structuralizations, which is based on the polarity of inside and outside, inclusion and exclusion. Thus he asks the cyclops for inclusion, hospitality, and all the considerations that the system reserves for insiders – those who know how to use language. This is, of course, a deception, since Odysseus seeks inclusion only to destroy his host: Odysseus arrogantly and insultingly invites the deformed to affirm the very language that excludes it and that it opposes.

The ensuing cannibalisation of his comrades makes Odysseus shrewder in his words, and to the monster's second question he is able to give the enlightened answer, "I am No-man" (*oudeis*). The blinding of the cyclops corresponds directly to the hero's declared nothingness, for as Odysseus' transcendence of self-affirmation to metaphysical negation occurs in the narrative, it is betokened and paralleled in Polyphemus' passage from one-eyed to blind. Odysseus and Polyphemus play out a dialectic of cataphasis and apophasis on both the level of narrative and the level of image. The Greek moves from affirmation to negation, thus approximating the state of the cyclops and crossing into his space; the monster moves from negation to transcendence as he embraces the blindness that allows him to declare that " 'No-man' causes my deception and death." Serres continues: "Polyphemus is, perhaps, the name for the world inasmuch as he is the bearer of universal language, of the totality of prescribed meaning. 'No-man' is the name for the unknown that hides or vanishes in order to pose the proposition 'The unknown = *x*,' element of that mathematical language that is futile in its unversality because it has no meaning at all. Thus remains the limitless game of universal language about nothing and universal language about the universe."[82]

In this way the monstrosity of polyocularity and that of monocularity are part of the same thing, the many eyes of the Argus connoting the *via affirma-*

tiva of discourse "from which nothing could be completely hidden," and the single eye of the cyclops connoting the *via negativa* of dissimilitude in which is revealed the incompleteness of what is seen and understood. The monsters of the eye pass from the Argus-state of "not completely hidden" to the one-eyed state of "not completely revealed," to the transcendent state of Polyphemus' full understanding in total blindness and negation.

The Middle Ages employed numerous one-eyed monsters in the tradition of the grotesque. While the classical cyclops remained the governing archetype, the significance of the deformed eye became more generalized in the mediaeval monster tradition. Thus, *The Book of the Monsters* identifies the one-eyed monsters of Sicily as cyclops, adding the detail that they surpassed the highest trees in height. Ulysses is identified in relation to his confrontation with Polyphemus, who, however, is referred to only as "a certain Cyclops."[83] Thomas de Cantimpré's *De Natura rerum*, a main source of knowledge of the monsters for generations of mediaeval students, depicts the monster both verbally and visually, naming it a cyclops, but without reference to the classical legend.

Polyphemus, like all other monsters, poses the question: "Who are you?" The answer elicited is always some version of one of the two given by Ulysses: "I am / I am not." The first, cataphatic response underscores the difference and separation of the interrogator and respondent and is betokened in the aggression of the one against the other; the second, apophatic response, represented by the molten stave that terminates the action of the narrative and fixes its direction on the deformity of the antagonist, unites hero and villain, speaker and listener, human and monster, in a negation of self, form, and language.

EARS AND LIPS

Head, eyes, mouth, ears, nose – no part of the body escapes the deforming process of monstrous symbolism. Wittkower tells us that long-eared races were unknown to the Greeks before Megasthenes (c. 300 B.C.), who borrowed them from the Indians. The mediaeval *Marvels of the East* depicts a race whose monstrosity is constituted only by the possession of enormous ears that they cleverly use to protect themselves against the chilly night, reclining on one ear and covering themselves with the other.[84] Many cultures possessing mythologies include in them beings with deformed ears: "In the Tuamotu Islands (Melanesia), for example, we encounter the belief in the Mokorea spirits, hairy men with ears so long they use them to catch fish; in China we find the Jen, men with long ears, and the Nie-eul-Kouo, whose ears are so long they have to carry them in their hands so as not to trip over them."[85]

A whole family of Panoti, or people who are "all ears," is depicted in the renowned tympanum of the Abbey of Vezelay. The early mediaeval representations, such as those of the Cotton Vitellius manuscript of the *Marvels of the East* (c. 1000),[86] are derived from Greek sources[87] and become, in

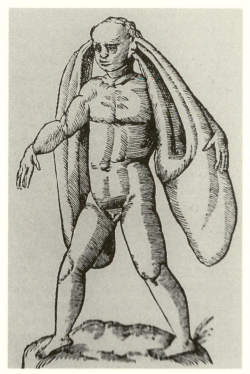

Panotus. Aldrovandi, *Monstrorum historia*, 10.
McGill University, Blacker-Wood Library

turn, the standard source for the continual representation of these monsters throughout the Middle Ages and the Renaissance.[88] Other discussions and depictions of the Panoti can be found in mediaeval encyclopaedias, such as that of Rabanus Maurus (c. 1023) whose *Encyclopedia* contains some of the most striking illustrations.[89]

Some monsters are constituted by the absence of a nose and other facial features,[90] others by an overgrown nose.[91] The monster lacking a nose also lacks lips, while others have a bottom lip so overdeveloped that it serves as a parasol during their siesta.[92] Each and every feature of the head, the index of reason and the origin of language, is modified, diminished, magnified, reduced, multiplied – deformed in every possible way in order to express a series of negations addressed to the limitations of natural form, in this case the form of the head and the concepts associated with it.

But no part of the body is neglected. If the head appears to be the most important index of monstrosity, because it is the most attended to, it is only relatively more prominent than other corporal parts. Trunk, genitals, and limbs also provide possibilities for the extension of the monstrous discourse.

Various deformities. Von Megenburg, *Buch der Natur*, 282v.
McGill University, Blacker-Wood Library

LIMBS

Arms

The deformity of the limbs is achieved in a manner similar to the deformation of other body parts. The multiplication of arms, for instance, or their
complete absence makes of the body thus modified a monstrous form. Similarly, the transformation of a human arm or hand into a limb of another species achieves the same transformation of the body from natural to monstrous,
as does the dislocation of the limb to an unusual part of the body. The innumerable "grylles" of mediaeval grotesque art are composed basically by

Fortune with many arms. Boccaccio. *De Casibus virorum illustrium* Codex Gallicus, Fol 200v.
Bayerischen Staatsbibliothek. Munich

eliminating or reducing the human or animal trunk and replacing it by a
combination of the remaining head and limbs. In such combinations the arms
are often eliminated or multiplied. Jerome Bosch seems to particularly
favour this type of grotesque, and he populates his canvasses with creatures
deprived of arms or legs.[93]

Eastern religions regularly employ the iconography of many arms to express the divine, and classical Western culture attributes similar characteristics to its mythic figures. Thus Baltrusaitis traces the existence of all western
examples to the influence of Buddhist art. According to him, the multiarmed
god found on the Island of Zipangri and described by Marco Polo is an example of Eastern composition.[94] The Greeks also had their version of this divinity; the "Hundred-Handed Ones" constitute a whole race of divine beings

who are the very first progeny born of Mother Earth in quasi-human form. They later assist Zeus in defeating the Titans. The Middle Ages adopted this symbolism and transferred it to the monster. Isidore of Seville's description of such a race is squarely based on his classical sources, but Boccaccio's fascinating employment of the iconography is more overtly philosophical and indebted more to allegory than history. He makes Lady Fortuna "a hideous monster of a hundred hands and arms with which she gives and takes away the goods of this world and with which she pulls down and raises up men in this world."[95] Among the monstrous races of the Middle Ages, there is a people with three sets of arms, as found in the fourteenth century allegorization of Thomas de Cantimpré's *De naturis rerum*, where the figure also symbolizes giving (virtues) and taking away (vices). A similar figure is also illustrated by Conrad von Megenberg in his *Buch der Natur* (Augsburg, 1475),[96] in the *Bestiaire de Gand* (1479),[97] and in Schedel's *Chronique de Nuremberg* (1493).[98] In the sixteenth century, Petrarch offers an example in his *Remèdes de l'une et l'autre fortune*,[99] and as late as the seventeenth century we find examples by Aldrovandi in his *Monstrorum Historia*.[100] In mediaeval teratology, of course, there are numerous monstrous births of multiple-limbed beings.

Legs

Although monstrous forms achieved through deformation of the legs are less numerous than others, they are more widespread: "The same are called the Umbrella-Foot tribe (Sciapodes) because in the hotter weather they lie on their backs on the ground and protect themselves with the shadow of their feet."[101] The sciapodes are one-legged, and their single foot is so enlarged that it can be used for the function that Pliny describes. Despite their deprivation, they are inordinately fast, as Pliny tells us, moving in jumps with surprising speed.[102] Every chronicler of the monstrous races includes the sciapodes among the world's monstrous peoples, and the geographers and map-makers of the classical and mediaeval periods locate that presence in the world. Every traveller of the Middle Ages returns to report an encounter with them, and to the mediaeval artist they become one of the most expressive and decorative figures in the entire programme of the grotesque. St-Parize-le-Châtel has what is probably the most beautiful representation in a twelfth century capital; another is found at the Cathedral of Sens. Numerous illustrated manuscripts contain them, and "scientists" up to and through the seventeenth century describe and picture them.[103]

The sciapode is usually represented seated and grasping his single leg in the act of pulling it up above his head, presumably to provide the shade he is reported to have been seeking. Artistic formalization of this pose tends to make of the figure a quasi circle, head to toe, reminiscent of the circular,

The sciapode. Capital of St-Parize-le-
Châtel. In Wittkower, "Marvels of
the East," 43

self-swallowing serpent, and, perhaps, iconographically suggestive of the
same symbolism.

In addition to the monstrous births of teratology involving superfluous
legs, the lack of them, or their misplacement, leg deformity is also found in
the purely aesthetic, decorative device of the circular arabesque composed,
for instance, of a single torso radiating several pair of running legs.

GENITALS

After the head, the most important index of monstrosity is the genitals and
related ideas such as sexual distinction, the sexual act, and reproduction.
Genital deformation, either effected directly through the representation of
abnormal organs or indirectly through anomalies in sexual phenomena, constitutes a monster of identity of the most profound sort. Selfhood, social
structure – indeed, our very sense of a logical reality – depend on this fundamental distinction between male and female. When it disappears or is confused, the necessary distinctions between all things evaporate with it, and the
rational structures of the real begin to collapse and to meld one into another
in a cascade toward the absurd. Also reminiscent of the monstrosities of the
head, the deformation of the genitals is one of the principle techniques of
monstrous representations of the divine.

Disembodied Genitals

Although restricted to the visual and plastic arts, autonomous genitalia were widespread representations in the Middle Ages, functioning both as magico-religious objects, usually worn as amulets, or as comic, salacious decoration in manuscripts and architecture. Disembodied genitalia appeared as *ex votos*, gems and medals, coins and various sculptures, and were in one way or another related to the pre-Christian fertility cults, particularly that of Priapus, which had survived in some Christianized fashion into the Middle Ages. Every imaginable combination of phallus with other body parts, human and nonhuman, was employed in order to produce this host of grotesque genital forms. One of the most grotesque and famous of the phallic deformations is the bronze in the Vatican museum composed of a human trunk and neck leading up to the head of a rooster whose beak is rendered as a large, erect penis, the scrotum of which forms the wattles of the bird. This monstrosity bears the inscription "The Saviour of the World," leaving no mistake as to its phallic, grotesque representation of Jesus.

Such representations of the divine have their origins in the concept of God as Creator and principle of generation. Not only were there static representations of this divine power, but in paganism, ritual bestiality expressed the same idea. Herodotus describes as "monstrous" (*teras/tepas*) the public coupling of a sacred goat with women of the city of Mendes. For the Egyptians this sacred bestiality represented divine incarnation. The bull was another animal of symbolic importance in the cult of Priapus, to whose head a phallus was attached in grotesque representations originally tied to this cult.

Winged phalluses are widespread and are undoubtedly an echo of the ancient cult of Priapus, who possessed as his chief attribute as Father of the Night a pair of wings: "Wings are figuratively attributed to him as being the emblems of swiftness and incubation; by the first of which he pervaded matter, and by the second fructified the egg of Chaos."[104] The winged phallus is often depicted as being ridden by a woman. This symbolism, originally a conscious part of the religious cult, formed the basis for the figure of the broom-riding witch of later magic cults in the Christian era.

The disembodied phallus is also formed into a cross, which, before it became for Christianity the symbol of salvation, was a pagan symbol of fertility. The association of cross and genitals was not uncommon; a number of metal representations found in the river Seine depict a Christian cross on one side and male or female sexual organs on the other.[105]

The deformation of the genitals was practised on both sexes indiscriminately. For instance, the female sex organ is represented in association with the cross, just as is the male. Divinity could as easily be represented by the vagina as by the phallus, and so it was. Often both symbols were united on pins and amulets. Oddly, however, it was only in Ireland that the representation

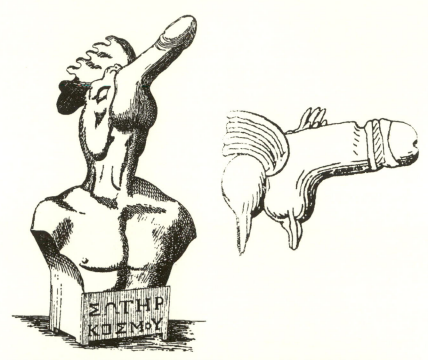

Left: Phallic rooster, "Saviour of the World," Vatican bronze; *right*: disembodied winged phallus. In Knight, *Worship of Priapus*, pl. 2, fig. 3 and pl. 10, fig. 2

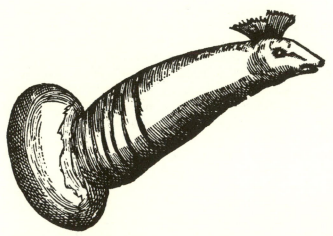

Grotesque phallus. Aldrovandi, *Monstrorum historia*, 389. McGill University, Blacker-Wood Library

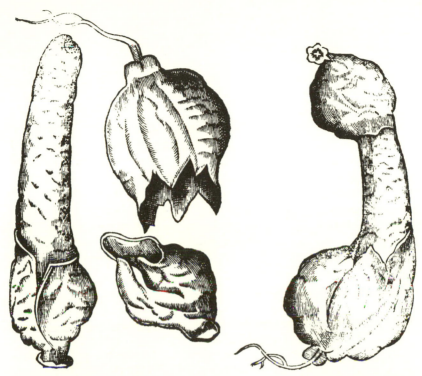

Plant phallus. *Histoire admirable des plantes*, 238–9

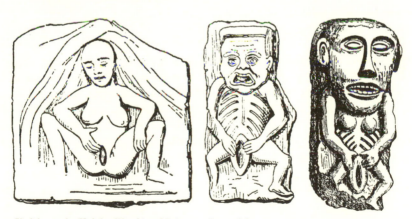

Shelah-na-gig. Knight, *Worship of Priapus*, pl. 5 and 6

of the female sex organ predominated over that of the male. In ancient Christian churches of Ireland there abound, so to speak, representations of women's genitals, figures known as *shelah na gig*, that is, "immodest woman."[106] And well-named they are, consisting as they do of a female figure, legs spread, displaying an over-sized, gaping organ. These *shelah na gig* would seem to be related to the later fish-tail representations of mermaid-like female figures exposing their genitals.

In the world of mundane reality, the process of generation, like all other processes, was one that operated on duality and on binary opposition, with male and female temporarily combining to produce further distinct beings: male and female offspring. In the monstrous world of negation, however, this process is broken, first by the detachment of the genitals from the body, thus denying identity through sexual polarity, and second through the combination of the distinguishing organs so as to transcend distinction. However, among the various negations permeating the grotesque representation of sexual organs, there is one so intense in its disorienting power that the few remaining examples of it are among the most heavily encoded and indirectly stated of all grotesque forms. It is to this deformity that we now turn.

The vagina dentata

One of the earliest allusions to the devouring female sex is found in the Scriptural story of the wedding of Tobias (Tobit 6–8). Features of the narrative make it sufficiently clear that the son of Tobit escapes the deadly fate of his predecessors through magic and prayer. The young Tobias, bathing in the river Tigris, is attacked by a devouring fish that, on the advice of an angel, he brings to land and eats, saving the heart and liver, which he keeps with him as he goes to the house of Raguel, his cousin. It is decided that Tobias should marry Raguel's daughter, Sara, who, alarmingly, has had seven previous marriages, each equally unsuccessful: "This maid has been given to seven men, who all died in the marriage chamber. And now I am the only son of my father, and I am afraid, lest, if I go in unto her, I die" (Tobit 6:13–14). The nervous groom goes on to specify that he has heard that there is a "demon" inside Sara who poisons the husbands mortally by stinging the phallus (Tobit 6:14). Again under instructions from the angel, Tobias burns perfumes in the bridal chamber with the heart and liver of the fish that would have devoured him and, just before penetrating his bride (Tobit 6:17), declares to God that he does so without lust (Tobit 8:7)!

Sara's predecessors are found in the Orient and reported by various sources. Aristotle frankly warns the young General, Alexander, to keep clear of women altogether or, should this prove impossible, to have congress only with a woman lovingly committed to him. For be sure, warns the tutor, by engaging in sex with women a man risks his life. To prove his point the

Philosopher reminds Alexander of the tribute sent him by the Queen of India, a gift of a beautiful virgin who, it was discovered, had been nurtured on snake venom from birth and was mortally toxic in all her secretions. Had he not examined her, boasts Aristotle, and discovered the danger, the young Alexander would have perished in sexual intercourse with her.[107]

Mandeville reports a practice he discovered in the the kingdom of Prester John in which young bridegrooms employ stand-ins on the wedding night in order to assure their safety in subsequent couplings. These professional deflowerers are in danger of their lives in the exercise of their craft because "in ancient times some men had died in that land in deflowering maidens, for the latter had snakes within them, which stung the husbands on their penises inside the women's bodies; and thus many men were slain."[108]

On the one hand, the figure of the *vagina dentata* suggests the common iconographic inversion of head and genitals in which the female sex as orifice becomes structurally analogous to the mouth, just as the male organ was analogous to the nose in the same iconographic inversion. Its monstrosity, therefore, is not only in the grotesquery of a disembodied organ, or a combination of unrelated organs (mouth and vagina), but also in the ultimate suggestion of castration through sexual cannibalism. The figure of the *vagina dentata* is the most overt identification of sex with eating, eating with sex, in which both acts, fundamental to life itself, become life's destruction. Mircea Eliade sees the vagina monster as the sign of the regression to the womb, and his investigation and analysis of initiation rites reveal the symbolic presence of the *vagina dentata* everywhere within the ceremonies having to do with symbolic death and return to the womb and rebirth: "The return implies the risk of being torn to pieces in the monster's jaws (or in the *Vagina dentata* of Mother Earth) and of being digested in its belly."[109]

The close association of the devouring mouth, like the mediaeval hell-mouth discussed earlier, and the *vagina dentata* in Eliade's discussion reinforces the idea of the association of cannibalism and sexuality that is present in the monster tradition. Eliade sees an encoding of the *vagina dentata*, or the devouring Mother Earth, in mythic narratives recounting the swallowing of the hero by a marine monster that is ultimately vanquished when the hero rips open the stomach and escapes into the world. Generally, all heroic adventures in which triumph over tribulation is signified by penetration involve the symbolism of the menacing female/mother, the destructive womb, with which is associated the castrating vagina.

The purpose of such symbolic conceptions and religious rituals was not the destruction of the hero or initiate, but his rebirth into a superior state: in the case of a youth, the initiation from boyhood to manhood, in the case of the literary hero (the archetype for the initiate), from manhood to a limited kind of godhood. Eliade describes the group of myths he calls the myths of "Paradoxical Passage" as functioning to allow the hero "access to a transcen-

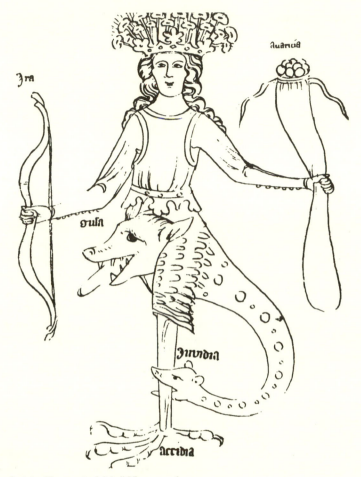

Vagina dentata. "Les sept péchés." Vienna, cod. 370

dental state." These narratives are characterized by the hero's passing between continually moving, wheel-shaped stones, between two rocks hitting
together, or passing over a bridge as narrow as the blade of a knife.[110] The
menaces of grinding, crushing, cutting contained in these narratives are the
symbolic expressions of the *vagina dentata,* the monster that chews away the
distinction and separation between self and other based on gender and re-
duces the plurality based on sexual identity to simplicity and nonidentity.
The hero who has successfully "negotiated" the *vagina dentata* has, of
course, made one of two, since it is the creative sexual act that betokens his
success.[111] Although in the sexual act, as in castration, the genitals "disappear," in the legend of the *vagina dentata,* this disappearance represents the
absorption of the male by the female and his destruction. In the normal sex-

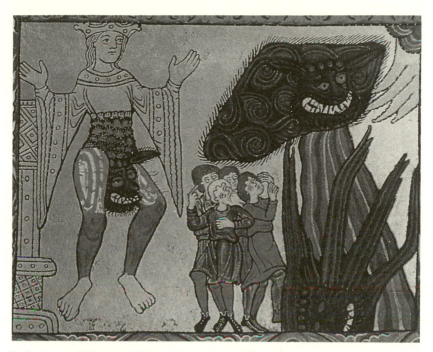

Vagina dentata. Hildegard of Bingen, *Scivias*, plate 32/III, 11

ual act such disappearance betokens the transcendence of both gender restrictions and, like the transcendence of the rational, it is temporary.

As rich as are myth and ritual in the symbolism of death from the womb,
they are not the only sources of its expression. Its presence in mediaeval al-
chemy, a discourse half way between myth and philosophy, suggests that the
idea of the *vagina dentata* also functioned in relation to more rational, less
primitive structures. Paracelsus says that "he who would enter the Kingdom
of God must first enter with his body into his mother and there die."[112]

Claude Kappler suggests the fourteenth century "Fish-Woman" as an encodement of the *vagina dentata*. Representing the Seven Deadly Sins, the
figure consists of a crowned female head and torso finishing in a serpentine
tail from whose genital area emerges a wolf-like head. Both the phallic-like
tongue and the sharp teeth of the wolf's maw are made very prominent in the
figure, encouraging agreement with Kappler that "we discover in this figure
the double symbolism of the toothed phallus-mouth which can be interpreted
in a number of ways."[113]

The allegorical employment of the figure of the *vagina dentata* finds one
of its most overt and startling instances in the work of Hildegard of Bingen.
The great German mystic's vision of the "Virgin Ecclesia" is troubled by the

intrusion of its opposite, the Antichrist who appears, not as a separate figure, but as the genital area of Ecclesia: "That feminine figure [Ecclesia] which I had formerly seen before the altar in the sight of God now appeared to me again, so that this time I could see her below the navel as well. For from her navel down to the place where a woman's sex is recognized, she had variegated scaly blotches, and in place of her privy parts there appeared a monstrous black head with fiery eyes, asses' ears, and the nose and mouth of a lion gaping wide, horribly gnashing and sharpening its terrible iron teeth."[114]

The illumination accompanying the text depicts Ecclesia's nether parts as a monstrous face with highly emphasized teeth; in the same illustration, this *vagina dentata* – the Antichrist – is seen detached from the body, exalting "himself on a heap of excrement."[115]

The Hermaphrodite

In contrast to the symbolism of the castrating vagina that eliminates sexual identity, the monster par excellence is the being deformed by the possession of both sexes. Plato makes the hermaphrodite the symbol of philosophy and identifies the Titans, giants of myth, as the race of androgynes that made war on the gods (*Banquet* 14–15). Unlike their fate in myth, the hermaphroditic giants in Plato's version are not defeated by thunder and banished but are divided into male and female and thus lose in this way their prodigious power. These weakened creatures are men and women; they retain an unconscious memory of their previous, glorious state, as well as an urgent desire to recreate the primordial unity from which it arose. For Plato, sexual intercourse between male and female is a sign of the transcendence of all opposition into the union and simplicity that is the perfection of human nature and intellect. Thus the androgyne stands as the ideal, yet contradictory, sign of the final goal of eros:

In its most profound aspect, eros embodies an impulse to overcome the consequences of the Fall, to leave the restrictive world of duality, to restore the primordial state, to surmount the condition of dual existentiality broken and conditioned by the "other" ... Here is the key to all the metaphysics of sex: "Through the Dyad toward the Unity." Sexual love is the most universal form of man's obscure search to eliminate duality for a short while, to existentially overcome the boundary between ego and not-ego, between self and not-self. Flesh and sex are the tools for an ecstatic approximation of the achievement of unity.[116]

The achievement of this union in the sex act is, however, imperfect, for the primordial oneness that is attained at the moment of orgasm begins to fade as soon as it occurs, and the loss of self in the other is fleeting, followed instantly by the reestablishment of the boundaries separating self and other.

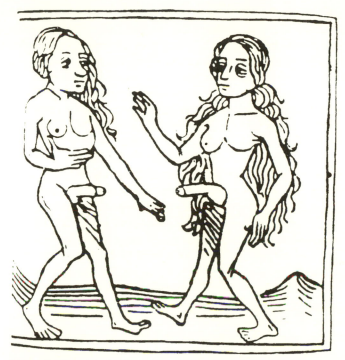

Hermaphrodites. Mandeville, *Travels*. In Kappler, *Monstres*, 145, fig. 36

The bisexuality of the giants who lay siege to heaven is significant both in Plato's rendition and in the original myth, for it suggests that androgyny is a characteristic not only of the aggressors but, as well, of those they would displace. The possibility of the Titans' divine rule rests upon their god-like androgyny as we see when they fail: their defeat and exclusion from divinity is signified by their loss of genital simplicity and unity.

The notion that the ultimate monster is God Himself is reinforced by the hermaphroditic representation of the divine. The mythic narrative attributes the origin of androgyny to Hermes and Aphrodite, who produced the god Hermaphroditus, who is sometimes identified with Eros himself. Hermes is the phallic god, his most common image being a phallus finishing in a human face. Aphrodite is the goddess of love; both therefore, given their intense genital signification, are highly appropriate as the parents of Hermaphroditus and the origin of the concept of androgyny.

Another side of the bisexual symbol is present, however, in one of the legends of Hermaphroditus that provides the archetype for the story of Narcissus and that relates androgyny and narcissism more explicitly. While most versions describe Hermaphroditus as being born bisexual, one depicts him as being born and passing his youth as an extraordinarily beautiful male. In this version he comes to the edge of a lake inhabited by the nymph Salmacis, who falls in love with him. Although he rebuffs all her sexual advances, Hermaphroditus eventually bathes in her lake, thus unwittingly putting himself under her power. Salmacis attaches herself to the boy so as never again to be separated from his body. In his bitterness, Hermaphroditus denounces the lake as a place of unmanning for any male who enters into it. In this version, bisexuality is not a transcendent union of opposites but a loss of virility, a demotion in the scale of being, and a realization of the dreaded loss of individual identity.

Eliade, in his famous study of the androgyne, *The Two and the One*, relates the bisexual figure to the nature of the cosmos and divinity itself, seeing in the "brotherhood" of God and Satan the point of origin of a whole set of double opposites: good and evil, time and space, inside and outside, life and death, unity and multiplicity, male and female. The union of these opposites, the *coincidentia oppositorum* of Neoplatonist, mystical thought, is a moment of transcendence, a fulfillment of man's most fundamental yearning, and has as its trope, the monster: "The attempt of Indian thought to arrive at a single Urgrund for the World, Life, and the Spirit, has attained equal success with Vritra, the exemplary ophidian monster. Vritra symbolizes darkness, inertia, and immobility, and at the same time the potential, amorphous and undifferentiated; in short Chaos."[117]

Eliade makes the important point that androgyny signifies, not the existence of two sexes in one being, but rather the transcendence of the oppositions and metaphysical limitations that maleness and femaleness signify. In the monster tradition the hermaphrodite is not a sexual, but an ontological phenomenon. The inability to perceive this difference betokens the loss of a valid understanding of symbolism itself and the tendency in certain cultures to materialize and sensualize the metaphysical: "French and English decadents occasionally return to the theme of the androgyne, but always in the form of a morbid or even satanic hermaproditism (in Aleister Crawley, for example). As in all the great spiritual crises of Europe, here once again we meet the degradation of the symbol. When the mind is no longer capable of perceiving the metaphysical significance of a symbol, it is understood at levels which become increasingly coarse."[118]

Speaking of the extension of androgynous symbolism into the area of ritual transvestism, widely practised in the classical, pagan religions, Eliade reveals the psychological and spiritual goal of the concept of the union of the sexes:

If we remember that transvestism was very widespread at Carnival, the spring festivity in Europe, and also in certain agricultural ceremonies in India, Persia and other Asiatic countries, we realize the principal function of this rite: it is, to be brief, a coming out of one's self, a transcending of one's own historically controlled situation, and a recovering of an original situation, no longer human or historical, since it precedes the foundation of human society; a paradoxical situation impossible to maintain in

profane time, in a historical epoch, but which it is important to reconstitute periodi-
cally in order to restore, if only for a brief moment, the initial completeness, the intact
source of holiness and power.[119]

Eliade supplies several examples of the Christian expression of divine androgyny and connects the concept to the mystical tradition of *coincidentia
oppositorum*, beginning with Denys the Areopagite and continuing through
(and reaching a high point with) Nicholas of Cusa. He cites the important
declaration of Jesus, as reported in Apocryphal texts, that each of us will
know God "when you make the inner as the outer, and the outer as the inner,
and the upper as the lower, and when you make male and female into a single
one, so that the male shall not be male and the female (shall not) be female,
then you shall enter (the Kingdom)."[120]

The Judaeo-Christian version of the origin of sexual distinction, like the
Greek, conceives of genital difference as part of the Fall, a consequence of
sin. The primordial state was one of gender unity, as will be the future state in
paradise. Several versions of the Creation present Adam as created bisexual
by God. In one, the first human being was double-faced, the male face looking forward vis-à-vis the torso, the female face looking backward, reminiscent of the Janus figures. Another legend has Adam as an androgyne
composed of two fully developed bodies joined back to back.[121]

In the Christian Middle Ages there were numerous literary references to the
first creature's bisexuality. Philo is one of the first to connect the tradition of
an androgynous Adam with the Scriptural assurance that God created man in
his own image (Genesis 1:27), and from that to deduce the androgynous nature of God Himself![122] Tertullian discusses the sex of God as an androgynous state that, while it is a transcendence of sexual distinction in the Divinity,
is nevertheless the origin of maleness and femaleness in human beings.[123]

Scotus Eriugena also conceived of Adam as androgynous and the separation into different sexes as the very sign of the Fall: "For he would be 'simply man' created in the simplicity of his nature, multiplied in intelligible
numbers, as the holy angels are multiplied, but, oppressed by the guilt of his
disobedience, he suffered the division of his nature into male and female"
(*Periphyseon* 2.532D–533A). More strikingly than in other sources, we see
in Eriugena the cosmic symbolism that the Middle Ages attributed to androgyny. Just as the process of creation from simplicity to multiplicity begins
in God, the matrix of unity, and proceeds (*editus*) into matter, so the multiplication of the sexes and the differentiation into male and female proceeds
from androgyny, the original state of God and man (remaining): "Since the
division of substances, which took its beginning from God, and, descending
by degrees, reached its end in the division of man into male and female,
(and) again the reunification of the same substances ought to begin from
man and ascend through the same degrees to God Himself, in whom, as

(Maximus) himself says, there is no division because in Him all things are one" (*Periphyseon* 2.532A).

In the world of time, humanity is continually in a process of returning to the original state of unity, sexually as well as in other ways. At the end of time, humanity will be fully returned to its androgynous state, and this has been foreseen in Christ's androgynous condition at the Resurrection: "It was not in the bodily sex but simply in man that He rose from the dead. For in Him there is neither male nor female" (*Periphyseon* 2.538A). Here Eriugena gives another echo of Christianity's insistence that discriminations in sex, class, and race are the results and emblems of human enslavement to the material and must be eschewed by Christians: "There is neither Jew nor Greek, there is neither bond nor free, there is neither male nor female: for ye are all one in Christ Jesus" (Galatians 3:28).

The connection of sexual distinction with the Fall introduces the further association of knowledge with sexuality. Mediaeval Christianity understood Satan's temptation of Eve "to know good and evil" as a temptation to opt for fragmented, discursive, analytic knowledge rather than the angelic knowledge mankind first possessed, knowledge characterized by immediateness and completeness, a oneness of knower and known, and, consequently, unselfconsciousness. For the Middle Ages the Fall was intellectual; sex was merely its sign. Androgyny was the sign of prelapsarian knowing; the sexuality of genital difference was the sign of discursive, analytic knowing. An illustration in one manuscript of Mandeville's *Travels* reveals the mediaeval conception of the prelapsarian human condition; Adam and Eve in Eden each bear fully developed male and female sex organs; Adam, however, is bearded and has a male chest, Eve has female breasts.

The hermaphrodite was not only symbolic, however. In the vast tradition of monstrous races, a bisexual people also existed. The Machlyes, Pliny reports, are androgynous and perform the sex act of both genders; they also have both types of breast, the right one being like a man's to permit manual labour, the left being like a woman's to suckle infants. Pliny attributes the origin of this last characteristic to Aristotle. *The Book of the Monsters* describes exactly the same race, repeating the idea that members of this race produce their offspring by alternating sexual roles.[124] Precisely the same description reappears some five hundred years later in Mandeville's account of his voyage.[125] Also reported are bearded women from an entirely different race in Armenia, where they live as huntresses using, in the place of dogs, tigers, leopards, and other beasts that they rear for this purpose.[126]

Bisexual representations of divinity were common in pre-Christian, classical times. Marie Delcourt, among others, points out that Zeus was anciently represented with breasts; Aphrodite was depicted bearded, and Venus was presented as bald in some Italian depictions. Valerius Soranus refers directly to Jupiter's androgyny when he calls him "*genitor genitrixque*," just as does Lavinius in referring to Venus, "whether he be male or female."[127] The encoding of divine androgyny is dispensed with altogether in the several representations of Venus adorned with a phallus.

In Christianity, however, representations of God with sexual attributes were rare and depictions of the Divine as androgyne even rarer. Although the Middle Ages had no inhibitions in theologically expressing God's transcendence of sexual distinction by the incorporation of both sexes, visual representation of the idea was another matter. Nevertheless, through various forms of encodement, the concept of an androgynous God the Father, as well as that of an androgynous Jesus were represented. The chief means of this encodement seems to have been through hagiography in which certain saints, usually extrahistorical, functioned as stand-ins for God and his various attributes. Perhaps the most extensive example of this is seen in what has been called the "Diana Complex," which groups a number of female saints whose legends resemble each other in crucial ways: a Christian girl disguises herself as a man in order to avoid marriage, becomes a monk, and in the process of the narrative is accused of sexual relations with a nun or a village girl. She suffers the injustice of the accusation in silence for the rest of her life, and only after her death is she discovered to be a woman; her innocence is thus established.[128] Some thirteen Christian saints' lives follow this pattern, including the famous Saint Margaret.

Scholars have seen in this phenomenon a Christian expression of the idea of the androgynous God, more overtly expressed in paganism, and at least one has gone so far as to identify in these saints elements of the cult of the bisexual Aphrodite of Cypress, whose devotees worshipped her dressed as women, if they were men, and dressed as men, if they were women.[129] The iconography of several other saints appears somewhat more overtly androgynous, but even here their symbolic connection to the divine remains highly encoded. The best known and most highly developed example is the barbate female, Saint Wilgeforte, an avatar for Christ and the origin of the bearded lady figure. She will be discussed in detail in part 3.

The Middle Ages commonly defined and described the monstrous in terms of the dimensions of the physical body. From Isidore of Seville and others came the idea that monsters were constituted by violation of the body's limits: excrescence of parts, deprivation of parts, and other abnormalities. This physical explanation could, however, be extended to a conceptual explanation that saw all these deformities as transgressions of logical categories. The scholastics following Aristotle conceived of limits as that which constituted the very form of the thing. "Thing" here, as elsewhere, is a metaphysically inclusive term designating everything that "is," and in this definition form is given the function of supporting being: nothing can exist that is not bounded; existence depends on boundaries; boundaries are form. From the point of view of Aristotle's description of "thing," transgression of the boundary (form) is a transgression of being itself.

As bounded form makes possible what is, boundless deformity makes possible what is-not. As we have seen in looking at monstrous taxonomy from the model of the body, the human "thing" is constituted and recognized by the boundaries that are the body; within that all-embracing boundary are numerous other boundaries making possible further and more specific distinctions: thus the extremities, the torso, the joints, orifices, organs – all constitute borders that define the general form. The transgression of any of these limits annuls the form and, in so doing, transforms the being. The multiplication of the number of heads, the immigration of the eyes to places all over the torso, the combination of male and female genitals – such "deformities" not only transgress the specific boundaries of the organs involved but negate the limitation of the being so bounded, creating a different, expanded being called the monster.

While for the Middle Ages, as for most cultures, both sexes could symbolize fertility and the generative powers, there was a difference in the exegetical nature of their symbolism, and this difference in the mode of fertility also determined differences in forms. By and large, genital symbolism was informed by the deepest human sense of difference between male and female and by the intellectual formulation of the very concept of difference. Difference consisted originally in the complementary principles of the active and the passive in generation, and from the earliest times, the female principle was associated with matter, the male with form: "The female always provides the material, the male that which fashions the material into shape ... We may safely set down as the chief principles of generation the male (factor) and the female (factor): the male possessing the principle of movement and generation, the female possessing that of matter."[130]

Thus from the biological combination of matter and form arises the being; from the intellectual combination of the concepts of body and soul is derived the basis of metaphysics. The final symbolic extension of this basic distinction between male and female is as a sign of the divine wherein the female, representing the passive in the first instance and matter in the second, at last comes to signify Nature; the male, first as active principle then as form, finally comes to signify the Divine: female and male, *Natura Genetrix, Deus Genitor*. "And the same argument applies to the universal nature which receives all bodies ... she is the natural recipient of all impressions and is stirred and informed by them."[131]

The monster of genital deformation is conceived of as belonging to a primordial moment of unity and wholeness of the psyche and the body, and this is signified by the combination in a single being of both sexes. However, one of the principal causes of all monstrosity was seen from the earliest times to be the isolation of sexual matter or the particular condition of one or the other sexual substance, sperm or menstruum. An overabundance of sperm produced monsters of superfluity, such as progeny with an excrescence of organs; a shortage of sperm or a feeble fluid produced monstrous offspring deprived in stature or in bodily organs. Intercourse taking place late in the woman's cycle risked a deformed offspring due to the closeness of the menstruum to a state of "nothingness," just prior to the woman's period. Thus one of the most frequently referred to sources of monstrosity and one of the most powerfuly monstrous phenomena is menses. Pliny expresses one of the most remarkable ideas concerning the origin of monstrosity that was constantly repeated throughout the Middle Ages: "But nothing could easily be found that is more remarkable [*monstrificium*] than the monthly flux of women. Contact with it turns new wine sour, crops touched by it become barren, grafts die, seeds in gardens are dried up, the fruit of trees falls off, the bright surface of mirrors in which it is merely reflected is dimmed, the edge of steel and the gleam of ivory are dulled, hives of bees die, even bronze and iron are at once seized by rust, and a horrible smell fills the air."[132]

This concept goes back to classical theories of reproduction and metaphysics in which, as has been said, the female furnished biological matter through ovulation upon which was imposed form, a male character carried by the sperm. The occurrence of menstruation suggested, theoretically, a physical existence of unformed life – the phenomenon of potential being without the binding limits of form, and therefore open to limitless deformations. Charles T. Wood, in his discussion of the mediaeval attitude toward menses, describes the link that menses provided between the closely related concepts of monstrosity and nothingness. "A scientific explanation, one that St Thomas Aquinas was quick to adopt, was thereby created to buttress the prohibition, so strongly put in both Leviticus and Ezekiel, of intercourse during menstruation itself, for that was an action which could produce only monstrosities at best, or, more likely at worst, that truly medieval and Augustinian horror, pure nothingness."[133]

The escape of matter from form is a return to chaos, the primordial state of undifferentiated being, which, after the imposition upon it of form, becomes the origin of order. To this primordial state of chaos, we long to return, while at the same time we strive to flee it through order and reason. Chaos, in this view, is menses, and menses is chaos. When separated from its corresponding principle (and polar opposite), powerful menses negates the form of things, disordering their ends and deforming their constitutions. Thus it is that mirrors cease to reflect, metals rust; seeds dry up, and fruit falls from trees. Menses, like chaos, negates the laws of existence, such as cause and effect, by the raw, undifferentiated power of being.

The human body is the field upon which the greatest number of monstrosities are worked. As life's physical realization, the body is simultaneously the incarnation of our being and, as form (with all its constraints), the limitation of the potential of our being. It is this paradox that encourages the play with corporeal form wherein the grotesque is constituted. All the deformations that we have discussed are achieved through this kind of reweaving of the fabric of various conventional garments into the seamless, shapeless, permanently unfinished tapestry of the monstrous, in which all the familiar designs and themes are present but skewed. The human body is the primeval matrix of all the chief figures and analogies by which human language seeks to understand reality; it is the model for the world and the universe, just as it is the chief source of metaphors for the other and our relation to the other. The deforming of this governing form negates the equating of the limits of the real to the limits of discourse and reveals the realm of the monster as the step beyond the borders of affirmative discourse into the realm of the real. But it is not only the human, corporeal form that the monster distorts. Other forms fundamental to human ordering and structuring that the monster dissembles provide the rest of the taxonomy of the deformed.

4 Nature Monstrous

The negation of the structural order of physical nature is another means of transgressing the affirmative limitations placed upon reality. Like the human body, nature's "body" provides a kind of text of the mind and its rational workings that, through rearrangement and deformation, can be expanded and rewritten to include its own negation. While the body as microcosm provided the key for the interpretation of the Cosmos, Nature as macrocosm governed the structure of the human body that was its reflection. Just as the human body was naturally arranged through a balance of corresponding limbs and parts – and grotesquely rendered by displacement of these parts – so nature, whose parts were fewer but more universal, could be ordered or disordered according to the expression desired. Fire, air, water, and earth were the fundamental components of nature's structure, and everything arising from nature was composed of these elements. In the Middle Ages, the ordering power of the four elements was total.[1] To them corresponded sets of quadruple ordering systems that together embraced and explained the entire universe: summer, spring, winter, and autumn were seen as the components of seasonal structure analogous to fire, air, water, and earth; the human body, similarly was made up of the four humours – yellow bile, blood, phlegm, and black bile – that corresponded in the same way to the four elements; human psychology was produced through the interaction of analogous states – choleric, sanguine, phlegmatic, and melancholic – each produced by one of the four humours.

Consistent with other mediaeval structures, the animal kingdom was built upon this same concept of four elements; beings were sorted out into animals of the air, of water, and of earth.[2] The elements, functioning as physical

realms, served to keep apart the denizens of each realm by providing boundaries to establish the distinct identities of bird, beast, and fish by isolating
them one from the other. The elements, then, acted as containers.

In the system of the four elements, each element possessed a certain
charge and existed in relation to the other elements in a dynamic of harmony
and opposition. Fire and air existed in harmonious relation to each other, just
as did earth and water, and so these elements, although separate, could share
proximity; this harmony had its expression in the physical structure of the
cosmos, in which air and fire were found together "above," and earth and
water were bound together "below." Fire and water, however, being binary
opposites, were forever divided: they were never to unite except in catastrophe. Air and earth existed in the same oppositional relation, and there was
the pre-Socratic belief that life itself was created by the cataclysmic interaction of these opposites. Just as the conflictual elements were in perpetual opposition and could never be combined, so the creatures of the sea were
forever separate and distinct from the beings of the air: in nature birds never
dwelt beneath the waters nor did fish enter the skys. Similarly, animals of the
earth could not dwell in these other realms, as their physical forms attested –
they had neither wings nor fins. Although in each realm and in each animal
kingdom there were natural forms suggesting a link to another realm – the
reptile approaching the state of water-being, the bat almost a bird – the union
of realms was never complete, and the gap between them was extended by
ever-finer differences in form. Nevertheless, these transitional beings gave
clues to the possibilities of transcending nature's limits.

The positive state of the world depended upon the proper relation between
the four elements in each ordering system. Harmony arose through a bal-
anced presence of each element, and such balance was realized, not by the
union of two or more elements, but by their separation. The healthy body
was constituted by an equilibrium struck between the contradictory forces of
the humours; a healthy mind was the result of a similar sorting out and balancing of the four temperaments produced by these humours. The physical
universe itself held together because earth, water, air, and fire were held
apart. The transgressions of these categories, any mixing or imbalance of the
four elements, caused, in the respective areas, conditions described then, as
now, as disease, insanity, and cataclysm. Such "disorders" are the monsters
of the mediaeval apophatic discourse.

The transgression of the order of physical nature was the source of a
seemingly limitless number of monstrous forms. Unwonted combinations included both teratological phenomena – natural creatures, such as amphibi-
ans, which, seeming to participate in two realms at once, were regarded by
the mediaevals as monsters – and "conceptual" beings, such as dragons –
which extended the phenomenon of natural transgression into speculation
about its significance as philosophical negation. In both cases, such mon-

strous beings contradicted the absoluteness of nature's order and categorical structures, exposing them as arbitrary, man-made, intellectual impositions. The representation of an ever-expanding kingdom of transcategorical beings implied a cosmos with monstrosity at its centre in which ataxy preceded eutaxy and negation was the hermeneutic of the real.

The transgression of elemental boundaries, like those of the body, was another source of monstrous form and, therefore, potentially a principle of monstrous taxonomy. Breaking the containers of fire, air, water, and earth and allowing a scandalous mixing of their inhabitants and principles not only engendered the grotesque beings that called into question the conceptual limits themselves but also menaced the other ordering categories based on the elements – the division of being into animal, vegetable, and mineral kingdoms.

COMBINED ANIMAL FORMS

Theriomorphic Combinations

Before venturing into the wider cosmos to search for boundaries to transgress, the Middle Ages explored the possibilities for the grotesque within the animal kingdom itself and among the denizens of earth. The violations of boundaries and transgressions of limits existing within the animal kingdom yielded numerous monstrous deformities. The monsters of earthly form may be grouped most broadly into combinations of human and animal, on the one hand, and, on the other, combinations of various animal forms. In the first category are found many of the most famous classical and mediaeval monsters: the sphinx, the centaur, the minotaur, and the satyr; less common are the borak, a combination of horse and man (differing from the centaur in the fact of its Arab origin and the fact that the horse is always a mare); the manticore, a lion with the face of a man; the scarab, a man in the form of a beetle; and what for the Middle Ages, at least, was a monster, the monkey, considered a deformation of the human type.

In the second category we easily recognize such well-known figures as the unicorn, a combination of horse and rhinoceros; the viper, a horned serpent related in Eastern tradition to the rhinoceros; and the scorpion, a strange union of reptile and insect. Less familiar are the aegipan – a fish-tailed goat – and the amon – a serpent-tailed wolf capable of taking human form. Here we shall discuss only a few of the more familiar examples of deformed earthly figures.

On a first level of signification, the sphinx is a symbol of sexuality, but the sexuality it connotes is itself a sign of something further. Cultural anthropologist and disciple of Gaston Bachelard, Gilbert Durand, speaking of the phallic force of the animals of the Bestiary, identifies the sphinx as the archetype of such signification: "The sphinx consitutes the sum of all sexual symbols, the 'terrible animal, derived from the Mother,' and is related to the incestuous

The Unicorn. British Museum, Royal 12f. XIII, fol. 10b

Oedipus."[3] Since the sphinx will be discussed further in connection with Oedipus in the next section, we may defer the subject until then.

Satyrs and centaurs are essentially the same monster, differentiated only by the stories in which they appear; the satyrs' adventures are consistently trivial and vulgar in comparison to the exploits of the centaurs. This powerfully sexual sign that combines a human, male torso and an equine body, is personified in the child sired by Ixion on a phantom of Hera, created by Zeus. This Centaurus, as he was named, sired progeny in his turn, but through the illicit congress with mares, producing the monstrous combination we have come to identify as centaurs. Georges Dumezil, in an extended study of the centaurs, discusses them in the context of comparative mythology and sees their origin in religious celebrations of the winter solstice involving the figure of the horse.[4]

Clébert believes that the cultures using the figure of the centaur understood that the monster disposed of two phalluses; one human, with which to violate the human women kidnapped by them, the other a stallion's sex, for the penetration of centauresses.[5] It is, perhaps, this genital power, in combination with the numerous stories of rape associated with them that gives the centaurs their highly sexual charge.

Satyr. Bodleian, Ashmole, 1511 fol. 19a

Centaurs battling griffins. *Livre des merveilles*, pl. 180. McGill University, Blackader Library

Centaur warriors. Dante *Div. Com.* Vatican, Lat. 4776, 42v.

Tradition describes two types, or families, of centaur, the violent, brutal, and rapacious ones defeated by the Lapiths, and those of greater intelligence and sentiment such as Cheiron. It is, however, not so much the story of Heracles' massacre of the centaurs and his accidental wounding of Cheiron that focuses their monstrosity as it is the earlier story of their debauch at the wedding of Hippodameia. Unused to wine, the uncivilized centaurs – half rational man, half beast – become so drunk that upon the entrance of the bride they rape her and all the other women and boys at the celebration.

From that time forward, wine, a symbol of civilization and its technology, is forbidden to them. When Heracles is entertained at the cave of Pholus, he is served roasted meat, while his centaur host dines on raw meat; the distinction between cooked food and raw further emphasizes the division between the civilized and the uncivilized, personified in the centaur. It is the smell of the wine served at this same feast that drives the centaurs into a frenzy, ending in their defeat and death. The iconography of the centaur is among the most perfectly stated of all monstrous forms: just as the figure itself is composed of half man, half beast, so its meaning expresses the tension within the human psyche, divided in half between the forces of intellect and of instinct. This symbolism is extended by the figurative force of wine, which suggests the civilized agricultural technology that makes it possible, and the Dionysiac frenzy of its inventor.

One of the most intriguing centaurs is the mediaeval adaptation of the figure that associates it with language. The *Book of the Monsters,* for instance, presents the centaur as a monster that cannot establish and maintain the borders between sounds that constitute language and that distinguish man from beast: "Hippocentaurs have the mixed natures of horses and men and in the manner of wild beasts have a head which is hairy but in some part most similar to the human form in that they are able to begin to speak, but lips inexperienced in the human way of speaking mark off no sounds into words."[6]

Like their physical form, which welds two normally distinct species, the centaurs fail to keep apart the different sounds that constitute words and the different words that constitute sentences, thus presenting the antithesis of discourse in the unified, monotonal howl of the wild beast.

Earth and Water

Monstrous combinations of the forms of the denizens of earth and of water are so numerous that only a few may be described. As in all other mediaeval paradigms, the pivotal figure is man who, while regarded as an inhabitant of earth, is also seen as a transitional figure, placed between the angels and the animal and sharing characteristics of both. Human form is combined with a myriad of other forms from the animal kingdom to create theriomorphic monstrosity. Thus the melusine and the echnida join the human form to the serpentine.

Originally Celtic water fairies, the melusine are found not in the sea but more often in and around fountains. Always female in the upper part of the body, they appear as sea-serpents in the lower portion. Gilbert Durand sees the melusine as the European version of the universal ophidian symbolism in which "the motif of wings completes the figure's ophidian malevolence."[7] Echnida, another woman-serpent who emerges from her ocean cavern to devour sailors, is, in one version of the legend, killed by Argus. She is credited with giving birth to such celebrated monsters as Cerberus, the hydra, the chimera, and the dragon.[8]

Other mingling of creatures of earth and water include the orobon, a combination of cat and crocodile, the sea-horse, combining the equine form with ocean habitat, and the hydra, whose monstrosity consists not only in its mingling of the realms of water and earth but also, as we have seen, in its multicephalic condition and, in Homer, its unnatural ability to regrow its nine heads as they are cut, and thus to forever resist death.

Still another monster presented primarily as female is found in Homer's personification of a treacherous, ship-wrecking rock. Charybdis is represented as a voracious, man-eating, female sea monster, and her symbolism is strongly sexual. Her habitat, the strait of Messina, is conceived as a threatening passage, a watery "virago" in which whole ships have been consumed.[9]

The melusine. Miniature, fifteenth century. In Lascault, *Le Monstre*, 309

Crocodile. Bodleian 764 fol. 24a

Glaucus. Paris, Bibliothèque Nationale, engraving

The themes of narrow passage, female menace, and consumed male suggest, both to the Middle Ages and to modern psychology, as well, the symbolic expression of the fear of castration. Three times a day this female monster sucks in great quantities of the sea's waters, causing a whirlpool that swallows the men of the sea and their ships that are in the vicinity. It is interesting that Ulysses escapes being devoured in this manner by holding tight to a fig tree lying just outside Charybdis' cave as the waters rush in. The fig is the common mediaeval symbol of the male genitals.

Other mediaeval inheritances from the classics include Glaucus, the fish-man-god. It is Glaucus who causes the transformation of Scylla into a marine monster with a devouring, canine tail and six heads. Glaucus loves this partner of Chabyrbdis who also devours sailors as they cross the Messina strait, but she spurns him. Glaucus was born human, the son of Sisyphis, and had been the King of Corinth (Ephyra). In one legend he is devoured alive by two of his mares who have gone mad because Glaucus has prevented them from mating. In another, he is transformed into a god by drinking water from a certain fountain. To prove his divinity to doubting subjects, Glaucus hurls himself into the sea, in which he remains as a menace of death to all sailors. Glaucus is represented as a fish-tailed man with widened shoulders and green beard.

Closely related to Glaucus is Triton, son of Poseidon and Amphitrite. The name is sometimes applied to a group of divinities who attend Poseidon, sometimes it is used as a proper name for the sea god who assisted the Argonauts. The visual representation is the same for both, a figure consisting of a human, male torso, with the lower parts of a fish.

From Hebrew tradition comes the monster Leviathan, usually identified as the whale, but originally as the dragon in its origin as a sea creature. In the

Leviathan (whale). Gesner, *Historiae animalium*, 4:18. McGill University, Blacker-Wood Library

Old Testament, Leviathan is the epitome of all the monsters of the sea, just as, in the same tradition, Behemoth is the epitome of terrestial monsters, and they are conceived of both as antagonists and as elemental opposites. From Leviathan's nostrils comes smoke, from its mouth comes fire; its body is covered with serpent-like scales (Job 41). But the centre of this creature's monstrosity is its combination of earth and water, for while Leviathan is clearly a fish, it is also a mammal. In order to depict visually its mammalian constitution, the female of the species is usually featured in representations of the monster, and she is suckling her young.[10]

Behemoth, on the other hand, is described in Scripture with heavy emphasis on his maleness. God invites Job to admire the monster's phallic power: "Low now, his strength is in his loins, and his force is in the navel of his belly / He moveth his tail like a cedar: the sinews of his stones are wrapped together" (Job 40:16–17). This contrast between the monster of land and the monster of sea is further emphasized by the addition of sexual difference, but this opposition is gradually dissolved in the emerging symbolic significance of Leviathan. Psychology has seen in the legends of the whale and Leviathan representations of male sexual anxiety concerning the "devouring" female, but the Middle Ages found more commanding the figure's paradoxical nature, a creature of both land and sea (fish and mammal), a monster of both hindrance and enabling, both female (as it "swallows" Jonah) and male (as it spits him out to "disseminate" the word of the Lord).

Leviathan is the marine representative of a group of monsters whose chief significance is in their devouring activity. They are differentiated according to whether they chew the victim up and thus cause his disintegration in the process, or whether, as in the case of Leviathan, the victim is swallowed whole and thus preserved, although transformed, in the belly of the devourer. Durand describes the dynamic of the symbolism involved in the figure of Leviathan as a process of double negation by which the menacing aspect of the figure is turned into its opposite, and, as a by-product of this transformation, a kind of *coincidentia oppositorum* is achieved: "The procedure consists essentially in reconstituting the positive through the negative, through a negation or a negative act one destroys the effect of a preceding negative."[11]

Just as Leviathan is opposed to Behemoth in terms of habitat, so, too, is it opposed in terms of ingestion: Behemoth is described as a chewing animal (Job 40:15), Leviathan, the whale, is a swallower. The victims of the whale, such as Jonah, go through the process of being devoured, sometimes even dying, but without, in fact, being annihilated. While they descend into the abyss (of death, of sexuality), their reemergence is made possible by the fact that they are not dismembered and disintegrated. The double negative that Durand identifies consists in the negation that is death itself, signified by the devouring beast, which is annulled by a second negation, the vomitous expulsion of that which was swallowed, still intact. The symbolic antiphrasis inherent in swallowing/expectorating changes negative for positive, life for death. The encoded inversion contained within this monster is clearer when we consider the Jewish belief that at the end of time, Behemoth and Leviathan will be served up at the celestial banquet for the people of Israel to feast upon: the devourers will be devoured, the devoured will devour, the container will be encompassed, the contained will contain; that is to say, death will die.

But the reversal contained within the symbolism is not limited to the psychological experience of the fear of death, for within the figure of Leviathan, negations are extended well beyond the psyche. The fundamental division of water from earth is also negated by the double negation personified in monstrosity itself: Leviathan is not not a mammal, not not a fish. Just as the negation of negation causes the merger of opposites in the mediaeval perspective – death becomes life in that it is a passage to immortality, life is death in that it is a mortal prison – so, the monster teaches us, affirmation and negation themselves are antiphrastic reversals, each one a version of the other. The figure of Leviathan, like other monsters, begins with a process we might call the "double positive," which produces a negative (as if a parody of the logic of double negative) and which is reminiscent of the cataphatic process of naming in Pseudo-Dionysius: Leviathan is a fish, Leviathan is a mammal. The process continues in the negation of these assertions: Leviathan is not a fish, Leviathan is not a mammal. It ends in the transcendence of affirmation and negation as opposites. The most complete expression of this way of conceptualizing is to be found, not in the psychological significance of the figure, but in paradox and the philosophical language of negative theology.

Probably the most widely represented monster of earth and water is the siren.[12] Half woman and half fish, the siren is sometimes winged, suggesting

Siren. *Hortus sanitatis*, "De piscibus," chap. 82
McGill University, Blacker-Wood Library

the harpy. The incident in Homer in which Ulysses puts wax in the ears of his companions and has himself tied to the mast of his ship so as to resist the temptation of the siren's song made a long-lasting impression on the Middle Ages and provided rich material for allegorical representation. Durand remarks that the siren is a feminization of the beast-monster placed in the element of water, which fluid signifies menstruation, and the siren herself, the fatal power of woman-matter.[13] Thus the mediaeval description of the siren emphasizes the beauty of the upper portion of her body, calling it "human" and "virginal," while her nether parts (including, of course, the genitals) are described as "scaly," "fish-like," and "concealed." In all mediaeval descriptions there is a strong emphasis on the contradiction between the visual beauty of the upper part and the repulsiveness of the lower part of the siren; the same contradiction is extended in the contrast between the harmony and sweetness of the sirens' song and their murderous intentions and acts. Indeed, the sirens seem to be figures of contradiction: "Sirens are girls of sea, who, with their most beautiful form and the sweetness of their song, deceive sailors, and from the head down to the navel they have a maiden's body and are most like the human species; nevertheless, they have the scaly tails of fish which they always hide in the sea."[14]

While in the original versions in Hellenic and Oriental cultures, the sea monster signified, generally, the passage of the dead to the afterlife, the fe-

Left: sirens. *Hortus sanitatis*, "De piscibus," chap. 27 McGill University, Blacker-Wood Library
Right: siren. British Museum, Sloan 278

male, theriomorphic monster in Western thought bore a different, more menacing connotation. In the siren is signified the luring destruction of matter and the annihilating power of the flesh as signified by the feminine. She is a strongly sexual representation and often presented as a virtual shelagh whose primary effect is to suggest the female sexual organ as a gaping void capable of annihilating its victims.

There were two kinds of sirens. Combining the characteristics of the denizens of earth and the denizens of air, the winged-siren is charged with all the connotations of the avian and the feminine.[15] The fish-siren, linking the elements of water and earth, carries with it the symbolic associations of water and the feminine. Represented together – as they usually were in the West – as a woman with wings and fish tail, the siren's three elements symbolize the transgression of air, water, and earth.

In her activities the siren employs principally voice and language, usually in the form of song. Her avian characteristics evoke the theme of the human soul's separation from the body and voyage to the afterlife, but, as Clébert points out, the siren's particular iconography specifies her symbolic role in a more negative way: "She is the soul of the dead who has not found the pathway to heaven because of a lack of virtue. She lingers between earth and sky, perched upon her crag, exiled from both the living and the dead, in eternal quarantine."[16] Just as she hangs between the animal and the human, so the

Ulysses and the sirens. British Museum, Greek vase

siren hangs between bird and fish, heaven and earth, simultaneously transgressing these boundaries and unifying them by constituting the bridge
between their divisions. Her ironic association with beautiful music, the
symbol of harmony itself, belies the disharmony of the monster's discordant
form. The siren's cataphatic song draws the listening travellers into the lan-
guor produced by the harmonious relations of order itself.

Instructed by Circe, arch-symbol of destructive femininity, Ulysses protects his crew from the sirens by preventing them from hearing their song.
But the hero himself must attend to this monstrous discourse, and so his ears
remain open but his body is bound. Thus while the many either never experience the contradiction of fatal delight or, having experienced it, are destroyed, the hero hears the discourse composed of positive and negative,
assertion and contradiction, similitude and dissimilitude, but transcends its
limiting, intellectually enervating dialectic. Attracted to the shores of rational structures and logical affirmation, the man who puts to port there perishes through the sweet death of self-assurance and contentment, and never
finishes, with Ulysses, the voyage "home."

The monstrous figure of the siren contains its own dynamic contradiction,
the cataphatic melody of its song continually negated by the apophasis of its
grotesque form. Such a dynamic produces the transcendence to which all monstrosity points, the transcendence of all discourse and the limitations of logic.

Earth and Air

The transgression of the boundaries of earth and air introduces the theme of the combinations of spirit and matter more specifically than the inordinate union of other realms. The identification of air as the realm of the spirit is universal, as is the association of earth with matter and dross. Human beings, again, are pivotal in the relation between air and earth, for in humans are found both spirit and fleshly matter, coexisting but remaining separate. Western thought is characterized not only by its description of the human existential situation as constituted by the opposition of matter and spirit but also by the ideal of synthesizing this contrariety. The war of the flesh against the spirit was seen in much of early Western thinking to be resolvable only through a victory of the spirit and its dominance of the flesh; in modern thought the problem has been handled, in general, by denying existence to the spiritual altogether. In both cases, the dualism of the solution merely repeats the binary oppositions of the problem, suggesting the tautological and unsatisfactory nature of such solutions.

The mystical tradition suggested a different view of opposition in general and of that between the spirit and the flesh in particular, a view that harmonized spirit and flesh and signified that harmony in various combinations of opposites. The mystico-spiritual combination of the opposition of spirit and flesh can be seen to correspond to the transgression of the natural realms of air and earth represented by the monster: in this analogy, combination is transgression, transcendence is the monster. The interpenetration and mixing of the denizens of earth and air through monstrous forms negates the order that separates and thus opposes them.

More marvel than monster, the sea urchin in its fossil state was thought to be an unnatural invasion of earth by a heavenly phenomenon. Called "thunderstones," the strangely marked, round objects were thought to fall from the sky at the time of thunderclaps.[17] It was quite otherwise with the bat, a monster par excellence, unnaturally combining earth and air. Flying mammal, creature of the dark, the bat was thought of in the Middle Ages as a monstrous bird possessing wings but no feathers, a creature that suckled its young and slept upside down, signifying, perhaps, the inversion of the natural realms that it personified. Probably because of its avoidance of the light and its generally repulsive appearance, the bat carried with it a highly negative symbolism.

The monstrosity of the ibis was established more through its associations than its physical form. The Middle Ages confused the Egyptian belief that the basilisk was born from the ibis' eggs with the idea that the ibis fed upon serpents' eggs and, because of this diet, sometimes brought forth young formed of a combination of ibis and snake. The ibis was sacred to the Egyptians who were grateful because the bird kept them free of serpents. It was the symbol of the Egyptian god Toth and the Greek god Hermes, patrons of

Bat. Rabanus Maurus. *De universo*,
"De Avibus," 7. McGill University, Blacker-Wood Library

Pegasus with the nine muses. British Museum, Harley 4431 f. 183a

prophetic speech; it represented intellectual power and esoteric understanding and became the emblem for the science of interpretation.

The representation of the union of earth and air through the combination of the forms of horse and bird is widespread, and the most famous is that of Pegasus, especially in his adventures with Perseus and Bellerophon. Pegasus' orgin, like all monsters, is in the sea, for he is the fruit of the passion of Medusa and Poseidon. It was because of her relations with Poseidon that Medusa was transformed into a monster by Athena, and it was at the moment of their mother's decapitation by Perseus that Pegasus and his twin, Chrysaor, were delivered from her dead body.

Pegasus is pitted against another monster, the Chimaera born of Echidne, when the fratricide Bellerophon saddles him to do battle with her. Pegasus triumphs by flying above the Chimaera so that Bellerophon can shower down arrows upon her. It is by the same strategy that the Amazons are defeated. After the death of Bellerophon, Pegasus serves Zeus by carrying the high god's thunderbolts for him.

The symbolism of the horse is as extensive as the symbolism of the bird, and in the figure of Pegasus, the symbolisms are combined. This combination is not, however, a simple adding; the winged horse expresses the contents of both symbolisms but in a deformed mode that points toward their negation and consequent expansion of meaning. Speaking of the vast symbolism of the horse, Clébert underlines its fundamental ambiguity: "The role of the horse is ambivalent, pure and impure, solar and funeral, uranian and chthonic, sign of happiness, agent of death. He rises up from the shadows as the serpent-horse and ends his race as the winged-horse. He precedes the human and continues it."[18]

There is an indirect association of the horse with still another important monster of earth and air. The harpies, combination of woman and bird, give birth to the horses of Achilles and those of Hermes, and they themselves take on the form of mares.[19] In their avian form, Virgil describes them vividly: "They are birds with girls' faces, and a disgusting effluvium comes from their bellies. Their hands have talons and their faces are always white with hunger."[20] Cousins to the sirens, the harpies are hideous creatures composed of the head and face of a woman and the body of a bird. They were born of the winds and embody them, being originally personifications of the Cretan death goddess in the form of a whirlwind.[21] They are specifically associated with two activities: the snatching of humans, whose body and soul they devour, and the simultaneous eating and spoiling of food. The former is derived from such stories as the kidnapping of Pandareus' daughters,[22] the latter from the story of Phineus and the Argonauts, in which the Harpies invade Phineus' dining room at every meal, snatching up the food and maliciously befouling what they cannot steal. The idea of monsters that simultaneously eat and defecate is associated with the harpies throughout the many discussions of them.

Pegasus with other animals. *Livre des merveilles*, pl. 60. McGill University, Blackader Library

Pegasus. *Hortus sanitatis*, "De animalibus," 103.
McGill University, Blacker-Wood Library

Harpy. Aldrovandi, *Monstrorum historia*, 337. McGill University,
Blacker-Wood Library

The association of this monster with food and appetite is predominant in
the mediaeval representation of her. *The Book of the Monsters* describes food
theft as her main activity, but adds to the tradition the harpy's ability to speak
all languages: "It is read that certain harpies, monsters existed [sic] in the
Strophades Islands on the Ionian Sea, in the form of birds, nevertheless with
the face of a maiden, who were able to speak the languages of men and always were insatiable with ravenous appetites and with their hooked feet
snatched food from the hand of those eating."[23]

Beryl Rowland points to the paradoxical symbolism of the figure:

Like the Sphinx, the Gorgon, and the Sirens, who also have bird attributes, the Harpies
bring death and destruction. They are psychopomps who carry off the soul to the underworld, the personification of human guilt and fundamental fears. At the same time, like
Medusa and even Demeter herself, they give birth to horses, and this equine association
points clearly to their extraordinary sexual potency. But while these creatures embody a
double conception, being the givers of life as well as of death, their destructive capacity
is emphasized and they represent the most terrifying aspects of Mother Goddess.[24]

The griffin, as a combination of lion and eagle, each considered as the noblest and greatest denizens of earth and of air respectively, is associated with

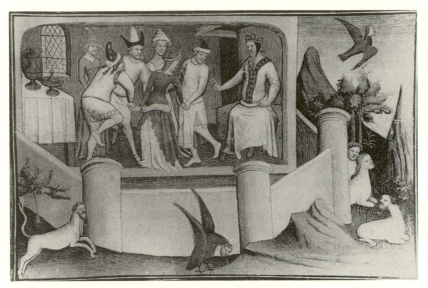

Harpies with other monsters. *Livre des merveilles*, pl. 183. McGill University, Blackader Library

Griffin. *Hortus sanitatis*, "De avibus," 56. McGill University, Blacker-Wood Library

Griffin. Aldrovandi, *Monstrorum historia*, 342. McGill University,
Blacker-Wood Library

power and knowledge. Herodotus reports that the griffin guards gold mines,
and this became for the Middle Ages the symbol of the denial of occult knowledge to the human mind.[25] The mediaeval story that hunters camouflaged
themselves in animal skins to be taken off by the griffin to his gold-filled nest
is an encoding of the idea of overcoming the obstacles to knowledge and the
possession of understanding, for once in his nest, the hunters slay the monster
and claim his treasure.

Mandeville tells us that the griffins are neighbours to the ten lost tribes of
Israel, who are enclosed in the Caspian mountains.[26] His description is typical of the mediaeval exaggeration of the power of this figure: "Nevertheless
the griffin is bigger and stronger than eight lions of these countries, and bigger and stronger than a hundred eagles. For certainly he will carry to his nest
in flight a great horse with a man on his back, or two oxen yoked together, as
they work together at the plough."[27]

Although often a symbol of Satan in the Middle Ages, the griffin was also
a symbol of Christ. In *The Divine Comedy* Dante depicts him pulling a chariot brighter than the sun, a symbol of the Church. (*Purg.* 29.130f.). The griffin is also represented drawing the chariot of Apollo, and Alexander is pulled
aloft to heaven by two griffins.[28]

The monstrosities produced by the transgression of boundaries between
earth and air suggest the paradox of an identity founded on the opposition of
spirit and matter and a nature constituted by the constant striving to unite these
contraries. The harpy, the griffin, and the other monsters of this kind transcend
the polarity inherent in the two constitutive realms and everything these realms
and their corresponding elements can represent. They accomplish this through
the monstrous sign, the transgression of the structural limits of intellectual classification and the deformation of the figures that represent that classification.

Earth and Fire

In the opinion of many, the element of fire was the ultimate matrix of the monster, especially because of the association of fire with spirit and the association of the monsters with the etherial, the abstract, and the divine. Hedelin, a natural scientist of the early seventeenth century, refers to an ancient Egyptian tradition that the sea was brought into existence by fire's transgression of the limits of its own sphere. Fire, then, was seen as creating its own opposite by leaving its natural realm and joining earth: water was thus fire's perverse mode of existence, and through the violation of the natural limits of its realm, fire invested itself with a new and monstrous form. The sea was universally identified as the immediate origin of monstrous forms; that its own origin was the element of fire was less often mentioned. It was for these symbolic reasons, Hedelin tells us, that monsters, hermaphrodites and parricides were thrown into the sea as "social excrement."[29]

The combination of earthly forms and forms associated with fire creates a conjunctive monster expressive of energy, spirit, and life, as well as the idea of arcane and mystical knowledge. Thus the empuse (also called the "lamia") is an extreme polymorph having one foot made of metal, the other in the form of an ass's hoof, and the power to appear as a cow, a dog, a viper, or a woman; in each shape her head is encircled by fire. This monster also has cannibalistic habits. In Isidore of Seville's *Origines,* the lamia eats children,[30] and in Keats' poem, Lamia devours her lover as soon as he is empty of passion, an act that echoes the theme of the paradoxical relation of sex and death. Clébert describes the empuse as "*le démon du midi*," coming into action at that ambiguous moment when time is neither ascending nor descending, neither ante meridiem nor post meridiem, a being that both exists and does not exist, like that moment in which time stands still. Her connection with fire is established by the burning halo that surrounds her hideous head: "She can adopt the diverse forms of woman, dog, bull, and viper. She has a flame surrounding her head and two odd feet, one like a donkey, the other made of brass."[31]

The phoenix is as often described as a wonder or marvel as it is described as a monster, possibly because of the emphasis placed on its great beauty. Nevertheless, its peculiar relationship to fire separates it from the nature of all other avian creatures, and, as for so many other monsters, its monstrosity is related to its representation of paradox, its "showing forth" the *coincidentia oppositorum* of time and eternity, matter and spirit, earth and fire.

Although an Arab phenomenon, the phoenix became one of the most powerful and widespread symbols of Jesus, mainly because of the theme of death and resurrection so prominent in the legend of the phoenix.[32] Van Den Broek's recent study of the myth of the phoenix in classical and early Christian times gives us an idea of the enormous fascination that this legend has

Phoenix. Greco-Roman mosaic. Paris, Louvre

produced from the earliest times, as well as showing that well into the seventeenth century, serious and extensive scientific investigation was devoted to discovering the real identity of the bird.[33] Although there are many variations on the legend of the phoenix, the common view is of a magnificently beautiful bird of very long life that, when it is ready to die, appears for the first time in the human world and then sacrifices itself in the flames of a pyre that it has itself prepared. A variation asserts that the regenerated phoenix arose, not from its ashes, but from its own rotting corpse. It is not uncommon to find aspects of both versions in one account.

The Egyptians considered the phoenix as the bird of the Sun, the fiery deity to which the bird offered up the dead body of its father. Herodotus describes the phoenix as wrapping its sire in an egg made of myrrh, which it places in the temple of the Sun. Several versions of the mediaeval Physiologos describe

Phoenix perishing in its nest. *Hortus sanitatis*, 48.
McGill University, Blacker-Wood Library

the flight of the phoenix from India to Heliopolis, the city of the Sun, where it immolates itself and rises from its own ashes. Pliny, however, reporting an older tradition taken from Manilius, tells us how, from the bone marrow of the moribund sire, rather than from its own ashes, a tiny white worm, "a sort of maggot," emerges to grow and to become the new phoenix.[34] Clement of Rome, in different manuscripts of his *Letter to the Corinthians* (I Clement 25), provides both versions: the phoenix builds a nest of thyme and myrrh that becomes his grave, and from his rotting body emerges the white worm that will metamorphose into a young phoenix. This heir places his father in the egg of myrrh and bears it off to the altar of the Sun.[35] The later Clement manuscripts contain the immolation theme.

The great literary tradition of the phoenix may be taken as beginning with Lactantius' *De ave phoenice,* a poem that attempts to combine the themes of cremation and decay: the bird dies a natural death in its nest of herbs. Only after death does its body combust, and from the ashes arises the new phoenix. Oddly, the element of transporting its dead parent to Heliopolis remains. Later mediaeval literary versions of the phoenix story were largely derived from Lactantius, including the beautiful Anglo-Saxon poem, *Phoenix.*

The general force of all phoenix symbolism depicts its immolation as the liberation of the spirit and the transcendence of the limits of the body and all material phenomena. The phoenix's ability to regenerate itself signifies the triumph of the spirit over death through the burning away of the material body, which is the locus of change, decay, and death. It is clear in many versions of the myth that the phoenix is the embodiment of the Sun, or of divinity in general; in its nocturnal passage through the underworld, beginning at sunset, it is incarnated in a physical body from which it is liberated at the end of the journey at sunrise. It then manifests itself in its true nature as pure spirit and in its true form, pure fire. Such is the symbolism of the phoenix, but the monstrous quality of that symbolism is found, not in the simple idea of the triumph of spirit over matter, nor in the affirmation of life over death, but rather in the continuing reality and force of each of these contraries even in transcendence. The phoenix is a monster because it is one and the same being that is dying and that is coming to life in the conflagration of oppositions that erupts in its nest of curative herbs and gives birth to the paradox of simultaneously being and not being.

Another aspect of the phoenix symbolism that is crucial to its signification is that of its cyclical appearance in the world and its resulting commentary on time and the relation of time to matter. In its own life the phoenix follows a fixed cycle: an adult life of a specified time, followed by death, followed by resurrection. The significance of this cycle is attested to by the great debate and variety of opinion that surrounded the number of years constituting it. For Herodotus, 500 years completed one cycle, and thus the monster appeared in the world every 500 years; for Solinus, as for Pliny, it was every 540 years.[36] The various assertions concerning the number of years in the cycle each bore symbolic significance, all pointing to the same idea: the completion of a cycle (of however many years) at the end of which the planets have returned to the positions they were in at the very moment of the origin of time.

The "Great Year" was, as Van Den Broek tells us, a Platonic idea that held that time was created by the heavenly bodies, which, over an enormous number of human years, moved through a cycle back to the point of origin and alignment that had existed at the moment when time began.[37] The journey of the phoenix is the personification and reenactment of the course of this Great Year and of the creation of time. It is to the very cusp of the moment when time both does and does not exist that the phoenix's immolation corresponds. On one side of that moment resides stasis, eternity, and spirit; on the other begins the movement of growth and decay, the essence of matter.

The salamander was considered monstrous in the Middle Ages specifically because of the element of fire in its constitution. According to Pliny, the salamander's ability to inhabit fire arose from its own extraordinary coldness; it was, in other words, the opposite of fire, and a contrary so powerful as to be able to extinguish flames by its touch. In addition to Pliny's view, another version described the monster as having its natural dwelling in fire, upon which it also fed. Not surprisingly, living on such a diet the salamander exhaled flames. The animal's ability to pass through or even inhabit fire was, again, taken as a sign of the transcendence of the material to the spiritual. It is likely because of this symbolism that the cabalists proposed the salamander as the sire of Zoroaster: "Composed of the most subtle elements of the sphere of fire, they are perfect creatures and were the companions of Adam before he sinned ... Noah, one says, having learned from the example of his ancestor, Adam, agreed that his wife, Vesta, give herself to the salamander, Oromasis, in order that the earth be repopulated as quickly as possible by beings both beautiful and mighty. In mythology this Vesta was the protectress of Rome, while the child she conceived by the salamander was Zoroaster."[38]

As a serpent closely associated with fire, the salamander suggests the more complete version of its own monstrosity in its relative, a figure considered to express the essence of monstrosity, the dragon: "The lunar animal, par excellence, is, of course, the polymorphic animal, par excellence: the Dragon ... This monster is, indeed, the symbol of totalization, the complete enumeration of all of nature's possibilities."[39] Its form combines all that nature has kept separate, and upon this separation humans have constructed their cognitive systems. This monster is simultaneously a being of water, earth, air, and fire, and thus the sign of the potency and plenitude of being itself. At the same time, the dragon is a powerfully negating sign, since by combining the four realms constituting the phenomenal universe, it denies the distinctions between them. Transgressing the borders between the fundamental principles of the world, the dragon erases their identity and destroys the efficacy of our cognitive schemes.

The Hebrew tradition identifies the dragon with the original sea drake, Leviathan. It is said to have existed before creation, but it is also described as having been created on the fifth day out of fire and water. It is both male and female, but God destroys one or the other sex (depending on the commentary) preventing reproduction. This facet of the Hebrew tradition makes possible the combination of the symbolic themes of creation and anticreation. In fact, the dragon originally contained within it the two ur-monsters of Jewish culture, Behemoth and Leviathan, the former being its male identity, the latter its female self. At the end of the world the angels will do battle against the monster but will fail to destroy it. Then the contraries that it contains within itself will attack each other and destroy the whole.

All cultures possess the dragon, and so rich is his lore that even a description limited to the Greek, Roman, and mediaeval traditions must remain sketchy and incomplete. A salient feature of the dragon stories in classical culture is the monster's association with cities, and, more generally, with enclosures and social spaces. Ladon, who had the power of human speech, was the dragon that resided in the garden of the Hesperides and guarded the golden apples that grew there. The iconography of the myth pictures the gar-

Dragon with seven heads. British Museum, Royal 196, XV fol. 22b

den as walled (accomplished by Atlas fearing destruction of the apples) with the apple tree in the centre around which is coiled the dragon. Precisely the same iconography accompanies the mediaeval representation of the Garden of Eden: walled garden, tree, apple, serpent.[40] Thus we have the first association in western thought of the dragon with the garden paradise and with gold. These significations become the basis for the extension of the dragon figure to the association with knowledge and death.

The dragon defeated by Cadmus continues the identification of the monster with enclosures and is the first specific association of the dragon with the city. Searching for his abducted sister, Europa, Cadmus comes upon a great dragon that kills his men but is in turn destroyed by Cadmus. Following the orders of Athena, the hero sows the serpent's teeth in the ground from which springs a crowd of disputatious, warring men. Cadmus fixes the dragon's body to the trunk of a tree with his lance. On this spot is founded the city of Thebes. The first great city of the classical world has its symbolic foundations in a monster whose menacing teeth populate the social space they define with murderous citizens, and thus the paradigm for social disharmony is established. Like Enoch, the first city in the world according to Scripture, founded by Cain,

Thebes is a monument to fratricide and bloodshed, and the dragon is its origin and emblem. Moreover, in the story of Cadmus, who pierces a dragon with his spear, we see the origin of the *typos* that the Middle Ages will represent principally by St George.

The legend of St George, which is of mediaeval origin, invokes much of the dragon's symbolic power. The monster menaces a city in which he has incarcerated the inhabitants. His rage and appetite are mollified by the daily sacrifice of one of the citizens, and at the moment of the hero's arrival, it is the King's own daughter who is sent out beyond the city walls to become the dragon's food. The figurative opposition of inside and outside is strong in this story, and the monster is seen initially as excluded from the city, an enemy outside, trying to get in. But the dragon, like the city from which it is exiled, is also a container and thus both similar and dissimilar to the city it opposes. The movement of the early part of the hagiographical narrative describes the passage of the ill-fated inhabitants from inside the container of the menaced city to inside the fiery stomach of the monster. It is significant that when George first confronts the dragon, he subdues it but does not kill it. This allows the principle action of the second part of the tale to occur: the maiden leads the beast into the city by her girdle. The obvious significance of the taming of the wild and destructive is extended through the figurative and iconographic details, and psychoanalysis has not been slow in noting the sexual symbolism in the warrior's lance and the maiden's girdle as they come together on the iconographic field of the dragon. Only these two objects touch the monster and transform it from conqueror to conquered, from an exile to an inhabitant, from deadly menace to passive captive. The entrance of the dragon into the walled city emblematically presents the coincidence of opposites in which the outside becomes the inside and the container the contained.

It is not only the literature of St George and the dragon that is heavily symbolic but the visual representations as well. The numerous illustrations of the legend reveal common iconographic elements: the scene contains a gaping cavern out of which the monster has emerged; a female figure stands by as the male battles the dragon; objects in the foreground usually include the lance, the sword, and the girdle; the background is constituted by the walled and turreted city, seen often on the pinnacle of a mountain beside a tree and surrounded by water. While the phallic and vaginal symbolism is insistent, the dragon speaks to more than the sexual. In her analysis of a fifteenth-century altar painting from Colmar, which depicts St George slaying the dragon in the presence of Christ and John the Baptist, Claude Kappler perceives the function of the monstrous serpent as referring to divine and human adventures in different moments in time.[41]

The dragon is simultaneously a denizen of land, air, and sea. Its fish-like scales remind us of its aquatic origins and serpentine character, while its wings suggest, in contradiction, an avian nature. But it is especially the fire vomited

Dragon and angel. *Bamberg Apocalypse*, Bamberg, Staatsbibliothek

forth from its insides that fulfills its monstrosity in completing the totality of its transgression. Confounding the identity of the four natural elements by combining earth, air, water, and fire, the dragon also negates the specificity of locus by mingling land, sea, and sky. Heaven and hell, suggested by the presence of its wings and of its fiery mouth, are both contained in this monstrous form; indeed, the dragon was used in the Middle Ages as a symbol both of Satan and of Christ in a dynamic of oppositions characteristic of mediaeval iconography.[42]

Dragon devouring babies. *Livre des merveilles*, pl. 128. McGill University, Blackader Library

The dragon is the monstrous version of the concept of place because it de-
stabilizes boundaries. Relentless in its opposition to the city, with its walls,
moats, gates, and other structures of exclusion, the dragon is both the affirmation of the city – for the city exists to keep the dragon out – and its negation – as he devours its inhabitants one by one. His own habitation is the
cavern, the tunnel, or the tomb, out of which holes he emerges to attack civilization. In Germanic culture, he lives in the ruins of the great cities "built by
giants," and it is his blood that fortifies the weapons of war. He is the chaos
and destruction that lies outside the walls of ordered society; he is wilderness, lawlessness, disorder, and, as such, he creates the need and thus the
possibility for civilization, law, and order.[43]

The dragon also hoards gold, and this treasure, conceived in Germanic culture as bearing an ancient curse, is often seen as an image of wisdom. Treasure and understanding are associated in western discourse, often through
analogies of lost or undiscovered understanding as hidden treasure; thus
Ecclesiastes (20:32): "Wisdom that is hid, and treasure that is not seen, what
profit is there in them both." That the dragon sits upon a mound under which
is buried ancient treasure suggests the monstrous image of paradox, which
must be penetrated in order to attain the wisdom that heroic gold represents.
That the dragon's wisdom is something more than rational analysis or logical
affirmation is seen in the story of Siegfried, who, having drunk the blood
of the dragon, transcends the limits of human discourse and understands the
language of all creation, including the beasts of the field. Siegfried is the
Germanic avatar of Perseus, who rescues the bound and naked Andromeda

from a dragon, a legend also paralleled in Heracles' rescue of Hesione. All the stories would seem to be related to the Hebrew story of God's destroying of the dragon monster Rahab (Isaiah 51:9). The serpentine monster is life and death, a totalization so complete that these fundamental contraries are no longer distinct. He is both the end of the world and the banquet of the chosen people; he is both the bane of the maiden and the phallic possibility of her fruitfulness; he ingests and spits forth: "Little drop of death, source of life! Used at exactly the right time, under precisely the right astrological conditions, the venim provides youthfulness and healing. The serpent swallowing his tail is not just a thread in circular form nor a simple ring of flesh, it is the material dialectic of life and death, death which arises from life, life which arises from death, not as in the Platonic logic of contraries but as an endless inversion of the matter of death and the matter of life."[44]

VEGETAL COMBINATION

Not only the animal kingdom but the plant and mineral realms as well were subject to the deformation of teratology. The common mediaeval image of the world as a book filled with signs expressive of the intention of the divine author rendered the entire cosmos a text constructed of both similitudes and dissimilitudes, of cataphatic and apophatic language, which required both an affirmative, hermeneutical reading beginning with the beautiful rhetorical "surface," as well as a negative and deforming reading that "sees through" the affirmative. This is the sense that Hugh of St Victor gives to his extended image of the world as a book and its reading: "The world can be likened to books written by the hand of the Lord (that is, through the power and wisdom of the Lord) and each creature is like a word in those books, showing the power and wisdom of the Lord. The unwise look only at its outward beauty and the comeliness of the beautiful creation, and cling to it with love. But he who is wise sees through the beauty of the exterior and beholds the wisdom of the Lord."[45]

Hugh's semiotic universe is reflected by Mandeville in his travels "beyond Cathay" when he instructs the inhabitants of these exotic lands that the whole world is the context for monstrosity: "There there grows a kind of fruit as big as gourds, and when it is ripe men open it and find inside an animal of flesh and blood and bone, like a little lamb without wool. And the people of that land eat the animal, and the fruit too. It is a great marvel. Nevertheless I said to them that it did not seem a very great marvel to me, for in my country, I said, there were trees which bore a fruit that became birds that could fly; men call them bernakes and there is good meat on them."[46]

Thus there are birds that the Scots call "cravans," which are unengendered, rising spontaneously from rotting wood that has fallen into the sea. Claude Duret relates an ancient identification of oysters as the origin of certain monstrous birds. He also reports on the cravans, which he calls "klakis" and

Vegetable lamb. *Histoire admirable des plantes*, 330. British Museum

speaks of several other wonderous trees on a certain island, including one
whose leaves become animate and walk about when they have fallen to the
ground.[47] But of all the monstrous interpenetrations of animal and vegetable
life, the most spectacular and best known is the Vegetable Lamb of Tartary.
Also called the Borametz, this creature is described under one name or another by numerous mediaeval and Renaissance writers. In his extensive study
of this monster, Henry Lee provides a fascinating seventeenth century illustration that depicts Adam and Eve going about Eden, admiring its plants. In
the background is seen the vegetable lamb – the sole animal form in this depiction of paradise. The association here of monster and paradise, the presentation of the deformed as indigenous to God's creation, echoes an ancient
identification of the monstrous as originary and as divine. Lee also conve-
niently translates Virgil's verses on the vegetable lamb:

> The traveller who plows the Caspian wave
> For Asia bound, where foaming breakers lave
> Borysthenes wild shores, no sooner lands
> Than gazing in astonishment he stands;
> For in his path he sees a monstrous birth,
> The Borametz arises from the earth:
> Upon the stalk is fixed a living brute,
> A rooted plant bears quadruped for fruit.[48]

Lamb-bearing tree. *Livre des merveilles*, pl. 179. McGill University, Blackader Library

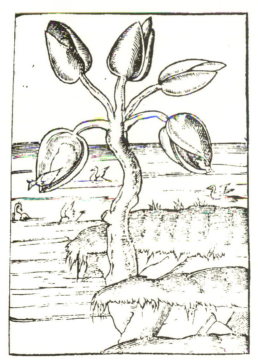

Wak-Wak. *Histoire admirable des plantes*. British Museum

Nearly sixteen hundred years after Virgil, the same monster inspires no less wonder but greater piety: "This description of zoophytes, or animal-plant combination, is not so much fabulous as a reflection of the glory of the Sovereign Creator for whom all things are possible."[49] Specific association of this monster with Christ is found in the description of it as the Agnus Dei in, for instance, the correspondence between Louis XI and Lorenzo de Medici.[50]

Trees, bushes, and plants that bore human beings were also known to our ancestors. Apparently of Arab origin, the tree with human fruit is a marvel known generally as the wak-wak, named after an island on which it grows or, alternately, after the cry that it emits at birth. The legend describes a tree like a fig tree, the fruit of which changes little by little – organ by organ – into human beings. As summarized by Baltrusaitis, this tradition has several versions: in one, the tree bears fruit in the form of the heads of the sons of Adam, which at the beginning and the end of the day, sing "Wak, wak" in praise of God; in another, whole human bodies – all females – grow on the trees and cry "Wak, wak" as a bad omen.[51] Still another has the tree growing on the Isle of Wakwak, where the beautiful women who are its fruit scream "Wak!" as they fall to the ground in full ripeness. Maimonides describes a head bearing tree, and in the *Roman d'Alexandre* as well as in Mandeville's *Travels* the Trees of the Sun and the Moon speak from star-like faces.[52]

Other trees, while not producing human fruit, enjoy the most human of powers in possessing the gift of speech. In the empire of Prester John, Mandeville tells us, grow the Trees of the Sun and Moon, in the middle of a desert, guarded by "a great number of wild beasts that there are in that wilderness, like dragons and different kinds of serpents and other ravening beasts."[53] These trees spoke to King Alexander and foretold his death.

Of all the anthropomorphs in the panoply of monsters, perhaps the most compelling is the mandrake. This mysterious monster is a flowering plant the root of which is a human being; some are male, some are female. Its stems and its blue and white flowers emerge above ground from its head as part of its hair, while its human form remains subterranean. In the Middle Ages the mandrake was revered throughout Europe as a miraculous medicinal plant, especially effective in curing barrenness. So popular and precious was it that an industry thrived in the cultivation of false mandrake produced through elaborate horticultural procedures.[54]

The legend that explicates this monster states that when pulled from the ground the mandrake screams with such pain and anguish that anyone who hears it dies instantly, or within the year, emitting the same screams. Thus the method of harvesting the anthropomorph required that a dog be tied to it while its master removed himself out of earshot of the undertaking. When the master calls the dog, the plant is removed from the earth without loss of human life. The dog, of course, perishes.

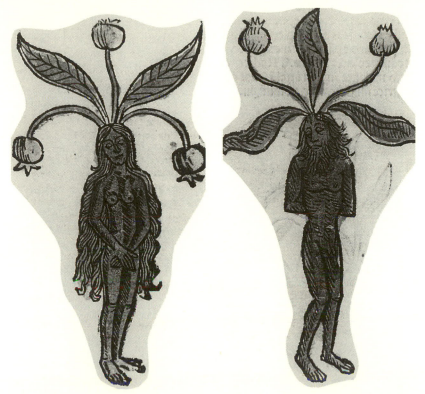

Female and male mandrakes. *Hortus sanitatis*, "De herbis," 276-7. McGill University, Blacker-Wood Library

Another legend has it that the mandrake grows beneath the gallows, wherever such a structure is set up and that the plant-monster springs from the mixing of the hanged man's semen with the earth. In Wales, it was the tears of an innocent hanged man that caused germination. In contrast to this association with death, the mandrake is at other times a token of sexuality, fertility, and life. It is called "Great Lady" and "Good Mother." The Middle Ages referred to its healing powers as a sign of the Virgin Mary.

Eliade discusses at length the cult of the mandrake and the rituals surrounding its harvesting in modern Romania, where offerings are made to forestall the cry of the monster plant.[55] He sees it as the preeminent erotic plant and perceives, as well, its paradoxical signification. It is "the herb of life and death."[56]

Aphrodite was sometimes called "mandragoritis," and the plant itself was known in Greek as *circeium*, from the goddess, Circe, bearing out its long-established relation to eros in both its beneficent and malevolent aspects.[57] In fact, the plant was an aphrodisiac, and so it is described in Scripture when Leah and Rachel use it to excite Jacob and conceive sons by him (Genesis

Mandrake being drawn by dog. *Tacuinum sanitatis*. Nationalbibliothek, Vienna, Ms. 2644, fol. 40

30:14–17). An ancient Jewish legend recounts that this mandrake was found by Reuben lying beside the dead body of an ass that apparently had accidently uprooted it and suffered the traditional consequences.

The mandrake was originally a hermaphroditic monster, its differentiation into two sexes being a later development. It is simultaneously a phallic symbol and a sign of androgyny. Its powers are life-giving, but it also kills. Indeed, its vivifying and fertile virtues must be tricked out of it. As a botanical monster, then, the mandrake harnesses the contraries of male and female and contains within its deformed being the powers and principles of life and of death.

MINERAL COMBINATIONS

The lowest order of existence in the hierarchy of being devised by logic is the mineral kingdom, characterized by a solid, inert, and inorganic state. But even this ontologically humble reality was invested with power and wonder by the Middle Ages. As in the case of other kingdoms, or divisions, there were transitional figures between the lowest kingdom and the categories above it, beings that combined charcteristics of the mineral kingdom with those of higher realms and were thus, paradoxically, neither one nor the other, yet both. These were the monsters of the mineral realm.

Gems were considered cosmic monsters in the Middle Ages and were so identified in the lapidaries. Although denizens of the mineral kingdom, they provided a transition, not only between the different realms of mundane life but between Earth and the Heavens themselves. The peculiar mediaeval view of the interpenetration of being between one reality and another is succinctly expressed in the *London Lapidary* of King Philip, which relates the mineral world, the botanical world, and human language in asserting the divine origin of the power of certain beings that we have called monstrous: "And wyse men shulde not doute but god hath put vertu in stones & herbes & wordes."[58]

The lapidaries were a main source of ancient knowledge, and because they descend directly from premediaeval texts, they preserve Egyptian, Arab, and Greek knowledge. By and large, however, the mediaevals were unaware of the origin of the ideas and histories contained in the lapidaries and took them as Christian truth. Fernand De Mely, who has studied the engraved stone of the Middle Ages, argues that because the Middle Ages was ignorant of the historical details of the pre-Christian past, and particularly of the technique of carving gems, the mediaevals concluded that the image-bearing stones that they discovered in abundance in the rubble of the Mediterranean lands were cosmic wonders and deformations of nature in which human or animal forms had become imprinted on inorganic minerals, as if in parody of the imposition of form on matter in the combination of sperm and egg. In a world where an ideal form existed for every kind of thing, the "accident" by which one or another of these forms became imprinted on stone rather than flesh, or upon one type of matter rather than another, was easily comprehensible.

But it was not only in the Middle Ages that the mineral world was viewed as characterized, like the vegetal and animal realms, by monstrous deformations intended to increase human understanding. We see, for instance, that Pliny considered the existence of certain carved gems as quite independent of human artifice – and therefore the more valuable: "After this ring [a sardonyx belonging to Polycrates of Samos], the most renowned gemstone is that of another king, the famous Pyrrhus who fought a war against Rome. He is said to have possessed an agate on which could be seen the Nine Muses with Apollo holding his lyre. This was due not to any artistic intention, but to nature unaided; and the markings spread in such a way that even the individ-ual Muses had their appropriate emblems allotted to them."[59]

It was, perhaps, not so much mediaeval ignorance as the allegorical world-view of the Middle Ages that made possible a certain universal and trans-historical perception of truth. One student of ancient carved stones describes this attitude as eclectic and points to the existence of amulets used by the early Christians employing pagan themes; one example is an engraved amu-let of the early Christian period bearing on one side the portrait of Alexander the Great, on the other, an ass, a scorpion, and the name "Jesus Christ."[60]

The typical subject for engraving on stones was, as Baltrusaitis has amply shown, the monstrous and the grotesque, and one of the richest sources of grylles in ancient art was the Greco-Roman glyptics. It seems that in the very combination of the inherent virtue of the particular stone and the inherent signifying power of the distorted forms was born a force embodying the es-sence of the monstrous: "Doubtless, stones engraved with these effigies had magical powers. A supernatural force sprang from the displacement and rep-etition of a monstrous growth and mix of living forms."[61]

Gems were the signature of the cosmos, veritable texts within the world describing the structure and meaning of the universe they reflected. The exe-gesis of these texts showed a reality in which the unnatural was the basis of nature, the grotesque the origin of form, and the monster a key to meaning. Even uncarved gems exhibited behaviour characteristic of other forms of life and defiant of the ontological limits placed upon them. So Mandeville, assur-ing us of his frequent experiments in the matter, describes the nutritive and reproductive ways of the diamond: "They grow together, male and female, and are fed with the dew of Heaven. And according to their nature they engender and conceive small children, and so they constantly grow and mul-tiply."[62]

The pearl was monstrously conceived through a mingling of realms, by in-tercourse of the highest with the lowest. Pliny, who considers the pearl the greatest of all things of value, clearly describes its origin as a kind of reversal of the hierarchy, for this mineral form is the progeny of an animal: the oyster. This shellfish is made pregnant by the sky as dew descends upon it. The size and purity of the pearl is determined by the amount and purity of the dew received by the oyster.[63]

The sponge was monstrous exactly because it was an intermediate being. All sponges, Pliny tells us, grow from rocks, and yet they eat and are, there-fore, animal.[64] The sponge is the transition between plant and animal, born of the foam of the sea, matrix of all monstrosity. Clébert reports an associa-tion of this creature with the paradox of language itself. Certain people at the other end of the earth possessed sponges that had the power to absorb the sounds of spoken language, like water, and retain them until needed. Thus, to communicate with their neighbours, these people spoke slowly and distinctly into a sponge and sent it off. The recipient, holding the sponge to the ear, squeezed it gently to expel the message.[65]

Snails were considered mineral to the extent that it was the shell, rather than the inhabitant, that was referred to by the name. As Clébert notes, the wondrous aspect of the snail was found in the perfection of its form, a flawless spiral, turning always toward the right.[66] The spiral was noteworthy for two reasons: it was the longest possible distance between two points and thus suggested discourse; also, it was considered a natural maze which, in turn, symbolized logic. In the Middle Ages, this same perfect form, albeit a sign of logic and order, was also considered a fertile source of monstrous forms. As if in contradiction and parody of the shell's rational structure, anthropophytes of every kind emerge, zoophytes of greatest deformity, and limitless tendrils, shoots, and plant forms.

Of all the creatures of the mineral realm that qualify as monstrous, the most "deformed" – because the most heterogeneous – is the coral. Like the dragon, the coral is a creature, not so much between two realms, but – impossibly – "between" all three: a totalizing monster, it is mineral in that its consistency is adamantine, vegetal in that it is tendrilous and alive but stationary, and animal in that it is carnivorous. But one does not simply deduce the teratism of the coral from its strange characteristics; its very origins are rooted in the monstrous. After having slain Medusa and severed her head, Perseus encounters the dragon that menaces Andromeda. At the very moment of slaying the leviathan, the hero lays the Gorgon's head upon a clump of seaweed that he has taken from his sack to use as a weapon. Impregnated with the monster's blood, the seaweed is transmogrified to coral.

According to legend, as soon as the plant has soaked up the blood of the Gorgon, its branches and leaves are invested with a hardness and rigidity previously unknown to nature. Nymphs, fascinated by this prodigious event, sprinkle the wonderous blood on other algae lying out of the water along the beach, with always the same result. Even to this day, Ovid tells us, coral retains this characteristic, that under water its stem and branches are supple, while out of water they harden and become brittle.[67] This participation in the three modes of life is also dramatically stated in the description of the genesis of coral in the *North Midland Lapidary*: "Corayle is a ston yt is mad of ye fom of ye se and ye dew; and ye wynd beres it vpe in-to ye eyr, & yer it sal congele & wex hard & be-comes a ston."[68] Lapidaries generally ascribe to coral the power of making possible good beginnings and good endings. Describing it as a prodigy as early as the second century, the author of the Greek lapidary, *Orphei Lithica*, identifies coral as the greatest marvel of all the beings on earth![69]

5 Monstrous Concepts

The practice of constructing letters of the alphabet out of the forms of plant, animal, or human body parts was widespread in the Middle Ages. Such a practice suggests, in the first place, a view of letters and thus of writing and, further still, of discourse as a whole as having some ontological character; thus the abstract forms that these letters are given in the roman alphabet are distorted into forms derived from animate reality. These representations are inevitably grotesque, the transmogrification of animal to letter, letter to animal, and when they employ the human body, they are often erotic. The grotesque alphabet is an incarnational monster, a putting of flesh upon abstraction, and it demonstrates among other things the Platonic idea of the origin of the material in the conceptual, for it is the "idea" of *A*, *B*, *C*, and other letters that generates the grotesque physical forms assigned to them.

At the same time this deformation of the normal appearance of the letter establishes, like all deformations, a contradiction, a negation, of that which it deforms, presenting a kind of parody of discourse. The transformation of letters of the alphabet into twisted human shapes or contorted animal forms can be seen as a "liberation" of the letter from the restrictions of geometrical lines, a blossoming or evolution into living, moving shapes, which further suggests the liberation from discourse itself through the transcendence of the separation of sign from signified. When the forms that constitute the world become the very signs with which the world is represented, that which is signified and that which signifies it have merged, and the mediation of

Anthropomorphic alphabet. *Les heures de Ch. d'Angoulème*. Paris, Bibliothèque Nationale, Lat. 1173

discourse between the speaker and the thought, the knower and the known, is surmounted.

For centuries the mediaeval monster had dwelt in the margins of the illu-minated manuscript, looking in toward the centre, where writing expressed the message, the reasoning and wisdom of human thought. This very cen-tredness of the written inscription surrounded by margins that were popu-lated by the deformations of teratology suggested the usurpation by intellect of a privilege inappropriate to its powers. Early on, the exile began its invasion of the text through the decorated initial, in which we see an increasing use of cacogenous subjects until, in the fourteenth century, the monster penetrates the centre from the margin by transforming the very symbols of written language into its own deformed discourse as it anamorphizes the alphabet itself.

Baltrusaitis describes certain late thirteenth-century manuscripts in which the ends of lines turn into animal shapes, body parts, and botanical forms. It is probable, as Baltrusaitis claims, that it was the decorating of capital letters in manuscripts that led to the animation of the entire alphabet.[1] This explains the "how" but not the "why" of the phenomenon of the grotesque alphabet. Why, for instance, should the letter *U*, reproduced by Baltrusaitis, spawn a dragon, a sciapode, a blemmye, and a griffin – rather than a flock of natural forms, or geometrical ones, or any other device that would fulfill the desire for decorative extension of the letter?

Other forms were, of course, used, and deformity is by no means the exclusive principle of mediaeval decoration. But so prevalent are grotesque illustrations of capital letters that one might imagine that the mediaeval artist, confronted with the letter – foundation of the word – may have responded with its perfect contradiction – the teramorph, foundation of silence. This contradiction is embodied in the paradox of the deformed letter. Baltrusaitis makes this point in describing the invasion of the central script by the marginal figures of the manuscript, identifying with a striking metaphor the "negative" force of this process: "The margin penetrates the letter, which, reversing its tones, reproduces in a way its negative."[2] It is not, however, the representation of letters of the alphabet as monstrous creatures that is required to create a grotesque alphabet. The deforming of the letter in any way so as to suggest through this dismantling of its formal structure some other, alien form renders the letter – and by extension the alphabet – grotesque. Baltrusaitis describes a charter of Charles V (1380) in which the monarch's name – KAROLUS – is integrated into a scene of the Virgin and Child. The same monogram in another document gives rise to a brood of misshapen monsters.[3] Fully developed animated alphabets appear at the end of the fourteenth century and the beginning of the fifteenth. A work of considerable beauty, the Bergamo alphabet combines human and animal forms as well as teratological figures in a style suggestive of Bosch. It is probably the most complex of animated alphabets. A somewhat later example, the alphabet of Master E.S., intensifies the monstrousness of the letters, at the same time increasing the use of religious themes. In this alphabet the figure of St Christopher, represented as a monster in both legend and iconography, is used to deform no fewer than three of the letters.[4] In the world where all is possible, the sacred is written with monsters. *Ave Maria Gracia Plena* in the manuscript of Israel van Mechenhem is written with plant and animal grotesqueries and unnatural human

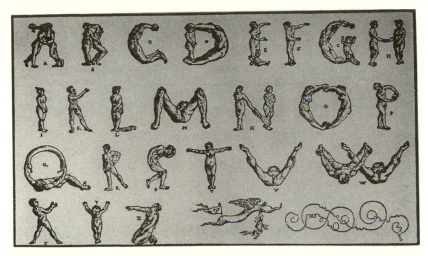

Anthropomorphic alphabet. *Menschenalphabet*. Peter Flettner (Flötner), in Geisberg, *Einblatt-Holzschnitt*, pl. 22

combinations. In the same manuscript, the Incarnation is expressed in signs composed of dragons, griffins, and deformed human bodies.[5]

Interestingly, the postmediaeval continuation of the animated alphabet abandons the monstrosities popular in the Middle Ages in favour of the normal human body. Here the letter as sign is transformed not through replacement by a grotesque form but rather by a normal form in an abnormal posture. The monstrous alphabet of an earlier period deconstructed the very process of signification by creating a surcharge of meaning akin to a kind of discursive hysteria. In normal written signification, sound is represented by a letter and letters are combined to represent words, which in turn represent a meaning. In grotesque writing, each letter functions as a letter and each word as a word, but the process of signification is confused, short-circuited, by the fact that each letter is already a thing – a human body, for instance, in a given posture – and thus the letter, before it is ever connected to the next letter – that is, before the normal signification process has got under way – already communicates some kind of complete meaning, however incoherent. Words made up from these grotesque letters present the same contradiction in exacerbated form; sentences so created result in a hypertrophy of meaning, with one level of meaning being communicated by the word itself and several other wholly foreign meanings being communicated simultaneously by each of the word's letters. The communication of the discursive meaning through grotesque signs does not eliminate or necessarily directly contradict this discursive meaning as such but, rather, negates discourse itself as the sole authoritative form of knowledge and suggests a possibility of limitless meaning, albeit at the cost of logical coherence.

Zoomorphic letter. Zacharias of Besançon, *Concordances*. Douai, fol. 101

For instance, in the van Mechenhem manuscript, the representation of the *M* in the name Maria as a wild man riding a dragon-like monster and a grotesque perched on top of another takes the sign *M* beyond the limits set for it as a letter and a sound, and forces us to read the letter as if it were in itself some kind of narrative. But it is not. The various deformities that make up the first letter of the Virgin's name tell no story, nor is their relation, one to the other, in any way significant; they do not *mean* but rather call attention in a rather mocking way to the very idea of meaning. The grylle that forms the *G* in the word Gracia is composed of nether parts devoured by a dragon – itself part of a human, male figure – and the severed head of a werewolf-like figure. Such a construction obviously transcends the limits of the sound "g." Taken as a whole, the letters also go beyond the word *Gracia* that they

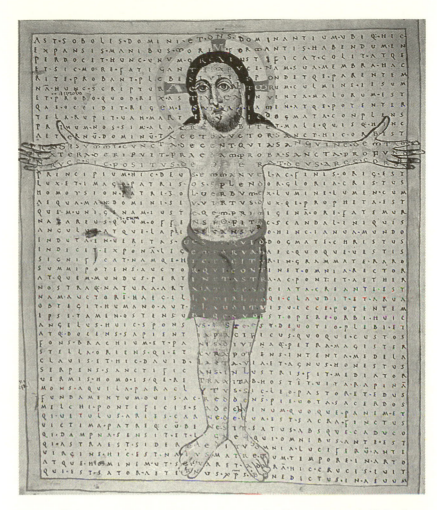

Christ crucified on a field of letters. Rabanus Maurus, *De laudibus sanctae crucis*. National-bibliothek, Vienna

make up, as well as transcending the idea of grace that the word signifies. In their deformed state the letters seem to exist in their own right and as an end in themselves.

But they do not mean. Highly realistic in style, the letters simply play with forms, all the while deforming the original sign. The *r* in *Gracia* is built from the figures of an owl-like grotesque holding a crossbow and a woman whose raised arm is swallowed by a fish to whose tail is attached a dragon. Here the sign, while standing for the sound it represents, also comes into existence in its own right as a scene, a fantasy emerging out of unusual relations between signs. No longer abstracted out of existence as sign, the letter freed, from the limits of form, takes on a whole other function, while continuing to do its job as the letter *r*.

In the animated alphabet the deformation of signs hints at the possibility of the transcendence of the limits of discourse, beyond which resides the union of sign and signified. The frequency of the combination of the monstrous and the sacred in this deformation may be seen to parallel another example of the unification of sign and signified, the person of Christ – sign of God in the world of history and signs, but also God Himself. The eucharist, both sign and reality, becomes the extension of this fundamentally and formally monstrous concept.

PRODIGIOUS NUMBERS

In mediaeval thought the most elemental and originating concept is number. Prior even to form, number is the foundation of reality itself, and an understanding of its science is the closest thing to an understanding of God's mind. The entire Christian, Neoplatonic system of creation through God's going-out and His return to Himself was understood as a mathematically structured system. St Augustine, who contributed heavily to mediaeval number theory, considered number to be inherent in and constituent of form, and the Neoplatonists generally viewed number as, before all else, the original principle:

If you look at something mutable, you cannot grasp it either with the bodily senses or the consideration of the mind, unless it possesses some numerical form. If this form is removed, the mutable dissolves into nothing; do not, then, doubt that there is some eternal and immutable Form which prevents mutable objects from being destroyed and allows them to complete their temporal course, as it were, by measured movements in a distinct variety of forms ... Through eternal Form every temporal thing can receive its form, and, in accordance with its kind, can manifest and embody number in space and time.[6]

If, as is argued here, the mediaeval concept of the monstrous concerns the necessity to deform in order to liberate being from the limits of form and to negate so as to free understanding from the limits of logic, then the relation of number, as origin of form, to the concept of the monstrous is pertinent. An examination of mediaeval number theory reveals that the Middle Ages indeed had a teratology of number.

In a seminal study of the mediaeval language of numbers, Russell A. Peck points out the relation of mediaeval number theory to the Neoplatonic concept of universals and particulars. Number is conceived in the Middle Ages as the fact, the phenomenon, the truth that indisputably exists in and of itself, utterly independent of the human mind. The truth of number never changes, nor is it in any way related to the human context in which it is considered. Peck cites Augustine: "To ascend the path toward Wisdom, we discover that numbers transcend our mind and remain unchangeable in their own."[7] As if anticipating the idea that all we can know are our own verbal representations of reality, Augustine retorts: "If a man comprehends number, it is not changed; yet if he fails to grasp it, its truth does not disappear; rather it remains true and permanent, while man's failure to grasp it is commensurate with the extent of his error."[8]

Number is the basis of all order. Time is sired by number, and it is number that makes possible the physical universe. In its various uses, number would seem to be the foundation of everything that the monstrous seeks to negate through its promotion of disorder, deformity, and transtemporality; but at the heart of the concept of number, just as at the heart of nature, there is revealed a fundamental monstrosity. Peck economically describes the Pythagorean and Platonic ideas of number in which monad and dyad, the male and female of the "species," are considered elemental. All numbers originate in the monad, but odd numbers, especially, share in its nature, while the dyad is seen as more closely related to even numbers. Three, the triad, is viewed as the "progeny" of the monad and the dyad and as the first real number – real in the sense that "1 designates point, 2 designates line, 3 designates space, and 4 designates volume. In the world that our senses tell us is real, we perceive reality only as space and volume."[9]

It is probably in Boethius that we find the fullest expression of the mediaeval concept of number. Derived principally from Nichomachus, the *De Institutione Arithmetica* of Boethius was the single most influential mediaeval treatise on arithmetic and, secondarily, on number theory. Typical of his culture, Boethius conceives of number in ontological terms. He speaks of male and female numbers, of their marriage and procreation, and, importantly, of their virtues and vices. Beauty and ugliness, form and deformity, are for Boethius first and foremost a question of number, but number itself is something that has being:

Boethius, who transmitted the Pythagorean esthetic system to the Middle Ages, could not resist the temptation to pass from mathematics to metaphysics. For if the unit and its derivatives, the odd numbers, are the foundation of identity, indivisibility, simplicity, equality, immutability, massiveness, and virility, duality and the even numbers that derive from it represent the principle of multiplicity, divisibility, composition, infinite variety, fluidity, nimbleness and all that is feminine. Seen in this perspective of the dissolution of quantity into quality, a form is beautiful in so far as opposing characteristics – stability and movement, unity and multiplicity, odd and even, masculinity and femininity – are integrated and harmonized therein in correct, simple proportion.[10]

The mediaeval understanding of number as expressed by Boethius is complex. On the one hand perfect numbers – those that are equal to the sum of their constitutive parts – are "virtuous," just like those men, designated "wise," whose mental and spiritual "numbers" are so ordered as to put them in harmony with the cosmos (it is these who hear the music of the spheres, also a product of number). Perfect numbers are also beautiful, providing further truth about the unity of truth, beauty, and goodness. However, the definition of a perfect number given by Boethius reveals it as an even number:

Between these two kinds of numbers [those whose parts when totaled are less than the number and those whose parts are more], as if between two elements unequal and intemperate, is put a number which holds the middle place between the extremes like one who seeks virtue. That number is called perfect and it does not extend in a superfluous progression nor is it reduced in a contracted reduction, but it maintains the place of the middle; the sum of its parts is not more than the total nor does it suffer from a lack in comparrison with the total, as are 6 and 28 ... Within the first ten numbers there is only one perfect number, 6; within the first hundred, there is 28; within a thousand, 496; within ten thousand, 8,128. These perfect numbers always end in one of two numbers, 6 or 8.[11]

In contrast, odd numbers are somewhat disparaged by Boethius, presumably because, although not all even numbers are perfect, no odd numbers can ever be such. In this view perfection itself seems to be a limiting concept, and it would appear that Boethius and the Middle Ages regarded the lesser and derivative even numbers as representative of the human concepts of virtue and beauty, while admitting that odd numbers, with their origin in the One, are ultimately superior: "There is in these a great similarity to the virtues and vices. You find the perfect numbers rarely, you may enumerate them more easily, and they are produced in a very regular order. But you find superfluous or diminished numbers to be many and infinite and not disposed in any order, but arranged randomly and illogically, not generated from a certain point.[12]

The Middle Ages clearly recognized, however, that the odd numbers, not the even, perfect ones, were of the divine: "God takes joy in the odd numbers."[13] It is also from the ranks of the odd numbers that the monsters emerge. By definition, an odd number is one that has a remainder when divided and, important for its symbolism, one in which the parts add up to something greater than itself or less than itself. It is this excess or deficiency that constitutes the monstrous in the world of numbers, just as in biological nature:

The larger numbers surpass by means of an immoderate plenitude, in terms of the numerosity of parts, the size of their own total bodies; the smaller numbers, as though needy and oppressed by poverty, suffer a certain slight lacking of their nature ... So these numbers, those whose parts added together exceed the total, are seen to be similar to someone who is born with many hands more than nature usually gives, as is the case with a giant who has a hundred hands, or three bodies joined together, such as the triple-formed Geryon. Or this number is like some monstrosity of nature which suddenly appears with a multiplicity of limbs. The other number, whose parts when totaled are less than the size of the entire number, is like one born with some limb missing, or with an eye missing, like the ugliness of the Cyclops' face. Or the number is like one who is born naturally deficient in relation to some member, who emerges short of his total fulness.[14]

It should be noted that Boethius' concept of the monstrous number is directly comparable to Isidore of Seville's idea that two of the indices of monstrosity in nature are superfluity of body parts and deficiency in body parts.[15]

The symbolic system of numbers itself suggests contradiction and becomes a kind of mirror for the principle of paradox that informed mediaeval thinking about being and knowing. God prefers odd numbers, but only even numbers can be perfect. Unnaturalness characterizes these odd numbers that He prefers, virtue and propriety mark the even. And yet, that which cannot be divided – that is, all odd numbers – signifies the indissoluble and the incorruptible.

In terms of signification, it is only through addition and multiplication that the mediaeval exegete arrives at the "meaning" of numbers, not through subtraction or division. The monad plus the dyad produces real number. The first real number, 3, which is male, added to the second real number, the female 4, produces 7, the figure of totality and the basis of the physical world. The multiplication of 3 and 4 (considered "better than" addition) produces 12, the figure of spiritual fullness. It would seem from the various interpretations of number and the procedures by which the interpretations were arrived at that addition and multiplication in the world of number are analogous to the procedures of logic and affirmation in the world of discourse and to divine *editus* in the creation of the cosmos. Indeed, by its movement through discrete units of meaning, linguistic discourse may be seen as analogous to incremental arithmetic. But just as in discourse there is negation and in cognition there is the apophatic mode, so in number there is subtraction and, through the minus, the significance of what is-not. As negation and the transgression it makes possible are the source of the monstrous in the physical world, so in number, subtractive procedure and factorial imperfection are the source of monstrosity in the numeral world.

In numerology, as in all mediaeval allegorical systems, each figure possesses two contradictory significations: just as Venus was a sign of fruitfulness, love, and life in her role as *Venus Genetrix*, as *Venus Fornitrix* she denoted self-indulgence and death. Whereas the number 5 betokens the world and all creation, it is also the first monster in the decade. A deficient being, because its factors add up to less than its "body," 5 is nevertheless a powerful and mysterious digit, because it is the sum of the dyad and the first real number (2+3). Thus it may function as a figure for the legendary incest of Eve (the first female, the dyad) and Cain (the first "real" man – that is, born of woman), the unnatural act that throughout mediaeval tradition was identified as the origin of all biological monsters and the ultimate cause of the Flood. Cain's later bestiality in the land of Nod and that of his descendants may also be suggested by 5, since it is the number directly associated with animality.

Still another monstrous characteristic of the number 5 is its self-generating power, in the sense that it repeats itself in the last digit when multiplied by a kindred odd number ($3 \times 5 = 15$; $5 \times 5 = 25$; $7 \times 5 = 35$) and through addition to the product when multiplied by an even number ($2 \times 5 + 5 = 15$; $4 \times 5 + 5 = 25$; $6 \times 5 + 5 = 35$). In this strange self-duplicating and self-representing power, the number 5 recalls the monstrous dimension of the self-swallowing serpent and, as Russel Peck points out, it anticipates a related monster in the decade, the number 9.

Nine is defective in itself because it is short of 10, the number of completion, unity, and inclusion. It is seen as contradicting 10 by refusing its completion, by just retaining its own rag-tag parts of 4 and 5, which, taken together, symbolize earth, time, space, animality, and imperfection. It is also a monster of deficiency in regard to its factors, since these produce a mere 4 (1+3), well short of its whole. Yet, like 5, this monstrosity lends it power for it, too, reproduces itself endlessly in multiplication, and the sum of the product is also itself ($2 \times 9 = 18$ [$1 + 8 = 9$]; $3 \times 9 = 27$ [$2 + 7 = 9$]; $4 \times 9 = 36$ [$3 + 6 = 9$]; and so on). This self-producing, self-reflexive monster is the last real number and, as such, bears a special relation to the originating monad. Nine is the furthest extension of the monad before it returns and repeats itself and the rest of the decade in 10 (the monad plus 0), 11 (the monad plus itself), and so on. Symbolically the Middle Ages saw 9 as the furthest *editus* of the One before it begins its return, its *reditus*, to the simplicity of self. As such, 9 is the terminus of the multiplying Unity and a mirror in which the monstrous paradox of the One is "shown forth."

The most monstrous of all numbers, however, is found just beyond the decade in the number 11. Just as the dragon grotesquely contains all the elements of biological form, so too the number eleven contains both of the basic elements of numerical monstrosity; it is both deficient and superfluous, the first in falling short of twelve, the second in exceeding ten. Ten and twelve provide important boundaries in number symbolism, and 11, coming before 12, is seen as refusing the rational totality that it represents; as the double of 6, the first perfect number, 12 is the multiplication of perfection; 12 is completion, being the product of 3, the spiritual form, and 4, the material universe. Falling short, 11 is seen to defy this completion. At the same time, 11 is a transgression of 10, the sign of unity; it defers the closure that 10 proposes, the closure of affirmation. If the decade is the fullness of the extension of the monad, its going out from its own simplicity and unity to greater and greater multiplicity, then 10 is the completion of its voyage. Thus, in analogy with the neoplatonic theory of God's *editus* into Creation, 10 rightly signifies the complete, the finished. The further analogy is to affirmative discourse, the language appropriate to *editus*. If the intellect stops its search with the understanding of the created universe, it limits its understanding to matter, to the affirmations of logic and language, or, metaphorically speaking, to the decade.

The monster 11 represents the *reditus*, God's return to Himself (where He always remains), the soul's return to God, multiplicity's return to simplicity, the return of language to silence. In the decade 11 is the return of 1 into itself. It is the very possibility of 12, but deferred, a fullness created by the transgression of the limits of 10. Like so many monsters of the physical world of nature, 11 is a transitional being providing a bridge between one rational category (here represented by even digits) and another. Figurally, 11 is the reduplication of the character 1. Symbolically, the monster of simultaneous superfluity and deficiency emerges as the perfect representation of the One.

It is interesting that in gematrics, the equating of numbers with letters and vice versa, the Greek word for monster, *teras* (τερας), produces 606, which mediaeval number symbolism would have analyzed as: the first perfect number (6) raised to the centile (600) and added to itself (+6). The Latin word for monster, *monstrum*, yields 1200 gematrically: the two perfect 6s of the Greek gematria added together and raised to the centile.

PART THREE

Texts

Christopher carrying Christ and the world. Rome, Fresco,
San Clemente.

6 Three Heroes

ALEXANDER

In the various stories of Alexander the Great, we see one of the original Western models of the epic hero. From this series of narratives concerning the Macedonian world-conqueror flows the worldview in which the mighty win and hold dominion over all peoples and every continent, a power justified by concepts and values that are the underpinnings of the saga of Alexander the Great.

The original Greek version of *The Life of Alexander*, known as the Pseudo-Callisthenes, is contained in three manuscripts, each recounting the same basic story but with important variations regarding certain episodes. Several Latin versions descending from the Pseudo-Callisthenes and other Greek renditions carried the story over to the Middle Ages, expanding it in several ways.[1] The numerous mediaeval versions descend from these adaptations of Pseudo-Callisthenes and take several forms: vitae, romances, letters, histories, courtesy books, and encyclopedic entries. The story of Alexander is found in practically every genre of mediaeval literature.[2]

Although established early on as a cultural trope, the Alexander theme experienced a resurgence of popularity in the twelfth century. The character of Alexander and his exploits served as model and authority for the heroic personifications of Western culture, such as Charlemagne, Roland, and Orlando – all of whom are to some degree versions of Alexander the Great. Others, indirectly related to the Greek hero, reflect the archetypal heroic elements of his character and circumstance.[3]

Alexander's parentage is confused. The illegitimate offspring of an Egyptian mage, the young Alexander himself believes he is the son of King Philip of Macedonia. Olympias, his mother, had been seduced by the Egyptian's magic into believing that she was visited and impregnated by the god Ammon (the Egyptian Zeus), and throughout the narratives Alexander is identified as having been sired by this horned, ram-headed monstrous divinity. Alexander's birth is accompanied by wondrous, unnatural cosmic events, and the child himself is physically deformed: he is unnaturally small, has the mane of a lion, and his pointed, sharp teeth are compared to the tusks of a beast. But it is the eyes that are the strongest index of Alexander's monstrosity: one is blue, the other black and heavily lidded. Out of both shines an eerie light making his eyes like fiery stars, and reminding us, perhaps, of the hallmark of the monsters of mixed human and divine natures descended from Cain according to mediaeval exegetical legend.[4]

The significance of Alexander's particoloured eyes is related to the ancient worldwide tradition of the "evil eye." Often independent of the will of the possessor, the "evil eye" destroys whatever falls under its withering glance, spewing out an invisible poison liquid, whence the Italian *jettature* or *gettature*. It is the organ of desire, but a desire out of control, insatiable and perilous. Those who possess the "evil eye" are quickly identified, since they are all in some way deformed: "All those among the ancients who in any way surpassed conspicuously the common standard, as, for instance, in athletic or physical strength or size, were dreaded as possessors; on the other hand, anyone specially defective, particularly a dwarf; the latter, if hunchbacked, was dreaded still more. Squinting or differently coloured eyes were always certain marks of what is now a *jettature*."[5]

Just as it functions as the symbol of desire, the "evil eye" is also the sign of death, for only in death is its longing satisfied and its searching light extinguished. This is precisely the role played by Alexander's eyes in the saga; they signify his persistent yearning to see, to know, and to possess as his political ambition carries him from one military conquest to another. As is made plain in the episode known as the *Iter ad paradisum*.[6]

Alexander is as prodigious intellectually as he is physically, thus justifying the extravagance of having Aristotle as his principal tutor. This element of the story is structurally important because it makes possible the narration of many of the hero's adventures in the form of letters addressed to his teacher, Aristotle. The epistolary form constitutes large portions of the various texts for, in addition to the correspondence with Aristotle, there are letters to and from Olympias and between the hero and his royal opponents. *The Letter to Aristotle*, a text exchanged between the mightiest in physical prowess and the mightiest in intellect, was sufficiently stimulating to the mediaeval imagination that it detached itself from the longer saga and took on an independent existence.

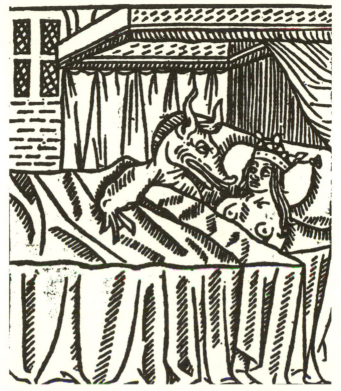

Siring of Alexander. *Alixandre le Grant*. Paris: Michel le Noir, 1506.
Fol. Bii

Prominent throughout the narratives is Alexander's relation with his father
and various father-figures. In an early episode Alexander attacks Nectanebo,
his biological sire, for no apparent reason and thus becomes a parricide when
Nectanebo perishes after revealing the secret of his paternity.[7] In a later scene,
Alexander attacks Philip, his legal father, and menaces him because he has
taken another wife. He renounces Philip as father, while offering him "friend-
ship." Curiously, one of Alexander's principal enemies, Darius of Persia,
addresses him as "son," and, like a son, Alexander carries him to his funeral
pyre on his shoulders, according to the customs of the time, just as he had carried the cadaver of Nectanebo. The text describes him as "inheriting" Darius'
realm, rather than as having conquered it. Alexander the Great appears to be
constantly in search of a father, repeatedly killing fathers and surrogates and
carrying them to their pyres with filial duty.

From the moment of his first exploit at the age of twelve, Alexander is a
figure of action, a maker of history and shaper of the world. This dynamism
is most clearly seen in the text through his expansion of the Macedonian

empire, an expansion marked and symbolized by Alexander's founding and construction of cities. The text of Pseudo-Callisthenes ends with a litany of names of Alexander's triumphs commemorated in the names of cities: "And he built twelve cities which still remain today, rich and complete and populated by countless people: Alexandria, which he built on the bullheaded horse; Alexandria Kattison; the Alexandria for Poros; Alexandria of Undranikos; Alexandria of Scythia; Alexandria of Mesopotamia; Alexandria on the Dklat River; Alexandria of Babylon; Alexandria of Troy; Alexandria at Massagyrs; Alexandria near Xanthos, and Alexandria near Egypt."[8]

The fact that Alexander has named all his constructs after himself emphasizes the nature of his exploits as self-affirmation and, even more specifically, as a projection of self into time and space in order to create the world and its history and, in so doing, repeatedly to create the self anew. The hero is quite conscious of this intention, as is the author of the *Wars of Alexander*, and Alexander's instructions to the carpenters for the building of Alexandria are explicit:

> Then he called for carpenters, commanded them swiftly
> To build a city as a memorial to himself,
> And he names it with his own name that never since changed,
> But Alexander forever, after himself.[9]

At the same time that the text presents Alexander as the builder, inaugurator, and fashioner of the world, it also portrays him in an even more fundamental way as destroyer, as a force for pulling down what human ingenuity has built up. This occurs in two ways: through the recounting and depiction of the champion's defeat of his enemies and his levelling of their cities, and through Alexander's own exegesis on the narrative of his acts. Both ways are seen when the gates of the great city of Thebes are closed to Alexander: "And the advancing Macedonian hand did not tire of intoxicating the slaying sword with blood."[10] The seven gates of the world's most renowned city are cast down, the walls demolished, and all its buildings razed. While this dismantling is taking place, a Theban poet recites to Alexander the story of Thebes in the hope that the city's glorious history and the rhetorical splendor of his discourse on it may convince Alexander of Thebes' incomparable value. Thus the poet-historian Ismenias, "a man wise in speech," recites the city's saga in order "to offer the great man moralizing song and sweet speech."[11]

In his history of Thebes, Ismenias affirms the famous deeds and the prestige of such figures as Heracles and Dionysos, Cadmos, Acteon, and – most emphasized of all – Oedipus. This is the "official" history of the foundation of Western civilization and the mythological representation of origins that the Middle Ages knew and accepted. But far from being mollified, Alexander is offended by this affirmative version of history, and he retorts with a negative reading of the same events. The justification of his destruction of the city is articulated in the conqueror's long denunciation of Theban glory and Ismenias' misuse of rhetoric to create desired meaning: "What are these fairy tales? You most evil offspring of the race of Cadmus, wild and wicked offshoot of a wretched stock ... Did you mean to beguile Alexander by recounting these artful fabrications? I shall still devastate this entire city; I shall ravage it by fire; I shall turn to ashes the roots of those ancestors."[12]

Alexander the builder, the affirmer and sustainer of the worldview of the West, is also Alexander the destroyer, the negator and reviser of this tradition. The same negative analysis is found in Alexander's treatment of Athenian history. He gives a negative reading of the biography of the glorious Athenians by emphasizing incidents that the official tradition minimizes: "You shut up Euclides in prison ... you vilified Alcibiades ... Socrates ... you slew."[13] Alexander is particularly suspicious of texts, not only of the verbal rhetorical texts such as that of Ismenias in praise of Thebes but even of the written texts of Homer. The warrior goes so far as to suggest that the epic dimensions and heroic glory of Greece were more a product of the power of words than of heroes' deeds: "And he entered the very city of Ilion itself and sacrificed to Hector and to Achilles and to the other heroes. And when he saw the Skamondros River across which Achilles had leaped, and that its width was not five paces, and the seven-skinned shield of Eandos, and that it was not very big nor as wonderful and amazing as Homer had described, Alexander said: 'Fortunate are you who happened upon a minstrel such as Homer. For such as you were, you passed into his work and were inscribed among the great; although in actual fact you fell short.' "[14]

Such a critique suggests not only the possible pretence of the Greek heroes but, by extension, the fraudulence of mimesis itself, since Homer is here described as one who, being unable to imitate a reality that did not exist, invented it.

For his part, Alexander refuses the Greek poets' offer to record his own exploits in heroic verse, for the Macedonian hero claims to have no need of textual authority – a delightful irony for the reader of *The Romance*, a text purporting to be written by Callisthenes, who accompanied Alexander on his exploits. The monstrous eyes of this deformed hero, he seems to claim, read the world at a level beyond that of human rhetoric, comprehending the metalanguage of anagogy that transcends apparent meaning by negating it. But other elements of the text suggest that Alexander ultimately stops short of this transcendence, shying away from the *via negativa* and merely substituting his own rhetoric and his own anthropology for those of others. Both in *The Romance* of Pseudo-Callisthenes and in the mediaeval *Wars of Alexander*, the text seems to suggest a natural division of structure into books or sections. The narrative covers three periods: the first section recounts

Alexander's birth, youth, and education, along with his early exploits up to his destruction of Thebes; the second section is constituted by the hero's arrival in Athens and concludes with his defeat of the great Emperor Darius, his marriage to the Emperor's daughter, Roxianne, and Alexander's own long summary of deeds; the third section begins with Alexander's invasion of India and recounts his war with Poros, his final victory, and his death.

The Sk'andar's encounter with the monsters occurs in the central book and is described by Alexander in a letter to his mother. Coming at the conclusion of part 2, the monsters form a bridge to the concluding section, in which the saga of Alexander and the monsters is continued. Thus, it is at the pinnacle of his success, at the very moment when he has achieved the longed-for name of "King of Kings," when he has extended his control of the world to its penultimate point, that the hero encounters a reality that he cannot control or contain and that gives the lie to his totalizing naming and controlling.

Not satisfied with ruling the Mediterranean and "the whole Persian world which Darius, the great, ruled," Alexander turns his eyes beyond the known world toward the wasteland that lies beyond it. There, at the furthest reaches of India, at the edge of the "real" world, Alexander confronts the Plantings, slender giants with long, swan-like necks. Although he slays many, he can capture none. The Oxoli, whom he next encounters, are red giants whose hair flows out in a fan shape, six feet long. Sk'andar also fails to capture any of them. Fleas as big as turtles, hairy, barking men, invisible monsters and disappearing trees, fire breathing fowl – one prodigy after another – elude the control of the world-conqueror.

Many-limbed, multi-eyed beasts abound in the vicinity of the headless men, blemmyes with faces on their chests. Although his soldiers plead with the King of Kings to turn back, he persists because he "wished to see the end of that land."[15] But the locus of the monsters, like Alexander's own quest, has no end. The warrior has been told twice in oracles that he will never return home but will die young, before the conclusion of his adventures. The hero's quest for containment, finality, and for meaning through closure – the Macedonian's struggle "to get to the end of the world" – is reversed in his passage through the land of the monsters, where he is unable to conquer and possess a single race, where the kind of rational control he seeks is utterly elusive: "And when we advanced fifteen miles, two birds with human faces met us, and they were larger than our birds at home. And they were crying from above in Greek: 'Why do you tread the earth looking for the home of the gods? For, you are not able to set foot in the Blessed Islands of the skies. Why do you struggle to rise to heaven, which is not within your power?' "[16]

The question posed by these monsters hints at an association between Alexander's quest in the land of the monsters and the later Babelonian project "to rise to heaven." Various biblical tropes of power seem to reinforce the idea of reckless arrogance so often found in scriptural stories, beginning with the defiant building of the tower of Babel. Directly after this encounter with the avian monsters, Alexander slays his last and greatest opponent in a scene of single combat highly reminiscent of the battle of David and Goliath. Like the Philistine, the last of Cain's monstrous descendants, Poros of India is also a giant. All the versions emphasize Alexander's smallness and juxtapose it to Poros' height, the one measuring approximately four feet, the other approximately eight: "Thre cubettis fra þe croune doun his cors had a lenghte. / Þe person of ser Porrus past him þat hiȝt twyse."[17]

Immediately after his defeat of this foe, the occasion of his ultimate victory, Alexander goes to meet the gymnosophists,[18] an episode of crucial importance in the story and the subject of the "spin-off" texts such as *The Letter of Alexander to Aristotle* and the Brahman episodes of Paladius and of St Ambrose. Like all heroes, Alexander faces not only physical challenges but intellectual challenges as well. It is to be recalled that the famous Gordian knot, dedicated to Zeus and described by an oracle as the knot to be "unravelled" by the future ruler of Asia, is not, in fact, ever unravelled – that is to say, the hero does not attain the wisdom signified by the undoing of the knot – rather, the knot is petulantly cut in half with the conqueror's sword by the wrathful Alexander. Another form of the Gordian knot is presented to Sk'ander by those skilled in posing conundrums, the Brahmans.

This crucial encounter is constructed through a set of questions posed by Alexander and answered by the "Naked Wise." Just as these questions arise out of Alexander's experience of the world, the answers he receives constitute cumulative denials of the worldview that the hero assumes and pursues. In the Greek versions Alexander is said to have packed up all his gold and silver and precious possessions to bring to these hermits who pride themselves on possessing nothing and who underscore the irony of Alexander's lack of understanding by taunting him with a conundrum: if you conquer us, you conquer nothing, because we possess nothing, assert nothing, are nothing. The entire episode of the Brahmans is composed from the point of view of negation, and Alexander, himself a composite of affirmation and negation, construction and destruction, fails the test of unifying the contraries.

To Alexander's peculiar opening question, "Do you not have graves?" the Brahman responds with paradox: "This place we live in is my grave."[19] Because the Oxydrakes in fact make their dwelling in underground caves, the answer is comprehensible on the literal level, but it provocatively recalls Serapis' prophesy concerning Alexander's demise and initiates a dynamic of similitude/dissimilitude between the hero and the philosophers: "For you shall dwell there both when you are dead and when not yet dead; for this city you are building is to be your grave."[20] Thus the hole in the ground, symbol of death, is where the Brahman "lives," a trope that joins the contraries of life and death and resolves the opposition between growth and decay.

Alexander's exploits reinforce the opposition: his constructs are a building up of material monuments to immortalize his name, and his extension of his control of the world is a means of overcoming death by denying it. The way in which the Brahman's grave is his dwelling is the ironic opposite of the way in which Alexander's dwelling is his grave. Indeed, the fundamental contrast between Alexander and the Gymnosophists is in desire: Sk'andar flees death by keeping desire alive; the Naked Wise, who have achieved the state of *apathia*, have thereby conquered both desire and death at one stroke. This difference is clear in Alexander's retort.

Armand Abel, whose study of the Alexander sagas ranges from the Pseudo-Callisthenes through all the mediaeval versions, has pointed out that the encounter with the Brahmans falls exactly in the middle of Alexander's confrontation with the monsters and that these Naked Wise are physically located at the exact centre of the monstrous lands traversed by Alexander. Seeing it as a kind of relief from the fantastic "foolishness" of the passages on the monsters, Abel describes this literary device as a sort of counterpoint to that which surrounds it: "A welcome relief interrupts, at last, this succession of extra-human adventures: crossing an island discovered along the banks of the river, the Greeks encounter the Oxydrakes or Brahmans, a wise and virtuous people with whom Alexander and his men engage in long and pleasant discussions."[21]

Rather than providing a deliverance from the ridiculous and meaningless episodes involving "foolish" monsters, the philosophical exchange with the Brahmans may be seen both in its content and in its strategic structural position in the composition as the theoretical centre of the text for which the monstrous deformations provide the necessary exegesis. Like the mediaeval manuscript with its discursive message occupying the middle of the parchment, surrounded by the grotesque visual commentary of the decorated borders, the Alexander narrative is structured so as to comment upon its own meaning through a monstrous bracketing of the central scene.

The English *Wars* is doubly apophatic, establishing two negative poles of discourse – the encounter with the giant, Poros, and the penetration of the land of the monsters – between which falls Alexander's physical and intellectual encounter with the deformed. Everything that Sk'andar has affirmed to this point through word and action is negated by the Naked Wise,

> Since we have joy *neither* in gems *nor* in jewels,
> *Nor* furs, *nor* stones, *nor* pearls, *nor* have we beautiful clothes,
> *Nothing* except what is sustained by our own simple crafts.[22]

Crossing the dark desert, Alexander and his men meet with warrior women, dragons, a monstrous sea bull, bearded women, amphibious people, and, after a storm in which the sky rains fire upon them, they reach the

Ganges and the land of the Brahmans. Alexander's letter to Didymus, the Brahman King, and his subjects introduces Alexander as "King of Kings" and specifies that his interest in the Brahmans is sparked by their very *difference* from all other men and from himself,[23] and, he further specifies, it is knowledge and understanding of this difference that he seeks. Didymus obliges with a response that echoes the method of the *via negativa* of Pseudo-Dionysian apophasis:

> We *do not* keep horses, we *do not* plow, *neither* have we oxen,
> *Nor* do we turn the earth, we *do not* plant,
> We *do not* seek sustenance to keep alive.
> We *do not* cast nets, we *do not* fish at all,
> *Neither* do we hunt *nor* hawk, we *do not* take birds,
> But seek what grows in the ground without man's interference.
> We eat that and fill our tables with it,
> For we *do not* desire dainties.
> We *do not* need cures, we *do not* have rich stews.[24]

Didymus goes on to enunciate a long series of negations, ninety lines of them, in all: the gymnosophists do not overeat, they do not have a science of medicine, they do not use fire, and do not accept any technology. They do not build, and they do not seek "knowing." In summary, Didymus' apophatic declaration identifies the Naked Wise as rejecting civilization in all its manifestations:

> We *do not* read rhetoric, we *do not* complicate language;
> But in complete simplicity we order our words,
> So that *never* from our lips spring lies.
> We *do not* follow theorists *nor* any school of philosophy,
> Such as sophistry and the like to befuddle the people.[25]

The Brahmans, then, reject learning as acquisition, as well as all other ambitions of the human intellect. Instead, their way is a rigorous application of the *via negativa*. The scene of the encounter with the Brahmans proceeds in almost dialectical fashion, with the Brahmans supplying the necessary negations to Alexander's version of the *via positiva*, a version that condemns all negativity as weakness and passivity. King Didymus has offended Alexander not only by his own "difference" but by his direct condemnation of Alexander's way of life and way of understanding. Alexander's violence and covetousness, says the Brahman, has blotted out the light of the sun. What has been presented up to this point in the text as Alexander's heroism is now described in highly negative terms as the madness of war, the killing of children, and unquenchable cupidity. He builds, he makes, he produces images and signs, and in every manner imposes himself upon the world. Nor are the hero's intellectual affirmation and physical aggression a lapse; they are the result of his worldview, and Alexander defends himself: "And even if I wished to stop making war, the master of my behaviour would not let me. For, if we all behaved the same way, the world would be idle and empty. There would be no navigation on the ocean; houses would not be built; marriages would not be consummated; there would be no children born. For a great many men have been ruined by my wars and have lost all their possessions; yet others have become prosperous on the riches of others. For all men grasp at everything, and in turn we leave it all behind to others; and there is nothing (permanent) anywhere."[26]

The defense is one that is characteristic of the mentality of progress, and it enjoins many of the values of occidental society, such as the superiority of the dynamic, the privileging of change, and the trick of turning mutability to profit. In the English version, Alexander's response is even more aggressive:

> All this I call living like beasts
> Which have no intellect nor any joy in the good.
> But we who have form and substance & free will,
> Differ in our qualities and are far from your kind.[27]

Alexander portrays "his kind" as free because they change, moral because they choose – regardless of the nature of the change, regardless of the consequences of the choice. Western man develops his five wits, Alexander claims, for freedom consists in doing *everything possible*.[28] Sk'andars' ultimate rejection of the Naked Wise – and, along with it, of the *via negativa* they espouse – is most decisively expressed in the self-assertion of his construction of a pillar of marble in the land of the Brahmans on which he orders inscribed in both Latin and the 'letters of India',

> I, son of Philip the Great, founder of Greece,
> Alexander the Noble, ruler of the barbarians
> Since the death of Darius and Porus.
> Thus far have I pursued my foes![29]

The contradiction inherent in Alexander's saga and in the nature of the hero himself – his building up and tearing down – is drawn out and brought to the foreground in the text through his encounter with the monsters, and the hero's dialogue with the contemplative Didymus functions as a sort of philosophical commentary on these encounters with the grotesque. Directly after an oracle has told him that he will never return to Macedonia but refuses him details of his approaching death, Alexander encounters a horde of griffins that attack his army and cause extensive harm; these creatures are grotesque in the extreme:

Then they came to a place of perilous beasts
With cloven claws like the hoofs of hogs.
They were thick and heavy, three foot across,
And they fought with them and killed knights,
They were quick as a flash, burly and grim.
Each had a boar's head full of fierce tusks
Which formed their front, but behind they seemed
Like a leopard and a lion both, with tails
And there was a flock of vultures and of griffins among them
that flapped in the faces of our soldiers.[30]

From these monsters, who tear men out of their saddles and carry them away as prey, Alexander and his army barely escape to continue their journey to the end of the world. But further obstacles are immediately encountered: women ten feet tall with hair to their feet inhabit a great river where they keep watch for sailors:

Dwelling in these waters were creatures like women
Who were pretty of face but with hair to their heels.
Any man who strayed there or sailed by their shores
They dragged down into the deep and drowned them forever,
Or else they lured them into the woods where, as the book says,
They used them for their pleasure so long that the men expired.[31]

Alexander's explorations beyond the civilized world have brought him into a reality that eludes his governance and his understanding. Just as he himself embodies the contradictions of builder and destroyer, big and small, understanding and misunderstanding, so the beings he encounters as he approaches the end of the earth are composed of analogous contradictions – a bird-lion, a fish-woman, and other such grotesque unions. The monsters function not only narratively and didactically to teach Alexander that conquest is not the highest value but, far more importantly, to provide for this prince of princes a "cognitive" mirror in which his own monstrosity is made manifest. What eludes Alexander on the field of battle in the land of the monsters is what in the Brahman episode eludes him on the terrain of the intellect – the nature of paradox. Paradox, as it appears in the Alexander legend, is the true *end of the world*, that is, the beginning of the real and the discovery of the self .

At the physical limits of the known world, Alexander finds only ocean and sky. Not satisfied with having reached the goal of his journey, Sk'andar conceives what the English text calls a "foolish fantasy": having marched to the ends of the earth, he will now rise to heights of the heavens. With griffins attached to his throne, Alexander rises up beyond the limits set for man:

Alexander ascends to the sky. *Alixandre le Grant*. Paris: Michel Noir, 1506.
Fol. Kii

"So high in the heavens they bore him up that in an instant / Earth, like a
millstone, appeared to him."[32]

While the text suggests that Alexander has transcended even the limits of
nature through his boldness and wit, and perhaps, as well, that he has gained
moral perspective as he gazes down upon the littleness of the earth he has
conquered, another, quite contradictory and negative reading is made possible by the presence in the text of what might be called apophatic "hints":
the description of the world as a "millstone" inevitably echoes the Biblical
menace against whoever shall give scandal: "it were better for him that a
millstone were hung about his neck, and that he were drowned in the depths
of the sea" (Matt. 18:6). Not only does the allusion suggest Alexander's possession of the world as a scandal and remind us of the punishment for such
transgressions, but it anticipates his next exploit in which, paralleling his rise
to the heavens, he descends to the bottom of the sea.

The second apophatic hint arises from a certain insistence on the detail
that the author supplies concerning the hero's contrivance: with pieces of

liver on the ends of hooks as bait, the power of the monsters is harnessed to bring the quester to God. The nature of the project as well as its technology is likely to have reminded the mediaeval audience, and others, of the exploits of Daedalus, and therein lies the second hint.

In the same line that describes transcendence, perception, and union with God, there is simultaneously expressed a bathos that utterly demolishes the emerging mystical sense of the text. Having risen to the "highest heavens," Alexander and his whole ridiculous contraption is, like Daedalus, dumped to the ground: "The power of the Very God surrounded him for an instant, / And then they fell in a field far from the army."[33]

Balancing the description of this feat as a "foolish fantasy," Alexander's next and last exploit – diving to the depths of the sea – is called a "wondirfull witt," a strange, or even monstrous, conception.[34] With the same concern for detail, the author describes the glass box strapped with iron in which Alexander is lowered into the depths:

> Then he had men go and make him a barrel
> Of green glittering glass all girded with iron,
> So he could sit therein and see the sights,
> One, another, and all the things that lived outside it.[35]

Alexander declares that in searching out the depths of the sea his intention is to discover the marvels and strange creatures that he hopes live there. He is not disappointed, for at the bottom of the sea, just as at the end of the world, the locus of the deformed is attained:

> There he saw shapes of fishes and forms diverse
> Of so many unknown kinds and unlikely hues.
> Some like land beasts went on all fours,
> But fled as fast when they spied this fellow.
> And other marvels he saw, more than he wished,
> That were so strange as to exceed man's understanding.[36]

Thus it would seem that at the extremities of all physical realms and on their margins resides the monster, that deformed version of the being that occupies the centre. Alexander, the conqueror of the "known" world, discovers at the outer limits of land and sea the unknown and the uncontrollable, which is the monstrous. His discovery at the limits of the sky, "the verray god," is by extension the unknown, the uncontrollable, the monster. At the end of every direction of space – upward, downward, and across – lurks the paradoxical being who cancels out the hero's quest as well as the physical space in which that quest occurs and who obliterates the hero's very identity by merging with him in a union that negates all identity and all separation.

Armand Abel finds that the heaven-and-sea adventures illustrate more clearly than other episodes the intention of the text to valorize human curiosity and to authorize intellectual confidence. Moreover, claims Abel, these feats constitute a kind of challenge to God's omnipotence: "We have demonstrated how the Roman mentality, from its Judeo-Byzantine origins up to its modification by Arab influence, is utterly dominated by fear of the divinity, by aversion to everything that is beyond human measure. This mentality is particularly manifest in the treatment of the two episodes of [Alexander's] descent to the bottom of the sea and [his] ascent into the heavens."[37]

This timidity in face of the divine dimension of nature, so evident in early versions of the Alexander saga, had quite disappeared by the thirteenth century when, bolstered by the growing domination of the affirmative sciences of logic and dialectic, confidence in the definitive powers of the human intellect swelled sufficiently to anticipate, at least faintly, thinks Abel, the full-blown "humanism" of the Renaissance: "The curiosity of a courageous man is satisfied, without any cost or inconvenience to him! We find ourselves here far from the impious temerity of the Byzantine Alexander who, all alone, makes three attempts at his audacious undertaking until Leviathan himself carries him back in his terrifying maw to the river's banks. The spirit of the thirteenth century has already begun to look favourably on that lust to know that will characterize the Renaissance when the fear of transgression will no longer hinder the harvest of the delicious fruits of science."[38]

This is the affirmative reading *par excellence* of a text that, despite Professor Abel's ability to find sweet fruits, contains a large dose of bitter dregs for those committed to the anthropocentric. The Daedalus echo, one of the apophatic hints in this episode, was not regarded in the Middle Ages as a romantic example of courageous daring, but rather as a lesson against the vanity and arrogance of overconfident and misdirected intellect; thus it was a homily on pride. Alexander's feat immediately invites comparison not only with Daedalus' catastrophic undertaking but with the similar and more overtly sacrilegious storming of heaven by the giants in their war against Jove. Considered by the Middle Ages as the distorted pagan versions of the same accounts found in Scripture (Genesis 6:4), such associations ultimately summon the trope of the Tower of Babel and introduce it, once again, into the narrative of the Alexander legend.

The Alexander-Daedalus association seems more than casual. It is Daedalus, the archetype builder and sculptor, who in Greek mythology forms and fashions many of the most significant constructions. Daedalus it is who builds the labyrinth for Minos, and it is Daedalus, too, who constructs the wooden cow for Pasiphae to conceive the Minotaur. His name means "cunningly wrought," and to him is attributed the invention of the tools of carpentry and construction. Most significant, perhaps, it is Daedalus who first anthropomorphizes the gods by fashioning human limbs of bronze and fixing them to the previously amorphous representations of the divinities. In his best known exploit, his ascent to the One, Simple, Unknowable is, like Alexander's, achieved through a multiplication of complicated devices and technologies: in both cases, it is all a vaguely embarrassing matter of feathers, hooks, and contraptions.

Moreover, the association of Alexander with still another archetypal builder is also established in this episode and helps to advance the negative reading. Alexander's incessant constructing of pillars, monuments, thrones, and cities, echoes the Scriptural version of the origin of such enterprises in which Cain and his descendants introduce building into the world. After the city of Enoch, the most infamous of Biblical cities is Babylon with its tower, founded by Nimrod, a monstrous descendant of Cain. The city is the symbol of war, weaponry, and bloodshed, while the tower itself, as we have seen, symbolizes defiance of God and the fragmentation of human discourse through the division of language into many incomprehensible tongues. Alexander's marble pillar, on which he inscribes his name in many languages, finds its certain archetype in the Babylonians' tower, erected so as to "make us a name" (Genesis 11:4). The Macedonian's attempt to explore the depths of the sea and heights of the heavens may also be compared to the Babylonians' attempt to storm heaven, and the comparison is enhanced by the presence in both of the monstrous: the identification of Babylon and the fallen tower as the origin of all monstrous deformities and Alexander's encounter with them at the furthest limits of the world.

The most compelling association between Alexander's ascent and descent and the tower of Babel is, however, the text's description of the hero's last adventure. Directly after emerging from his plunge to the bottom of the sea, Alexander attacks and conquers his last city, Babylon. Here, according to the English alliterative poem, Alexander contrives a final monument to himself, a throne in the middle of Babylon made of solid gold, twelve cubits high, accessible by twelve steps; twelve strange images support the structure. Twelve, the number of completion, even and affirmative, is the key factor of the King of King's celebration of the self. All over the throne in numerous languages are inscribed names: names of vassals, names of provinces, names of countries, the names of all that Alexander has conquered and controls. *The Wars of Alexander* concludes with a litany of the names of over sixty countries vanquished by Alexander the Great.[39]

Sk'andar, fated never to return home, dies in Babylon where, in a symbolic sense, he has always lived amid the rubble and babble of human affirmation. His throne, erected in the very place where human understanding lost its simple unity, where sign was severed from signified, is a cataphatic riot of names and naming, defaced, like some already abandoned monument to absent glory, by a kind of royal graffiti declaring for all of Western history the origin of its hegemony.

The monstrous typology appears at crucial moments in the narrative: at Alexander's birth, at each pronouncement of an oracle, at the hero's arrival at the end of the known world, and finally at the end of Alexander's life. Most versions of the saga preserve the episode of the hero's death omen: a Babylonian woman gives birth to a monster (who in one version has been sired by Alexander himself), a child whose nether part is a swarm of grotesque shapes: "When one of the local women gave birth to a child, the upper part of its body, as far as the navel, was completely human and according to nature, but the lower extremities were those of a wild beast. And its general appearance was like that of Scylla except that it differed in the kinds of animals and in the great number of them. For there were the shapes of leopards and lions, wolves and wild boars and dogs. And these forms moved, and each was clearly recognizable to all."[40]

On the surface level, it is clear that this omen betokens Alexander's immanent death, and the chief magus confirms this when, through the skill of his science, he has read the message encoded within the twisted forms: "So just as it has left its living state, so have you too departed to those who are no more."[41]. But there is still another message contained within the monster, one that goes beyond the prophesy of future narrative events and directly to the heart of the negative meaning of the text: this monster, like so many others, is a deformity of superfluity, a union contradicting all the boundaries of nature and human science.[42] In the first place, it joins life and death in a single, grotesque being. In order to interpret this teratological text, the magus separates it into two parts, declaring that the lower, living, animal part represents Alexander's army, and the dead torso the great army's leader himself, thus signifying Alexander's demise. It also joins stasis and motion, for while the dead child is still, its deformed lower part is constantly moving. It unites the many and the one, one human form and several animal forms. It further binds two natures, human and animal, a fundamental composition of the grotesque.

While the exegete has separated the monster in two, dividing signs and meanings in order to produce a discursive reading, the truth of the monstrosity is exactly in the union of what is not unifiable and in the indivisibility of distinct things. When the omen reader says, "O bravest of all men, you are the human body, and the wild animal forms are the soldiers who are with you,"[43] he normalizes and "re-forms" the abnormal, deformed text that he has been assigned to interpret and thereby produces an affirmative reading, one that advances the narrative and leads the text toward conventional closure.

But another, negative reading inheres. What the monster (who, as his son, is an extension of Alexander himself) reveals is not principally the chronological fact of Alexander's demise, but rather Alexander's own monstrosity: the King of Kings is the monster he beholds. Just as Alexander and his army are one in the tumult of battle and the bloodbath of history, so the monster correctly joins the dead human form to the squirming, inhuman parts below it. The dog-heads, mermaids, dragons, griffins, and other monsters that eluded Sk'andar both physically and intellectually in his march to the end of the world are here recalled in this new monster, which provides Alexander with another chance for fuller understanding, if only he can surpass his exegete's logical exposition of the text. Just as the gymnosophists urged Alexander to embrace paradox through the negations that they welded to his affirmations, so now in the shocking epiphany of the monstrous Babylonian birth, the world conqueror is invited to look upon and understand the nature of paradox and to discover therein his own identity and the reality he has so long pursued.

That he has, in fact, finally embraced his own paradox and the monstrosity of the real may be signified in Alexander's negative description of his heroic quest when he prays to his god for assistance in his *reditus*: "Aramazd, you have brought the fraudulent game to an end for me. So if such is your desire, take me, this mortal man, to you also."[44]

One of the functions of the Alexander legend was to provide a source and a rationale for the cultural and political hegemony sought by the Western world and, more fundamentally, for the affirmative, rational, and logical worldview that was gaining prominence in the Judeo-Greco culture inherited by mediaeval Europe. Professor Abel sees the Alexander legend as crucial in the creation of the historico-literary authority needed for the establishment of the scientific rationalism of this culture: "It introduced all at once into the thought and consciousness of the Greek world and in turn bequeathed to the entire civilized world a plethora of concepts ... Most important of all, the expanded world attains new dimensions, new coherence."[45]

Doubtless, the narrative of the Alexander legend promotes a view of the world, as Abel describes it, enlarged to its very limits, in which there no longer exist unexplored regions. In such an affirmative reading of the saga of Alexander the Great, there is no such thing as the unknown, and the world, which in this reading is the extent of the real, is governed by a single, rational, mighty rule. The youthful Alexander is the enemy of the disordered, the separate, the confused and the unknown. He brings the light of reason and the rule of logic to the previously dark terrain – identified as India, as Ethiopia, the Antipodes, or the desert – where impossible and ungovernable beings exist.

Such a reading must, however, ignore, or at least marginize, all of the text that features the monstrous, the chaotic, and the contradictory. It must minimize, as well, the words and attitudes of the older Alexander, who looks back on his glorious victories and declares them a "fraudulent game." To a certain extent, this is precisely what we see happening already in the Middle Ages when the Brahman episode and the descriptions of the lands of the monsters are separated from the Alexander legend itself, leaving that legend to propagate the purely martial figure of the hero and to monumentalize his conquests. Reincorporated into the text, such episodes, along with the iconography of the gods, oracles, and omens, the non sequiturs of the narrative, and its negative allegory on cities, weapons, boundaries, and war, constitute an apophatic reading that does not eliminate but corrects and completes the more accessible affirmative reading.

The mystery of the Alexander legend takes on its fuller proportions outside of texts when we consider the significance of this figure in mediaeval Christian culture. As George Frederick Kunz has pointed out in his study of mediaeval gems, among the Christian faithful there was a quasi cult surrounding the pagan warrior: "In Roman times the image of Alexander the Great was looked upon as possessing magic virtues ... Indeed, even among Christians coins of Alexander were in great favor as amulets, and the stern John Chrysostum sharply rebukes those who wore bronze coins of the monarch attached to their heads and feet."[46]

The reason for this reverence toward the heathen conqueror is less likely to have been a lapse into heresy than a recognition of Alexander's symbolic significance. It is not impossible that in Alexander the Great the people saw shadows of a prototype of Jesus, a manifestation of the paradox of divinity in which the unnatural, even monstrous, combination of distinct natures, human and divine, unite in a single being. This certainly was the perception of, at least, the thirteenth century Armenian scribe who openly compares Alexander to Christ and who attaches to his poem a plea to be excused for this audacity.[47] The analogy between Alexander and Christ would seem to lie, on the one hand, in the recognition of Alexander as himself a monster of paradoxical unions and, on the other, in the recognition of monstrosity as the fullest manifestation of the divine.

Alexander is both the force that battles the monsters as he attempts to extend civilization to the ends of the earth, and he is the monster itself, demolisher of cities, reviser of history, debunker of rhetoric. Monster and antimonster, hero and villain, large and small, Alexander incorporates a series of contradictions that identify him as the central paradox of the text, a condition that allows him to "show forth," like the monster, the nature of being and the real.

OEDIPUS

The earliest representation of the Oedipus story in Greek culture is made up of mythic legends arising presumably from the oral culture of the people and the literary versions of these myths, such as those of Homer, Sophocles, Pausanias, and others.[48] Roman writers pick up the basic narrative and pass it on to the Middle Ages, for which the single most important source is Statius, through his *Thebaid*. For the mediaeval audience, the story of Oedipus is part and parcel of the founding legend of western culture, the epic movement through history of the founding and destruction of human societies, symbolized by their cities; this movement leads from Thebes and its fall, to Troy and its fall, to Rome and its fall, and thence to the great mediaeval cities of Bologna, Paris, and London.[49]

One example of the mediaeval representation of the Oedipus story is Lydgate's *Siege of Thebes* and another, his *Fall of Princes*, where we find one of the fullest literary representations of the Oedipus story in the Middle Ages. But in addition to these "formal" literary versions, the intentional product of individual authors, there existed in the Middle Ages, just as there had before, the folkloric, legendary renditions of the Oedipus myth. As the great French scholar of hagiography, Hippolyte Delehaye, long ago observed, the story of Oedipus was widely read throughout the Middle Ages, circulated through the various saints' lives that facilitated the transference of the pagan story to Christianity.[50]

The broad outline of the story is the same in all versions: Laius, King of Thebes, is warned by an oracle that he will be killed by his own son; Oedipus is born and is mutilated and exposed, or the equivalent, so as to cause his death; he survives, grows up, and unwittingly kills Laius, his father, whose homosexuality has brought upon his kingdom the scourge of the monster Sphinx.[51] Oedipus solves the Sphinx's enigma and destroys the monster. He marries his mother, Jocasta, and sires children; upon discovery of his identity and thus his "crimes," he blinds and exiles himself.

The hero's encounter with the monster in the legend of Oedipus occurs between the episode in which he kills his father and that in which he marries his mother. This narrative structure emphasizes the centrality of the sphinx, which emphasis, in contrast to the modern concentration on the lateral episodes, the pagan Greeks and the Middle Ages seem to have intended. From the earliest versions down at least to the renditions of Lydgate, the young hero's encounter with the monster is presented as the key to the meaning of the myth.

The figure at the heart of the myth is the Ethiopian sphinx, a monstrous combination of differences that mixes and unifies bird, lion, serpent, and human forms. In Egypt the sphinx is male; in Greece, female. Just as its form is an enigmatic combination of dissimilitudes, the sphinx is the source of the enigma itself, the intellectual riddle based on the combination of similarity and dissimilarity. The sphinx is a monster because it embodies enigma; it is an enigma because it is constructed monstrously.

In the story of Oedipus, as in most stories involving monsters, the deformed figure is only briefly on stage. Her function is propaedeutic and is accomplished through the demonstration of the ultimately enigmatic nature of the reality in which she resides. The awareness of the incompleteness of the rational and the self-assertive similitudes that sustain a corrupt Thebes is brought about in the literary process through the gradual revelation of the priority of paradox. By a sustained, repetitive contradiction of the apparent meanings and significations of the literal narrative and the figurative devices used to create that narrative, the apophatic sense emerges.

The sphinx's enigma, like many riddles, operates on a certain irony: what being goes first on four feet, then on three, then again on two and afterwards on three, then on four, and finally returns from whence it came?[52] The surprise contained within the answer resides in the thwarting of the expectation that such a creature must be one that undergoes radical metamorphoses, changing its form at each stage described by the riddle; the question seems, indeed, to call for the identification of some kind of fantastic creature, but, instead, the answer is the most natural of creatures, the very measure of the normal and no monster at all. Or so, at first, it seems.

The irony arises through our difficulty in recognizing one of the simplest and most obvious realities, that the locus of the existence of contraries and differences is the single, unified subject. Thus the person, when conceived as an ontological subject, is the answer; this being, as a process of growth from birth to death, is the object of the monster's inquiry. But the legend has in store for us a further irony, a second level of paradox in which this image of normalcy is reversed and the human being is revealed as, indeed, the arch-monster. But it is as much the intellectual process required to answer the riddle as the answer itself that reveals the riddle's meaning. In order to understand what being it is that travels down the road of life in such a peculiar way, one's mind must travel down the less explored road of the *via negativa*, for the riddle operates by asserting in the interrogative, What creature goes on four, goes on three, goes on two? and then moves to its conclusion by negating these assertions: What creature (does not go on two but) goes again on three, (does not go on three but) goes again on four, (does not go on four but) returns whence it came? It will be noted that not only does the riddle parallel the process of negative theology but at the same time imitates the Dionysian process of emanation/remaining/return; humans come into being, proceed through the stages of life, and "return whence they came."

Nevertheless, in the context of the Oedipus story, one is bound to wonder why this particular riddle is asked and how this enigma is appropriate to the story. Marie Delcourt, in a now-classic study of the Oedipus myth, points out that the enigma as test is a common feature of both myth and folklore and that the answer to it is often the name of the questioner: "As soon as Apollonius of Tyane named the name of the Empuse, the evil spell with which she menaced Menippus vanished."[53] Naming the being, Delcourt goes on to say, furnishes control of it and power over it. Only in the case of Oedipus is it not the name of the questioner but that of the respondent that is the correct answer to the enigma: "The Sphinx asks Oedipus to name the animal that has four feet in the morning, two at midday, and three in the evening. The answer he must give in response is not in this case the name of the questioning Sphinx, but his own name – Man!"[54]

Although Delcourt dismisses this "highly curious" feature as simply that, the reversal it contains may be significant if it can be shown to work with other reversals in the narrative, as I believe it does. Delcourt herself moves in this direction by demonstrating that the hero's own name, *oidipous*, contains within it the word *dipous* (biped), the common name of the human species. In an alternate version of the episode, Oedipus does not utter the correct answer at all but, seeing him touch his own forehead in a pensive gesture and believing he is pointing to himself, the monster accepts this as the correct answer. Through the reversal of the usually correct answer, the Oedipus story identifies questioner with questioned, tester with tested, by an exchange of names that transfers the monstrosity of the Sphinx to Oedipus, as a metaphor of his own monstrosity. Thus, the convention of using the questioner's name as the answer to the riddle is not changed here but rather made a vehicle for identifying the hero with the monster. Further, by identifying the hero with humanity itself, by relating his name to the answer to the riddle, monstrosity is further extended to all humanity. The answer to the riddle, then, is only apparently not the same as the answer to the other riddles, for when the hero is identified with the sphinx, the correct response is his name, is her name, is our name: and the single name for all is "monster." Just as he insists upon knowing his identity by seeking names – the name of his father, the name of his mother, and even his own proper name – so the hero (dis)solves the paradox by naming its subject, humanity. Ironically the seeker has named his identity in his own response, but despite the emphasis on the image of feet in the riddle, Oedipus, "monster-foot," does not recognize himself.

In a story where sire is slayer, where male couples with male and son with mother, the reversal of the usual solution to the enigma suggests reversal itself as a central theme of the text. Just as the usual answer is the name of the monster, so the answer given by Oedipus names the monster, but the monster is now man himself. The function of reversal here is to extend the character of monstrosity from the deformed figure of the sphinx to humanity, otherwise the arbiter of normalcy and of form.

The sphinx is Oedipus, and Oedipus is the sphinx. This identification of Oedipus with the monster was not uncommon. Seneca, in his play *Oedipus*, a source widely known in the Middle Ages and one cited by Lydgate, has Laius called up from the dead to explain Thebes' ongoing pestilence; he does so by identifying Oedipus as his own monster: "He plied his own source and begot unholy issue upon his own mother. His own brothers he fathered, a thing wild beasts avoid – a tangle of evil, a monster more baffling than his own Sphinx."[55]

If the central episode of the hero's encounter with the sphinx functions to reveal him as similarly monstrous, the story of his birth and exposure has already accomplished this in another way. In fact, as Delcourt has stated, all the episodes of the narrative that one can distinguish (she distinguishes six)

Oedipus and the sphinx. G. Moreau. New York, Metropolitan Museum

tell the same basic story and present the same meaning, each by a different symbolic pattern. Delcourt convincingly reads that basic story as the prehistory of power and its attainment in Greek civilization. But it would seem that the Oedipus story also reveals something more general about the nature of human beings and their relation to the world. While the Oedipus myth reveals to us the nature of power and human accession to it, it also reveals its ultimate meaninglessness.

What is the narrative function of the detail concerning Oedipus' feet? This question has been asked by many who have analysed the story because, although this characteristic is the basis of the hero's name and in some versions, including the mediaeval ones, the means by which his patricide and incest are discovered, the maiming has always seemed a poorly integrated and unnecessary feature for the development and denouement of the story. Indeed, Delcourt declares the dimension of the pierced feet totally meaningless and absurd at the rhetorical level of the story.[56] At a deeper level, the level of an apophatic reading, however, the mutilation has exactly the same function as the enigma and is its trope.

The fate of the baby born to Jocasta parallels the procedure of exposing deformed children either on the sea or on a mountain top, so as to let the gods decide their survival. Delcourt's thesis is again persuasive: by the fact that Oedipus is exposed at birth in the same way as monsters, he is symbolically one of them. The incident in which his feet are pierced functions as a kind of token of deformity, and his scars remain as a sign, not primarily of his undergoing physical abuse nor of any other element of the narrative, but of an original state of monstrosity.[57]

All of the ways employed by the ancients to destroy the monsters born to them had symbolic content. The Spartans abandoned what they considered evil omens in a field full of holes; in Athens they were hidden in a "secret place." In Rome, as Delcourt tells us, "they are brought to the sea in a chest and set afloat far from the shore without ever having come in contact with the earth. If their deformity is such that it completely effaces human resemblance, they are burned and their ashes thrown into the sea, thus suffering the same fate as monstrous animals."[58]

The exposure of deformed children, as distinct from infanticide, expresses an ambivalence toward monstrosity itself. On the one hand, the monster is thought to be a sign of the displeasure of the gods and thus a presage of their hostility toward the society into which the malformed is born. On the other, the monster is a marvel whose force is equally capable of beneficence and of malevolence; it is, after all, the monster that is the favoured form of theophany. How, then, to tell whether the grotesque and unnatural new-born shape belongs to a divine being sent as a boon or to an evil spirit sent as a curse? Exposing the child to the forces of nature allows the gods to save the monster if he is, indeed, one of them.

There is a certain amount of evidence that many of the exposed monsters survived the ordeal and grew to adulthood, as in fact did Oedipus. The possibility of survival was no doubt related to the lessening of the degree of peril in the method of exposure. In other words, the Greeks insured the survival of those whom they ritually threatened with death by manipulating the ceremony:

Little by little in classical Greece the exposing of deformed infants ceased. In Rome Titus Livius refers to adult abnormal individuals, indicating that they must have been spared at birth although we cannot be sure of the conditions surrounding this situation: did the parents care for their deformed offspring, or did they expose them in such a manner as to ensure their survival? I suspect that it was more than pity that led to the maximum chance for survival being afforded the monster and the scapegoat ... He who had been consecrated and who had been chosen by the gods to be saved has become a source of good fortune. The reality with which he is charged remains grim, but there has been a change of sign.[59]

This "change of sign" functions doubly, for by the fact that the monster survives, either as a deformed child or as a privileged sign, not only is the abnormal tolerated and accommodated but the absolute precedence of the normal and its criteria is put into question. In one way, not only does the survival of Oedipus guarantee the end of the pestilence that has befallen Thebes because of his father's sterility, but, more fundamentally, the denial of this monster child who will become king also betokens the flaw at the very foundation of that civilization. Although Oedipus, who bears only the traces of monstrosity, also finally denies himself, it is through him that the limitations of human intellect and ingenuity that have conceived and constructed Thebes are made manifest.

The sign of the monster is thus ambiguous and paradoxical, communicating at one and the same time the malevolent forces of divine anger, with consequent catastrophe, and the benevolent grace of divine favour. In this way the monster is the ideal religious sign, for, as Delcourt again shows, in the transcendence of the limitations of logic, the religious discourse passes through ambiguity toward the completeness of paradox:

"Thus one can explain how the same sacrificial mechanism can serve such utterly different religious requirements. It carries with it the same ambiguity that religious forces themselves carry; the victim represents death just as he represents life, disease as well as health, vice along with virtue ... It is the means of the concentration of the religious; it expresses it, it incarnates it, it is its vehicle. Acting upon one, we act upon the other; directing it we either attract and absorb it or we expel and eliminate it." This complexity exists not only in ritual but also in legend, for example, in the Oedipus story. First expelled from the community as a bad omen, then chosen by the gods, the hero becomes as powerful as he had been miserable.[60]

Although in the classical myth Oedipus is abandoned on a mountain and not in a chest upon the sea, we will see that in certain mediaeval versions of the story the child is, in fact, sent to sea in a coffin-like contraption. All versions of the Oedipus story have the child carried away by a servant of some type to be slain, and the servant's softness of heart that saves the baby is the equivalent of divine intervention in earlier (nonextant) versions. The piercing of the feet is variously explained in the literature as a way of keeping the baby out of reach of beasts by hanging him in a tree[61] or, most ingenuously in the French *Roman de Thèbes*, as a way of making blood drip down over his body so that the servants can report truthfully to Laius that they left the baby "cut up and bloody."[62]

The function of the pierced feet is also to supply an etymology and significance to the name *oidipous* – "feet swollen, enlarged, or misshapen." Thus the trace of the original monstrosity is borne by the hero not only in the lesions on his feet but also in a name that heralds deformity. It is here, as we focus more and more on the hero's deformed feet, that the more obvious meaning seems to begin to go astray. From this perspective, what Sophocles composed as a tragic vision of fated kingship in the history of a great and powerful civilization emerges increasingly as a meditation on the limits of human will and intellect and the paradox of existence. The narrative direction of the story that in classical culture moves toward the mythic and tragic and in mediaeval, Christian culture, toward the heroic and didactic, is diverted away from these meanings toward a radically different, apophatic sense by the eccentric element of the feet. The narrative of the Oedipus legend belies the logico-tragic meaning that it assumed in the Greek rational, classical period, as well as the logico-moral meaning it tended toward in the mediaeval period. The feet are, in fact, the medium by which monstrosity is transferred; through the original maiming of the feet at his birth, the hero is associated with the infant monsters abandoned to death or redemption on the mountains and seas of Greece and by this association becomes a monster like them. In mediaeval Europe, unlike classical Greece, a still further transference is possible in association with another hero bearing the mark of wounded feet.

Oedipus' wounded feet further suggest the injured phallus, for the foot, like the nose, is an organ having a sympathetic physiognomical relation to the phallus. The father's murder of the son, foiled in the surviving versions of the Oedipus story, is replaced by the mutilating of the son's feet, and this substitution itself signifies Oedipus' monstrosity. According to Delcourt, the evil that the misshapen birth is supposed to represent is often the displacement of an ancestral infirmity incurred in an earlier moment of history, before the birth of the unlucky child.[63] Laius' maleficent disorder is his homosexuality, metaphorically a phallic distortion. The child marked with the sign of such unnaturalness survives to become the scourge and executioner of his criminal sire.

Leopold Constans, who has made one of the most extensive studies of the Oedipus legend, points out that the immediate cause of the parricide in the narrative, according to some authors, is a new injury to Oedipus' foot: "According to Euripides and Hygines, [Oedipus] has his foot crushed by one of the wheels of his father's chariot. Enraged, he tears Laius from his seat and kills him."[64]

The dynamic of teratological transference from monstrous births, to mythic hero and finally to humanity is powered by the sign of feet, infantile and unsteady, pierced and deformed, and old and failing – the very element that Delcourt rightly declares absurd in the tragi-mythic ethos of the classical versions of the story. The function of the monstrous is, however, precisely the reversal of this meaning, or more correctly, the negation of the intended meaning in favour of a sense that is significantly absurd and wholly apophatic.

The identification of the monster with Oedipus (and *as* Oedipus) is further strengthened through the genealogy of the sphinx. She is a product of incest. The progeny of Orthros, a multicephalic watchdog of the giant, Geryon, and of his own mother Echidna, half woman, half snake, the matrix of numerous monsters, the sphinx is an appropriate interlocutor for Oedipus and has much to teach him. But for all his naming, Oedipus does not learn the lesson, and although he supplies the right answer, his own understanding falls far short of it. As one of the readers of his own legend, Oedipus remains on the literal level of understanding of the text, supplying the correct cataphatic answer, but never capable of the necessary apophatic exegesis. In relation to the riddle, a text within a text, Oedipus' intention is to *solve* it; that is, to supply a totalizing interpretation that replaces the text. Constans reports a relevant popular expression: "The Sphinx rends us in pieces with its enigma; no one can destroy the enigma.[65]

In an effort to understand the deepest sense of the Oedipus story, as well as the function of the monstrous that encodes that meaning for the Middle Ages, we must consider several peripheral elements connected to the major episodes. In the first place, the pestilence that befalls Thebes is a form of agricultural infertility, and it is related to the appearance of the sphinx. In one way or another it is specified as a punishment – both of Laius and of his people – for the King's homosexuality. In some versions it is Hera herself, goddess of marriage, who sends the monster to ravage the city of Thebes; in the Latin versions it is Juno, Queen of Heaven and patroness of marriage, who fetches the sphinx out of that ancient matrix of monstrosity, Ethiopia. The fact that it is through Oedipus' exchange with the sphinx and his destruction of her that he is able to marry his mother and thus fulfill the prophesy of incest gives to the monster a strong sexual charge. The sexuality of the monster and her relation with Oedipus, although nowhere specified in the legend, has nevertheless been sensed by audiences of the myth. This is, perhaps, nowhere more evident than in the painting by the nineteenth century French painter Gustave Moreau in which a voluptuous sphinx poses her enigma while clinging to a naked Oedipus almost as if a part of him; the couples' eyes are identical in their sensual expression.

The monster becomes paradoxically the articulation of perversity and its punishment; she is the agent for the passage of a Thebes ruled by a homosexual king to a Thebes ruled by an incestuous one. Laius' homosexuality has significance beyond the moral level.The symbolic nature of its punishment – agricultural sterility and death through the devouring of the society's youth – suggests that the sexual aberration is a sign of something beyond itself. While in some versions retribution does not occur until after the death of Laius, in others it is while travelling to consult the oracle about how to rid Thebes of the pestilence that Laius encounters his son and is killed.

The mythic representation of the introduction of homosexuality into the world signals the obsession with likeness and the rejection of the other. Just as in the myth of Narcissus, so in the story of Laius and several others, homosexuality is seen as a celebration of the self and the sexual icons of the self through the rejection of the other. It is erotic isolation in which the self seeks out its similitude and embraces it to the exclusion of all difference and all dissimilitude. Just as the lack of issue condemns the homosexual act to sterility and the unfruitful spending of seed in that act suggests loss and death, so the extension of the significance of the sexual metaphor to the level of cognition connotes the limitation and closure of cataphatic rationality. Homosexuality symbolizes the rejection of the union of contraries, the refusal of the *coincidentia oppositorum* of the sexes, represented conventionally by the union of male and female in marriage. The goddess of marriage answers the Theban rejection of the marital *coincidentia oppositorum* by sending the monster, a grotesque union of contradictory forms, into that society. It is only in answering its enigma, a verbal form of itself, that Thebes can be freed of its devastation.

If the monster is Oedipus, she is also Laius, for she has come directly in response to his fault, and like him she attempts to bar Oedipus' return to Thebes and to kill him. The sphinx, then, embodies Laius and his actions: she is a sign of his sterility, albeit as its punishment, and an emblem of his persecution of his son. The sphinx is also Jocasta. Marie Delcourt analyses the sphinx as a kind of succubus/incubus which, like so many other spirits of its kind, is a figure of excessive female sexuality: "The sirens, Keres, Erinyes, Harpies, the birds of Stymphalos, are the spirits of the dead ... They all have one trait in common: they are avid for blood and sexual pleasure."[66] Delcourt goes further: the defeat of the sphinx is betokened in the sexual submission of the female to the male, as accomplished in the marriage of Jocasta to Oedipus. Thus the triumph of the new ruler is symbolized, in this myth and in many others, by the killing of the old king and the possession of the royal female, usually the princess, but here the Queen herself.

Delcourt clearly identifies Jocasta as the monster overcome by Oedipus. Jocasta is an echo of the ogre-queen who must be defeated before the young warrior can ascend to power, and in this light it is significant that in most versions of the story a considerable amount of time passes between Oedipus' murder of his father and his overcoming of the sphinx, for, in such versions, it is Jocasta who occupies the throne during this interim. Thus it is she, not Laius, who is replaced as ruler by Oedipus, and this detail reinforces the archetypal theme contained in the figure of the ogre-queen. Lydgate's version, like others, makes it clear that Jocasta's marriage to Oedipus is tantamount to relinquishing power to the male. It is precisely this that the citizens of Thebes desire:

> They were without a governor,
> Against their foes, no succour,
> No man to defend them, only a queen;
> ....
> So all the lords by one assent,
> Within the town held parliament,
> Decided there with the Queen to treat,
> That this manly man in marriage she meet.[67]

Were this not clear enough, Delcourt reveals that, alternately, in some versions of the story it is to be understood that between the reigns of Laius and Oedipus it is, in place of Jocasta, the sphinx herself that rules Thebes, and that it is Oedipus' defeat of the monster – not of Laius or of Jocasta – that wins him the throne. Indeed, modern Greek versions of the story have Oedipus wed, not his mother, the Queen, but the sphinx herself who, as Delcourt says, is one and the same with Jocasta.[68] Oedipus' incest is both a fulfillment of the oracle and an enactment of the enigma posed by the sphinx, an enactment made possible by Oedipus' failure, in the first place, to understand the riddle in any but the most literal way.

Several heroes representative of their cultures are marked by incest: Cuchulainn in Celtic, Siegfried in Germanic, and Gawain in British culture are all heroes whose triumphs are signalled by the trope of incest, and Delcourt strongly suggests Alexander as a type of Oedipus.[69] It is reported that Caesar, before crossing the Rubicon, dreamt of incest with his mother and that this was interpreted as a sure sign of victory; that is, it symbolized the Earth submitting to the Conqueror.[70] The mythical function of incest is found in the theme of the marriage of the cosmocrator to a mother or sister in order to keep the royal bloodline pure so as to retain control within the group and exclude "others." Oedipus returns to the womb from which he emerged – on the symbolic level, upon death, and on the literal level, through the act of incest. A fourth century epigram found on two funeral vases summarizes the paradoxical "return" to the locus of life and death: representing

Oedipus' tomb, the epigram reads: "I contain Oedipus, son of Laius, within my womb.[71]

The enigma presents the nature of human existence, which is both linear – depicted in six stages from birth to death – and, simultaneously, circular – returning to the point of origin in the "womb." Existence is a process characterized both by motion and by stasis, and the enigma of the sphinx represents it as a fundamentally apophatic process. This process, as mentioned earlier, parallels the Neoplatonic process of *editus-reditus* in that its single (remaining) subject goes through the triad 1, 2, 3 (emanation) to arrive at the first real number 4, at which point it returns, 3, 2, 1: that is to say, the subject of the monster's paradox comes forward at birth into a world in which he first crawls (1), then toddles (2), then walks upright (3); at the zenith of his strength (4), the subject then begins to toddle (3), then crawls (2), then returns to whence he came (1). The latter half of the process follows the *via negativa* in a *reditus* to the point of origin, for it is an apophatic version of the first three stages. As a whole, both processes are ones of *remaining*, since the point of arrival is the point of departure.

Ignorant of the popular wisdom that "no one can solve the enigma," Oedipus short-circuits the paradox contained within the enigma and dissolves both enigma and monster with his answer. He similarly short-circuits the process of ontological *return* through his sexual return to the womb, metaphorically suggesting the refusal of the entire apophatic dimension of life.

Lydgate's use of the theme is found in two versions, *The Siege of Thebes*, derived from an Old French prose romance, and his *Fall of Princes*, which he composed about a decade later, in 1431. In addition to Lydgate's version and the French *Roman de Thèbes*, there are several other mediaeval versions that associate Oedipus with saints and other figures in the religious tradition.[72] The principal one is the deeply encoded version of Oedipus found in the legend of Judas, which will be discussed below.

Lydgate's *Siege of Thebes* is projected as an extra story of Chaucer's *Canterbury Tales* recounted by the poet, who imagines himself as a latecomer to the pilgrimage, summarily ordered by the Host to tell a tale as the group leaves Canterbury for the return journey. Lydgate's *Thebes* is literally a verbal construct before it is an architectural one, built by King Amphion, who raises the walls simply by the force of the poetry he recites to the accompaniment of a harp:

> But how the walls were raised on high
> It is a wonder and a marvel to tell.
> ....
> How Amphion, this prudent king,
> With the sweetness and the melodious sound
> And the harmony of his sweet song,

Built the City that was betimes so strong
By virtue of the warbling sharp
That he made on Mercury's harp,
Of which the strings he played not soft,
Whereby the walls were raised aloft,
Without the skill of any man's hand.[73]

The poet specifies that Mercury, god of eloquence, gifted Amphion at birth with the "craft of Rethoric" (1.219), so that there was none like him in the world for the use of words. He taught all the citizens of Troy to revel in language, and Lydgate makes clear for us that this teaching had nothing to do with music *per se*, but rather that it was "the crafty speche of this kyng" (226–7) that charmed men to labour at the construction of the city. Enthusiastically Lydgate compares this speech to the work of poets who, with the same powers, construct their texts. Thus Thebes is presented at the outset of the poem as a monument to the power of speech.

Laius is the first descendant of Amphion mentioned, and with him begins the story of Oedipus. Through minute astrological calculations, Laius discovers that his long-awaited heir is doomed to slay him, and he orders a grief-stricken Jocasta to kill the child as soon as he is born. The servants charged with this task find the child so beautiful that they are unable to carry out the Queen's order, and they hang him in a tree by holes pierced through his feet. The story continues along the conventional lines with the poet explaining that the name Oedipus means in Greek "with bored feet." This detail is added to a description of an adolescent Oedipus in the court of Polybus, depicted as arrogant, proud, and disdainful, an interpolation that will make possible the moral sense that the mediaeval author intends in his text.

After he has learned from a playmate that he is not the natural son of Polybus, the hero consults an oracle described by Lydgate as containing an evil, unclean spirit that lies to all those who interrogate it, thus again laying the groundwork for a moral and rational explanation of the later events of the poem. The sphinx is found in a setting characteristic of the locus of mediaeval monsters, a wasteland filled with numerous deformed and menacing creatures of which the sphinx is only the worst.[74] Strangely, the monster, although female in appearance, is referred to throughout as male:

Body and feet he had of a fierce lion,
But like a maid, in truth, was head and face,
With a ferocious expression, full of menace
....
Worse than tiger, serpent, or dragon.[75]

The mediaeval Oedipus insults and upbraids the monster before destroying it, and its greatest offense seems to be the riddle itself, for which the sphinx is called false and a fraud. The mediaeval hero seems to have nothing but contempt for this enigma:

> Thy false fraud shall now be quit.
> I have no inclination to play with runes,
> But shall your problem now expound
> So clearly that you shall not go hence![76]

Oedipus decapitates the monster and is rewarded with the rule of Thebes and with its queen. Lydgate's moral understanding of the meaning of the story leads him to project Oedipus as a simple warning to his audience against the hideous sins of parricide and incest, for, as the author says, if Oedipus, who committed these acts in ignorance and innocence was punished as he was, what may they expect who deliberately and knowingly do such deeds. But the text itself goes well beyond this lesson. The hero is presented first as an innocent victim of a devil-oracle, mutilated and abandoned; he is then seen as an arrogant and abusive youth. Later his image is rehabilitated when, heroically, he defeats the monster; immediately after, however, he is an arch-sinner siring children upon his own mother. This unstable perspective is due in part, to be sure, to the lesser artistry of Lydgate, but it also has to do with the material of the narrative itself, and the difference between the anomalies of the mediaeval romance and the anomalies of Sophocles' tragedy is only one of degree.

Among all the anomalies of the narrative, only the detail of Oedipus' feet is salient in Lydgate's version and in all others. After a long and merry life with Oedipus, with whom she has had four children, the hero's wife suddenly notices the scars on his feet and bursts into tears. She reveals to Oedipus that long ago she bore a son whom Laius ordered slain but who survived due to the tenderness of his assasins; rather than kill the child, they had only pierced his feet to hang him from a tree. Due to the exigencies of the plot, Jocasta cannot, of course, know about the maimed feet or even of her son's survival, so the use of this detail in this way seems more an attempt to provide a logical function for the detail of the deformed feet rather than an attempt to move the plot toward its denouement. Oedipus responds by recapitulating his biography from the point where Jocasta has left off in the story of her son; the single common point in both narratives is the piercing of the feet:

> *Jocasta*: And forth they go [the servants] to the forest wide,
> Adjacent to this country,
> Pierce his feet, hang him on a tree.

> *Oedipus*: Unto the queen he told his story,
> First how he was to a forest taken,
> Wounded in the feet, and all the rest.[77]

Astonishingly, our author tires of the story at this point and says so, rec-
ommending Seneca to any of his audience who might wish to pursue the narrative of Oedipus' blinding and exile and that of his disloyal sons.Thus
Lydgate in his naivety articulates what so many audiences of the Oedipus
legend have instinctively felt: that the real story ends with the hero's discovery of his identity and that the ensuing punishment of his acts is so much
treading water in the hope of arriving at some reasonable closure adequate
either to tragedy or homily. The real structure that emerges out of the infelicities of Lydgate's rhetoric is again one of a narrative bound by parricide at
the outset and incest at the end, in the centre of which – and central to which
– is the enigma that identifies the hero and all humanity as monsters existing
in a reality of which the deformed is the first principle. The controlling deformity in this text is the feet.

Lydgate's second version of the Oedipus story is found in the *Fall of
Princes,* a text which is, if anything, more didactic in intention than the first.
Its focus is as much on Jocasta as on Oedipus, emphasizing her grief as
mother when the baby is exposed, as wife at the violent loss of Laius, and, finally, as woman at the discovery of her incestuous relation with her second
husband. Oedipus' childhood arrogance, the trait that in other texts provokes
a playmate to reveal his true origins, is here eliminated. The Prince's name is
more developed; he is not named at infancy, but "when he in age gan to wexe
more" (3259), and when the wounds on his feet are healed, he is given the
name that best describes him:

> According to his wounds was he named.
> For Edippus is a name that means,
> For those who know the etymology,
> "Pierced through both feet."[78]

Oedipus' name, then, stands as a constant reminder of his deformity, verbally functioning in precisely the same manner as his bodily scars, as a sign of
a monstrous origin and his inevitable return to that same monstrosity. Such a
device assures that even to those who cannot see his feet, there is available a
sign that, interpreted correctly, reveals the prince's true identity. In addition to
this innovation, Lydgate has Jocasta suspect Oedipus' true identity early on;
the function of the deformed feet is as a confirmation of her fears.

Curiously, the sphinx's riddle is described as unnatural, for the author
states that the creature was a monster that spoke against nature (3373). The
parallel between the process of human life, which is the riddle's first level of
meaning, and the distorted version of it, which Oedipus mocks in his incestuous "return" to the womb, possibly clarifies the sense of Lydgate's description of the enigma as unnatural speech. This is perhaps reinforced by the
gloss that the author provides on the meaning of the sphinx's words:

This enigma may be summarized,
That which the sly serpent proposed,
That at the very moment of birth, alas,
Nature leads us toward our death,
Every day a step closer, no other gloss there is;
Experience teaches from the beginning of time,
That this world here is but a pilgrimage.[79]

Viewing Oedipus' incest symbolically and in parallel to the enigmatic figure of the process of growth and decay that is life, the hero's unnaturalness may be seen as a desire to curtail the process of life represented by the sphinx. His sexual return to his place of origin suggests a literalism that attempts to "reconceive" the self endlessly so as to undo the paradox of death as life, life as death.

Typically, Lydgate tries to resolve the problems of his text morally. A long diatribe against Fortune follows the event in the narrative in which Oedipus weds his mother; the act is blamed on some evil influence of the stars, and the text is projected as one bounded by didactic intention and meaning. But the tropological element is woefully inadequate to the weight of the text. Tiresias' description of the origin of the pestilence that haunts Thebes and his identification of its cure is, in and of itself, enough to prevent a purely didactic analysis of the poem. At the moment of Tiresias' pronouncement that only through the deposition of an incestuous and patricidal king can Thebes be cleansed, Jocasta directs her eyes toward Oedipus' feet, and the denouement is triggered. As in other versions, it is the totally "dysfunctional" narrative element of the feet that sweeps away the bounded reading of the text and makes possible another.

Notwithstanding Lydgate's versions of the story, the Middle Ages did not restrict the saga of Oedipus to its moral significance, but, as in the case of Alexander, saw in this deformed figure a sign of the ontological and the divine. As in all such apophatic representations of the holy, the associations of Oedipus with the sacred are more deeply encoded in the Middle Ages than the tragic or the didactic uses of the theme. One such example, contrasting sharply with Lydgate's forthright handling of the story as history, is the extra-Scriptural legend of Judas.

This strange story of Judas may be summarized as follows. Having dreamed that she would conceive a son who would be the destruction of the entire Jewish race, Cyborea gives birth in Jerusalem to a son. Together with her husband Reuben, she sets the child adrift on the sea in a wooden chest that is eventually washed up on the island of Iscariot. Judas is adopted by the Queen and brought up with a son born to her later whom Judas hated and persecuted. In a fit of anger at this behaviour, the Queen reveals to Judas his true origin, provoking him to slay her son in vengeance and to escape to Jerusalem. He joins the retinue of Pilate, who one day orders him to steal fruit from a nearby orchard, and while carrying out the theft, Judas is confronted by the guard, Reuben, his unrecognized father, whom he slays.

In an effort to silence the protests of the widowed Cyborea, Pilate marries her to Judas in order to provide her with support, and they have children. When the identity of Judas is discovered (rather casually by Judas himself), he goes to Jesus to seek forgiveness. He becomes a disciple and is assigned the post of treasurer of the group of apostles. The legend links up with the Scriptural story when Judas eventually betrays his master for thirty pieces of silver, experiences remorse, and hangs himself.

Thus it is that the mediaeval legend of Judas, clearly based on the Oedipus story, preserves a possibly older version of the monster-birth theme in having Judas exposed, not in the wild like Oedipus, but on the water in a container. The other significant difference is that in most versions Judas bears no scars or other physical sign of monstrosity. If we see Judas as a proto-Oedipus, we would expect that Judas' feet would function as sign, whereas in fact it is only the exposure, patricide, and incest incidents of the narrative that create the connection. This is, I believe, because Judas is not a proto-Oedipus but rather a means by which the original monstrosity of the sphinx is transferred to still another figure dramatically absent from the legend.

Paull Baum, in an early study of the mediaeval Judas legend, exhaustively analyses the several versions of the story.[80] As Baum correctly states, the evident intention of these stories is to blacken the name of Judas, on the one hand, and, on the other, to demonstrate that for the truly repentant forgiveness is absolute. Indeed, those who are used to mediaeval exegesis can readily see the rich allegorical possibilities of the text: Judas, the Synagogue, elder child of God, who slays his younger brother, the Church, and progresses in sin to slay his own father, Jesus/God, and dishonours his mother, the Law. However, Baum also accurately perceives the complete inadequacy of this level of meaning in the text:

The man who first told or wrote down the life of Judas, and those that repeated it after him, lacked a command of narrative sufficient to make their meaning perfectly clear: and beneath the surface, whether the writers themselves were conscious of it or not, there may have been, as some think, an uncomprehended notion of the *ineluctabile fatum*. But if any part of the original intention of the Judas legend was to inculcate the moral of divine forgiveness ... it may be thought to bespeak very little intelligence in the minds of its authors that they overlooked the true nature of his sins ... From the early Fathers and homilists down, there was ample precedent for finding instructive illustrations where they did not exist, as well as for appending morals that did not fit with extreme accuracy.[81]

Clearly, however, the Middle Ages had no need of a secular text in order to propagate this allegory, since it was the most common reading of the Scriptural Judas story of the time. By the same token, the secular Judas legend itself clearly requires more than this standard scriptural exegesis to be understood in any coherent way. The second part of the narrative is basically the scriptural story of Judas' role in the Crucifixion, widely known to all; the first part, however, is an innovation, indeed a rather eccentric one, functioning obviously to illuminate the second part and to set its usual meaning in a different direction. What is that direction?

In the earliest English and French versions of the legend, the story of Judas' betrayal of Christ is expanded for the apparent purpose of providing a logical explanation for that treason. As Christ's treasurer, Judas is paid ten percent of all the transactions that the Twelve make. This, too, is a detail initially motivated by a concern for verisimilitude and logic, for, as explained in one version, Judas was forgiven his parricide and incest by Jesus but required to continue to support his wife and children. It is specifically for this purpose that Jesus paid him the tenth of all the company's transactions.

Taking its clue from John's Gospel, the literary text explains that Judas' inherent meanness was excited by the waste of the pound of precious ointment by Mary, a substance worth three hundred "pence" (John 12:3–5; see below). Had it been sold to give alms to the poor as Judas wished, the treasurer would, of course, have taken his percentage of the sale. Mary's exorbitant act cost the disciple thirty pieces of silver, and Judas protests. The influential version of the story in *The Golden Legend* offers this explanation and the following explanation:

Shortly before the Passion of our Lord, Judas was angered that an ointment which was bestowed upon Jesus was not sold for three hundred pence; probably he had planned to take this sum for himself. He went therefore to the Jews, and betrayed Christ to them for thirty pieces of silver. Of this fact two interpretations are given. One is that the pieces of silver that Judas received were each of them worth ten pence, and thus made up the sum which he would have had of the sale of the ointment. The other explanation is that Judas was accustomed to take a tenth part of all monies that were entrusted to his care; and thus the silver given to him by the Jews amounted to the profit which would have come to him had the ointment been sold.[82]

The story is thus expanded not merely to create the link between the sum of thirty pieces of silver lost in this way and the sum for which Judas sold Christ, thus providing a logical motivation for the betrayal. But more importantly, the elaboration furnishes access to an anagogic level of the narrative. John's gospel story of the unction at Bethany contains the same central trope as the story of Oedipus. That which is conspicuously lacking in the legend of Judas is conspicuously present in both Scripture and myth, and thus the legend forms the bridge between the two:

3 Then took Mary a pound of ointment of spikenard, very costly, and anointed the feet of Jesus, and wiped his feet with her hair: and the house was filled with the odour of the ointment.

4 Then saith one of his disciples, Judas Iscariot, Simon's son, which should betray him,

5 Why was not this ointment sold for three hundred pence, and given to the poor?

6 This he said, not that he cared for the poor; but because he was a thief, and had the bag, and bare what was put therein.

7 Then Jesus said, Let her alone: against the day of my burying hath she kept this.
(John 12:3–7)

The central image of the passage is Jesus' feet, upon which is poured the precious ointment and over which is passed Mary's hair. Jesus, who has just raised Lazarus from the dead, interprets this as a sign of his own approaching death not only, we may assume, because of the idea of embalming but as much for the suggestion of feet pierced upon the cross. In any case, in the context of the mediaeval Judas legend it is the reference to Mary's act that invokes the image of the feet and associates with Oedipus and his tragedy, not Judas, but Christ. In the Greek legend of Oedipus, as we have seen, it is the child's feet that provide the sign of monstrosity necessary for the contextualizing of all the other details of the story that makes them comprehensible. In the dialogue with the enigma-posing monster, the feet reveal the basis of Oedipus' own name and provide a bridge between Oedipus and the sphinx by which the monstrosity of the questioner is transferred to the respondent. In the mediaeval version, this transference of deformity is continued, always by the same imagistic vehicle, the feet; thus in the Judas version of the Oedipus symbol, when the traitor sells his master for thirty pieces of silver, this sign calls forth the sign of the ointment which, in turn, yields the sign of the feet; by this process of semiotic evocation, the monstrosity originating in the sphinx is transferred to Jesus.

Jesus' next act is to wash the feet of his disciples over the famous protest by Peter, which emphasizes the inappropriateness of the act: "Know ye what I have done to you?" Acting as his own exegete, Jesus explains that he has inverted the normal relation of master and disciple, just as he has inverted all other structures of the world and dissolved their binary oppositions; his meaning is always reversal: "For I have given you an example, that you should do as I have done to you" (John 13:12, 15).

Just as the Greek myth recognized the basic monstrosity of human beings and expressed it through the image of paradox and enigma, the Christian mediaeval text extends this perception to God Himself and so makes of the human monster a reflection of the ultimate monster, God. Once again, the aesthetic use of the deformed gives expression to the Neoplatonic conception of the Real in which the metaphysical takes precedence over the logical, but in which that metaphysics, in turn, gives precedence to that which is beyond being, that which is-not. In both the Oedipus story and the story of Judas, the life/death reversal is accomplished in a paradox that echoes numerous other reversals and inversions throughout the texts, and that reveals the monstrous coexistence of contraries at the heart of what is most real.

The heroic qualities embodied in figures such as Oedipus and Alexander were reflected for mediaeval English audiences in the native King Arthur. Like his predecessors, Arthur represents the achievements of human ingenuity as reflected in the bygone culture he ruled and, again as in the case of his figurative ancestors, those achievements are ultimately seen as dubious.

GAWAIN

The difference between the function of the monstrous in the encounters with it by Oedipus and Alexander and the similar encounter in *Sir Gawain and the Green Knight* is that Gawain's confrontation with the deformed and deforming more specifically engages the failure of language to manifest the real. The principal, but not the sole, monster in the poem bursts upon a scene of social intercourse in which the phenomenon of speech is strongly emphasized and into which his presence brings an equally emphasized silence. The hero responds to the monster's challenge in terms of language when, in replacing Arthur in the contest with the giant, he demands Camelot's approbation, not of his bravery, but of his rhetoric: "And if I speak not handsomely, let all the court judge."[83]

It is precisely in these terms that the hero is later challenged in Bercilak's castle through a series of tests of his ability to use language to resolve the double binds that the Lady creates for him. The entire court of Hautdesert acclaims Gawain's fame for wit and discourse and looks forward to witnessing "perfect expressions of noble talk" from "the father of civilized conduct."[84] The conundrums of "courtly conduct" that he experiences are framed by the larger, more symbolic paradox of the beheadings and scarrings that begin the story and end it.

The mythico-historical context of the poem is established at the very outset when the poet connects Arthur's court to the great cities of the past, identifying it as the last in a chain that has come to be known as the "Babylonian succession": "When the siege had ceased at Troy, / The city demolished, burnt to brands and ashes."[85] At the eschatological end of the mediaeval trope of the succession of earthly cities lies the New Jerusalem, but at the other lies Babylon, and by beginning the work with a gaze backward, the poet links Camelot to this ancient locus that was before Troy, before Thebes, and in the middle of which stood the broken tower of failed discourse. The cities of the world are the architectural equivalent of language; both are symbols of the assertive and controlling constructs of intellect, the paradigms of which must be deconstructed through negation – the one physical, the other verbal – in order to gain understanding and wisdom.

What Gawain must learn from the monsters he meets in his adventure is that his verbal constructs, brilliant though they may be, are not coequal with the real. This understanding is brought about as the monster gradually negates the logic and its discourse that Gawain employs to escape the paradoxes that confront him. Many readers of the poem have seen its theme as a critique of human pride and the artificiality of culture. These interpretations have usually grounded the theme in a religious authorial intention, emphasizing the didactic dimension. Indeed most audiences have readily recognized the Green Knight as teacher, the monster whose sudden appearance in society carries with it a revelation and a lesson. In a recent study, Martin B. Shichtman sees that revelation as a lesson in history – taught, one might add, in a highly apophatic way. Shichtman sees the Green Knight as undercutting the security that Arthur's court finds in ritual and the mythic cycle: "He forces the central characters to abandon their imitations of paradigms and to become involved in a history which unfolds syntagmatically, as a narrative sequence, one which emphasizes the individuality and responsibility of its participants."[86]

Thus the monster leaps into the middle of the history of Babylon-Thebes-Troy-Rome-Camelot in order to break its continuity. This saga of human social achievement, the author tells us, is not without ambiguity:

> On banks full broad Britain he founds
> > With joy,
> But war and woe and wonder
> Have there all coexisted,
> Both bliss and blunder
> have there been all mixed up.[87]

It is precisely this violent history that King Arthur insists be recounted as literary entertainment before he allows the New Year's feast to begin. Arthur demands a poetic celebration of the tradition of which he, himself, is the personification:

> Some adventurous thing, some strange tale,
> Some great marvel to be told that he might believe
> Of kings, of armies, or other adventures.[88]

This insistence by the King is described in seemingly negative terms for the poet calls him "childish" ("childgered," 86) and "wild-brained," "crazy" ("brayn wylde," 89), adding that he could never sit still for long! The entire scene at Camelot is frenzied, for in addition to Arthur's agitation, noise of all kinds dominates the court: the blare of trumpets, thundering drums, pipes, lutes, laughter, and – above all – talk! Robert Blanch and Julian Wasserman note the importance of noise in Camelot and relate it to the description of the court of Belshazzar in the Pearl Poet's *Purity*, where it represents "the chaos underlying the inverted festivity." They point out that through this symbol of noise the poet connects the courts of Belshazzar and Sodom. On the other hand, as they also show, the noise and clamour of Camelot is sharply contrasted with the quiet, calm, and orderliness of Hautdesert.[89]

All this is brought to a sudden stop with the appearance of the giant, and the instant silence that his monstrous form creates accentuates his role as contradiction to the babble of all that is social and discursive. The Round Table, the poet tells us, thought he was a spirit or other kind of monster, and it is that thought that brings them to utter speechlessness:

> For phantom or fairy the folk there took him,
> Therefore to answer they were too afraid,
> Astonished by his voice, stone still they sat.
> Dead silence through the hall hung heavy,
> As if all had slipped off to sleep, so squelched was their noise![90]

The intruder's salient characteristics are his size and his colour, and it is these factors that are the index of his monstrosity. The Green Knight is called "aghlich" (monstrous, 136) and "half etayn" (giant, 140), which accounts for his size, "one of the tallest on earth" (137). This identification of the Green Knight as an "eoten" relates him to the British tradition of Cain and his distant biblical descendants, Nimrod and the giants who ruled the earth until, having constructed the tower of Babel, they provoked the sweeping away of their constructs by the Flood. They are monsters of exaggeration as well as creatures of mixed nature, sired by angels upon the "daughters of Cain."[91] The Green Knight does not function specifically in relation to the details of this tradition; rather the details of the tradition function to place him in the general iconography of the teratological.

The monster's greenness has been associated with vegetative myth,[92] with demonism,[93] and with Christian colour symbolism,[94] and Martin Puhvel, in his study of the folkloric origins of colour significance, reminds us of the connection of the colour green with British Faeriedom.[95] The unnatural skin colour is understood by the audience more generally as at least wonderous, and so the poet tells us: "For wonder of his hue men had" ("For wonder of his hwe men hade," 147). This index of monstrosity is extended from the giant's body to his clothes and further to his horse. Colour contrast is created not only by the gold trim of his costume but also by his mysterious red eyes. As discussed earlier, mediaeval teratological tradition gave considerable prominence to the sign of fiery eyes, or eyes from which a light shines. In this text the eyes establish a further association with the descendants of Cain, father of all monsters, whose red, blazing eyes were understood as one of the characteristics inherited by his descendants from their angelic sires. The Green Knight's eyes are not only red, but they look out on Camelot from under "bristling eyebrows, gleaming green" ("bresed brozez, blycande grene," 305), and like the eyes of other monsters, they seem to hypnotize their victims:

> His gaze dazzled like lightening,
> So said all who could see him;
> It seemed no man could
> Under his power endure.[96]

Thus the Green Knight is both a monster of excess, by his unnatural size, and of combination, by his mixed nature. It is perhaps this trace of the mixture of human and divine in the Green Knight's distant past that leads Lawrence Besserman to perceive him as a paradoxical combination: "From start to finish he is both godlike and demonic. At Camelot, where he appears to be both "lovely" (l.433) and "ugly" (l.441), he functions as a type of the slain and risen Christ, expunger of aristocratic pride and also as a demonic, beheaded-but-still-living wild man, driven by a witch's lust for mortal revenge."[97]

The Green Knight is, then, an enigmatic monster, in some ways reminiscent of the sphinx. Rather than composing an intellectual riddle, like that posed to Oedipus, the Green Knight presents Gawain with the moral conundrum of how to preserve his honour and his life in a situation that seems logically to require the foregoing of one or the other. Long before that test and as if in preparation for it, when the monster first appears at Camelot the hero is confronted with what might be called a foreclosed paradox: Gawain, trusting in the efficacy of his own reason and rhetoric, thinks that there is no risk to him in accepting the terms of the Green Knight's contract, a stroke for a stroke, for how can a dead man claim his rights? But what had seemed a sure bet turns out to be a paradoxical trap for the unsuspecting Gawain. The monster both dies and lives:

> The head in his hand he holds up high,
> Toward the best one on bench he twists the face.
> Eyelids lift, gaze grimly at Gawain;
> Mouth opens, croaks out this order:
> "Gawain, get ready your promise to keep,
> And seek sincerely until, sir, you find."[98]

Things are not what they seem, as Gawain now begins to discover through the agency of a deformed creature he thought he controlled by outwitting the

Head-carrier. Dante, *Div. Com.* British Museum, Egerton 943, 51r.

creature at the creature's own game. But if things are not what they seem, how can they be represented? How can they be contained in words? It is precisely this conundrum that the hero will face in his second test. The audience is already prepared for this slippage between appearance and reality through Gawain's inflated rhetoric, for instance, by which he creates a self-portrait built on false humility and in which he depicts himself as what he is not:

> I am the weakest, I know, and slowest of wit,
> Thus less my life's loss will be of concern,
> But only because your blood's in my body,
> And you be my uncle, have I any worth.[99]

The Green Knight has been direct and to the point about the reason for his challenge: Arthur's court represents the highest point of human civilization and human discourse that exists; triumph in battle, excellence of manners, and refinement of language all characterize this zenith of human achievement, and it is all this that the monster wishes to expose as hollow, deceptive, and limiting:

> "What, is this Arthur's house," howled the hobgoblin,
> "Whose fame flows throughout the world's realms?
> Where is now your great pride, your victories,
> Your fierceness, your force, and all those great words?"[100]

Civilization itself is contradicted in the challenge to Camelot. Gawain acts as surrogate for Arthur and, as such, represents society as a whole in the challenge thrown at it by the monster. Because of his fame for flowery talk and discursive skill, Gawain's replacing of Arthur expands the object of the giant's negation to include not only social constructs represented by the king but the intellectual and rhetorical achievements represented by the courtier, as well.

The hint that the monstrosity of the poem is not limited to the Green Knight and the first suggestion that it may be extended to the hero himself come with the introduction and description of the pentangle on his shield. This figure is presented insistently as an enigma, a *coincidentia oppositorum* in the world of geometry: this ancient symbol of perfection was "a sign that Solomon set" ("Hit is a syngne þat Salamon set sum quyle," 625), that is, as the geometric basis of the Temple of Jerusalem; it has five points and "each line overlaps and locks into the other" ("And vche lyne vmbelappez and louken in oþer," 628). The dominant feature of the figure is that it is, in each of its five points and through all the lines that join them, "Everywhere endless" ("And ayquere hit is endelez," 629). Gawain bears an emblem that denotes the mysteries of the union of opposites: the beginning is the end, multiplicity is unity, and similarity is difference:

> Based on the five that failed folk never,
> Which never met in any direction, yet never separated,
> Without end in any point anywhere.[101]

The number five itself, as discussed earlier, is the first monster of mediaeval number symbolism, because it has the paradoxical quality of self-replication when "mated" with a kindred odd number, so that in every such multiplication the product is always 5 or a number ending in 5. It is also the product of the dyad and the first "real" number, 3, a product suggestive of incest in that the dyad is the "mother" of 3.

Nevertheless, the number five also expresses affirmative ideas. It is quintessence, the very foundation of the world with its five zones, five animal species, and it is, as the poem reiterates, the number of Mary's joys and

Christ's wounds. It is significant that it is to the affirmative symbolism that Gawain is attentive, since he bears Mary's image on the inside of his shield (which, as carried, is, of course, always visible to him) so as always to think upon the joys: "And when he looked there his confidence failed not" ("Þat quen he blusched þerto his belde neuer payred," 650). As so many commentators on the poem have noted, it is precisely the overcoming of this "belde" (confidence, rashness)[102] that the hero must achieve, through the agency of the monsters, in order to gain humility and to see rightly the shallowness of Camelot's behaviour.

Whereas the affirmative expression of the number five in the pentangle is tropological and found in the unification of the five virtues that Gawain embodies (generosity, pity, charity, chastity, and courtesy), the hero himself experiences these as separate and distinct, and the drama of the temptation scenes consists in Gawain's confronting the dilemma of unifying the disparate and of accepting the enigmatic. Gawain's lack of awareness of the paradox of the pentangle does not prevent the transference to him of the qualities of that sign, both affirmative and negative, for the shield bears his emblem and is thus a sign that stands for him and signifies what he is. As Shichtman has shown, Gawain *is* the pentangle, and the pentangle is he.[103] The hero must rid himself of the overconfidence that the affirmative aspects of the shield furnish and enter into the process of negation that will lead to the substitution of the pentangle by the girdle.

This begins at Hautdesert, the castle where the Green Knight, now revealed as a shape-shifter, appears as the generous host Bercilak de Hautdesert. The hero's transition from the security of Camelot to the trials of the court of Bercilak is prepared for in his passage through a lonely wilderness inhabited by monsters:

Now rides the royal one through the realm of Logres,
Gawain, on God's behalf, and thought it no game.
Always alone, without friends his nights he passes.[104]

The hero's solitary condition is emphasized, and it is this state, it seems, that prepares him for the encounter with the monster:

Many cliffs in the countries strange he climbed,
Far from his friends as a stranger he fared.
At each bank and brook that he broached
A foe opposed him, of fantastic nature,
So foul or fierce that to fight it behoved him.[105]

Battling his way through a landscape filled with dragons, satyrs, wild wolves, and giants, Gawain comes upon the most beautiful castle ever seen, a contrast between edifice and setting that lends an ominous quality to the castle and a sense of magic to the adventure. Insecurity replaces the grotesque; does the audience find itself, with Gawain, in a monster-infested waste or in the semiparadise surrounding the charming castle of Bercilak? Just as the landscape is and is not what it seems to be, a savage wilderness filled with monsters, a noble palace in a splendid garden, so the interior of the castle is and is not what it seems to be. Inside, illusion is extended through a series of deformities: things are not what they appear to be, but neither are they not what they appear to be. Hautdesert, refuge from deformity, is at the same time the very matrix of the monsters that surround it.

It has often been noticed that the scene that introduces Lady Bercilak gives the first hint that she, like her shape-shifting husband, is unnatural. Described as the most gracious lady Gawain had ever seen, more beautiful even then Guinevere, the Lady is led forth to Chapel by her physical opposite:

> Another lady her led by the left hand,
> Older than she, even ancient she seemed.
> She was highly respected by all about,
> But as dissimilar as could be those two were.
> The young one was winsome, withered was the old;
> Red rosey cheeks the regal one had,
> Rough wrinkled jowls trembled on the other.[106]

The beautiful woman, representing everything positive, shows herself as much as possible within the limits of decorum; her throat and her breasts she "bare displayed," while her contrary, presented as a physical negation of the lady's positive qualities, is covered, hidden, and as nonapparent as possible. The old hag wears a covering that hides her throat, wrapped under her black chin in white folds; nothing about her is unhidden, says the poet, except her face, and even that was "strangely blurred" ("sellyly blered," 963).

The descriptive structure throughout the poem is based on a juxtaposition that employs a dynamic similar to cataphasis/apophasis. The controlling trope of this device is inaugurated in the early lines of the poem when the monster, imposing apophatic silence in noisy Camelot, thereby establishes a tension between discourse and silence. It is again seen upon Gawain's departure from Camelot when he is dressed by his page, a process described in minute detail as each object of clothing and decoration is appended to his body. Immediately upon arrival at Hautdesert, we see the hero stripped naked, garment by garment, in a scene in which negative description unfolds into apophatic theme. Gawain's helmet is taken from him by those who greet him; then his sword and shield are removed. After being greeted by the Lord, he is shown to a richly decorated room where he is "despoiled" of his clothing "with speeches of mirth," and he seems to all present the most beautiful knight ever created (860–700). The contrast is emphasized not only between Gawain "dressed," in Camelot, and "undressed," in Hautdesert, but also between the stripping of Gawain's body by Bercilak's servants and the chamber in which it occurs, a room "dressed" to the hilt, as it were, with furnishings, hangings, and objects of all kinds, overladen with drapes, curtains, tapestries, rugs, and other cloth (853–9).

That the old hag functions as a negation of the youthful beauty, not only on the descriptive level but on the thematic level as well, is not, in and of itself, original or crucial. Mediaeval literature is full of such juxtapositions of youth and eld, of the beautiful and the ugly, and indeed, as Puhvel remarks, of protean Morgan-as-hag, Morgan-as-maiden.[107] More important than the contrast here is the realization, complete at the end of the poem, that the lovely Lady Bercilak and the old hag are one and the same, and no other than Morgan Le Faye. Thus Morgana, a shape-shifting monster of semidivine origin, contains within herself the contraries that she represents, and in designating her as the locus of the coincidence of opposites, the poet indicates the nature of monstrosity as inhering in paradox.

In Celtic lore and in literature she is represented not only as adopting the various forms of lovely lady/loathely hag but also the form of a bird. In the British tradition she is usually a crow, but with distinctly bat-like features. Roger Sherman Loomis points out that as late as the nineteenth century, ill-behaved Welsh boys were threatened with being carried off by Morgan to a watery dwelling.[108] Such a metamorphosis would associate her with the harpy, that lustful and savage monster bird of prey. In addition, Loomis reveals the interesting identification of Morgan, who is variously represented as female and as male, as a mermaid, which recalls her ancient connection with the island and the waters of Avalon. This depiction is complete with legends that exactly parallel the classical stories of the sex-starved Sirens who destroy their human lovers by drowning.[109] At the same time, Morgan is habitually depicted as a healer and comforter, most famously in her care for Arthur at Avalon.

The three hunts conducted by Bercilak are juxtaposed with the three temptations conducted by the Lady, and these operate, as well, on the principle of affirmation/negation. In the interior of the castle, Morgan the shape-shifter, appearing as the young and beautiful wife of Bercilak, tests Gawain's ability as the most famous knight in the world for civilized discourse and wit by placing him in the paradoxical situation of being either discourteous in refusing her or discourteous by cuckolding his host. Outside the castle, in the landscape invented by Morgan, the shape-shifting Green Knight appearing as Bercilak is contriving the other side of the paradox into which Gawain is placed by hunting the prey he will exchange with the young knight in the evening. Both the temptations and the hunts reflect the apophatic concept that underlies the poem and that is the essence of the monstrous.

Like the description of Camelot, the scene of the first hunt is one of frenzied activity and noise – the barking of the dogs, the bugle's blare, and the
cries of the hunters mix and grow while the monster knight "drove the day
with joy into the dark night" ("And drof þat day wyth joy / Thus to þe derk
nyȝt," 1176–7). The description of the butchering of the doe contrasts
sharply with the vibrant and assertive description of the hunt, which ends
with her death. Unlike the body of many men that make up the hunt, "a hundreth of hunteres" knitted together into a single band, the doe's body is taken
apart, chopped, cut, dismembered, separated, until she is virtually no more:

> They sundered the breast bone, tore out the stomach,
> Shaved it with knives, bound up the flesh;
> They cut off the four legs and pulled off the hide.
> Then they broke the belly and bowels took out,
> Skillfully pulling the flesh of the knot.
> They gripped the gullet, and quickly dispatched
> The throat and the windpipe and yanked out the guts.[110]

Fully forty lines are devoted to the detailed dismemberment of the deer;
interwoven into this description of butchering is the first encounter of the
hero with the lady. The contrast is sharp between the methodical reduction of
the form of the animal and the relentless piling up of words in the bedroom
conversation. Through his old device of self-deprecatory rhetoric, Gawain
succeeds in eluding the trap set for him by the shape-shifter, assuring the
Lady that she deserves much better than he; thus he respects his debt to his
host and preserves his reputation for courtesy toward ladies. That his very
identity is bound up in words is made manifest when Lady Bercilak declares
that she suspects that he is not, in fact, Gawain, a challenge that makes him
fear, "lest he had failed in forms of expression" ("Ferde lest he hade fayled
in fourme of his castes," 1295).

The triumph of language in controlling events is not, even in this first encounter, complete. Because he fears that words have, perhaps, failed, he con-
cedes the Lady a kiss, and for the first time, we imagine, there is silence in
the bedchamber. It is this kiss, the sign of concession, that Gawain delivers to
his host in the first exchange.

The same descriptive technique is used in the second hunt and temptation.
Now the quarry is a boar and the stanzas that describe its pursuit act as kind
of introduction to the second conversation in Gawain's bedchamber, just as
the hunting down of the deer preceded and prepared for the first encounter
with the lady. Once again the lady questions the hero's identity: "if you be
Gawain, it were a wonder" ("Sir, ȝif ȝe be Wawen, wonder me þynkkeȝ,"
1481), and once again Gawain identifies himself with his discourse. He succeeds in fending off the Lady this time with the same discursive skill he used

before, but even more concessions are necessary, and this time the lady extorts two kisses. She states bluntly that what she seeks is a true understanding of this strange man who is at once the most famous of talkers and yet, apparently, the most reticent of lovers. Gawain, having previously tested the effectiveness of rhetorical *deprecatio*, uses it again as a strategy to elude the Lady, rather than as a sincere self-revelation.

As Gawain constructs his rhetorical self in the day-long discussion with Lady Bercilak, the hunt of the boar builds to an end. The confusion of horns and hollering, the violence of the animal at bay, and the charged activity of the pursuing hunters come to a sudden halt as Bercilak drives his sword through the boar's body, straight to the heart. The building of excitement, of action, and of words seems now to begin to be undone in the description of the pulling to pieces of the prize:

> A hundred hounds ripped him asunder,
> Bit him to pieces with their savage teeth.
> ....
> First he [Bercilak] hews off the head, sets it on high,
> Then rips down the backbone roughly and rude,
> Flings out the bowels, casts them on coals.
> The dogs he delights with bread soaked in bowels;
> Then he breaks up the flesh in bright broad chunks.[111]

It has long been noted that the series of animals hunted by Bercilak is hierarchically arranged and represents a descriptive method of diminishment, the progress being from the most valuable and honourable, represented by the deer, to the least worthy, represented by the fox, which is killed in the third hunt. Such a method may be compared structurally to the cognitive system of negative theology, in which in the cataphatic stage of understanding one asserts the greatest of divine characteristics and procedes to the least; the inadequacies of this method are then corrected by reversal so that, beginning with the least and moving to the greatest, all of these assertions are denied.

So it is that on New Year's Eve the hunt of the fox begins, a prey that Bercilak characterizes as "foul," and worthy of the devil! The same commotion of human and animal sounds marks this last pursuit and, like the others, this turmoil is brought to an end by the death-dealing Lord who, holding up the dead animal, invites the crowd to strip away the fox's skin. The contrast between the third hunt and the third temptation is first noted in the brevity of the description of the hunt scene and the extended description of the bedroom scene.[112] But more importantly it is in this third encounter that Gawain's concessions to the inadequacy of language exceed the trivial and lead to betrayal. In the third test Lady Bercilak contrives to make it impossible for Gawain to equivocate:

That princess of praise pressed him so hard,
Pushed so close to the limit that either he must
Seize then and there her love, or offend her outright.[113]

Gawain still places his faith in words, however, and "with sweet talk he
parried her speeches, / Evaded her word traps with words of his own."[114]
Curious, perhaps, about his relations with Guinevere, the Lady asks Gawain
whether he is not already committed to some other lover, but he uses the
opportunity provided by the indiscrete question not only to deny his present
involvement in love, but to assert a commitment to chastity, thus outmanoeu-
vring his pursuer once again. In lieu of Gawain's body, the Lady then demands a souvenir of his presence, a token by which she can remember him
when he is gone. Aware that such a sign would constitute becoming the
Lady's knight, Gawain again successfully employs self-deprecation to steer
between the charybdis of rudeness and the scylla of entrapment. Nothing he
posseses, declares the silver-tongued Gawain, could possibly be worthy of
such a lady, so to avoid embarassment to them both, he gives her nothing.

Morgan Le Faye, even in her benign aspect, is not a mere human opponent, apt to be deluded by the illusions that language creates. If Gawain will
not concede her a sign of his presence, retorts Lady Bercilak, she will furnish
him with a trace of hers that will last forever: "Though I have none of yours,
/ Yet shall you have of mine!" ("Þaȝ I hade noȝt of yourez, / ȝet schulde ȝe
haue of myne," 1815–16). Gawain refuses a precious ring, and, at first, even
the green girdle that the Lady removes from around her waist. The sexual
charge of the symbols offered is both clear and appropriate, since they summarize the most obvious sense of the temptation that the hero has faced.[115]

But the temptation monstrously proffered in *Sir Gawain and the Green
Knight* is sexual only at the surface, and the flesh functions simply as a sign
of a deeper dilemma, the paradox of being itself. Thus, it is to the hero's existential anxiety that the Lady appeals by describing the girdle as a magical
protection against loss of life, the very predicament that Gawain faces and of
which, in fact, she is the author:

Forsake you this silk, said the sumptuous lady,
Because it is simple? So it does seem,
It is so little, less worthy you deem it;
But whoever knows the powers knitted therein
Praises the thing that belies what it seems.[116]

Gawain's preference for the elaborate, the complex, and the "big," so amply demonstrated in his discourse, is here exposed by the Lady as hollow, for
it is the little, insignificant trifle of the feminine undergarment that contradicts all of the hero's grand words and sophistical stratagems. Just as the an-

swer to every enigma is the simplest possible and just as every right response belies the complexity of the question, Gawain is at first misled by the banality of the object into refusing the girdle, just as the sphinx's victims were misled by the complexity of the question into misunderstanding the riddle. However, guided by one of the monstrous guardians of paradox, Britain's champion falls prey to this last temptation and, in so doing, paradoxically saves himself.

Victor Yelverton Haines has argued convincingly that the fundamental trope of *Sir Gawain and the Green Knight* is the Christian concept of *felix culpa*, the paradox of the so-called "fortunate fall," by which the incarnation of God and the redemption of humanity is made posssible through man's original sin. Haines' rich reading sees the poem as a series of juxtaposings of events in Christian history, primarily the Fall and the Redemption, through which dialectical oppositions are dissolved and the truer perspective of paradox is revealed.[117]

Humankind fell through the deception of the devil's offering of a form of knowledge – to know "like the gods" – a knowledge that, because it involves self-consciousness ("And they knew that they were naked" Gen. 3:7), is represented in Scripture under the figure of sexuality. This unhappy divorce of the unitive consciousness that existed between Adam and Eve is fully expressed in the discursive communication to which they are condemned: to represent in multiple and divided signs that which was once wholly and immediately present to them. But it is through this invidious "fall" into words that the Word is made possible, a paradox represented again in the "fall" of the postlapserian hero, the already loquacious Gawain, when he "sinfully" accepts the girdle that will be the means of his redemption and that will lead him to silence. The mysterious girdle not only saves Gawain from physical death, it also redeems him from babble by teaching him humility, the cure for our prideful conception of ourselves as the measure of the real.

The Gawain of Camelot suffers from that flaw of over-refinement so well defined by Cardinal Newman when he described, not the mediaeval courtier, but the secular 'gentleman' of four hundred years later. The same cultivation of *modesty* while ever eschewing *humility* by Newman's nineteenth-century man of intellect and manners reveals the essential fault of the fourteenth-century Gawain: "The embellishment of the exterior is almost the beginning and the end of philosophical morality. This is why it aims at being modest rather than humble; this is how it can be proud at the very time it is unassuming. To humility indeed it does not even aspire; humility is one of the most difficult of virtues both to attain and to ascertain ... This is true humility, to feel and to behave as if we were low; not, to cherish a notion of our importance, while we affect a low position."[118]

Lawrence Besserman traces the figure of the girdle in Scripture to establish the possible significance of the green girdle of the poem, describing it as a sign of such virtues as valour, prophecy, truth, and, especially, chastity.[119] The sign functions in relation to the concept of containment, for a girdle or belt is meant to bind. In a much older study, P. Saintyves discussed the phenomenon of the magic belt from evidence of popular religion in the Middle Ages and showed clearly the paradoxical element of the figure. The belts or girdles associated with St Margaret, St Honorine, and others all possess the power to protect pregnant women and to assist mothers in childbirth; churches consecrated to St Leonard are surrounded by chains in order to bind evil; St Thomas Aquinas was saved from lechery by a girdle miraculously furnished him in his sleep. Cities, too, could be belted, as it were, and Saintyves tells us that during a plague in the tenth century, the "Virgin Mary encircled the city of Valencia with a red cord, saving it from further disease."[120]

What is clear about the symbolism of the girdle is its fundamental contrariety; be it a belt of chastity, or of pregnancy, or of valour, the girdle binds in order to release. The pregnant woman is encircled with a cord that assists her in releasing the child that she contains; the warrior wraps his loins, source of his virility, in order to release his power against the enemy; the saint's body is ligated so that it may be freed. Just as Gawain's fall signifies the paradox of needing to sin to be saved, so the girdle, emblem of that fall, is a paradoxical sign of the binding that is liberation, the ligature that frees, and the constraint that makes expansion possible.

The three temptations in Hautdesert are the bridge between the two beheading scenes in the poem, and the second of those scenes is structured so as to recall the tripartite character of the temptations. Just as the hero did not fall victim to the temptation of the first visit of the Lady, nor to the second, so the first stroke of the Green Knight misses, as does the next. The third stroke, however, wounds Gawain's neck, causing his red blood to spatter the January snow on which he kneels:

> He lifts lightly his axe, then lets it down,
> The blade bites the bare neck, but only a little,
> And hurts the hero hardly at all!
> The steel sliced through skin, the flesh it slashed,
> And bright blood over his shoulders blotted the earth.[121]

The Green Knight, now revealing himself as Bercilak of Hautdesert, a shape-shifter and familiar of Morgan Le Faye, provides a clear exegesis of the events, telling Gawain that each feint represented the hero's two successful encounters with temptation, while the wound he now bears on his neck was given as a sign of his fall, the mortal condition that makes him "love his life." That this scarring of the hero takes place on the Feast of the Circumcision has been noted before and widely commented upon by students of the poem. In a fascinating recent study, R.A. Shoaf links the circumcision symbolism to the function of the arch-symbol of the poem, the Pentangle, and finds, as well, the typical sign of fallen discourse in the idea of circumcision:

Circumcision is a sacrament instituted *ante legem* and operative *sub lege* ... It is not a sacrament of the new *pactum* but a sacrament of the old *pactum* ... Circumcision in the flesh of Abraham and his seed is a sign and a sign only of their faith in the Mediator to come. Therefore, circumcision is the sacrament that retains and makes visible the essential differentiae of the sign: it is radically separated from its signified – *in carne venturi* – and it remains the presence of an absence – a mark or a trace in the flesh, of a reality absent temporally and materially.[122]

Shoaf sees Gawain's symbolic circumcision as a *rite de passage* leading to a mature and correct understanding of the nature of discourse and its limitations, as well as to an understanding of the relation of self to the real and the various mediations that such a relation requires. Shoaf's reading echoes remarkably Pseudo-Dionysius' analysis of the affirmative-negative dynamic of right speaking:

Circumcision is a rite that emphasizes the separateness of sign and signified; just so, Gawain, who had collapsed the ideal that he signified into identity with his own person, its sign, is circumcised so as to emerge from the ritual wearing a sign, the *syngne of surfet* and *token of untrawþe* which is a wisp of cloth indisputably separate from its signified. Gawain's error was finally the error of idolatry, the deliberate confusion of sign and signified. He is liberated from his error and purified through a rite or sacrament that was instituted, Aquinas tells us, against idolatry (in 4 *ST* 3a.70.2, *ad resp.* 1).[123]

Girdle and wound are closely associated in a poem that is overladen with signs. Based on Gawain's own direct statement that the girdle is a sign of the wound, Ross G. Arthur sees the two as interdependent: "This is the band of the blame I wear in my neck" ("Þis is þe bende of þis blame I bere in my nek," 2506).[124] Although Arthur sees Gawain's use of the girdle as part of a misconceived determination to consider himself in a permanent state of sin, one may see it less specifically as a metasign, as the sign of signification. Gawain's girdle, worn as a kind of *explicatio* of the scar that has replaced the wound on his neck, is *a sign of a trace of a state of deformity* that is both origin and terminus of all form, all affirmation, and all constructs of the intellect. Just as the name Oedipus signified the deformed feet of the King of Thebes and was thus *a sign of a token of the encodement of the monstrous reality* of which he was a part, so too, Gawain's emblem – which serves as a name if we accept it as the origin of the title of the Order of the Garter – reminds us of the hero's symbolic decapitation (circumcision) and associates him with all the headless, monstrous forms of teratology.

The monstrosity of the Green Knight is constituted not only by his gigantism but also by his headlessness. Such a deforming sign associates him with the cephalophores and the blemmyes of mediaeval monster lore, and several identifications of specific allusions to local decapitated saints in *Sir Gawain and the Green Knight* have been made.[125] The symbolic association between head and genitals underlies the metaphoric circumcision of Gawain by the slicing of the skin of his neck in a decapitation gesture. The sexual charge found in the figure of decapitation is explicated in the legend of Molus the rapist, and the practice of tatooing prostitutes with the figure of this headless god reinforces it. But, in addition to the sexuality suggested by the deformation of the head, we recall that the ideas of courtesy and hospitality are also invoked by the grotesque figure of the headless body. Baubo's comic method of entertaining Demeter by an illusion of headlessness expresses this aspect of the representation and suggests an archaic element in the Christmas entertainment in Camelot provided by the Green Knight.

The fundamental connotation of headlessness, however, is the negation of rationality, the uniquely human faculty that has its seat in the head. For this reason, the vast majority of martyred saints, having undergone the most extraordinary tortures with little damage, must finally be dispatched by decapitation. Eating and speaking, ingestion and expression – both functions of the mouth – are also negated with the separation of the head from the body, but in the case of the decapitated saint, this negation seems to inaugurate a transcendence to a higher form of discourse, for many of the martyrs put to death in this way speak anew from the severed head. St Denis and his companions sing the praises of God after decapitation, and Orpheus' sundered head becomes an oracle of Apollo.

The monstrosity of the Green Knight is transferred to Gawain both by the green girdle, which is the property of the monster, and by the wound that he inflicts upon the hero's neck, just as a trace of the prodigious was passed onto Alexander by his monster-god father and was to be found in his eyes and his stature, and just as Oedipus' monstrosity was betokened in his wound and encoded in his name. Gawain's symbolic beheading makes him one simultaneously with the blemmye and with the headless saint. As the text makes clear (2506), the garter is a sign of the scar, which is a sign of decapitation, and Gawain, in wearing this sign around his waist, emerges as a figurative cephalophore bearing the dislocated seat of reason and origin of discourse on his trunk. Such a metaphorical displacement betokens the new understanding that Gawain attains and that is expressed as humility:

> He bared the blemish on his naked neck
> That he had as a token of treason, sign of guilt.
> He suffered when he had to confess,
> He groaned for grief and shame.[126]

The reception that Gawain receives on his return to Camelot is one that, rather than reintegrating him as it is intended to do, further alienates him from the affirmative, discursive, conventional society that he once epitomized. Arthur and the court are unable to understand the transformation in the hero, and they all attempt to normalize and neutralize the sign of Gawain's deeper understanding of reality by adopting in a mocking and frivolous manner the green girdle that Gawain has earned at the cost of anguish and personal suffering:

> The King comforted the knight, and all the court
> Laughed loudly at it and lightly agreed,
> Those lords and ladies who belonged to the Table,
> That each brother of the band a baldric to bear,
> A green sash slung slantwise, nonchalant style.[127]

The poet does not fail to bring the poem, the narrative of which has progressed in a circle, back to where it began, to a full circumlocution in a figurative as well as structural sense. By once again connecting Camelot with the tradition of the Babylonian succession, he reminds us that the blindness of Arthur, and the more general arrogance of the human intellect, have an ancient pedigree:

> So in Arthur's day this adventure happened,
> The Books of Brutus bear witness abundant;
> And ever since Brutus first braved his way here,
> After the seige and assault was ceased at Troy.[128]

But he also reminds us that throughout this fallen tradition marked by the endless affirmations and misrepresentations of human discourse, the lesson of negation is always taught and learned. Thus the poem that has deconstructed the meaning of geometrical signs through the dissimilitude and simplicity of the circle ends, not with the tableau of the risible court, but with a final circumlocution:

> After the seige and the assault was ceased at Troy,
> Ah, yes,
> Many adventures ere
> Have gone like this.
> So may he who crown of thorns did bear,
> Bring us to Him in endless bliss! Amen.[129]

The affirmation of the geometrical pentangle is succeeded by the negating effect of the spherical girdle which, in turn, gives rise to another circular sign in the circumcisional scar of the hero. But this succession of signs is completed only in the ultimate lines of the poem, where all signification terminates and is fulfilled in the encompassing embrace of the crown of thorns. And here it is possible to see the final transference of monstrosity to the circular crown of thorns, and thus to its bearer, a transference that is effected through the vehicle of the succession of annular signs of monstrous paradox and deformation in the poem. Much as in the mediaeval legends of Judas, which encoded the Oedipus story, the transgressive and deformed is here discovered in the hero and is immediately transferred beyond the text, in an anagogical manner, to the Godhead who is its source. Just as Oedipus and Judas ultimately become vehicles for the discovery of the paradoxical and negatory identity of the One, so Gawain, albeit the hero of a narrative about his own self-understanding, is the mediator through whom we perceive, in that non-text lying just beyond the final lines of the poem and toward which the poem reaches, a reality accessible only through signs so deformed as to humble and chasten the intellect that rests confident in them.

7 Three Saints

> Since, therefore, such myths [i.e., those of Homer] arouse those
> naturally endowed to a longing for the knowledge hidden within them,
> and by their grotesque surface [*ten phainomenen teratologian*] provoke
> a search for the truth which has been set in its shrine, while at the same
> time preventing profane individuals from laying hands on what is
> forbidden them to touch, are they not, in an outstanding way,
> appropriate to the very gods whose substance they communicate to us?
>
> Proclus, *Commentary on the Republic*[1]

The propriety of the monstrous representation of the holy, as Proclus makes
clear, is constituted by the fact that the grotesque is the very mode by which
the divine has chosen to manifest itself, in order that the human mind may
have some understanding of it without confusing it with any of its own similitudes. This concept of the monstrous, fundamental to Neoplatonism, comes
into widespread use in the art of the Christian Middle Ages and particularly
in the hagiography and iconography of the time.

The saint's life is a particularly useful kind of text for the exploration of
the concept of the monstrous, since its literary structure is fully polymorphic,
involving the cult of the saint, the biography or legend, and the visual representation. Not surprisingly, it is in the fabulous, extrahistorical saints' lives
that grotesque elements are most prominent, and the question has long ago
been raised whether such legends come into being first through an iconographic representation that gives rise to a narrative that in turn creates a cult,
or whether the text begins as a story that produces visual representation that
becomes the object of a cult.[2] The question need not be answered here, but it
is a useful one in that it recognizes indirectly the tripartite structure of this
literary genre. Each saint's life, whether fabulous or historical, is a text composed of the narrative – usually the life, works, and death of the saint – the
iconography – illustrations of these narrative events as well as abstact representations – and the cult or rituals surrounding the veneration of the saint.
This latter is, in some cases, simply a prayer for intercession, but sometimes,
as in the case of our grotesque saints, the cult involves a more complex encoding of the dialogue between saint and petitioner.

The interrelation of these three elements constitutes the meaning of the text, and it is remarkable that in so many of the saints' lives the iconography goes beyond the visual illustration of the story by introducing additional, sometimes surprising, elements of the "Life." Similarly, in some instances the prayer addressed to the saint and the practices involved in the cult suggest ideas or associations quite distinct from the other elements of the *Vita*, as if something were missing from the narrative itself or from the iconography that the ritual supplied. Each element, then, informs the other, and the saint's life as text is constituted by a reading of all three parts: narrative, iconography, and cult. However, the order in which such a reading takes place may itself influence the understanding of the text, and in many cases it is necessary to reread in all possible directions to unravel the meaning of the text. As will be seen in the following discussion, the relation of narrative to iconography to cult is not one in which meaning simply accumulates in a logical pattern; rather, it would seem, it is one in which each element holds the key to another, where, let us say, the same narrative content is negated by details of the iconography, or where the words of the prayer illuminate details of the iconography and reinterpret incidents of the narrative, and so on.

The view taken here is that the monstrous saint's life, like all uses of the deformed in mediaeval culture, is an expression of the Neoplatonic, Pseudo-Dionysian principle that the most appropriate language for the revelation of the unknowable God, or for that matter, for the revelation of the fundamentally real, is negation leading to the ultimate transcendence of discourse itself. Saints' lives are particularly suitable for illustrating this because they are, by the very nature of their subject, overtly within the arena of the sacred and therefore less distanced as negative discourse from the source of negation in the One. Nevertheless, the sacred biographies and legends remain, like the epics and romances of the Middle Ages, symbolically encoded, the more deeply as their meaning approaches through a negative decoding an identification of the deformed saint with God Himself.

The saints' lives chosen here represent, to some degree, different aspects of the use of the monstrous to reveal the paradox of the real, but the similarity between them will be obvious. Denys the Areopagite described divine superabundance as the very matrix of negation, and the affinity of the monstrous to this concept is evident in the saints' lives: the gigantic size of St Christopher, the separated head and torso of St Denis, the androgeny of St Wilgeforte are the negations of physical and conceptual limits through excess and superabundance that allow these figures to take on a theophanic function.

ST CHRISTOPHER

By all accounts, the cult of St Christopher was one of the most widespread and most popular of the Middle Ages. His story shares many of the characteristics

St Christopher carrying Jesus. Book of Hours, Spain, ca. 1480. British Library, Add. MS 50004, fol. 64b

of the popular mediaeval saint's life: conversion to Christianity, miraculous adventures, converting of others, martyrdom for the faith. What sets the text apart are the fabulous details that have intrigued audiences for so long: Christopher is a dog-head, a member of the nation of such monsters celebrated throughout teratology in all the mediaeval texts that describe the deformed. He also practises cannibalism, a characteristic of his race, and is a giant. Most versions describe him as having a fierce visage, emphasized by his gleaming eyes.

St Christopher's story is reasonably consistent from one source to another; here we follow chiefly the account given in the *Golden Legend*.[3] A member of the race of the Canaanites, the twenty-foot Reprobus, for such was his heathen name, harbours an ambition to serve the mightiest of all masters. Discovering that his earthly master, the king, fears the devil, Reprobus abandons him and enters into the service of Satan. Confronted one day with a crucifix, however, Satan flees in fear, and Reprobus realizes that there is still one more powerful to be found. A hermit instructs him in the knowledge of Christ and attempts to find some appropriate task for him so that he might serve this most powerful of all masters. Reprobus refuses the first suggestion, which is to fast for Christ, as well as the second, which is to pray continually, describing himself as unable to accomplish either of these things. After considering the convert's physical size and prowess, the hermit finally assigns him the task of ferrying on his shoulders all those who want to cross a deep and dangerous river, a labour the giant enthusiastically accepts.

After "many days" at this job, he is awoken by the voice of a child requesting passage who is apparently so small that the giant cannot see him the first two times he responds, but on the third, he places the babe on his shoulders and with staff in hand wades into the familiar river. But as the ferryman progresses, the waters rise higher and more turbulent than ever before, and, even more strangely, the child becomes heavier and heavier, so that he almost crushes the colossus under his increasing weight. Safe on the other side, Reprobus complains: "Child, thou hast put me in dire peril, and hast weighed so heavy upon me that if I had borne the whole world upon my shoulders, it could not have burdened me more heavily!" But the babe explains all: "Wonder not, Christopher, for not only hast thou borne the whole world upon thy shoulders, but Him Who created the world."[4]

Reprobus is now Christopher, not only through the Christian baptism to which he alludes later in the narrative but also and more significantly through etymology: he is the "Christ-bearer (*phore*, meaning "bearer"). As further proof of his divinity, the child Jesus has Christopher plant his staff in the bank of the river where it quickens, blooms, and bears fruit. Abandoning his occupation as ferryman, the saint travels to the city of Samos in Lycia, seat of the pagan king named Dagnus in the *Golden Legend* but variously identified as Decius and as Dagon. Here Christopher receives the gift of tongues and begins to convert the people. The evil king torments him, sends prostitutes to

Christopher ferrying the child Jesus. Wall painting, Pickering, Yorkshire. In Whaite, *Saint Christopher*, pl. 21

corrupt him, tortures him, and finally dispatches him through beheading. Nevertheless, the king himself is converted to Christianity by a postmortem miracle authored by the holy cynophale he has martyred.

Christopher's connection with Anubis, the Egyptian dog-headed or jackal-headed deity, and with Herakles, who carries the child-god Eros on his shoulders, immediately suggests itself and has been widely commented upon in discussions of Christopher.[5] Hermes, patron of travellers (and rogues), is also strongly suggestive of the Christian saint. Anubis was the god of creation and of fruitfulness, as well as death, associated with Sirius, a star in the constellation Canis Major. Because the Nile began to rise on the twenty-fifth of July, with the rising of the star Sirius, the two were associated, and it was further asserted that on this date the world had been created and that the first rising of the Nile acted as a sign of this event. In contrast, on the ninth of May, when

Sirius sets, Hell was opened, and it was on this date originally that the antiworld had been created. It is significant in our discussion that the first rising of the "dog star," Sirius, during the first canicule, or "dog days," was also indentified as the moment of origin of all the monsters that inhabited the earth. This ur-moment was identical with the creation of the physical world, making the coming into being of the deformed the originary ontological event.

In his role as psychopomp, Anubis has his equivalent in the Greek Hermes, who separates the soul from the body, assists at its judgment, and leads those who are deemed pure to their reward. But there are other similarities. Hermes was appointed the herald of the gods of the underworld, Hades and Persephone, and acted, as well, as the personal representative of Zeus, his father. Thus he "stands for" the god of gods, just as Anubis "stands for" Osiris in the entire ritual treatment of the dead. His general function in mythology is as the divine amanuensis, expressing and enforcing the will of the gods. The iconography of Hermes includes the caduceus, a winged staff encircled by snakes, winged sandals, and a helmet. The white cock is sacred to him. He is sometimes represented carrying a lamb on his shoulders, but he is more frequently represented carrying the infant Dionysus. Many engraved stones bear the image of Hermes as god-bearer; in the museum of Florence, for instance, there is a stone depicting Hermes with the divine child on his left arm while in his right hand is a blossoming staff.[6]

Saintyves connects St Christopher not only to Hermes and to Anubis but also to Herakles, and, in fact, in combining the legends and attributes of these three gods, we get a rather full sketch of the Christian saint. Herakles was not always the name of the Greek hero and god. Originally called Alcide, his name connoted physical strength; he was given the name Herakles (glory of Hera) as he began the twelve labours dedicated to the goddess. In the last of these, the obtaining of the golden apples of the Hesperides, Herakles replaces the giant Atlas and takes upon his shoulders the support of the entire Heavens. It is on his shoulders as well that he carries Erymanthus' boar, another of his labours. However, the most celebrated use of this theme is found in the story of Herakles and Eros. As Saintyves points out, this theme was vastly popular in the visual arts representing classical themes, which usually depicted the giant hero on his knees with the infant god on his shoulders so as to express the idea of being crushed by the weight of "love." Eros is, of course, the "maker" of the world in that he promotes generation, and the theme corresponds closely to that of St Christopher weighed down by the "maker of the world" in the form of a child.

St Christopher was not only the patron saint of travellers but also the protector of orchards, particularly of apple trees, and Saintyves reports a prayer sung by French children on the evening of the first Sunday in Lent:

Envoyez-en des grosses pommes,
Des tiots cafignons
Pour manger en saison.[7]

New apples were blest on the feast day of the Saint, and at Amiens new plums were eaten to celebrate the day.

The date assigned to St Christopher in the mediaeval calendar is the twenty-fifth of July, the day also dedicated to Anubis and related, as we have seen, to the creation of the world through the rising of Sirius and the Nile. In the Greek calendar the ninth of May is the feast day of St Christopher, which, as we recall, is the date of the setting of Sirius and the inauguration of Hell. During the Middle Ages the cult of Christopher sometimes involved placing snakes at the foot of his statue. Saintyves remarks that hagiography has been unable to explain the significance of this element,[8] but we recall that one of the animals dedicated to Hermes was the serpent, two of which entwine his staff. Egyptian symbolism claimed that the spirit of God resided in the serpent.

In the fourteenth century there were protests concerning the pagan practice of sacrificing a cock to St Christopher on his feast day, but regardless, in Germany an even more elaborate ceremony was held: "In Germany on the 25th of July the people sacrificed cocks that earlier in the week had been made to dance in honour either of Thor or of St Christopher."[9] Just as Hermes has the white cock as his sacred emblem, so Anubis sometimes received in sacrifice a white cock, symbolizing purity, sometimes a yellow cock, representing diversity and multiplicity.

The similarities between these pagan gods and the Christian saint are, then, numerous and have been widely noted. How, though, do they make any clearer the force and meaning of the grotesque saint? The story of Christopher, like his visual representation and cult, is a presentation of what is-not. Christopher himself never existed, of course, but that is only the point of departure for the series of dissimilitudes that progressively reveal him apophatically. In all versions of the legend, the saint changes his name in the course of his adventures, in the Greco-Latin versions from the Greek equivalent of "Reprobus," and in the Coptic *The Contendings of the Apostles*, from "Hasum," meaning something like "The Abominable."[10] The transformation in the names suggests something paradoxical, for the Cynophale's pagan names are clearly negative, at least in the moral sense: "reprobatus" suggests profligacy and damnation, although closer to its etymology it bespeaks testing and trials; "abominable" signifies in its metaphorical extension that which is detestable or loathsome, yet its basic meaning would be something similar to "shun signification" (*ab*, meaning "away from"; *omen*, meaning "sign," "announcement," or "truth"). The saint's Christian name naturally appears at first glance to be a positive change, from "reprobate" or "abominable" to "Christ-bearer," and therefore suggests a reversal of the process of negative theology whereby we first state the cataphatic and afterwards the apophatic. Indeed, we recall the Areopagite's opinion that such descriptions of God as "drunkard" and "hung-over" (not far from "reprobate" and "abominable") are better than "mighty" and "wise" because such grotesquerie protects the mind from its own anthropocentric errors.[11]

At the tropological level of the text, the development of nomenclature is clearly positive. The hero goes from pagan to Christian, from barking to rational speech, from unnatural eating habits to natural, and his new name denotes this evolution toward Christianity. But at the level of language itself, the names progress from one level of negation to another. The Coptic text makes this clear: "And the man with a face like unto that of a dog said unto him, 'My name is "Hasum,"' i.e. the "Abominable." And Andrew said unto him, 'Rightly [thou speakest], for thy name is even as thyself; but [here] there is a hidden mystery which is both honourable and pleasant, for from this day onwards thy name shall be "Christian."' "[12]

The saint's name is changed, according to this text, because of its similitude and resemblance to that which it signifies, and the transformation to "Christopher" thus constitutes a negation of similitude and a movement to the higher stage of dissimilitude; the hero is *nothing like* a Christian at the moment he receives the name. But just as in negative theology a third step following assertion and negation must occur, one that transcends even the superior understanding of negation, so, too, here, the name of Christopher will be transcended by reducing it from name to metaphor. The name "Christopher" is no name at all, or, as Dagnus his persecutor says, it is a "fool's name."[13] Just as "Reprobus" or "Hasun" are *metaphors*, so the name that replaces them is a *christophor*, we might say, indicating not a specific person, but a theophany, a making present of Christ, or the One, through a series of negations and the subsequent transcendence of all names.

St Christopher's monstrous head associates him with death and the various deities that preside over death as psychopomps, but both his cult and his iconography contradict this idea. The staff that is so prominent in his miracles is transformed from dead wood to living and blossoms into a symbol of life and fertility. A primitive phallic symbol, the flowering staff is familiar in hagiography and regularly signifies life-giving. The saint is prayed to not to ensure an easy death, as might be expected and for which there were many prayers available, but to avoid death. It is said that St Christopher's statues were erected on hills or other high places and built as high as forty feet because his devotees believed that all who cast their eyes on the colossus would not die that day.[14]

While Anubis and Hermes guide the dead souls to the final judgment and reward, Christopher does just the opposite: he is asked by the hermit who instructs him in the faith to prevent pilgrims from perishing as they cross the river, and so he does. He is invoked as the protector of travellers, and their journey may easily be seen as the journey of life, thus a voyage toward death; and yet it is not. His role as life-giver and protector against death contradicts his role as patron of travellers if we see their voyage as the iconographic passage from life to death: the paradox is that Christopher thus becomes a guide who protects travellers from getting to their destination. Nowhere in the legends of the ferrying saint do we witness him transporting anyone over the river except the baby Jesus, and in that case, strangely enough, when the two have reached the other side of the river, they seem to be back where they started. It is on the "other side" that Jesus tells Christopher to plant his stave in the ground so that it blossoms. But in the visual representations of this incident when the flowering staff is not found still in the saint's hand, it is seen planted beside the house from which Christopher set out to carry the child across the river, thus putting Christopher and his passenger back where they started. Through the confusion of "this side/the other side" the journey is a nonpassage.[15]

The negation of Christopher as psychopomp is, perhaps, most strongly expressed in the conclusion to the *The Contendings of the Apostles*, where he is depicted not only as protector of life, but as life-giver: "And a voice cried from heaven unto the man whose face was like unto that of a dog, and said unto him, 'O beloved Christian, thou hast received the gracious gift of power to raise up those who are [dead].' "[16] This ability, it will be noted, goes further than associating Christopher with life and fertility, it attributes to him the divine power, usually reserved only to God Himself, of raising the dead. Thus it is that the saint both is a psychopomp and is not. He is clearly significative of death, but he is equally the symbol of life, and it is precisely through such paradox that the full significance of this holy monster is made manifest.

Christopher's enormity and prodigious strength are also radically negated in the central episode of his encounter with Christ, the rhetorical force of which depends upon the irony of juxtaposition and the surprise of reversal: the greatest of men is weighed down by the smallest; seeking the mightiest of masters, the giant finds him in the slightest. In addition, the iconography that always depicts the divine child upon the shoulder of the giant tends to merge the two visually. From this point of view Christopher should now be taller and mightier, if anything, given the added stature of the child now hoisted above his head and the hidden power of the divine to which he is proximate. And this is, in a sense, so, for Christopher is made mightier spiritually by the child as well as being made weak physically. In his *Divine Names*, Pseudo-Dionysius discusses the coexistence of the opposites, great and small:

God is called great because of that characteristic greatness of his which gives of itself to everything great, is poured out on all greatness and indeed reaches far beyond it …

This greatness is infinite, with neither quantity nor number, and it reaches a flood as the result of the absolute transcendent outpouring of incomprehensible grandeur. "Smallness" or subtlety is predicated of God's nature because he is outside the bulky and the distant, because he penetrates without hindrance through everything. Indeed smallness is the most elementary cause of everything and you will find no part of the world without its share of smallness, which is why we use the word in this sense in regard to God ... This smallness has neither quantity nor magnitude. It is unconquerable, infinite, and unlimited, comprehending everything and itself never comprehended. (*DN* 909C–912B)

The paradoxical descriptions that characterize Denys' discussion of divine greatness and smallness are also applicable to Christopher. In his encounter with Christ he, too, is great and small; mighty enough to carry the "weight of the whole world on his shoulders," but so weak as to be crushed by a child and made small. Just as Denys describes God in terms of the paradox of this coexistence of opposites, so too Christopher's might and giganticism are negated in favour of the small. The text goes on to present Christopher as simultaneously giant and dwarf, mighty and weak; unlike Samson, a suitable counterpart to Christopher, he offers no resistance to arrest or to torture, except in the versions that do not include the Christ-carrying incident (for example, *The Contendings of the Apostles*), and never uses his strength or the advantage of his size in his encounter with the enemy.

The saint's monstrous head creates a similitude with other figures of such deformity and provides part of the significance of the Christopher figure, but that similitude is nevertheless negated in order that we will understand still more. The saint's inordinate size is to be read in the moral sense as the enormity of faith and the greatness of virtue, but this, too, is negated by the dynamics of his legend in order to reveal Christopher as his own opposite, a small child, thus making him the locus of the coincidence of opposites and of the demonstration of the precedence of the negative over the positive: that which is large is conceived of as positive or "more," while its opposite, that which is small, is conceived as "less" and thus negative.

A further reversal that is itself subsequently reversed is the saint's mode of discourse. Much is made of the fact that while the cynophale understands human speech, he can himself only bark and howl. As discussed earlier, the key test in teratology for determining the nature of a being was the ability to speak, itself the primary sign of rationality. In considering a claim to humanity, the Middle Ages was willing to put aside even outer form if only rational discourse could be detected. In the Irish *Passion of St Christopher*, it is specified that the cynophale speaks only the language of his kind, and it is through the intervention of an angel who blows upon his mouth and strikes his lips that human discourse becomes available to him.[17] But neither in the Irish version nor in any other does Christopher go on to use discourse in

order to convert the people to Christ. Rather, he teaches by example, amazing his audiences by his own grotesque appearance and convincing them
through miracles, not words. Thus in the *Passion*, he first converts Decius'
soldiers, not by addressing them in word, but by silently praying that his staff
be turned into a living stalk. Immediately afterward, he is heard "moaning"
as he sits in a temple at prayer. Similarly, it is his fierce canine appearance
that wards off the prostitutes sent to corrupt him, and they are first moved toward conversion by the wonder of it, not by words.

In the *Golden Legend* there seems even to be a question as to whether the
replacement of speech for barking was ever completed. In his conversation
with the evil Dagnus, Christopher's speech seems enough like yapping for
the King to say: "Thou art reared among the wild beasts, and speakest wild
things, not to be understood by men."[18] The fact that Reprobus already possesses intellect before he achieves discourse is evident from the descriptions
of his mental life as a dog-head. The Irish *Passion* states: "He meditated
much on God, but at that time he could speak only the language of the Dog-
heads."[19] Thus the ability to speak is not itself what constitutes reason but is,
rather, its sign. In the narrative of the saint's life, Christopher needs this sign,
not in order to possess the intellect signified by it, but rather to make his
monstrosity more acceptable to men. It is remarkable that the gift of speech
received by the saint is consistently juxtaposed to his deformity. In the
Golden Legend, at the very moment that he becomes discursive, the cynophale hides his face: "After this he came into Samos, a city of Lycia; and
not understanding the language of this place, he prayed the Lord to give him
understanding thereof. And as he prayed, the judges, thinking him mad, left
him alone; and having obtained his request, *he covered his face*, and went to
the circus, and there comforted the Christians who were being tortured for
the faith."[20] The parallel scene in the *Contendings* is strongly suggestive of
the theme of the *Deus absconditus*: "And when the apostles were wishing to
enter into the city, the man whose face was like unto that of a dog said unto
them, 'Cover over my face before ye enter into the city, that the people may
not see me, and may not flee from me.' "[21]

Christopher's monstrosity is obscured not only by the veil he draws across
his deformed face but by discourse itself, for it is language that is the sign of
the rational and the rational that constitutes the "norm." Just as in the theme
of the *Deus absconditus* one of the masks that God hides behind is language,
a mask that can only be pulled somewhat aside through apophasis, so in the
Christopher story the saint's acquisition of discourse is not a sign of his
transformation from monster to man but rather a sign that conceals his monstrosity and difference and identifies discourse itself as so much "barking."

While Christopher's barking is transformed into human speech through
the intercession of an angel, the dog's head from which this speech emerges
never changes; it is merely hidden, creating an association of the monstrous

with the rational in which the former takes precedence. And yet it is by the presence of the very sign of discourse and its subsequent negation that the process of revealing that which is-not can occur.

It has been claimed that both Herakles and St Christopher, in their respective cultures, approached the status of God, particularly in their universal protective functions,[22] but such an opinion may not go far enough, and we must ask why these two figures, in two cultures so different and distanced, should be identified as God. In Christianity it is understood that one of the many ways in which God reveals Himself is in the person of angels, that is, disguised as an angel; Jacob's wrestling with the angel is one example. Similarly, it would seem, God may reveal Himself through other figures, and the fantastic saints of Christian hagiography would seem prime candidates for theophany. Since they have no existence of their own, they become suitable signs of that which is-not, He who is beyond being and nonbeing and is their source. It is the fantastic saint's monstrosity, his negation of form through deformity and his very inability "to be," that allows him to manifest apophatically a portion of the divine. In so doing, the grotesque figure reveals much about the dynamics of monstrous representation and its links to negative theology.

St Christopher's monstrous head and barking initially negate the identification with human ideas and values that would be possible without such deformity, as well as pointing to the limitations of discursive rationality as the means to understanding. But even these perceptions are negated or transcended, for while Reprobus the pagan barker is transformed into Christopher the Christian speaker, this progress is reversed, in ways we have seen, in order to suggest the negation of the limits of names and words. Christopher as theophany signifies that truth about the One that Pseudo-Dionysius expressed thus: "Mind beyond mind, word beyond speech, it is gathered up by no discourse, by no intuition, by no name"(DN 588B). Our Saint's "foolish" name is no name, his words are no speech, mixed as they are with inarticulate sound, and his reason has a basis beyond discourse; in this he is a theophany.

In the negation of his bigness through smallness and in the symbolic transcendence of this reversal we see the coming together of opposites that Nicholas of Cusa thought the best definition of God. Christopher as divine avatar is both big and small and neither big nor small; he is mighty and gentle, as well as neither mighty nor gentle, suggesting through such paradox the divine transcendence of cataphasis and apophasis as well, a transcendence to where assertion and denial are left behind.

In his confusion of the roles of psychopomp and life-giver, Christopher reveals God as Being and non-Being, source of both and beyond both, the state that Denys calls "supra-existent Being" (DN 588B). Elsewhere, the Areopagite elaborates: "It falls neither within the predicate of nonbeing nor of being"

(*MT* 1048A). God is the source of life and of death, just as Christopher and Anubis signify these contraries, and, as such, the One is the source of these and other opposites. It is only in tracing back the assertions of life and of death through their negation that their sameness in a single source can be discovered and, thence, their transcendence achieved.

ST DENIS

The monstrosity of St Denis of Paris is perhaps more accurately described as a wonder, that of having carried his severed head several miles to the site intended for a cathedral to be built in his name. But his is a miracle unlike others, one that involves a gruesome suspension of natural laws and that produces an iconographic image of remarkable bodily deformation. Nor is St Denis' postmortem accomplishment an eccentricity unique to his individual legend, but rather, it is one occupying an important place in teratology.

Like St Christopher, Denis' primary index of monstrosity is his head, but in his case the deformity is achieved through displacement. Denis, or Dionysius as he was more commonly called in the Middle Ages, is a member of the class of grotesques discussed in the previous chapter and designated as cephalophores; they are found throughout mediaeval legend and nowhere more frequently than in hagiography, where Saintyves has discovered as many as one hundred and thirty.[23] Over and above this crowd of head-carriers, however, we know that the vast majority of martyrs whose stories contain fabulous elements end their earthly lives through decapitation. The familiar pattern is that after days and days of excruciating tortures of the most diverse kinds, the frustrated persecutor dispatches the saint quite easily and quickly by beheading. The act of separating the body and the head seems to be understood as the definitive means of ending life, and archeology points to neolithic cults that apparently involved the decapitation of cadavers before burial, presumably to guarantee the release of the spirit from the body and its safe passage to the otherworld.[24]

In his now classic study of the phenomenon, Saintyves investigates the origin of the concept of the cephalophore, considering, among other explanations, the opinion that the legend was inaugurated by the image. This explanation has it that, in an effort to communicate the type of martyrdom suffered by the decapitated saint, the visual artist simply depicted the saint with head in hand. Based on such images, the theory goes, the "credulous spirit of the common people" fashioned fantastic stories to explain the images. The disadvantage of such explanations is that they tend to drain all significance from the event they attempt to explain, reducing it to phenomena of historical error and intellectual misunderstanding. But considering only the historical criteria upon which the theory rests, the theory founders, for, as

Saintyves points out, the texts containing the legends are in general older than the existing images.[25]

The three oldest versions of the life of St Denis are in Latin and date from the seventh century in the case of the earliest, called the *Gloriosae*, and the ninth century in the case of the later two, the *Libellus antiquissimus* and the *Post beatum*.[26] Among the several later mediaeval versions in French is a fourteenth-century play, *Geu Saint Denis*, derived ultimately from Hilduin's *Post beatum* version, but perhaps more immediately from elements of the St Denis story permeating the popular culture of the time.[27] It is principally to that text that we will refer in this discussion, as well as to the version contained in the *Golden Legend*.

The story of St Denis, generalized from all of the sources, is as follows. Confused by the darkening of the day that occurs when Christ is crucified, the eminent Greek philospher Dionysius announces that the event, scientifically incomprehensible though it is, signifies by its darkness the coming of the true light of the world. Accepting his explanation, the Athenians erect an altar on which they inscribe "To the Unknown God." St Paul, arriving in Athens, debates the philosophers and particularly Dionysius to whom he explains the identity of the "unknown God" through the person of Jesus, and, with the help of a miracle, converts Dionysius and his wife to Christianity. This part of the legend is the basis of the widespread mediaeval identification of St Denis of Paris with Dionysius the Areopagite, who claimed to have been converted by hearing St Paul preach.

Later, together with Rusticus and Eleutherius, brothers in the faith, Dionysius is sent to Paris to convert its pagan population and establish the Church. After extraordinary success in his mission, Dionysius is arrested along with his companions by the pagan Emperor Domitian, who subjects the trio to extensive torture. At the beheading that ends the sufferings of the three missionaries, Dionysius springs from the ground, picks up his head, and, accompanied by two singing angels, walks the two miles from the place of his execution to the place chosen for his remains, the severed head all the while pronouncing the praises of God.

All versions include what appears to be the anticlimactic reference to the fate of the bodies of Rusticus and Eleutherius. Thrown into the river Seine by the pagans, they are retrieved by a holy Christian woman, Catulla, who brings them to rest beside Dionysius.

The story of Dionysius combines two wonderous elements, that of the carrying of the severed head and that of the so-called *lingua palpitans*, the disembodied tongue that speaks. The events of decapitation and the speaking of the severed head are related to the subjects of death and life and to the nature of discourse and understanding, not only in the story of St Denis but in the many mythical uses of the severed head theme that precede the hagiographic version. Polycritos, an Etolian leader who died four days after his wedding,

St Denis, Eleutherius, Rusticus. *Gospels and Collects*. St Omer, MS 342bis, fol. 63.

returns as a spirit to devour his new-born, hermaphroditic son, who is threatened by the crowd with death. The child's head, the only body part left by the
father, begins to prophesy and specifies the locus of its own resting place. The
head of the Welsh King Bran continues to converse with his companions after
it is cut from his body, and, later ensconced in London, it exercises a magical
resistance against invasion. The Scandinavian god Odin regularly consults the
severed head of Mimer, a wiseman, which he has had encased in gold.

St Denis and companions and the decapitation. MS St Omer, 342bis, fol. 63.

The most famous classical example of the speaking head is in the story of Orpheus, referred to earlier, and a comparison of the figure of this pagan poet with St Denis indicates that his relation to the Christian saint is more extensive than the single theme of decollation. Orpheus' murder and dismemberment occurs after his descent to the underworld, his loss of Euridice through lack of faith, and his subsequent founding of the Eleusian mysteries based on his experiences in the otherworld. Indeed, it was in vengeance for having excluded women from the celebration of these mysteries that the women of Thrace, members of the Dionysian cult called Maenads, assassinated the patron of music. Everything about Orpheus identifies him with the mystical, and it is precisely because of his own passing into the otherworld that Orpheus is able to bring back to earth the secret understanding that he then begins to teach: "It is on the basis of this myth that Orphic theology is constructed. From his descent into the Underworld in search of Eurydice, Orpheus is supposed to have brought back the knowledge of how to get to paradise and to eschew all of the obstacles and traps that await the soul on this journey after death."[28]

It is this suprahuman knowledge that the disembodied head of Orpheus expresses as an oracle at Lesbos in a discourse so far beyond the mundane that its author is honoured by poets as the inventor of their art. The understanding possessed by Orpheus is gained through transmissions associated with death, as reflected in his descent into the land of the dead in search of Eurydice. He speaks "from the other side," as it were, and the disembodied head signifies at one and the same time the world of the living – in that it speaks – and the world of the dead – in that it is lifeless. Thus the severed head becomes a medium through which the otherworld communicates to this world and through which its special language is translated into the discursive language of humankind.

Credit for the inauguration of the Eleusian mysteries – rituals which, we might note, address death and the afterlife – Orpheus shares with the god Dionysus. The relationship of the two is one of identity through opposition. Orpheus refuses to honour Dionysus and, in opposition to the Dionysian cult, preaches the serene, ordered, rational, "Apollonian way." This opposition, some say, caused the jealous god to inspire the Maenads to tear Orpheus to pieces.[29] The narrative itself is an encodement that uses the story of enmity between a man and a god to veil the theophany of that god through a *coincidentia oppositorum*. Proclus breaks through this code, as Robert Graves explains: "Thus Orpheus did not come in conflict with the cult of Dionysus; he *was* Dionysus, and he played the rude alder-pipe, not the civilized lyre. Thus Proclus (Commentary on Plato's *Politics*: p. 398) writes: 'Orpheus, because he was the principal in the Dionysian rites, is said to have suffered the same fate as the god,' and Apollodorus (i.3.2) credits him with having invented the Mysteries of Dionysus."[30]

Just as Orpheus may be seen as the man "twice perishing," so Dionysus is known as the god "twice born," having been torn from his mother's womb at six months, having been planted in Zeus' thigh and having been "born" again three months later. The story of Orpheus' descent to death to rescue his wife is a version of the story of Dionysus' descent into Hell to bring his mother back to life. Dionysus and Orpheus are the principal figures representing mystical ecstasy in both the initial approach to that ecstasy through calm reason and the eventual attainment of it in the orgiastic derangement of reason. Thus Dionysus bears the title "god of the vine" and is credited with the invention of wine and the euphoria of its intoxication – the divine unreason that loosens the tongue and makes possible the ethereal discourse of poetry, Orpheus' art.

The connection between these mythical figures and the mystical knowledge that they represented with the St Denis of hagiography is not a loose or slightly analogous one. The French prose *Life of Saint Denys*, as well as the Latin *Vita et Actus*, begins with a genealogy of the saint identifying him as a descendant of the Greek Dionysus, who discovered the vine and invented wine. He is identified with intellectual understanding, and as if to offset the Dionysian associations, he is called Theosophus – he whom God knows. Both texts give the impression that the great wisdom of the Christian saint and the brilliant insight of his mystical writings, which are identified by title in many of the versions, are due to his consanguinity with the mythical Dionysus as the figure presiding over the mystic ecstasies in the world of man.

The temerity of the Christian authors' identification of Dionysius the Areopagite with Dionysus the pagan god need not be explained by postulating their ignorance of history. The mythical symbolism of Apollo and Dionysus as dimensions of human understanding, the one rational, the other irrational, suggests a general parallel of a metaphoric kind with the system of negative theology enunciated by Pseudo-Dionysius in that the Apollonian represents a kind of *via positiva* in which the orderly assertions of human logic lead the intellect to a certain point in its quest for communication with the divine, while the Dionysian represents the superior *via negativa*, in which reason, order, and assertion are surpassed. The bond of these two dimensions, epistemic contraries, is the human arch-poet, Orpheus, amanuensis of Apollo, from whom he received his lyre, and cofounder with Dionysus of the Eleusian mysteries; both "gods" are incarnate in Orpheus.

In addition to the nominal similarity of the Christian mystic and the pagan god of divine mysteries, the mediaeval authors would likely have been encouraged by the feature of Orpheus' speaking head to see in the myths a parallel to the story of St Denis of Paris who, of course, was thought to have been the Areopagite. Orpheus' death is brought about for a particular reason and in a particular manner, symbolically expressed; his propagation of the rational, orderly process of understanding provokes the opposite procedure of the dismantling, undoing, and negating all of the assertions brought about through similitude and relation. This procedure is figured in the Maenadian frenzy that dismembers Orpheus, unconstructing, as it were, piece by piece, the physical structure of the body and negating, part by part, the architectural whole that signifies being and form: except for the head!

Orpheus' head, like St Denis' and those of all the many other cephalophores, remains in the world of human construction, producing a discourse unlike any other, as a token of the reality perceived only through the transcendence of human discourse. While Orpheus' head, placed in a cave sacred to Apollo, speaks for that god as oracle, St Denis' head, carried to a sacred place by the saint himself, expresses nothing informative at all, but only sings repetitively ritual praises of God and, through such divine pleonasm, functions likewise as divine spokesman.

A further connection between Dionysius and Dionysus that would not only have encouraged the peculiar genealogy of the *Vita* but also one that would explain one of the more awkward features of the Denis legend, the function of the saint's two companions, was illuminated long ago by S. Baring-Gould.[31] The narrative and plot of the legend of St Denis is in no way advanced by the presence of his two companions, Eleutherius and Rusticus, as many have noted, perhaps most recently Charlotte Lacaze.[32] Neither saint receives any characterization and both remain virtually mute in all the versions, even, somewhat astonishingly, in the *Geu Saint Denis*, where the two, although on stage for practically the duration of the play, utter six lines between them.[33] Why then does every version of the life of St Denis preserve this apparently useless element of the story?

As Baring-Gould reveals, the pagan inhabitants of Paris worshipped Dionysus, or Bacchus, as part of their cult of the vine, and gave the god a surname, Eleutheros, "founder of first mysteries."[34] The day of celebration of this god of wine was the eighth of October, the same day that was to become the feast of St Denis, or St Dionysius, in the Church calendar.[35] This celebration was a double one: celebrated within the city walls, it was known as the festival of *Dionysus Eleutheros Urbana*; conducted in the countryside, it was called the festival of *Dionysus Eleutheros Rusticus.*

It would be difficult not to see the Christian martyr trio, St Dionysius, St Eleutherius, and St Rusticus, as a metamorphosis of the god of mystical ecstasy, whose ritual compelled the dismemberment of the god himself. However, unlike the comparative religionists, we need not explain the relation between the two through presuming the ignorance of the Christian authors or the unconscious expression of the folk. The fact that the texts openly identify St Denis as a descendent of the god Dionysus renders the easy explanation of a mindless *volksgeist* inoperative. Rather, the story of St Denis, like the many other texts that invoke the monstrous, is so constructed as to obscure one level of its meaning: it is in the deformity of the severed, speaking head that the meaning is both obscured and revealed.

Whether or not the confusion of St Denis, the third-century Bishop of Paris, with Pseudo-Dionysius the Areopagite, who is believed to have lived and written in the fifth century, was a deliberate deception or an understandable confusion of similar names, the identification of the two begins in the ninth century and is commonly accepted throughout the Middle Ages and (by many but not all) even up to the seventeenth century.[36] This is, of course, explained in part by the prestige and advantage to be gained in being able to claim as the founder of Christianity in France a figure who had been St Paul's interlocutor and convert and who, with several of the original apostles, had been at the death bed of the Virgin Mary, as Pseudo-Dionysius himself claims.

As early as the sixth century, the writings of the Areopagite had begun to make their mark on Christian thought, and by the twelfth century he was, with Augustine, perhaps the greatest influence in Christian theology. The belief that France possessed the remains of so eminent a figure along with the original manuscripts of his writings, sent to Pepin the Short by Pope Paul I in 758, gave to that country enormous prestige and influence in the Holy Roman Empire and helped to earn for France the eminent title "Eldest Daughter of the Church." Within France the politics of the situation greatly favoured the Benedictine monks of the Abbey of St Denis, to whom the Emperor Louis the Pious confided another manuscript of the works of the Areopagite, and these monks, under the direction of their Abbot, Hilduin, took every possible advantage of the situation, propagating the identification of the Bishop of Paris and the Greek theologian through their authorship of most of the documents now extant concerning the life of St Denis.

Jacobus de Voragine's version of the St Denis story in *The Golden Legend* begins with an almost incantational listing of various names for the saint, as if in imitation of the cataphatic system delineated by the Pseudo-Dionysius whom Jacobus, like others, believes to be St Denis of Paris: "Dionysius is interpreted one who flees swiftly ... For Dionysius fled swiftly from the world by his perfect renouncement ... Moreover, before his conversion he had many forenames. He was called the Areopagite after the place where he dwelt, and *Theosophus*, one wise in the knowledge of God. Even today he is known to the learned men of Greece as *Pterigiontuurani*, which means wing of Heaven ... He is also called Macarius, which means blessed. After his homeland he is called Ionicus."[37]

Jacobus' specification that Dionysius' polyonymity existed before St Paul had converted him to Christianity allows us to speculate that as a Christian he shed all but the pseudonym he is now known by, an appropriate divestment for the prophet of negation. Thus the portrait of the Bishop of Paris is heavily influenced by an understanding of the Areopagite's theory of knowledge as expressed in his writings. A somewhat different emphasis, although still emanating from these writings, colours the character of St Denis in the dramatic rendition of the *Geu*.

The play begins with Denis' decision to leave Greece and seek a martyr's death in Rome, but arriving there, Denis is ordered by Pope Clement to go to France and convert the native pagans. From the first encounters with the Parisians, Denis describes the divinity he wishes to communicate to them in terms of paradox:

Second Parisian: Sir, this God of yours,
Is he new or old?
Saint Denis: Friend, our God is true God and true man,
Both old and new.
Second Parisian: New, but yet not new.
This is pure contradiction!
Saint Denis: Yes, indeed, and without fiction!
New he is and yet not new.
Second Parisian: Thus he is like both "Peppy" and "Plodder" who pull the plow together.
Third Parisian: Not at all! When he goes out
He has old clothes and new clothes,
And so he appears both old and new.
First Parisian: He's a trickster logician! ...
Lisbie (the most noble citizen): All your sophistry is useless.[38]

The attempt to explain the nature of God through logic is branded in the play as "sophistry," a characterization entirely in tune with the apophatic vision of Pseudo-Dionysius and thus attributable ironically also to his proxy, Denis of Paris. This missionary's method of conversion is to explain God in terms of what He is and what He is not and to depict the divinity as simultaneouly both and neither: new and not new, old and not old, end and not end, beginning and not beginning. Thus the author of the play, like the authors of the texts that are his sources, not only gives the missionary to the French the name of the great mystical theologian but carefully puts in his mouth the details of that theology. The insistence on images of coexisting contraries gradually identifies Denis with paradox itself:

Our lord is old without age
And He is young without youth,
Beginning and end,
Without beginning, without end.[39]

It is clear from the text that the conversion to the truth that Denis brings depends upon the ability of the listener to understand and accept paradox without attempting to "solve it" by dissolving it in logical analysis. That understanding is first brought about by freeing the mind from its own anthropomorphic images of reality. Lisbie, the character destined to receive this new understanding, is taught by St Denis: "How can two all-powerful beings exist as one? What do you think?" Lisbie replies: "Sir, one cannot exist as two!"[40]

But Lisbie is, as he himself puts it, led step by step by the saint to grasp these concepts that are deformities of logical thought, and he passes through such theoretical problems as hypostatic union and pantheism to a proper understanding of what is conventionally "improper": "Since you have led me to this point, / That there is no God but the One God, / Explain whence come so many Gods / That the world produces?"[41]

Denis has little difficulty in answering these objections because Lisbie, "the noblest citizen," has an aptitude for the paradoxical: "Sir, these reasonings are good, / Subtle, deep, and elevated!"[42] But not all spirits are as open as Lisbie's, and the three villainous Parisians, who have tried to answer Denis with logic, go off complaining that the Christian "destroys," "confounds," and "denies" all that is familiar to their culture.[43]

To Fescennin, Provost of the evil Emperor Domitian, these plotters describe St Denis as crazy, a senile Greek come to envenom France. Their representation of Denis' paradoxical description of God turns his negative abstractions into concrete images of material things, attributing to God the various experiences and characteristics of man, while ironically preserving in a crude, cataphatic way a similar sense of contradiction.

The first Parisian:
Sir, at Paris he preaches one God
Who made the mountains and the valleys.
He rides on horseback without a horse,
He makes and unmakes, all at once.
He lives, he dies; he sweats, he trembles.
He weeps, he laughs; he wakes and sleeps.
He is young and old, weak and strong.
He makes a cock into a hen.
He plays tricks of Toledo, Spanish sorcery!
It makes no sense at all.[44]

Whereas the tortures of the three martyrs are briefly and matter-of-factly described in the *Golden Legend* and most other texts, not so the *Geu*. Due doubtless to the dramatic genre, the hapless trio is mocked and tormented in what must be called sadistic hyperbole by three superbly drawn comic villains, the henchmen of Fescennin. The silence of Rusticus and Eleutherius throughout the ordeal contrasts with St Denis' hortatory addresses to the crowd.

When at last the pagans tire of abusing Denis, Fescennin declares the Saint drunk, mad, and delirious. That the three respond for the one addressed is as curious as the response itself: "In heart, in mouth, in works, / We three the Holy Trinity / Declare One God."[45] In addition to restating the mysterious theological concept of the Trinity, the lines here associate, if only by the awkwardness of the syntax, the human trio with trinity, helping to explain, perhaps, the superfluous presence of Rusticus and Eleutherius. The same vague suggestion that the missionary trio is meant to connote the Trinity can be detected in the representation of St Denis and his companions in the Gospels and Collects of the Saint-Omer manuscript (c. 1000), which places Denis in a slightly elevated position with his two companions on each side of him – an iconographic composition regularly used to depict the Trinity.

From the myth of Dionysus we recall that he possessed a triple identity, bearing three names metaphorical of his function. In another hagiographic legend featuring a cephalophore, now considered the prototype of the figure, we find the child martyr, Iustus, his father, Iustinus, and his uncle, Iustinianus.[46] The renowned Belgian scholar Maurice Caens points to two other sets of triple martyrs: Faustus, Faustinus, Faustinianus and Cantius, Cantianus, Cantianilla.[47] In the story of St Denis the element of the names functions so as to lead the reader away from the paronomasia of the mythic names and toward theological identification of the mystery of unity in multiplicity. The odd syntax of the trio's response concerning the Trinity – spoken in unison by the three – strengthens the suspicion that the reader's identification of Denis, Rusticus, and Eleutherius with the Trinity and thus more generally with the divine, was intended by the author.

The deformation present within the St Denis legend is thus contained not only in the cephalophory of the tale, but, prior to that prodigy, in the representation of the saint as a kind of triune figure. The trinity, we may recall, was considered a monstrous concept in the Middle Ages and was often represented visually by a three-headed figure. Here, the hint is established through the silent presence of Denis' two companions and the etymology of their names that they form a similar grotesque group signifying deity.

Just as Denis' triplicity is meant to tell us something about the nature, not of the third-century Bishop of Paris, but of the God we cannot know, so, too, the grotesquerie of the martyr's head-carrying posture acts as an amorphosis through which we perceive divinity through distortion. The blemmyes of mediaeval teratology struck the same pose as our headless saint, except that where he holds his head before his chest, their head has been absorbed, as it were, into the chest. The headlessness of both figures suggests, above all, silence, the removal of the body's locus of speech. Thus the severed head that speaks compounds the monstrosity by adding a contradiction to it: the cephalophore represents speech in silence and silence in speech. The missionary who in all the versions of the story, but particularly in the drama, has talked on and on in his effort to explain "the unknown God" is finally silenced by beheading, only to have that head immediately resume its chatter. But there is a difference; the discourse of the disembodied head is overtly nonexpository, abandoning the effort to explain in favour of the purer activity of simple lauding. The ultimate demonstration of the paradoxical relation between the *via positiva* and the *via negativa* that the saint was thought to have expounded is now "shown" through the monstrous representation of a speaking head that communicates nothing.

The significance of the monstrous deformation in the legend does not reside in the biography of St Denis, nor does it address the historical or even philosophical contents of the story. Rather, as we have seen in the case of St Christopher, the monstrous element reveals another subject altogether, the subject of the nature of the divine, and it is through the presence of the deformed in both texts that the reader is able to decode the hidden sense of the text and discover its other subject. Thus toward the end of the drama, just before he is to be mutilated and killed, Denis utters a prayer in language so eccentric that it encourages the audience to wonder whether more is not being said than is first apparent:

Sweet Jesus who me did *form*
Who by your grace has me *reformed*,
Who yourself were all *deformed*,
Who in your law have me *informed*,
....
Receive my soul through your goodness.[48]

Creating the rhyme through the repetition of the root word "form" gives an insistent quality to the verses. The forming, reforming, informing, and deforming that constitute the prayer also summarize the Pseudo-Dionysian dialectic of going out, remaining, and returning, through which, according to the Neoplatonist, both world and intellect were created. More remarkable still, this linguistic extension of the word "form" identifies the Godhead as itself "deformed." On one level this refers to the crucifixion of Christ and his physical mutilation, but on another it refers to the first person of the Trinity, maker of all forms but beyond form, and it refers to the Trinity as a whole, that formless coexistence of multiplicity in unity.

At the close of this prayer, Denis is decapitated and, through decapitation, transformed, not, as we would expect, from living to dead, for his actions suggest that he lives on, but instead, from man to monster. Such a transformation has been inconspicuously prepared for in the text through the elements of the three names of the god of mystic rapture, through the accumulation of paradoxes in the speeches of Denis to the pagans, and, most of all, through his final prayer. These preparations, or hints, emerge clearly and point to their meaning only with the fall of the executioner's sword, for at that moment, he who was formed, as he is described in the prayer, is deformed and merges with the deformed whom he himself has identified in his prayer as God.

In a way similar to that of St Christopher, St Denis becomes a monstrous theophany. In his *Life*, however, there is the added strangeness of the interaction of history and legend, for, identified with Dionysius the Areopagite, Denis becomes a symbolic representation of the ideas in his own works. Both figures illustrate Proclus' opinion that the monstrous is the most appropriate expression of the substance of the divine, for, as the Areopagite argues, the deformed is the least misleading expression of that which is-not.

ST WILGEFORTE

Possibly the most spectacular of the grotesque saints and certainly one of the most important is the Portugese virgin martyr, Wilgefortis, whose widespread cult reached its height in the fifteenth century. Unlike the cult of St Denis, which was literary in origin and propagated by the educated, devotion to St Wilgeforte was rooted in popular piety and flourished particularly among the peasantry of rural Holland, Belgium, northern France, Germany, and Italy. In England she was known not only as Wilgeforte but also as "Uncumber," which is related to the Dutch and German names "Ontkommer" and "Kumernis." All three are derived etymologically from the German word "kummer," meaning "grief," "pain." In French she is known as Viergeforte, Livrade, and more popularly, Débarras; in Italian she is called Liberata. The first good clue to her grotesque significance is found in the sense of these names: the one – the "uncumber" type – signifying release, deliverance, and unfettering; the other – the "viergeforte" type – metaphorically announcing her bisexual character through the contradictory combination of a female designation, "vierge," with the masculine modifier "fort(e)," in the sense of virile.

The iconography of the saint presents her as a bearded woman, fully clothed, usually crowned, nailed to a cross. She is almost always accompanied by a kneeling violinist at the foot of the cross, before whom lies one of her slippers. Often a cup or chalice is placed beside the discarded slipper at the foot of the cross. Despite her long robe, one can notice, in some representations, that her legs are bound.

Wilgeforte's legend, much despised by historians, relates the vicissitudes of a Christian convert, one of seven daughters, usually septuplets, of an unnamed pagan King of Portugal, who has been betrothed by her father to the King of Sicily, despite her vow of virginity. In answer to her prayers for assistance to remain faithful to her vow, God grants her the ability to grow a beard. Her enraged father has her crucified as a fitting consummation of the marriage with Christ, the bridegroom whom she prefers.

Wilgeforte was invoked as protectress of crops, of travellers, and of the marriage bond, so that her image, in addition to being displayed at rural

St Wilgeforte crucified. In Baron Sloet, *Heilige Ontkommer*.

crossroads, was hung over the marriage bed. Above all, however, she was patron saint of monsters and of all those who suffered deformities. Through her
intercession such unfortunates were either made normal during childhood or
prospered as monstrous adults under her protection. She was prayed to by
women as a source of fertility, and as a sign of this, votives in the form of a
toad were hung under her image. Women also invoked her to cure the stutter-
ing and shyness of their young children and to help them to stay on their feet
as they crossed the threshold between infancy and childhood.[49] And women
appealed to her for assistance in getting rid of old, abusive, or impotent husbands. Thus her French name, "Débarras," inspired by the prayer: "Débar-
rasse-moi de ça," or, just across the channel, "Uncumber me of this."

Hagiography and art history seem to have agreed on an interpretation of
this legend and its iconography that tends to explain them away. Stated early
on by Father Cahier[50] and continued by Louis Réau,[51] this "logical explanation," like the solution to many scholarly cruxes, appeals to the theory of error, in this case not to scribal error but rather to a confusion of the faithful.
The confusion is assumed to have been caused by the introduction into conti-
nental Europe of a Byzantine crucifix on which Christ is clothed, not in the
usual loincloth of the West, but in the long robe traditional to eastern representations but identified in the West as a feminine garment. This variation,
according to the historian, led the simple folk to assume that the crucified
figure was female, and, it is further imagined, to avoid the scandalous idea of
a female representation of the deity, the faithful shifted the identification of
the crucified figure to a wholly imaginary woman martyr, thereby inventing
from scratch, as it were, the bearded woman. A closer look at Wilgeforte's
typology and the nature of her cult suggests, I believe, a very different development and meaning.

Far from being the product of a confusion of Christological iconography,
Wilgeforte may be seen more informatively as a symbolic encodement of the
concept of a hermaphroditic Jesus as God. Her fantastic story functions, not
as history, but as the key to the symbolic language of her iconography; her
iconography, in turn, reinvests the legend with the uncovered clues required
for a true reading of the text. In addition, Wilgeforte's cult and the prayers
addressed to her by her devotees confirm these symbolic senses and fill out
the hidden dimensions of the text.

As the crucified Christ, the image itself asserts its hermaphroditic nature
not only by the protrusion of obvious and ample breasts but, as well, by the
presence of the votive toad hung beneath the cross by members of the saint's
cult. In the Middle Ages the toad signified, among other things, the vagina,
as Clebert indicates in his explanation of the mediaeval use of toad votives.
Wilgeforte's discarded slipper has a similar function. The shoe or slipper,
especially when empty, has long been taken as a symbol of the female sex
organ; we know it best, perhaps, as part of the psychological stucture of the

St Wilgeforte and the fiddler. In Baron Sloet, *Heilige Ontkommer*

Cinderella story. The hermaphroditic character of Wilgeforte is emphasized by the one-shoe-off, one-shoe-on element of the composition, while another part of the legend provides the allegory on this symbol.

A poor and hungry wandering minstrel, inspired to pay homage to our saint, knelt before her cross and played his fiddle. As a reward for his devotion, Wilgeforte let fall one of her golden slippers, which the musician took away with him; in most representations it is the left slipper that lies empty at the foot of the cross. The usual significance of the cup in the vicinity of the crucifix as a symbol of the agony at Gethsemene is here expanded in its reference to become a symbol of the female based on its function as container, like the shoe. When the villagers discover the minstrel with the precious shoe they arrest him and before hanging him for theft and sacrilege, grant his request to play before the statue once more. At the end of his performance, the saint releases her second slipper and saves the minstrel's life. The shod-unshod, shoe-on, shoe-off animation of the statue in the legend tends strongly to direct attention to the union of male and female signs, followed by their separation, which, in turn, recalls the male/female amalgamation of the hermaphroditic composition itself.

The choice of fiddler and fiddle to expand the narrative is significant as well, since in the Middle Ages the bow and the fiddle were common scatalogical metaphors for the male and the female and their erotic relation. Moreover, the standard mediaeval symbolism of the string intrument is of harmony through multiplicity, the several strings making a unified sound by means of a pick or bow. The cithar, for instance, was taken as a figure for the harmony between body and soul. The early mediaeval commentator Arnobius is one of several who compares the fiddle to Christ crucified, its wood being the cross, its strings, made of catgut (that is to say, consisting of organic tissue) being the stretched-out body of Jesus, and the pick or bow representing the Evangelists and their Scriptural interpretations: "The cithar signifies the wood of the cross; its cords are got from the innards of sheep; its plectrum signifies the Evangelists."[52] Hugh of St Victor also states the identification directly: "The cord is the body, stretched and tortured, as it were, signified both through the suffering of the body and in the sorrowful sounds of the notes.[53] A text attributed to Thomas Aquinas takes the fiddle as a figure for the body and all its members.[54] Helmut Giesel, in his extensive study of the symbolic value of musical instruments in the Middle Ages, points to the etymological origin of this symbolism: "The word 'chorda' from its Latin root stood for both 'nervus' and for 'fides.'"[55]

The iconographic composition involves the significant arrangement of signs of the virile and the feminine: beard, breasts, empty slipper, filled slipper, cup, bow and fiddle. These emblems are applied to the Deity by associating them with the figure on the cross. In some representations the phrase *Salvator Mundi* is even added for good measure, presumably to guarantee the viewer's identification of the figure as a hermaphroditic Christ encoded by means of a legend about a female saint – and a sufficiently fantastic one to provide the means of its own decoding.

It may be noted that the androgynous key to the code seems not to have been misunderstood by many, and there is evidence that, despite modern scholars' lack of confidence in their intelligence, Wilgeforte's audience understood quite well that it was Christ who was being represented as a hermaphrodite. Indeed, for the less symbolically minded, the message was so clear as to be offensive; for instance, the clergy of the church of St Etienne in Beauvais, which possessed a wooden statue of the saint, decided to avenge the sacrilege and eliminated Wilgeforte's identification with Christ by sawing off her beard.[56]

At its simplest conceptual level, the hermaphrodite betokens doubleness, the masculine and the feminine, combined in a single being. By its doubleness it is a monstrous form, since the members of the pair are taken as contraries. The name comes from a combination of Aphrodite, goddess of love, and Hermes – not as patron of travellers as referred to in connection with

St Christopher – but as the phallic god; these two were in myth the parents of Hermaphroditos. The story told about Hermaphroditos and the nymph Salmacis represents little more than the sense of the name itself, a figure for the combination of Aphrodite, the feminine principle, and Hermes, the masculine principle, but in relation to our image of Wilgeforte, Hermes is an interesting correspondent. His image is that of a phallus, the top part of which consists of bearded head, the lower of exaggerated virile organs.This image, like that of Wilgeforte, was established at crossroads. Again, like our saint, Hermes was a patron of travellers, and his amulets were worn to guarantee fertility. His most distinctive emblem is his slippers which, especially when the god appears as Mercury, are winged. What pagan mythographers expressed through the combination of foot, the sign of humility and the flesh, and wings, the symbol of divine mission, the mediaeval Christian iconographer achieved through the play on the relation between naked foot and crucifix.

Aphrodite is, of course, the principle of eros in ancient mythology. Her union with the phallic Hermes to produce Hermaphroditos speaks to the primal unity, not merely of the sexes, but of human consiousness. It is a powerful symbol of the synthesis of dualities and the transcendence of multiplicity to the fullness of simplicity, the manifestation of the whole in the unity of parts. Such a concept is, of course, sympathetically received in the religions of all cultures, and Christianity describes angelic knowledge and the divine mind in precisely this way. The idea of primal unity is alluded to continually in the representations of the gods and in the details of their stories. Besides her union with Hermes, Aphrodite is represented as herself endowed with male organs; she is represented at Cypress as a bearded woman; and she is found in Italy as a bald Venus.[57]

Many other bisexual representations of the gods exist, as we have seen in the previous section. In Christianity we have, in addition to the androgynous representations of Jesus and the saints representing him, the significant depiction of the Virgin Mary as a bearded woman: "In the Carolingian period we find an iconographic tradition of the bearded Mary, the Mother of God with a male attribute."[58] The hermaphrodite, in these cases and in others, is clearly not the sign of a physical state, but the symbolic representation of an intellectual and spiritual concept.

Another figure from Greek mythology particularly pertinent to the Christian saint is Jason, who throughout the Middle Ages and the Renaissance was taken allegorically as a prefiguration of Christ. In one of the accounts of his adventures, Jason is invited to a feast by the god Poseidon and arrives with one bare foot, having lost one of his sandals as he swam across the river Anaurus. The more detailed and popular version, however, connects the loss of the shoe to Jason's inheritance of his father's kingdom. Aeson has been disposessed of his kingdom by his half brother Pelias, who has promised to return the rule to Aeson's son, Jason, when the child has reached majority.

St Wilgeforte identified as Saviour of the World. In Baron Sloet,
Heilige Ontkommer

In the meantime, an oracle warns Pelias to beware of a one-sandaled man.
Jason, fully grown, returns to his birthplace and encounters Pelias on the
banks of the Anaurus river, in which he has lost his left sandal. Pelias buys
time by sending his nephew to find the Golden Fleece, but eventually Jason
inherits the kingdom.

The details of how Jason lost the sandal are provocative: an old woman
who had waited in vain by the banks of the Anaurus for someone to help her
across is offered assistance by Jason, upon whose back she mounts as he
wades across. Half way, however, he feels himself weighed down to the point
of drowning and discovers that it is the goddess Hera in disguise whom he is
ferrying. George Arthur Gaskell, interpreting Jason as a mythic prefiguration
of Christ, describes the Greek hero's shod-foot, naked-foot iconography as
an emblem of the dual nature of Jesus as Son of God, human and divine.[59]

This recalls the symbolism of the fiddle in which the humanity of Christ is
figured in the living animal tissue of the stretched gut, his divinity figured in

the music produced by the bow harmonizing all the strings as it is manipulated by the Evangelists. Thus the function of the feet, one covered, one laid bare, to express a fundamental duality, encourages us to see in the Wilgeforte portrait a fantastic combination of iconographs betokening the synthesis of these dualities figured under the sign of androgeny.

Although hermaphroditic representations of Jesus are rare, Wilgeforte is not the only example. Professor Bynum points out that female representations of Jesus began as early as the twelfth century and were produced constantly, if sparingly, through the thirteenth and fourteenth centuries.[60] While these feminized images of which Bynum speaks were produced by men, women authors were also drawn to the androgynous depiction of the divine. In the mystical writings of Julian of Norwich we discover clear descriptions of the Godhead as simultaneously father and mother and, further, depictions of Christ, whom Julian of course understands as male, as also female: "I beheld the working of all the blessed Trinity. In which beholding I saw and understood these three properties: the property of the Fatherhood, and the property of the Motherhood, and the property of the Lordship – in one God."[61]

Julian specifies that for the representation of the idea that God has taken on human nature and united it to his own divine nature, androgyny is the appropriate sign: "And furthermore, I saw that the second Person [Jesus], who is our Mother substantially – the same very dear person is now become our Mother sensually. For of God's making we are double: that is to say, substantial and sensual ... For in our Mother Christ, we have profit and increase."[62]

In Julian's vision the double nature of humanity taken on by God is most aptly expressed through the doubleness of the sexual identity of father and mother. Concomitantly, the hypostasis of Christ's divine nature, consisting in the coexistence of man and God in Him, is also most fully expressed through the grotesque coexistence of maleness and femaleness in a single body.

Wilgeforte's fettered legs, seen in some, but not all, representations, probably explain her patronage of toddlers but, more importantly for our purposes, they also signal her role as an aid to women in labour. Prayed to for an easy delivery, the saint's bound legs suggest just the opposite, the dolorous labour in which the woman fails to expel the child. The martyr's German name, Kumernis, probably also bespeaks her association with the pain of childbirth. Thus, the dynamic of the cult of the saint, in this and other cases, involves the iconographic representation of the opposite of the prayer. To a figure depicted as bound, one prays to be "uncumbered"; to a personage whose name connotes pain and suffering, one prays to be spared pain and suffering. The successful petitioner to St Wilgeforte will, therefore, be unbound, delivered, freed from pain, and the new-born will spring quickly from the womb in which he has been constrained. The interplay of cult and icon – prayer and picture – is based on the devotee's ability to recognize in the gro-

St Margaret bursting the belly of the dragon.
Valenciennes 838, fol. 55v.

tesque sign its contrary and the contrary of its signified. This idea of containment and bursting provides the link to another figure functioning in much the
same way as Wilgeforte.

Saint Margaret is another holy woman who displays distinctly virile characteristics, albeit less extravagant than those of Wilgeforte. Like our Portugese martyr, Margaret was the daughter of an eminent pagan, not a king, but
the High Priest of a pagan cult of Antioch. Converted to Christianity by her
nurse, Margaret incurred the hatred of her own father, a theme that appears
constant in the stories of these female martyrs. In this legend, however, the

father is replaced as persecutor by the local prefect who lusts after Margaret and tries to force her to worship pagan gods. Imprisoned for her refusal, the courageous maiden is tortured and then displayed to the crowd: "Thereupon she was bound upon the rack, and beaten cruelly, first with rods, then with sharp iron instruments, so that all her bones were laid bare, and the blood poured forth from her body as from a pure spring. And all those who stood by exclaimed: 'Ah, Margaret, how we pity thee! Oh, what beauty thou hast lost by thine unbelief!' "[63]

This detail of the torture becomes important in the cult of St Margaret since, believing that she had staunched the flow of her own blood so as to be able to undergo the remaining tortures, her devotees applied a pearl, the etymological origin of her name, to the patient suffering from an outpouring of blood. Thus was Margaret invoked principally by women hemorrhaging in menstruation or in childbirth. However, the chief power of the saint and the one that most strongly associates her with childbirth and reveals her androgeny, is acquired later in her tortures.

Like Wilgeforte, Margaret prays in prison, not to avoid marriage – a theme that, although present in Margaret's legend, fades to the background as the narrative progresses – but she prays, rather, that God may make manifest the Enemy who strives against her. Immediately there appears a ferocious dragon who swallows her. From the centre of the monster's belly the saint makes the sign of the cross, the beast explodes, and the maiden inside him issues forth unharmed. To complete the idea of the saint's prodigious power, the dragon opponent is quickly replaced by a handsome young man who is understood to be another manifestation of the Enemy but who, this time, employs seduction in lieu of violence. Her defeat of this opponent puts extraordinary emphasis on the saint's gender: "But Margaret laid hold of him by the head, stretched him on the ground, and put her right foot upon him, saying: 'Proud demon, lie prostrate beneath a woman's foot!' But the Devil cried out: 'O Margaret, I am conquered! And to complete my humiliation, my conqueror is a young girl, whose parents were my friends!' "[64]

The masculine element of the Margaret portrait is thus internalized and more subtle, consisting in her unnatural physical strength. Her androgyny is, therefore, more fully metaphoric. The extreme intertextuality of hagiography is seen in no more striking an example than that of the androgynous saints for, to a large degree, seizing the full sense of the St Margaret story depends on the various analogies between her legend and cult and those of Wilgeforte. The bound legs of the bearded woman correspond iconographically to the constraining of Margaret in the belly of the dragon and, later still, in a tub of water; in this way both saints are seen as figures of release from constriction and appropriate to be invoked at childbirth, especially if the birth is difficult. As the contained Margaret transcended the confinement of the

St Margaret emerging from the belly of the dragon. Kraus 75/88, fol. 196.

dragon's maw and the tub's structure, so the child under her protection will be released from the confinement of the womb.

In this capacity the manly Margaret took on, during the Middle Ages, a status approaching the divine. As Saintyves explains, only in the case of Margaret was the saint's very narrative thought to have supernatural power: "Throughout the entire Middle Ages no legend proved more popular. From the end of the thirteenth century on, eight verse versions were produced, one of which is the work of the illustrious poet, Robert Wace … Moreover, this is the only legend to which is attached in popular piety a supernatural power, not simply through the invocation of the saint, but merely through proximity to the text of her life and martyrdom. Women in labour, having had the narrative read to them, then had the book itself placed upon them so as to relieve the pangs and hasten their end."[65]

THE ANDROGENOUS TYPOLOGY

An entire complex of saints of the Wilgeforte type exist; in addition to Margaret, there is her Greek counterpart, St Marina, related to Venus Marina, as well as St Pelagia, related to Aphrodite Pelagia. The fact that the Church calendar sets each of their feasts on the same day, 20 July, encourages us to see them all as versions of each other. Only three, however, are bearded; in addition to Wilgeforte, Saint Paula avoids unwanted marriage by growing a beard. However, in the legend of the widow, Saint Galla, the iconographic growth functions in an opposite way; while the beard still signifies the unmarried state of the woman, in this story it serves almost as a penalty for celibacy. Warned by her physicians that if she does not wed, she will grow a beard, Galla accepts this burden in order to lead her life as a nun caring for the poor.[66] Saint Galla's monstrosity is defended in the remarkable treatise on beards by Burchard of Worms.[67]

The adoption of androgenous saints as patrons of childbirth suggests more than the fertility cults of paganism; by invoking the paradoxical presence of natural contraries in the context of coming to be, the monstrous trait of bisexuality articulates an ontological preoccupation with unity and identity. The legends of these "unnatural" saints contain several monstrous deformities, all of them hinting at the paradox of being itself. Wilgeforte raises the fundamental conundrum of human identity and the problem of alterity in addressing the primary set of opposites by which self-consciousness is achieved, the sexual contraries of male and female. In the iconograph of the bearded maiden the audience encounters simultaneously the imperative of gender as the basis of identity and knowledge and the imperative of negating gender as a means of transcending identity and knowledge in order to become one with the known, *of knowing from the inside*, as Pseudo-Dionysius put it. This is accomplished through the narrative's establishment of androgyny as sign and by the manipulation of that sign through the iconography and the cult to signify a monstrous Jesus as incarnation of the One, the *coincidentia oppositorum*.

In an age posterior to the Middle Ages, when the knowledge of a common symbolic language is less widespread, more direct statements of the previously encoded meaning are required. So, for example, the van Usuard Martyrology, an early seventeenth century document, specifies for those who contemplate the representations of the bearded maiden that, "Those who look upon Wilgefortis, perceive in heart and mind a maiden-like figure and, indeed, Christ Himself, who was in both and in both concealed!" If such literal statements seem somewhat gratuitous, they at least provide a useful gloss on the oft-times too shadowy sense of teratological symbolism, and statements like those of the van Usuard Martyrology provide important literal confirmation that Wilgeforte and other hermaphroditic deformations have ultimately nothing to do with sex per se, nor are the invocations addressed to her limited to fertility, childbirth, child-rearing, or even protection of the misshapen. Rather such monstrosity permits us, through encodement, to express the otherwise prohibited intuition of the need to transgress the limits that, through the polarity of opposites, make possible identity and knowledge, and such monstrosity enables us, thereby, to negate and transcend the self, so as to enter into the paradox of the *coincidentia oppositorum* and thus fulfill the most terrifying of human desires.

In sixteenth-century England, the devotees of the cult of St Wilgeforte, mindful of her legend, knelt in front of a cross bearing her androgynous image and recited the following prayer: "Just as you, Lord, granted to your servant Wilgeforte, the gift of the beard for which she yearned, we ask that you grant through your high grace the *deepest desire of our hearts.*"[68]

Unlike the historical figures canonized by the Church because in their lives they carried out and advanced God's "plan," the fantastic saints function not as divine agents but as divine images. If, as the Middle Ages was so fond of imagining, Creation is a book containing a story that moves steadily toward the fulfillment of its author's intention, then the historical saints act like characters whose actions establish the nature of the narrative and constitute the plot. The fantastic saints in such an analogy assure the symbolic level of the text and are themselves the "figures of speech" that expand the significance of characters and plot by raising the discourse to a trans-historical, allegorical level. They are the Author's avatars.

Just as in the text we "identify" with characters and tend to search out among them the author's "voice" so as to pin down the meaning more certainly, so in the great hagiographical program of the Church, readers are meant to identify with the historical saints, understanding through them the nature of the Christian life and even modelling personal behaviour on the virtues and actions of the heroes, martyrs, virgins, and others. Far less prominent is the moral level of the fantastic figures in the same hagiographical texts; figuring out how to model one's life on that of Wilgeforte demands considerably more imagination and interpretation than is usually required of the reader, and it is especially its insistence on its own anagogical interpretation that sets apart the fantastic figure from the historical in the literary genre of Saints' Lives. This hermeneutic imperative arises largely from the fact that the mode of the fantastic employed in the representation of these saints is the grotesque.

Deformed, unnatural, and wonderous, the fantastic saint represents the divine, not through the human and familiar as do the historical actors of hagiography, but through the negation of the human as the criterion of understanding and through the negation of similitude as the basis of representation. Like the epic tales of various mediaeval heroes, these saints' lives are constructed in a manner that undermines their own apparent meaning,

and in each text the thread by which the tight fabric of the narrative is unravelled is the thread of the monstrous; we tug, as it were, at the discoloured fi-
bre running throughout the larger pattern, precisely because of its unnatural
clash with the colour and design of the rest of the cloth. Oedipus' deformed
feet, Alexander's unnatural eyes, and Gawain's scar correspond heuristically
to Christopher's canine head, Wilgeforte's beard, and Denis' disembodied,
speaking head in the sense that each of these monstrosities checkmates the
anthropomorphic reading that its text invites by preventing an identification
of the figure – hero or saint – with the similitudes of the human mind. The
monstrous vetoes mimesis and points beyond to the freer understanding of
anagogy.

8 Conclusion

Whereas at the beginning of the Middle Ages St Augustine found in the monsters a rich source of philosophical meditation,[1] at the beginning of the Renaissance St Thomas More was loathe to defend the "superstycyous maner and vnlefull petycyons yf women there offer otys vnto saynt wylgefort in trust yt she shall vncomber them of theyr housbondys."[2] The decline in the fortunes of the deformed beginning in the sixteenth century is in its way as informative about the concept of the monstrous as the contrasting mediaeval enthusiasm for what has been called here the deformed discourse, and, while it is not the central concern of the present discussion, that decline may also reveal as much about the intellectual culture of the postmediaeval period as the embrace of the deformed and the grotesque reveals about the Middle Ages.

Wittkower has already posed the question that arises so insistently in discussions of the concept of the monster in the West:

While the Augustinian conception had made the monsters acceptable to the Middle Ages and monuments like the tympanum at Vezelay had given them their due share in the creation, while the later Middle Ages had seen in them similes of human qualities, now in the century of humanism the pagan fear of the monsters as a foreboding of evil returns. We are faced with the curious paradox that the superstitious Middle Ages pleaded in a broad-minded spirit for the monsters as belonging to God's inexplicable plan of the world, while the "enlightened" period of humanism returned to Varro's *contra naturam* and regarded them as creations of God's wrath to foreshadow extraordinary events.[3]

Clearly the nascent empiricism of the neoscientific Renaissance has much to do with the disappearance of the monster from both the philosophic and literary discourses of "the modern," but it was hardly the mere practice of dissection or the invention of the microscope that in and of themselves inaugurated the new mentality hostile to the fantastic. Indeed, as the subject of human inquiry becomes narrower and more focused, dissection and the microscope are perhaps more fittingly conceived as themselves metaphors destined to replace the metaphors of the monstrous and the deformed. Heidegger, in his famous discussion of the *Weltbild*, or "World Image,"[4] identifies this moment as a watershed when the mind, hesitating briefly between the mediaeval and the modern, begins to turn gradually from a contemplation of the world and reality as the subject of human understanding to a contemplation of itself as the sole subject and locus of the real. For the Middle Ages man is the observer-knower, all reality the *subjectum*.[5] With the development of science, humans themselves become the subject of cognition and eventually the first and only subject of "science." With this shift, the human takes the place of reality, and reality becomes identified with human conceptualizations: "For the Middle Ages being is *ens creatum*, that which has been created by the Creator, the personal God acting in the mode of Supreme Cause. To be a being signifies, therefore, a belonging to a certain degree, to the order of creation and signifies corresponding – inasmuch as being is 'caused' – to the creative Cause (*analogia entis*). Never could a being exist in that which, being made present to man as object, is fixed and finalized in its mode of presentation, becoming being only in this manner."[6]

Further, in contrast to what might, then, be called this mediaeval "direct experience" of being, Heidegger describes the modern "scientific" worldview as essentially a *concept* of being:

Here, where World becomes a conceptual image [Bild], the fullness of being is contained and fixed as that by which man can orient himself so as to make present and hold before himself, hoping in that way to capture being in a decisive way within a representation. "*Weltbild*," the world according to a "concept," does not, however, mean merely an idea of the world, but rather, the world itself siezed upon as that about which one can "have an idea." Being in its fullness is thus taken in such a way that it is really and only being to the degree that it is fixed and contained by man in his representation and production.[7]

The demotion of the monster in the intellectual and cultural life of the West was neither sudden nor complete. One has only to consider such monumental texts as Spenser's *Faerie Queene* or Milton's *Paradise Lost* to confirm how frequently and dramatically the "modern" poet has recourse to the deformed. Similarly in the self-declared "scientific" discourses so prominent after the Middle Ages, fascination with the deformed went unabated. Thus the sixteenth-century man of medicine, Ambroise Paré, became the author of what is now one of the best-known treatises on the monster, and the authorial commentary on the subject throughout the text identifies Paré's attitude toward his subject as thoroughly mediaeval.

Nevertheless, the conceptual shift, if subtle, is already present even in these examples. If Spenser's Error and Milton's Sin are monsters of the first descriptive and dramatic order, they seem to have lost something of their rank in the narrative order, for their function now is as foil to the respective heroes, heroes whose challenge it is to destroy the monster, both within and without, so as to free the world and the self of the nagging presence of negation.[8]

Spenser's monsters, like Milton's, are didactic artifacts functioning at the tropological level of the text and having nothing to do with the ontological status of the hero. Rather, they define his psychological condition – in Red Crosse's case, before his attainment of the heroic state, in the case of Milton's Adam, after his fall from that state. In both instances, however, the monster has ceased to function as the embodiment of paradox that must be encountered and embraced.

Whereas Ambroise Paré's *Des monstres et prodiges* was enormously popular in the sixteenth-century (as were so many other texts on the same subject, several of which were his sources), its condemnation by the intellectual establishment of the time reveals the beginnings of the tendency to exile to the ranks of the popular the monstrous representations that once functioned at the highest levels of intellectual discourse.

Paré himself had no doubt as to the philosophical efficacy of the deformities he so enthusiastically presented. In the earlier versions of his text, the author elaborates several reasons for the existence of monsters, the first being the glory of God, and concludes, "there are other causes that I leave aside for the moment, because in any case human reason can never provide sufficient and probable explanations for such beings."[9] Thus, in the investigation of the deformations of mundane nature and of the prodigious beings that fill the world may be discovered whole dimensions of reality to which human reason has no access. Such understanding, Paré seems to realize, requires a symbolic and negative communication, and he therefore resorts to the idea of the body as microcosm. The human body, God's greatest creation, "contains the perfections of the Whole, which represents the great body of the universe."[10] For Paré, it is the monstrous body, the deformed form, that completes this representation by adding to nature and to logic the outer dimensions of being.

But this was hardly the spirit in which the Paré's work was received by his colleagues or those who considered themselves his superiors. The second edition of *Des monstres et prodiges* in 1575 provoked a vigorous attack by the Faculty of Medicine at Paris on the author's competence and integrity, as well as upon the very existence of the work itself. Details of this condemnation furnish informative examples of the new "scientific" attitude, which eschewed "wonder" for fact and which was willing, even eager, to accept the limits of human reason as its boundaries.

A decree in 1535 gave to the Faculty of Medicine the right to inspect any publication that touched upon its disciplines, a right that Paré had apparently not respected, and he was therefore obliged to answer charges at a hearing. As Céard suggests, these charges included, in addition to the objection to having published in French rather than Latin, the offense of having published on the subject of monsters at all.[11] In this sense, the Faculty's attack was an attack upon the entire concept of teratology, since as Paré himself pointed out, there existed a long and venerable tradition of discourse on the monstrous, some of it even in the vernacular; to censure Paré was to censure the whole tradition. But this seems to be precisely what, in the last quarter of the sixteenth century, the intellectual climate was ready for.

Estienne Gourmelen, eminent Professor of Surgery at the College Royal, probably expressed for all his colleagues the attitude toward the deformed that was considered appropriate for science and that Paré had violated. Gourmelen stated before the hearing "that M. Ambroise Paré had composed a book containing many things abominable, as well as harmful to good behaviour and to the State."[12] The inability of Paré to understand why he should be singled out for condemnation and ridiculed simply for having continued in a path trod by Aristotle, Plotinus, Augustine, and others held eminent even by his attackers is rooted in a kind of naivety so complete that it cannot recognize scandal even when it is itself the origin of that scandal. Totally misunderstanding the temper of his times, Paré protested in vain that he had merely represented what was everywhere to be beheld, both in literature and in the world: "As to your charges touching the Monsters, I merely gathered them from Rondelet, Gesnerus, Cardan, Boaistuau, authors who, these days, are commonly found in the hands of ladies and young maidens. What is more, is it not quite possible to observe these monsters in the flesh every day in this city of Paris and elsewhere?"[13]

The cause of scandal, however, lies not in lying, but in telling inconvenient truths. Paré ran into difficulties because he became an obstacle to the new "scientific" spirit of inquiry, which, as Heidegger suggests, takes the human as both its subject and its criterion; in a world which has become a human "concept," the marginalization of the monster is essential. The publication in the late sixteenth century of descriptions and pictures of forms that constituted the iconography of apophasis and insisted on the limits of human reason could only embarass and irritate the sophisticated scientists Paré had wished to impress, since the new intellectual program had, by necessity, to ignore or to trivialize the ever-appealing monster in order to erase the obstacle that the monster continually erected: the *neant*. One of the more indignant condemnations of Paré expressed at the inquest says it best with its confident binary metaphors of old and new, child and man, philosophy and science: "It is one thing to treat of civilized customs in moral philosophy in order to educate tender youth, and quite another to speak of natural phenomena in real medicine and surgery for the education of full grown men."[14]

The fragmentation of discourse into the affirmative, on the one hand, and the negative, on the other, begins in the Middle Ages. But it is also in the Middle Ages that an integrated discourse of ordered cataphasis and apophasis existed, for however brief a time. It is clear that by the sixteenth century, however, the groundwork is laid for an entirely affirmative, rational approach to the real by relegating the negative to the arenas of the popular, the childish, and the "poetic."

This separation of two parts of the whole and the motivation for marginalizing one of them are not without a certain hubris. Indeed, it may be argued that it is, ironically, with the centralization of the human as the measure of all things that the truly invidious distinctions between humans become possible. Whereas a common culture and shared intellectual language existed in the Middle Ages, although socially structured along hierarchical lines, beginning in the sixteenth century there is a withdrawal of the learned from the ignorant, of what will come to be known as "high culture" from "low." In an intriguing study of the cultural implications of the monstrous in the sixteenth and seventeenth centuries, Katherine Park and Lorraine J. Daston have observed that, parallel to the demotion of the monster from the status of the sacred to the status of the natural, there is in this period a disintegration of culture into "educated" and "popular":

In the early years of the reformation, the tendency to treat monsters as prodigies – frightening signs of God's wrath dependent ultimately or solely on his will – was almost universal. By the end of the seventeenth century only the most popular forms of literature – ballads, broadsides, and the occassional religious pamphlet – treated monsters in this way. For the educated layman, full of Baconian enthusiasm, and even more for the professional scientist of 1700, the religious associations of monsters were merely another manifestation of popular ignorance and superstition, fostering uncritical wonder rather than the sober investigation of natural causes.[15]

Francis Bacon would seem to be a particularly important transitional figure in the changing mentality and the changing concept of the monstrous that serves as a sign of the new mentality. Like Paré, Bacon retains a sense of wonder in face of the deformed and prodigious, but it is an admiration directed now toward "nature," the force that, though enormous, is nevertheless within the intellectual containment of the human mind:

In the most popular literature such events [monstrous births, earthquakes, and other catastrophes] were originally treated as divine prodigies, and popular interest in them was sparked and fuelled by the religious conflicts of the Reformation. As the period

progressed, they appeared more and more as natural wonders – signs of nature's fertility rather than God's wrath. Bacon, strongly influenced by this attitude, adopted the
study of monsters as one of three coequal parts in his refurbished scheme for natural
history – a scheme which inspired the early efforts of the Royal Society. By the end
of the seventeenth century, monsters had lost their autonomy as a subject of scientific
study, dissolving their links with earthquakes and the like, and had been integrated
into the medical disciplines of comparative anatomy and embryology.[16]

Unlike Paré, however, who, as we see in his thirteen "causes" of monsters,
unselfconsciously mixed divine and natural origins of the deformed,[17] Bacon
strictly divided the two. It is significant that Bacon's readjustment of the
place of the monster is delineated in *The Advancement of Learning*, the work
that contains his revolutionary restructuring of human knowledge. Whether
intentionally or not, that readjustment marks an important step in the neutralization of the monster and its eventual exile from the arena of discourse
about the real. Even if, as Park and Daston illustrate,[18] Bacon retains the
monster as a distinct category, entitled *nature erring,* it is his very categorization that makes this exile possible.

While the scientific mentality of the postmediaeval world is increasingly
empirical, it is, as well, distinctly mimetic. It was not only the poets of the
sixteenth and seventeenth centuries, like Sir Philip Sidney, who conceived of
the sciences as imitators of nature:[19] the scientists themselves, such as Paré
and Bacon, wholeheartedly adopted the idea that nature was the source and
limit of what could be understood by the human intellect, and they thus further adopted the conception of their sciences as "imitations" of this force.
Thus, what is observable in the course of this shift of perspective in the postmediaeval period is not only the avid and hopeful pursuit of knowledge with
the promising new tools available, but, accompanying that pursuit, the steady
narrowing of the scope of the real through the marginalization and eventual
obliteration of phenomena that in any way inhibited the construction of what
Heidegger called the *Weltbild.* In relation to the monsters, this obliteration
seems to have proceeded in steps: first, as we see in Paré, the intermixture of
divine and natural causes of monstrosity in a kind of *omnium gatherum*, giving a certain equity to each; once endowed with status equal to the divine
(and with the divine demoted, as it were, by proximity to the natural) the two
are divided again, and sharply so, as we see in Bacon, so that each may stand
on its own. Finally the divine as cause is banished from intellectual discourse, and the monster is absorbed into the natural and logical, albeit as exception to the rule. In their description of Bacon's construction of this middle
step, Park and Daston anticipate the eventual demise of the monster: "Monsters now belonged wholly to natural history, the products of wholly natural
causes or 'general rules' … Although the 'miracles of nature,' including
monsters and the rest of the prodigy canon, could be 'comprehended under

some Form or fixed Law,' for Bacon they nonetheless constituted a coherent category rather than a miscellaneous collection of phenomena."[20]

The replacement of God by Nature as the source of deformation is not a simple substitution. For the Middle Ages, as we have seen, the existence of monsters did not constitute a contradiction of nature, but a contradiction "of what man understood of nature" – to paraphrase the mediaeval formula (*non contra naturam, sed supra*). For the Renaissance, however, nature is totally comprehensible, in theory at least. Thus the invocation of nature is a strategy by which the monstrous, as part of nature, is drawn into a definition wholly of human making, and paradox is corralled by logic and broken by rational affirmation.

Nor is it only science that strives in this way to domesticate reality, as it were. The function of mimesis throughout the Renaissance discourse on monstrosity indicates a general desire to control the deformed and the contradictory by assimilating them to the known; and what is better known, one imagines, than nature and the self: "We carry with us the wonders we seek without us: there is all Africa and her prodigies in us."[21]

The development of rationalism required, however, another step. Just as Nature had appropriated the Divine, so too, art and science would appropriate Nature. Where Sidney had seen poetic discourse as unlimited by nature, Bacon strove to erase all distinctions between the two. As art is a wholly human endeavour, drawing "Nature's errors" into its sphere completes the hegemony of the anthropocentralizing image. Indeed, it is not difficult to see in Bacon's conception of the relation of nature and art early glimmerings of technology, the manipulation even of the exception to the rule, so as to be its author and thus to control it: "For it would be very difficult to generate new species, but less so to vary known species, and thus produce many rare and unusual results. The passage of the miracles of nature to those of art is easy; for if nature be once seized in her variations, and the cause be manifest, it will be easy to lead her by art to such deviation as she was at first led by chance."[22]

In contrast, Christian rhetoric of the Middle Ages frankly admitted the difference between sign and signified and the consequent impossibility for discourse to make the self one with that which was known. As a sign of this fallen condition, specified in terms of representation, and simultaneously as an indication of the possibility of a semiotic "redemption," stood the deformed. The monstrous, inhabiting a space beyond the governance of human logic, assured a metadiscourse centred in negation and paradox that provided a corrective to, but not the exclusion of, conceptual, discursive constructs of the world. The connection between the function of monstrosity in science and its function in language, and the need to control both, is described by Gilbert Lascault: "In the same way that monstrous form reveals biological order at one and the same time as threatening and as essential, it also appears inseparable from a linguistic model which permits its conceptualization but which it challenges: monstrous form is comparable only to anomalies which can be encountered within the *order* of discourse. Obedient only to its own grammar, the monster transgresses all the normal grammatical rules, establishing a relationship with them that is as essential as it is polemical."[23]

Through science, nature, and art, then, the postmediaevals saw the route to the rational control of their world. By appropriating the monster to an image of the self – a knowing, controlling, totalizing self – the deformed, the apophatic, and the grotesque are all absorbed into the *subjectum* of intellect, and all science becomes an anthropology: "Indeed, the more completely the world appears accessible as world controlled, the more the object appears objective, the more the subject appears subjective – that is to say, peremptory – and the more irresistible the contemplation of the world, the more the theory of the world becomes a theory of man – an anthropology."[24]

Whereas Bacon extended value to the monsters as beings capable of unlocking the secrets of nature and of thus providing men with the power of invention, the anatomists, embryologists, biologists, and other scientists of the seventeenth century and later soon realized that such profits were not forthcoming; the study of monsters, if it served anything at all, served to highlight the structure of the normal. With the fragmentation of knowledge into numerous disciplines increasingly autonomous one from the other, the monster recedes to become part of the context in which the unchallenged *Normal* occupies the entire foreground. Like nature, the real is seen as an entirely regular phenomenon to which an "idea" is fully equivalent. The disciplines created for the dissection and ordering of the real become, in their turn, images of the self, now fragmented, projected upon the "category" of reality that each governs. The mediaeval *imago mundi*, which had been endlessly full of Being and beings, witnesses to God's plenitude, is now replaced by a world that has no meaning other than the meaning that humans permit it. In the climate of postmediaeval science, where the goal of intellect is the discovery and reinforcement of order – an order that is often the image of the mind's logical structure – the monster not only has less appeal; it is also an affront.

The history of the early modern period seen through the lens of the conception of the monstrous attests to a confidence in the human ability to control the world, an idea that, if not unknown in the Middle Ages, was much tempered and less uncritically asserted. This faith is by no means limited to the new sciences, nor even inspired by them; indeed, behind the assurance of the seventeenth-century scientist that nature can be fully known is the more fundamental confidence that the sign is fully adequate to the signified and that language, in whatever form it takes, will render the *thing* present, in itself, to the intellect.

The postmediaeval concept of the world redefines the monster as the "exception," making possible with this single utterance the neutralization of everything that hinders a fully affirmative discourse about the world. Such an idea, as Heidegger points out, arises out of a more fundamental intellectual process, the construction of similitudes through comparisons:

That which in the past is constant, that is to say, that because of which the historical explanation can support both the singular and the multiple in history, is that which always has been [*das immer-schon-einmal-Dagewesene*], the totality of the comparable. On the basis of the constant comparison of everything with everything else is constructed the comprehensible, which is then confirmed and consolidated as the plan of history ... The unique, the rare, the singular – in short, everything that in history is grand – is never accepted as such; it remains inexplicable. Historical research does not deny this grandeur, it explains it as "exception."[25]

With the increasing localization of the real within the mind and the thing within the sign, the original "grandeur" of the monster diminishes and the event that it forestalled occurs: the representation of being takes the place of being itself. The heuristic operation of the monster in "showing" a reality independent of human conceptualization is replaced by the scientific operation of representing the image of a reality delineated by intellect: "In relation to the Greek thought, modern representation signifies something quite different. It is expressed more accurately by the word *repraesentatio*. Represent in this instance signifies: to bring into the presence of the self, as opposed to [*Entgegenstehendes*] the simple existent, to draw it to the self which represents it and which reflects it in its relation to the self as the arena in which all proportion disappears."[26]

The alternate idea, that there is something in language beyond the sign's signification of a concept, that because of their difference there can be a kind of natural relation between the human intellect and the real, is the basis of the mediaeval concept of metalanguage. Stepping outside language in the direction of metalanguage is made possible through the poetic constructions of the paradoxes, ambiguities, grotesqueries, and monstrosities of mediaeval art and legend, which sufficiently transgress the normal process of signification and deform normal representation so as to urge the mind beyond its limitations, not by reducing the object of its understanding but, as Pseudo-Dionysius and Scotus Eriugena had taught, by liberating it from its own ascendency.

Notes

INTRODUCTION

1 Flaubert, *Temptation of Saint Anthony*, 220–1. Authors names and short titles in endnotes refer the reader to full bibliographic details at the end of this study.

2 See Seznec, *Nouvelles études sur la Tentation de St Antoine*.

3 Roques, *Pseudo-Dionysius*, 6–7.

4 Harpham, *On the Grotesque*, 11.

5 All references to Pseudo-Dionysius are to *The Complete Works* of 1987, unless otherwise indicated. Quotations from Pseudo-Dionysius are cited in the text with the following abbreviations: *DN*, *The Divine Names*; *CH*, *The Celestial Hierarchy*; *MT*, *Mystical Theology*; *EH*, *Ecclesiastical Hierarchy*.

6 For a clear and concise discussion of this aspect of the relation between scholasticism and the thought of Pseudo-Dionysius, see Leclercq, "Dionysius in the Western Middle Ages," 25–32.

7 The present discussion adopts, generally, the view of the main literary traditions so well described by Coulter in *Literary Microcosm*, particularly in his analysis of mimesis in the chapter "Mimesis: Eicon and Symbol," 32–72.

8 Mazzeo, *Renaissance and Seventeenth-Century Studies*, 23–4.

9 Colish, *Mirror of Language*, 2.

10 Ibid., 26, citing Augustine, *Ennaratio in Psalmos* 99.6.

11 Cassirer, *Symbolic Forms*.

12 Flaubert, *Temptation of Saint Anthony*, 220–1.

13 Augustine, *On Christian Doctrine*, 43.

14 Note, however, that even in what I would call the pseudo-literal tradition, there is a clue to the underlying fiction of the text: the "real" world existence of the races is always located in regions inaccessible to empirical verification.

15 Mazzeo, *Renaissance and Seventeenth-Century Studies*, 5.

16 Isidore, *Etymologiae* 11.3.1–2.

17 Ibid., 11.1.1–2.

18 Megasthenes, *Ancient India*.

19 Solinus, *Collectanea rerum memorabilium*; Pliny, *Natural History*.

20 Wittkower, "Marvels of the East."

21 Friedman, *Monstrous Races*.

22 Isidore, *Etymologiae* 11.3.7–39 and 4.1–3.

23 Paré, *Des monstres et prodiges*; Kappler, *Monstres, démons*.

24 See, for example, Mandeville's description of such a type in *Travels*, chap. 21, 134.

25 See, for instance, Wildridge, *The Grotesque*. An example of a more recent study that continues this approach is Kayser's *The Grotesque*.

26 For this approach see, for example, Daniel, *Devils, Monsters, and Nightmares*.

27 See Wittkower, *Marvels of the East*, 185.

28 See, for instance, Kayser's *The Grotesque*, which attempts to analyze the grotesque while concentrating exclusively on post-fifteenth-century literature. Arthur Clayborough has characterized this study as "frankly subjective" in his own work, *The Grotesque in English Literature*. Nevertheless, Clayborough himself, emphasizing eighteenth- and nineteenth-century literature, provides a thoroughly psychological analysis of the grotesque.

29 Todorov, *Littérature fantastique*, 69, my translation: "Si ce que nous lisons décrit un événement surnaturel, et qu'il faille pourtant prendre les mots non au sens littéral mais dans un autre sens qui ne renvoie à rien de surnaturel, il n'y a plus de lieu pour le fantastique."

30 Harpham, *On the Grotesque*.

31 Kappler, *Monstres, démons*, 298, my translation: "Dans un univers aussi fantastique, le monstre n'a pas le dernier mot; et bien qu'il ait une santé à traverser les siècles, il n'est qu'un éclat de lumière, aussi fulgurant que fugitif, auquel répondent d'autres éclats dans un clignotement sans fin ni commencement."

CHAPTER ONE

1 Generally speaking, philosophical realism holds that universals – justice, humanity, yellowness – exist prior to and independently of particulars – the just act, a person, a yellow pencil. For a fuller discussion of mediaeval philosophical realism, see Haren, *Medieval Thought*, 90f.

2 Thomas Aquinas defined theology as a rational science: "Sacra doctrina est scientia, quia procedit ex principiis notis lumine superioris scientia, quae scilicit est scientia Dei et beatorum" (*ST* 1.1, 2).

3 Rorem, *Pseudo-Dionysius*, 2.

4 See Roques, *Libres sentiers*.

5 See, for some of the many examples, *MT* 1000D–1001A, 1025B, and especially 1032D–1033D.

6 Leclercq, "Dionysius," 28.

7 Rorem, "Biblical and Liturgical Symbols"; Roques, *Libres sentiers.*

8 The passage cited by Dionysius from Judges (13:18) is significant. In the Vulgate the "name" in question is described as *mirabile*; In the King James, God's name is called *secret*; the Bible de Jerusalem translates it as *mystérieux* and an accompanying notes states: "Dieu est l'être que l'homme ne peut espérer comprendre en connaissant son nom (le nom révèle la personne)." (God is such that man may not hope to know Him through knowledge of His name [the name reveals the person].) While the sense of the Scriptural answer is, as Pseudo-Dionysius interprets it, that God is above the specification and limitation of name, He nevertheless has a name, but it is beyond understanding. While a name is, indeed, a revelation of the nature of the person, this name reveals nothing like all mysteries and secrets. It is a sign signifying only itself, and it is in this sense that Judges uses the word *mirabile*: wonder, prodigy, and so on.

9 Trouillard, *La Mystagogie de Proclus*; 197, my translation: "Avançant en cercle, la puissance s'étale en signification et la signification devient un symbole chargé de puissance."

10 Ibid., 206, my translation: "Loin d'être une trace inerte ou un simple objet, le signe sensible condense une longue procession sans rupture et se charge d'une puissance de conversion vers le principe sériel. Mais il ne livre son efficacité que si nous entrons dans son jeu, au lieu de le recevoir de façon passive."

11 See Proclus, *In Remp.* 1.3.19–25.

12 Rorem, "Biblical and Liturgical Symbols," 51.

13 Trouillard, *La Mystagogie de Proclus*, 50, my translation: "Entre le mythe et le prodige il y a échange formateur. Le mythe donne au prodige sa signification et son horizon, le prodige lui renvoie son actualisation. Le lien est le *rite théurgique*, qui est le symbole en acte."

14 Ibid., 49–50, my translation: "Les premiers auteurs de mythes ayant compris que la nature, qui élabore des images des idées immatérielles et intelligibles et qui emplit ce monde visible de leurs imitations variées, figure les indivisibles par du divisé, les êtres éternels par des processus temporels et les intelligibles par les sensibles, qu'elle représente de façon matérielle l'immatériel, de façon étendue l'inétendu ... ils signifient par ce qui est contraire à la nature ce qui la dépasse chez les dieux, par ce qui est contraire à la raison ce qui est plus divin que toute raison, par des images de laideur ce qui dépasse en simplicité toute beauté partielle."

15 Ibid., 203, my translation: "Dans l'un et l'autre cas il n'y a pas de commune mesure entre le signe et signifié. Et pourtant il y a un pouvoir d'évocation et une médiation signifiante au cours d'un processus de conversion et d'assimilation. Si le symbole prétendait tenir dans son clair-obscur ce qu'il médiatise, il serait un échec et une illusion. Mais s'il est un écart et un détour pour reconnaître ce qui est déjà communiqué au-delà de tout sens, il exerce une fonction nécessaire d'éveil."

16 Rorem, "Biblical and Liturgical Symbols," 105.

17 On hypostasis, see, for instance, Hardy, *Christology*. The theory of hypostasis was gradually distinguished from "ousia," which was reserved for what was common to the three persons. In the Council of Nicea (325) ousia and hypostasis are roughly equivalent, but with Cyril of Alexandria, the concept of a union of two natures in one person is advanced. See also Boethius, *De Trinitate* and *Utrum Pater et Filius*, passim.

18 Monad is a key term in Platonic and Neoplatonic thought and is defined by the *Oxford English Dictionary* as follows: "The number one, unity; an arithmetical unit. Now only *Hist.* with reference to the Pythagorean or other Greek philosophies in which numbers were regarded as real entities, and as the primordial principles of existence. b. applied to the Deity. an absolute unit of being; an absolutely simple entity."

19 Creation includes all phenomenal beings as well as that which "could be." Nothing that man can imagine has not already been conceived by God, and as such, many things already exist that are not actualized. The phrase "things that are-not" also includes human concepts – mental beings, called by the scholastics *ens rationis* and *fictiones*. The concept is especially important to the idea and function of the monster.

20 Marenbon, *Early Medieval Philosophy*, 19.

21 The subject of divine emanation was the occasion for the persistent heresy of "necessary" emanation associated with Neoplatonic excess.

22 Denys' complaint that humans strive to affirm the positive, the similar, and being as absolute and, in so doing, render reality incomplete, is echoed centuries later by Heidegger who, describing science as having impoverished itself by excluding the concept of "Nothing" from its investigation of the real, defines "Nothing" as that which completes our knowledge of what is: "The essence of Nothing as original nihilation lies in this: that it alone brings *Da-sein* face to face with what-is as such" (Heidegger, *Existence and Being*, 339).

23 Concluding his *Tractatus Logico-Philosophicus*, Wittgenstein expressed a similar idea: "My propositions are elucidatory in this way: he who understands me finally recognizes them as senseless, when he has climbed out through them, on them, over them. (He must, so to speak, throw away the ladder, after he has climbed up on it)" (189).

24 Armstrong, "Negative Theology," 180.

25 See, for example, *MT* 1033A–1033C.

26 See, for example, *DN* 592C; *CH* 336C–340B.

27 MacCormac, *Metaphor*, 36.

28 Rorem, "Biblical and Liturgical Symbols," 63.

29 Alanus de Insulis, "De Incarnatione Christi," Migne *PL* 210.579a: "Omnis mundi creatura / Quasi Liber, et pictura / Nobis est, et speculum."

30 Bersuire, in Gellrich, *The Idea of the Book*, 17.

31 Roques, *L'Univers dionysien*, 53, my translation: "Pour lui en effet, l'essentiel n'est pas d'expliquer le monde sensible comme tel, ce qu'avaient entrepris tous

les anciens philosophes et Basile lui-même. L'univers sensible sera plutôt con-
sidéré comme un champ de symboles qui peut et doit introduire les intelligences
humaines au monde intelligible."

32 Roques, "Symbolisme et théologie," 112, my translation: "Pour rendre symbolisme et théologie négative à la seule perspective qui les éclaire et au centre unique
de leur vertu, il faudrait les définir comme la rencontre de deux extases, si l'on
donne à ce terme son sens large et encore dionysien de "sortie de soi." La
première entraîne Dieu hors de lui-même [ἐξίστημι] et le porte jusqu'aux derniers
confins de la multiplicité: elle correspond à l'immense 'théophanie' des symboles. La seconde, de sens contraire, 'fait sortir les intelligences du dehors,' les
arrache à la multiplicité qui les divise … les fait tout quitter et se quitter elles-
mêmes pour retrouver l'Un. Or, c'est à la jonction de ces deux extases venues de
l'Un et commandées par lui que se situe l'effort anagogique de l'intelligence sur
les symboles."

33 Rorem, "Biblical and Liturgical Symbols," 102.

34 MacCormac, *Metaphor*, 36.

35 Marvell, "To His Coy Mistress." In terming poets such as Marvell "metaphysical," John Dryden intended to censure a certain intellectual excessiveness. Samuel Johnson was more specific in identifying (and condemning) the vision of the
metaphysical poets as *discordia concors*. Coming as he does at the very end of the
mediaeval tradition, Marvell may be seen to continue the apophatic tradition that
links Being and anomaly.

36 *In Remp.* 85.16–26, As cited in Coulter, *Literary Microcosm*, 57.

37 Geoffrey Galt Harpham discusses the same philosophy of Christian interpretation
in the context of contemporary critical theory and points to Saint Augustine. After
citing Augustine's question in the *Confessions*, "How can it harm me if I understand the writer's meaning in a different sense from that in which another understands it?" Harpham continues: "A property of every right interpretation, truth is
multiple (indeed, infinite), public, dispersed among readers who together must
try to assemble the totality God intended … Faith grants not the meaning of
the text but only the assurance that the text means, and that the meaning is true"
(*The Ascetic Imperative*, 129–30).

38 Lawler, *Celestial Pantomime*, 18.

39 Coulter, *Literary Microcosm*, 50.

40 Ibid., 77.

41 Not all discourses proceed from affirmation to negation, but rather only those that
contain abstract meaning.

42 This is, of course, merely a way of conceiving the redemptive events. Existentially, the Crucifixion has its independent and unique significance and need not be
considered as a continuation of another event. Similarly, the Resurrection is a totally uncaused explosion of divine power and cannot be limited to or incorporated
into another event as its conclusion.

43 Hopkins, *Nicholas of Cusa*, 6: "ubi contradictoria coincidunt."

44 See Aristotle, *Sophistical Refutations.*

45 Colie, *Paradoxia Epidemica,* 7.

46 Ibid., 6.

47 Ibid., 11.

48 Ibid., 32.

49 Alanus de Insulis, "De Incarnatione Christi: Rhythmus Perelegans," *PL* 210.577, my translation.

50 Cited in Michel, "Rhétorique, philosophie, christianisme," 43, my translation: "Les paradoxes sont des prodiges [*monstruos*] de la vérité."

51 See Colie, *Paradoxia Epidemica,* 22f; see also Klibansky, *Plato's Parmenides.*

52 As with other Dionysian descriptions of God, we are to understand that the Deity *is/is-not/is-beyond* paradox. Nevertheless, paradox is the fullest description of Him.

53 Colie, *Paradoxia Epidemica,* 24.

54 It should be underscored that what we are discussing is a difference of emphasis; Pseudo-Dionysius was aware of and had integrated into his thought elements that we would call "Aristotelian." Similarly, there is nothing in Dionysian analysis that Aristotle and his followers had not considered. This is not, however, to minimize the importance of the difference, which was crucial.

55 Chenu, *Understanding St Thomas,* 227–8.

56 Ibid., 228 n. 51.

57 Ibid., 228.

58 In *I Sent.* d. 3, *div. textus,* as cited in Chenu, *Understanding St Thomas,* 229 n. 51.

59 In *II Sent.* d. 14, q. 1, a. 2, as cited in Chenu, *Understanding St Thomas,* 227 n. 48.

60 An example of the tension that existed between the two parties over this point is seen in Salutati's description of an opponent as a "Thomistic enemy of poetry." See Salutati, *Epist.,* ed. Novati., vol. 4, 238–9.

61 See *Metaphysics* 1.9.992a–992b; 990–991.

62 Colish, *Mirror of Language,* 142f.

63 Anderson, *Analogy of Being,* 28, emphasis added.

64 Ibid., 48.

65 Colish, *Mirror of Language,* 114.

66 Ibid., 142.

67 Ibid.

68 *De Anima,* 8, in *The Soul,* ed. Rowan. Thomas states that the obscurity of poetic language had no value. See *ST* 1.1.9; 1–2.101.2.

69 Colie, *Paradoxia Epidemica,* 221.

70 For another view both of the nature of analogy and of St Thomas' use of it, see Saward, "Apophatic Anthropology."

71 Colish, *Mirror of Language,* 147.

72 *Processus Canonizationis Neapoli,* 267–407 (ed. M.-H. Laurent, O.P.), as cited in Weisheipl, *Friar Thomas d'Aquino,* 322.

73 Yannaras, *De l'absence et de l'inconnaisance*, 46–7, my translation: "Descartes est l'expression caractéristique de la tentation historique de l'Occident: consolider par la métaphysique et la philosophie la réalité de Dieu. Dans le classique chapitre IV du Discours de la Méthode (1637), l'existence de Dieu est prouvée en donnant une portée exclusive au pouvoir de penser du sujet. Le pouvoir de penser, par une démonstration abstraite, mène à l'idée universelle de l'être, et par là même, à l'existence de Dieu. Nous nous assurons de l'absolu en concevant le relatif et le fini. Et, puisque le seul moyen de nous assurer d'une vérité est sa conception rationnelle, nous démontrons l'existence de Dieu en concevant son idée, car l'existence est contenue dans l'idée de Dieu de la même manière que dans l'idée du triangle est contenue la vérité que la somme des angles est égale à deux droits." Yannaras identifies Descartes as the midpoint in a historical process of metaphysical demise, a process that he regards as always present in western philosophy, but which begins in earnest with the scholastics: "With Descartes, Spinoza, and Leibniz, the natural theology of mediaeval scholasticism, which is to say the system of reduction by analogy of natural entities to God, is fulfilled in its consequences with its historical production of rationalism. The anthropomorphism of natural theology had as its inevitable result the empiricism of Hobbes, Locke, and Hume, the transfer of the principle of authority, the reduction of understanding to sensation: 'There is nothing in understanding which has not first been in sensation.' Philosophy ceases to be a science of the transcendent and takes up its abode in the mundane with the human subject as its center, but also as its limit" (ibid., 49–50, my translation): "Avec Descartes, Spinoza, et Leibniz, la théologie naturelle de la scolastique médiévale, c'est-à-dire, en théologie, le système de la réduction analogique des entités naturelles à Dieu, aboutit historiquement et s'accomplit, quant à ses conséquences, dans le rationalisme. L'anthropocentrisme de la théologie naturelle eut pour suite inévitable l'empirisme de Hobbes, Locke et Hume, le transfert du principe d'autorité, de l'entendement à la sensation: 'Il n'y a rien dans l'entendement qui n'ait d'abord été dans la sensation.' La philosophie cesse d'être une science du transcendant, elle se situe dans le monde, avec le sujet humain pour centre, mais aussi pour limite."

74 Ibid., 50–1, my translation: "Ces deux fondateurs de la connaissance analogogique de Dieu prêchent en même temps le caractère apophatique de cette connaissance, l'inconnaissance essentielle de Dieu, et l'impossibilité de l'intelligence humaine d'approcher et de définir la vérité de Dieu. D'autres maîtres de la scolastique, comme Pierre Abélard (+1142), Albert le Grand (+1280), Jean Duns Scot (+1308) le grand mystique Maître Eckart (+1327), et Nicholas de Cuse (+1464), suivent également la tradition de la théologie apophatique. Mais leur théologie n'interrompt pas le cours historique de l'athéisme occidental. Elle lui appartient organiquement."

75 Denzinger, *Enchiridion symbolorum* 806.196, my translation: "Quia inter Creatorem et creaturam non potest similitudo notari, quin inter eos major sit dissimilitudo notanda."

76 Anselm of Canterbury, "On Truth," 2:101.

77 Burrell, *Analogy and Philosophical Language*, 47.

CHAPTER TWO

1 In Thorndike, *Magic and Experimental Science*, 6:408.

2 Caillois, *Babel*, 15–16, my translation: "La construction de la tour fut arrêtée. Petit à petit, le monument de l'orgueil, devenu celui de la confusion (on crut même que c'était là le sens du nom de Babel), tomba en ruines. Ce ne fut pas l'effet d'une intervention surnaturelle qui, suscitant soudain les différentes langues, empêcha chacun d'entendre ce que voulait son voisin. Cette tradition superstitieuse repose sans doute sur le fait que, parmi tant d'autres excès, les ouvriers s'avisèrent de ne plus se servir des mots dans leur signification usuelle, mais seulement dans celle qu'il leur plaisait à l'instant de leur attribuer. Fidèles à leurs maximes, ils ne souffraient pas que le sens des mots leur fût imposé."

3 Unless otherwise noted, all references are from *Periphyseon*, trans. I.P. Sheldon, revised John J. O'Meara.

4 "And this is why man is not inappropriately called the workshop of all creatures since in him the universal creature is contained" (*Periphyseon* 3.733B).

5 Cassirer, *Symbolic Forms*, 1:77–8.

6 Cassirer's divisions are, of course, all within what Scotus designates as the rational division.

7 Cassirer, *Symbolic Forms*, 1:76–7.

8 Jean-Claude Foussard, "Apparence et apparition," 339–40, my translation: "Jean Scot part du principe que dans sa condition actuelle, l'homme ne peut connaître aucune nature par une intuition directe (per seipsum). Il est donc nécessaire qu'un intermédiaire mette en relation l'homme et les choses. Cet intermédiaire entre l'extérieur et l'intérieur a pour fonction de faire apparaître la chose en fournissant une image. Telle est la *phantasia*: 'imago quaedam et apparitio.' "

9 Ibid., 340, my translation: "Les deux étapes du processus sont garanties par l'objet réel qui en est le point de départ: la *phantasia* est 'naturalium rerum imaginatio,' et rien ne peut apparaître en elle qui n'existe pas dans la réalité."

10 Ibid., 341, my translation: "En fait, c'est l'âme qui tout entière sent ('tota in sensibus sentit'), c'est l'âme qui se donne un corps et des organes sensoriels."

11 *Commentaire sur l'Évangile de Jean*, 117, my translation: "Nec solum hoc de hominibus, uerum etiam de angelis intelligendum. Nam et angeli deum suum, qui omnem intellectum exsuperat, in sua natura cognoscere non potuerunt, quia invisibilis et incognitus est; uerbo uero incarnato, dominum suum intellexerunt, dei videlicet filium, et in ipso et per ipsum totam remotam ab omnibus trinitatem."

12 Stephen Gersh, *From Iamblichus to Eriugena*, 116, referring to Proclus, *In Alcibiadem* 51.13–52.2. See also Porphyry, *ad Marc.* 24 and Iamblichus, *Protr.* 101.17

and *Comm. Math. Sci.* 55.19. Regarding the important differences between the Christian and pagan concepts, see Rosan, *Philosophy of Proclus*; Rist, *Plotinus*; Armstrong, "Pagan Eros."

13 Wolters, trans., 63.

14 Cassirer, *Symbolic Forms*, 1:88.

15 Armstrong, "Negative Theology," 179–80.

16 Roques, *Univers dionysien*, 220, my translation: "Elle 'L'Écriture' lui impose des caractères qu'il n'a pas et elle lui ôte, au contraire, ceux qui lui appartiennent en propre, ceux qu'aucun langage humain ne saurait adéquatement exprimer."

17 For an interesting discussion of this problem in the context of Augustine's *Confessions* and contemporary critical theory, see Harpham, *On the Grotesque*, 119f.

18 René Roques, "Symbolisme et théologie négative," 102, my translation: "Alors la vérité du symbole n'est plus recherchée dans sa signification véritable ... qui est nécessairement en haut: par paresse, par inconscience, ou par perversité, l'intelligence dissocie le symbole de sa signification connaturelle et sacrée ... pour ne retenir que la matérialité des éléments sensibles, en leur adjoignant peut-être une pseudo-signification de portée purement humaine."

19 *On Christian Doctrine*, trans. and intro. Robertson, 37–8.

20 D'Andrea, "L'Allegoria dei poeti," 71–78, my translation: "All' 'allegoria dei teologi,' che presuppone la verità storica degli eventi e dei personaggi dell'Antico testamento, quale risulta dall'interpretazione letterale, e mostra in essi l'anticipazione figurale, *in facto* e non *in verbis* (*De trinitate* XV. ix. 1), di Christo, della sua venuta e della sua opera, viene cosi sostituita l' 'allegoria dei poeti', che é tutt'altra cosa."

21 For instance, in Proclus the hierarchical structure of modes of understanding follows the general pattern of all other structures, including the structure of allegory:

Les dieux ἡνωμένως
Les esprits ἀγερισως, ὀλιχῶς   "unity"
La raison ἀνειλιγμένως, χαθολιχῶς   "intuition"
L'imagination μορφωτιχῶς   "discourse"
Le sens παθητιχῶς   "sensuality."

From Jean Trouillard, *La Mystagogie de Proclus*, 42–3, English added.

22 The descriptions that the author declares unbelievable are hardly those that most severely test the reader's credulity. The device is interesting as a negative reinforcement of verisimilitude for, if the author identifies as incredible those stories easiest to believe, he allows the reader to dismiss his objections as overly scrupulous; passing over without objection the far more fantastic accounts, the author appears to lend his approval and authority to literal belief in them.

23 *The Collected Dialogues of Plato, Including the Letters*. Eds. Edith Hamilton and Huntington Cairns, 1177.

24 *Apologia ad Guillem*, 12.28, in Leclercq and Rochais, eds., *S. Bernardi Opera*, 13:104, my translation: "Illa ridicula monstruositas, mira quaedam deformis formositas, ac formosa deformositas."

25 In James, "Pictor in Carmine," 141.

26 In *John of the Cross*, ed. and trans. Kavanaugh, 78.

27 "Our post-Babelian condition is more fully evidenced in *Finnegan's Wake* than in any other linguistic artifact" (Derek Attridge, "The Wake's Confounded Language," 264).

28 Aristotle, *Metaphysics* 4.1006a.34, W.D. Ross, ed., 1:265.

29 Girard, *Violence and the Sacred*, 44–5.

30 From this perspective it is, perhaps, not surprising that among the most severe forms of neuroses are those involving phobias of the disintegration or deformation of the form of the self, or even the loss of the form of the other; incorporation of the self into the other and the illusion of a disembodied self are examples of the pathology induced by the destabilization or weakening of the sense of self and its replacement by a "discourse of self" and by a schizoid desire for the other. See Hegel's theory of the *schöne Seele* (the good soul) in *Phenomenolgy*, 2:189. See also the note by Anthony Wilden on the *Belle âme* (good soul) in Lacan, *Language in Psychoanalysis* .

31 Girard, *Violence and the Sacred*, 49.

32 Catherine of Siena. *The Cell of Self-Knowledge*, 29.

33 Ibid., 30.

34 Ibid., 29.

35 Ibid.

36 Kuntz, ed., *Concept of Order*, xxxv.

37 Feibleman, "Disorder," 4.

38 *Sph.* 256d-e, ed. Hamilton and Cairns, 1003.

39 Feibleman, "Disorder," 10.

40 Livingston, *Disorder and Order*, 32.

41 For a fuller analysis of Cusa's concept see the valuable study of Hopkins, *Nicholas of Cusa*.

42 Feibleman, "Disorder," 10.

43 Gersh, *From Iamblichus to Eriugena*, 105, citing *In Parm.* 904:24–7.

44 Colish, *Mirror of Language*, 79.

45 Plotinus, *Enneads* 3.17.24–6.

46 Syrianus, *In Metaph.* Ed. Kroll, 107.5 ff. See also Gersh, *From Iamblicus to Eriugena*, 88–9.

47 O'Meara, introduction to *Periphyseon*, 15.

48 These categories John takes from Maximus the Confessor, as pointed out by O'Meara, introduction to *Periphyseon*, 16.

49 See *Periphyseon*, ed. Uhlfelder, 209.

50 Ibid., xxiv–xxv.

51 *On Christian Doctrine* 1.13.

52 Saward, "Apophatic Anthropology," 229.

53 Ibid., 229, citing *En. Ps.* 41.13 in *CCSL* 38.470.

54 The *Periphyseon* is thought to have been written between 862 and 866 and the *Expositiones* afterward.

55 Roques, *Libres sentiers,* 26, my translation: "Jean Scot va mettre en relief l'un de ses caractères, ou, plus exactement, celles de ses expressions qui justifient le plus rigoureusement sa dénomination de symbolisme dissemblable et où s'exerce avec le plus de force et d'efficacité sa vertu 'cathartique' et 'anagogique.' Il s'agit en effet des représentations proprement 'monstrueuses' qui 'brouillent' et détruisent en quelque manière les natures symbolisantes (*formarum confusio*), en 'bloquant' dans une seule et même image (*in una eademque imagine*) des éléments empruntés à plusieurs natures, voire l'intégralité de plusieurs natures qui sont en elles-mêmes distinctes, complètes et indépendantes (*absolutis*)."

56 Ibid., 16, my translation: "Pour lui, cet assemblage déconcertant de 'pieds,' d'ailes et de visages doit être interprété selon les mêmes normes que les images simples, bien qu'elles aussi 'dissemblables,' du lion, du cheval, des roues ignées, des passions [θυμός, ἐπιθυμία], de l'absence de raison ou de sensibilité [ἀλογία, ἀναισθησία], de l'ébriété ou du sommeil. À tous ces cas l'exégèse spirituelle [κάθαρσις, ἀναχάθαρσις, ἀνάπτυξις] appliquera un traitement uniforme, en soulignant l'altérité radicale qui sépare les réalités symbolisées des symboles banals, grossiers ou aberrants sous lesquels elles sont représentées: [ἀνομοίως ... τῶν ὁμοιοτήτων ἐχλαμβανομένων, χαὶ των αὐτῶν οὐ ταὐτῶς]. La symbolique 'tératologique' se trouve ainsi réduite à la symbolique 'dissemblable.' "

57 *Expositiones in ierarchiam coelestem*, ed. Barbet, 2.416–18.

58 Roques, *Libres sentiers,* 18, my translation: "Ainsi ce qui, dans tous les cas, fait trouver aux figurations bibliques une apparence d''absurdité' ou de 'monstruosité', c'est essentiellement un manque d'aptitude des intelligences restées plus ou moins profanes à entrer dans la signification intérieure et cachée de ces figurations ... La notion de 'monstruosité' ou d''absurdité' qu'il met en cause n'affecte pas de manière physique ou physiologique la nature même du symbole; ce qui est proprement 'monstrueux' ou 'absurde,' c'est de vouloir trouver une réalité ou une signification 'divine' dans des représentations d'ordre sensible, quelles que soient ces représentations."

59 *Expositiones in ierarchiam coelestem* 2.550–1, my translation: "In natura rerum visibilium pennatum hominem et volitantem nec vidi, nec legi, nec audivi."

60 Ibid., 2.551–2, my translation: "Est enim monstrosum et omnino humana natura alienum."

61 Ibid., 2.552–65, my translation: "Nam et poetica figmenta in falsissima fabula de uolatu Dedali non ausa sunt fingere plumas et alas de corpore ipsius hominis naturaliter creuisse; incredibile enim esset et deforme. Ac per hoc citius adducor ad negandum tali imagine omnino diuinas uirtutes ipsumque Deum circumscribi et deformiter formari – omne siquidem quod contra naturam est turpe atque deforme est – quam ad consentiendum tales figuras naturaliter in celestibus esse. Et

continuo, nulla mora interstante, perspicio illas imaginationes divine scripture significativas esse naturalium rerum, simplicium quidem, omnique forma atque figura sensibili circumscriptaque carentium, non autem ipsas naturas, que istis significationibus ad purgandas nostras terrenas cogitationes intimantur."

62 Roques, *Libres sentiers*, 29, my translation: "Au sens le plus radical de ce terme, la dissemblance érigénienne semble aller beaucoup plus loin. Elle entre au coeur des natures et trouve son terrain de choix dans leurs ruptures internes, dans leurs dislocations et leurs amalgames, dans cette sorte d'éclatement physique et on-tologique qui les dissout et dans cette fantaisie apparente qui les combine entre elles selon les normes irréelles. Ce qui revient à dire qu'une telle dissemblance est essentiellement étayée sur une 'tératologie': elle dissout la pureté structurale des natures (naturae absolutae, simplices – imaginationes mixtae); elle efface pour ainsi dire leurs traits en les insérant dans des ensembles ou elles perdent leur au-tonomie de natures (naturae omni confusione carentes – imaginationes confusae); au sens métaphysique du terme, elle attaque les natures dans leurs 'formes' qu'elle 'déforme' et contrefait (naturales simplicesque formae – naturalibus sim-plicibusque formis longe dissimiles, deformes imaginationes)."

63 In remarking that propositions cannot represent their own power of representa-tion, cannot describe "logical form," Wittgenstein used the German verb *zeigen* (to show) to indicate what language does instead: "Propositions cannot represent the logical form: this mirrors itself in the propositions. That which mirrors itself in language, language cannot represent. That which expresses *itself* in language, *we* cannot express by language. The propositions *show* [*zeigt*] the logical form of reality. They exhibit it" (*Tractatus Logico-Philosophicus* 4.121).

64 *Commentaire sur l'Évangile de Jean*, *Commentarius* 6.5.345a, my transla-tion: "Dans le Nouveau Testament aussi, le mystère du baptême, celui du corps et du sang du Seigneur, celui du chrême sont, d'une part, accomplis dans la réalité et, d'autre part, transmis et exprimés par des lettres. Ce type de signes visibles est justement appelé par les saints Pères 'allégorie des faits et du discours.' Il est une autre type d'allégorie, dont le nom exact est 'symbole' et qu'on appelle 'allégorie du discours et non des faits,' parce qu'elle consiste uniquement dans les discours de l'enseignement spirituel, et non en des faits sensibles."

65 Ibid., 6.6.346a–346b, my translation: "Les pains d'orge sont rompus par les disci-ples lorsque, dans les 'mystères' de la Loi de la lettre comme dans ceux de la Loi de grâce, on distingue la réalité historique d'avec sa signification spirituelle. Les hommes charnels sont nourris par le seul récit historique."

66 Ibid., 6.6.346b.

67 Ibid., 6.6.346d, my translation: "Qu'on apporte maintenant à cette même multi-tude les deux poissons, c'est-à-dire l'allégorie de l'enseignement spirituel qui est seulement 'allégorie du discours et non des faits historiques.' "

68 Ibid., 6.6.346d–347a, my translation: "Ce 'symbole' est lu par les yeux et en-tendu par les oreilles. Cependant, on ne peut pas le 'rompre,' parce qu'il ne s'agit pas d'un 'fait' historique, mais seulement d'un 'discours' allégorique."

69 *Enneads*, 8.6.1–9.

70 *Prologue de Jean*. Trans. Jeauneau, 1.283b–283c, my translation: "Par 'choses qui sont,' j'entends celles qui n'échappent pas entièrement à toute pensée, soit humaine, soit angélique étant inférieures à Dieu et comprises dans les limites des réalités qui ont été créées par la cause unique de l'univers. Par 'choses qui ne sont pas,' j'entends celles qui dépassent absolument les forces de toute intelligence. C'est ainsi que dans son vol, saint Jean le théologien, non seulement s'élève au-dessus de ce qui peut être saisi par l'intelligence et signifié par la parole, mais est transporté au coeur même des réalités qui surpassent toute intelligence et toute signification."

CHAPTER THREE

1 *The Order of Things*, xv.

2 *Etymologiae* 11.38–54.

3 Ibid., 52.

4 Isidore of Seville, *Sent.* 1.2.1, as cited in Brehaut, *Isidore*, 62.

5 Barkan, *Nature's Work of Art*, 10.

6 Douglas, *Purity and Danger*, 115.

7 Bakhtin, *Rabelais and his World*, 317.

8 Ibid., 317–18.

9 Canguilhem, "On the Normal," 65.

10 Ibid., 148.

11 Canguilhem, *Connaissance de la vie*, 173, my translation: "Mais dès que la conscience a été induite de soupçonner la vie d'excentricité, à dissocier les concepts de reproduction et de répétition, qui lui interdirait de supposer la vie encore plus vivante, c'est-à-dire capable de plus grandes libertés d'exercice, de la supposer capable non seulement d'exceptions provoquées, mais de transgressions spontanées de ses propres habitudes? En présence d'un oiseau à trois pattes, faut-il être plus sensible à ceci que c'est une de trop ou à cela que ce n'est guère qu'une de plus? Juger la vie timide ou économe c'est sentir en soi du mouvement pour aller plus loin qu'elle. Et d'où peut venir ce mouvement qui entraîne l'esprit des hommes à juxtaposer aux produits monstrueux de la vie, comme autant de projets susceptibles de la tenter, des grylles aux têtes multiples, des hommes parfaits, des emblêmes tératomorphes? Vient-il de ce que la vie serait inscrite, au sens géométrique du terme, dans la courbe d'un élan poétique dont l'imaginaire se fait la conscience en le révélant infini?"

12 Pliny, *Natural History* 6.22, 7.2, 10.30.

13 Odric de Pordenone, *Recueil de voyages*, 10:24, 345.

14 Mandeville, *Travels*, 140.

15 *Connaissance de la vie*, 172, my translation: "Il y aurait un éclaircissement à tenter sur les rapports de l'énorme et du monstrueux. L'un et l'autre sont bien ce qui est hors de la norme. La norme à laquelle échappe l'énorme veut n'être que

métrique. En ce cas pourquoi l'énorme n'est-il accusé que du côté de l'agrandissement? Sans doute parce qu'à un certain degré de croissance la quantité met en
question la qualité. L'énormité tend vers la monstruosité. Ambiguïté du gigan-
tisme: un géant, est-il énorme ou monstre? Le géant mythologique est prodige,
c'est-à-dire que sa grandeur "annihile la fin qui en constitue le concept" (Kant,
Critique du jugement, 26). Si l'homme se définit par une certaine limitation des
forces, des fonctions, l'homme qui échappe par sa grandeur aux limitations de
l'homme n'est plus un homme. Dire qu'il n'est plus c'est d'ailleurs dire qu'il l'est
encore."

16 Hesiod, *Theogeny*, 133–87, 616–23.

17 The corruption of the spiritual by the material is contained in the idea of the
"falling" of the divine (angels) to earth. It is paralleled in myth by the "falling" of
(divine) blood on the earth. Both falls are taken as the origin of monstrosity.

18 For discussion of the exegetical legends, see Williams, *Cain and Beowulf*, 19ff.

19 Clement, Homily 8, in *Clementine Homilies*.

20 *Book of the Monsters*, 56, quoted in Butturff, "Monsters and the Scholar," 103.

21 Cicero, *Acad. Post.* 2.39, 123.

22 *Book of the Monsters*, 99.

23 A full discussion of the tradition of the Antipodes may be found in Boffito's
"La leggenda degli antipodi."

24 More correctly, but awkwardly, referred to as the "wer-animal," since in locations
lacking wolves, the same phenomenon occurs with other animals as the target of
transformation.

25 Friedman, *Monstrous Races*, 26–36.

26 See, for example, Pierre L'Ancre, *Mauvais anges* 3.5.

27 Skeat, ed., 144, my translation: " 'Sire kniȝt, i am in þi kiþ & comen to þi owne, /
& þow makes me now but þis mene semblant. / to put þe of peril i haue ney
perisched oft, / & many a scharp schour for þi sake þoled, / to litel þow me know-
est or kinhed me kiþes.' / 'sertes, sire, þat is soþ' seide william þanne, / 'I ne wot
in þis world what þat ȝe are; / but i coniure ȝou, be crist þat on croyce was
peyned, / þat ȝe seie me swiþe soþ ho-so ȝe bene.' "

28 See Canguilhem, *Connaissance de la Vie*, 152–3.

29 Wakeman, *God's Battle with the Monsters*, 12.

30 Ibid., 50.

31 *Problemata Aristotelis ... cum Commento* 4.13, fol. 57v., as cited in Friedman,
Monstrous Races, 181, 252.

32 Aldrovandi, *Monstrorum Historia*, 375. On Aldrovandi, see Thorndike, *Magic
and Experimental Science*, 6:276f.

33 Rodkinson, ed., *The Babylonian Talmud*, 3:11, 41.

34 Ibid., 41.

35 Foucault, *The Order of Things*, 155.

36 Ibid., 156–7.

37 An additional legend, interestingly, provides a complementary opposite to this symbolism: the door of the temple of Janus is left open during war, closed only during peace.

38 Baltrusaitis, *Le Moyen âge fantastique*, 22.

39 Macrobius, *The Saturnalia* 1.20.1.

40 On the doctrine of hypostasis, see, for a general discussion and bibliography, *The New Catholic Encyclopedia*, *s.v.* "Hypostasis" and "Hypostatic union."

41 Pettazzoni, "Three-Headed Representations," 149.

42 Pettazzoni, *The All Knowing God*, 1–26, passim.

43 Just as God is represented as three-headed, a trinity of evil was represented in a parallel way by a tricephalic figure. See, for instance, Baltrusaitis, *Le Moyen âge fantastique*, 34–5.

44 See Pettazzoni, "Three-Headed Representating," 135.

45 *Letter* 7, 268; see also Pettazzoni, "Three-Headed Representations," 147.

46 Ibid., 151.

47 See Baltrusaitis, *Le Moyen âge fantastique*, 33; see also Pettazzoni, "Three-Headed Representations," 135–51.

48 Molanus, *De historia ss. imaginum et picturam.* See 2:4, 37.

49 Baltrusaitis, *Le Moyen âge fantastique*, 19.

50 For a summary, see Kappler, *Monstres, démons*, 274f.

51 *Book of the Monsters*, 98.

52 Pliny, *Natural History* 5.8.46; Macrobius, *De Nuptiis Philologiae et Mercurii*, 6, in Eyssenhardt, ed., 674; De Cantimpré, *Liber de monstruosis hominibus*.

53 Augustine *City of God* 16.8.

54 Baltrusaitis, *Le Moyen âge fantastique*, 33, my translation: "Les Blemmyes que l'on voyait déjà dans les Bestiaires romans et les Traités des Merveilles de l'Orient sont de nouveau fréquents au XIIIᵉ siècle et plus tard. On les retrouve dans la Mappemonde de Pierre (c. 1210), dans L'Image du Monde de Gautier de Metz (c. 1246), dans les récits de Marco Polo et de Jean de Mandeville ... Alexandre les combat dans l'Inde."

55 Von Simson, *The Gothic Cathedral*, 106.

56 The Bollandistes have described them as "suspect, fabulous prodigies" and as a "monstrous invention" by the Abbott Servieres: see P. Saintyves, "Les Saints céphalophores," 158, 168.

57 *Book of the Monsters*, 101.

58 See the discussions in Baltrusaitis, *Moyen âge fantastique* and *Réveils et prodiges*.

59 *Book of the Monsters*, 97.

60 Lascault, *Le Monstre*, 352, my translation: "Mais, grâce à Platon, c'est le langage lui-même qui devient le signifié du monstrueux et qui se définit en une métaphore complexe, ou plutôt qui, par cette métaphore, vient contester l'univers des définitions. Le recours à un système de parenté mythique (fils d'Hermes), le passage

par une étymologie plus ou moins hasardeuse aux yeux de Platon (autour de *Pan* et de *tragos*), la description du monstre comme unité des contraires viennent s'appliquer au langage."

61 Hart, *Trespass of the Sign*, 3–4.

62 For a discussion of farting as speaking and vice versa in Chaucer's "Miller's Tale," see my "Radical Therapy in the Miller's Tale,"

63 *Book of the Monsters*, 101.

64 See also *Book of the Monsters*, 97

65 Mandeville, *Travels*, 401.

66 This is one of the reasons that "beasts" (*beluae*) as opposed to "animals" (*animales*) are considered monsters and thus included in the *Book of the Monsters*.

67 *Les Trois Mondes*, as cited in Villeneuve, *Histoire du cannibalisme*, 70, my translation: "Puis celui qui le tenait prisonnier bien emplumé et qui n'aura paru tout le jour, se présentant avec son épée, lui demande s'il n'est pas des Margaias leurs ennemis. Il dit que oui et qu'il a mangé ses parents et qu'on le vengera bien. Ceci fait, l'autre lui donne si droit sous l'oreille qu'il le rend mort: et aussitôt la femme et ceux qui le servent, ayant un peu pleuré à ses pieds, sont les premiers à le découper et le manger."

68 His parents have prophesied his overthrow by one of his own children. See Appolodorus, 1.1.5; Hesiod, *Theogony*, 453–67.

69 *The Geography of Strabo*, vol. 2, 4.5.4, 259.

70 Herodotus, *The Histories*, 3:101.

71 Mandeville, *Travels*, 136–7. This is precisely the sentiment of the modern-day Mayoruna. See Tannahill, *Flesh and Blood*, 71.

72 Tuzin, "Cannibalism and Arapesh Cosmology," 62.

73 Barkan, *The Gods Made Flesh*, 92

74 *Book of the Monsters*, 100.

75 Klaeber, ed., *Beowulf*, 28.

76 Mandeville, *Travels*, 175.

77 Pliny, *Natural History*, 7.2.16–17.

78 *Book of the Monsters*, 101.

79 The same narrative is applied to the giants of Scripture who are descended from Cain, the first herdsman, and from angels. They are nomadic hunters, meat-eaters, cannibals, and creators of prehistoric monuments.

80 Serres, *Hermès ou la Communication*, 204, my translation: "Génie malin, dont les mots désignent tous les sens possibles, je m'appelle Polyphème. Je dis, et la chose réside ailleurs, et ici, à ma volonté, de sorte qu'il est impossible de sortir de mon antre, enserré que l'on est par les mailles de mon discours. Sur ce réseau partout centré, je vous place toujours sur un trajet préparé, prévu, piégé. La mort vous attend, au détour du chemin, parmi l'entrelacs de mes ruses."

81 Ibid., my translation: "Pour tromper ce trompeur universellement subtil, il n'est plus qu'une ruse, celle de parler en sorte que les mots soient privés totalement de sens ... Il est donc indispensable de me placer hors de la totalité des trajets, dans

le néant du lieu, du site, du mot, de l'être enfin: il faut que je m'appelle Personne. Face au ruse le plus subtil, Ulysse est plus fin que Descartes, il dit le
néant de son je, loin d'en affirmer l'être."

82 Ibid., 205, my translation: "Polyphème, c'est peut-être le nom du monde, en tant
qu'il est porteur de la langue universelle, de la totalité du sens prescrit. Personne, c'est le nom de l'inconnu qui se dissimule ou s'évanouit pour poser l'in-
connue = x, élément de cette langue mathématique, universelle en creux pour
n'avoir point de sens. Reste le jeu indéfini de la langue universelle vide et de la
langue universelle de l'univers."

83 *Book of the Monsters*, 95.

84 Wittkower, "Marvels of the East," 164.

85 Izzi, *I Mostri e L'Immaginario*, 156.

86 Cotton Vitellius A XV, fol. 104, a manuscript which, intriguingly, also contains
Beowulf.

87 See Wittkower, "Marvels of the East," 173–4.

88 Ibid., 81–2.

89 See Amelli, *Miniature sacre profane*; for other depictions see, for example,
Pigafetta, in Ramusio, *Navigazioni e viaggi*, 1:fol. 393d)

90 Mandeville, *Travels*, 343, 344.

91 *Book of the Monsters*, 97.

92 Mandeville, *Travels*, 344.

93 See above, p. 138 for illustrations of grylles.

94 *Moyen âge fantastique*, 198.

95 Boccaccio, *Decameron*, 1322.

96 In Schramm, *Der Bilderschmuck der Frühdrucke*, 3: pl. 465.

97 In Maeterlinck, *Le Genre satirique*, fig. 157

98 In Schramm, *Der Bilderschmuck der Frühdrucke*, 17: pl. 165, fig. 420.

99 Paris, B.N., ms. fr. 225, fol. 1 (c. 1503–18), in Ritter and Lafond, *Manuscrits
peints*, 38, pl. xvi.

100 "Homo sex brachijs refertus," 494.

101 Pliny, *Natural History*, 7.2.23.

102 Ibid.

103 Mandeville, Schedel, Lycosthenes, Herold, among others.

104 Knight, *Discourse*, 2:35.

105 Ibid., pl. xxxiii.

106 Ibid., 181d, pl. v.

107 "Of kepying of body," in the "Ashmole Version," in *Secretum Secretorum*, 45–6.

108 Mandeville, *Travels*, 175.

109 Eliade, *Rites and Symbols*, 51.

110 Ibid., 117.

111 Eliade points out (ibid) that in some primitive tribes, while boys are ritually "devoured" by a symbolic Mother Earth monster during their initiation into adulthood, the adults engage in sexual orgy.

112 Cited in Eliade, *The Forge and the Crucible*, 154.

113 Kappler, *Monstres démons*, 273, my translation: "On retrouve dans cette figure le double symbolisme phallus-bouche dentée qu'on peut interpréter de diverses manières."

114 *Scivias* 3.11, cited in Newman, *Sister of Wisdom*, 245.

115 Ibid., fig. 13.

116 Evola, *The Metaphysics of Sex*, 70. It is interesting to note the similarity between Evola's description of sexual ecstasy and Neoplatonic descriptions of religious ecstasy.

117 Eliade, *The Two and the One*, 92.

118 Ibid., 100.

119 Ibid., 113.

120 Ibid., 106, citing *The Gospel of Saint Thomas* as found in Grant, *The Secret Sayings of Jesus*. 143 ff.

121 See Graves and Patai, *Hebrew Myths*, chap. 10, i, j.

122 See "On the Creation," bk. 1, 24; "Allegorical Interpretation," bk. 2. In *Philo*, trans. Colson and Whitaker, 1:2.

123 Tertullian, "Septim Florens," *Lib. adv. Valentin.* chap. 33.

124 *Book of the Monsters*, 97.

125 *Travels*, 137.

126 *Book of the Monsters*, 98.

127 Marie Delcourt, *Hermaphrodite*, 18, 27, 29, 28.

128 Anson, "The Female Transvestite," especially p. 11.

129 See Delcourt, "Le Complexe de Diane," 7.

130 Aristotle, *The Generation of Animals*, 738b.20–5; 761a.6–10.

131 Plato, *Timaeus* 50b-51b. For mediaeval versions of this concept see, among others, Albertus Magnus, *Quaestionibus super de animalibus*, bk. 16, quest. 3 and *De Natura et Origine Animae*, chap. 4. See also the excellent discussion in Allen, *The Concept of Woman*.

132 Pliny, *Natural History.* 7.15.64.

133 Wood, "The Doctor's Dilemma," 716.

CHAPTER FOUR

1 For a more developed discussion of the four elements, see Buschinger and Crepin, eds., *Les Quatre Eléments*.

2 Beings of the first element, fire, were seen primarily as nonphysical, spiritual rather than animal; they were beings of pure intellect – angels and demons – as well as some of the animals associated with these beings, such as salamanders, lizards, and the like.

3 Durand, *Structures anthropologiques*, 74, citing Jung, *Métamorphoses et symboles de la libido*, 205, my translation: "Le Sphinx constitue le résumé de tous ces symboles sexuels, 'animal terrible, dérivé de la mère' et lié au destin incestueux d'Oedipe."

4 Dumezil, *Le Problème des centaures.*

5 Clébert, *Bestiaire fabuleux,* 83.

6 *The Book of the Monsters,* 94.

7 Durand, *Structures anthropologiques,* 365, my translation: "le motif des ailes vient de compléter le maléfisme ophidien."

8 For an exhaustive study of fairies and melusines with a very full bibliography, see Harf-Lancner, *Les Fées au moyen âge.*

9 See Kappler, *Monstres démons,* citing Jourdain de Séverac, 167.

10 Scripture uses the masculine pronoun for both Leviathan and Behemoth. The female persona of Leviathan is a mediaeval innovation.

11 Durand, *Structures anthropologiques,* 230, my translation: "Le procédé réside essentiellement en ce que par du négatif on reconstitue du positif, par une négation ou un acte négatif on détruit l'effet d'une première négativité."

12 The poetic derivation of the name "siren" is from the Latin *serenitas,* "calmness," "quiet," "fair weather" and the word for evening or twilight, that period between light and darkness. See Clébert, *Bestiaire fabuleux* 382.

13 Durand, *Structures anthropologiques,* 114–15.

14 *Book of the Monsters,* 94.

15 A distinction is sometimes made between the siren and the mermaid based on the former being winged, the latter not. See Rowland, *Animals with Human Faces,* 139–40.

16 Clébert, *Bestiaire fabuleux,* 376 my translation: "Elle est l'âme du mort qui n'a pas trouvé, faute de vertu, le chemin du ciel, elle reste entre ciel et terre, agrippée à son rocher, isolée du reste des vivants et des morts, en quarantaine éternelle."

17 Ibid., 286

18 Ibid., 101 my translation: "Le rôle du cheval est ambivalent, pur et impur, solaire et funéraire, ouranien et chthonien, présage de bonheur et porteur de mort. Il surgit des ténèbres comme cheval-serpent et termine sa course comme cheval ailé. Il précède l'homme et le prolonge."

19 Ibid., 102, 204.

20 Virgil, *Aeneid* 3.212f., as cited in Rowland, *Birds with Human Souls,* 75.

21 Graves *Greek Myths* 2:150.2, 232.

22 Ibid., 108f., 26–7.

23 *Book of the Monsters,* 101.

24 Rowland, *Birds with Human Souls,* 76.

25 Herodotus, *History* 3.116.

26 The ten lost tribes were imprisoned by Alexander the Great in these mountains and can never escape even though there are ways out of their valley prison (for instance, by ship over the Caspian Sea) because they are further imprisoned by language; speaking only Hebrew they neither understand nor are understood by others.

27 Mandeville, *Travels,* 167.

28 See Rowland, *Birds with Human Souls,* 71–2.

29 Hedelin, *Des satyres, brutes.*

30 MacFarlane, "Isidore of Seville," 70.

31 Clébert, *Bestiaire fabuleux*, 177, my translation: "Elle pouvait prendre diverses formes de femme, de chien, de boeuf, de vipère. Elle avait une flamme autour de la tête et deux pieds différents, l'un d'airain, l'autre d'âne."

32 For a catalog of the associations of the phoenix with Christ, see Texelius, *Phoenix visus et auditus.*

33 Van Den Broek, *Myth of the Phoenix.*

34 Pliny, *Natural History* 10.2.

35 See Kirchmaier, *On the Unicorn*, citing Clement of Rome, 61.

36 See Van Den Broek, chap. 5, for a summary of these opinions.

37 Van Den Broek, 72–3.

38 Clébert, *Bestiaire fabuleux*, 340 my translation: "Composées des parties les plus subtiles de la sphère du feu, elles sont créatures parfaites et compagnes de l'homme avant qu'Adam n'eut péché … Noé, dit-on, devenu sage par l'exemple de son ancêtre Adam, consentit que sa femme Vesta se donnât au salamandre Oromasis, afin de repeupler au plus vite la terre d'êtres beaux et forts. Cette Vesta mythique fut le génie tutélaire de Rome, tandis que l'enfant qu'elle conçut dans cette affaire devint Zoroastre."

39 Durand, 359–60, my translation: "L'animal lunaire par excellence sera donc l'animal polymorphe par excellence: le Dragon … . Le 'monstre' est en effet symbole de totalisation, de recensement complet des possibilités naturelles."

40 For the description of the garden of the Hesperides see Apollodorus, 2.5.2 and Graves, *Greek Myths* 1:133, passim.

41 Kappler, *Monstres, démons*, 295–6.

42 See Clébert, *Bestiaire fabuleux*, 168.

43 On this subject, see Kappler, *Monstres, démons*, 31–2.

44 Bachelard, *La Terre et les rêveries*, 280, my translation: "Goutte de mort, source de vie! Employé en de justes heures, dans la bonne conjonction astrologique, le venin apporte guérison et jeunesse. Le serpent qui se mord la queue n'est pas un fil replié, un simple anneau de chair, c'est la dialectique matérielle de la vie et de la mort, la mort qui sort de la vie et la vie qui sort de la mort, non pas comme les contraires de la logique platonicienne, mais comme une inversion sans fin de la matière de mort et de la matière de vie."

45 Hugh of Saint Victor, *Didascalicon.*

46 *Travels*, 5–16.

47 See Duret, *Histoire admirable des plantes*; see also Giambattista Ramusio, *Navigazione e viaggi*, 1:fol. 402a.

48 As cited in Lee, *Vegetable Lamb of Tartary.*

49 Duret, *Histoire admirable des plantes*, 329, my translation: "Cette description de Zoophytes ou Plante-animaux estoit moins fabuleuse, pour la gloire du souverain Créateur auquel toutes choses sont possibles."

50 Cited by Huizinga, *Middle Ages*, 181.

51 *Moyen âge fantastique*, 118.

52 See Baltrusaitis, *Moyen âge fantastique*, 118–27, passim.
53 *Travels*, 181.
54 See Thompson, *Mystic Mandrake*, 122–3.
55 Eliade, *Zalmoxis*, 210.
56 Ibid., 225.
57 See Thompson, *Mystic Mandrake*, 21.
58 Evans and Serjeanston, *English Mediaeval Lapidaries*, Evans and Serjeanston, 17.
59 Pliny, *Natural History* 10.37.3
60 Kunz, *Precious Stones*, 130–1.
61 Baltrusaitis, *Moyen âge fantastique*, 19, my translation: "Sans doute, les pierres gravées avec ces effigies avaient-elles des pouvoirs magiques. Une force surnaturelle jaillit du déplacement, de la répétition, d'un monstrueux agrandissement et du mélange des formes vivantes."
62 Mandeville, *Travels*, 118.
63 Pliny, *Natural History* 9.54.
64 Ibid., 9.68.
65 Clébert, *Bestiaire fabuleux*, 179.
66 Ibid., 180–3.
67 Ovid, *Meta.* 4.
68 Evans and Serjeanston, *English Medieval Lapidaries*, 53.
69 Halleux and Schamp, *Les Lapidaires grecs*, 110.

CHAPTER FIVE

1 Baltrusaitis, *Réveils et prodiges*, 197–239.
2 Ibid., my translation: "La marge pénètre dans la lettre qui reproduit, en renversant les tons, en quelque sorte son négatif."
3 Ibid., 224.
4 See Buhler, *Kupferstichalphabet de Meister E.S.* and Hermann, *Illuminierten Handschriften im Tirol*.
5 See Renouvin, *Progrès de la gravure*, 168 and Leroquais, *Les Sacramentaires*, pl. xxxiii.
6 *De Libero Arbitrio Voluntatis* 2.16.171, cited by Peck, in "Number as Cosmic Language," 15–16.
7 Peck, "Number as Cosmic Language," 15.
8 Ibid., 17.
9 Ibid., 23–4.
10 De Bruyne, *Esthetics of the Middle Ages*, 49.
11 Boethius, *De institutione arithmetica*, in Masi, *Boethian Number Theory*, 97.
12 Ibid., 98.
13 Jacobus of Liege, *Speculum musicale*, my translation: "Numero Deus impare gaudet."

14 Boethius, *De institutione arithmetica* 96–7.

15 See above, chap. 3.

CHAPTER SIX

1 Among the important versions are *Historia Proelis* of Leo Presbiter and *Res Gestae Alex.* of Julius Valerius. St Ambrose in his version of the Brahman episode used Palladius' *On the People of India.*

2 The standard work on this subject and the fullest is Cary, *The Medieval Alexander.*

3 The summary of the Alexander story given here is taken mainly from Pseudo-Callisthenes' *The Romance of Alexander the Great*, as well as from the mediaeval *Wars of Alexander*, edited by W.W. Skeat.

4 In the English alliterative version, Alexander's eyes are described "as blesand sternes" (line 604). In another version his eyes are black and gold.

5 Hastings, ed. *Encyclopaedia of Religion*, 5: col. 610.

6 The *Iter ad paradisum* episode involves Alexander, at the end of his world conquests, searching for the source of a stream whose waters have so invigorated him that his eyes glow; that source is Paradise. Demanding entry, as has become his wont (in some versions he demands tribute), Alexander is surprised to be refused and requests some token of his visit. What is given him is an eye (in some versions a stone, in some versions a stone cut in the form of an eye). Arriving in Babylon, Alexander is told by his sages (in some versions an ancient Jew) to place the eye upon one balance of a scale and on the other to put all the gold he has won in his campaigns. The eye outweighs the precious metal. The eye, Alexander is told, represents human desire, yearning after all that it sees but never satisfied when it possesses it. He is then told to cover the eye with dirt and to weigh against it a feather. The feather outweighs the buried eye, signifying, say the sages, that only in death is human cupidity ever fulfilled.

7 The magician seems to anger his son by giving a disagreeable interpretation of the stars, even though he has provided it at the request of Alexander himself.

8 Pseudo-Callisthenes, *Romance of Alexander*, para. 285, 158–9.

9 *Wars of Alexander*, 1117–20, my translation: "Ðan callis he to him carpentaris & comandis þaim swythe / In mynde & in memory of him to make a cite, / And neuens it his awen name þat never syne changid, / Bot Alexsander ay furth efter himseluen."

10 Pseudo-Callisthenes, *Romance of Alexander*, para. 127, 69.

11 Ibid., para. 128, 69–70.

12 Ibid., para. 131, 72–3.

13 Ibid., para. 146, 83.

14 Ibid., para. 122, 66.

15 Ibid., para. 209, 115.

16 Ibid., para. 209, 116.

17 *Wars of Alexander*, 3987–8.

18 In the English alliterative *Wars* the gymnosophists are distinct from the Brahmans. In the Pseudo-Callisthenes they are the same people.

19 Pseudo-Callisthenes, *Romance of Alexander*, para. 223, 121.

20 Ibid., para. 93, 54–5.

21 Abel, *Le Roman d'Alexandre*, 25, my translation: "Un intermède heureux allait couper, enfin, cette succession d'adventures inhumaines: en passant dans une île qui se trouvait en face de ce rivage, les Grecs rencontrèrent les Oxydraques ou Brahmanes, peuple sage et vertueux, avec lesquels Alexandre et les siens eurent, pendant plusieurs jours, des entretiens admirables."

22 *Wars of Alexander*, 4035–7, my translation; emphasis added: Sen at we Ioy *nouthire* gemmes *ne* Iuwels in cofirs / Pelour, pirre, *ne* perle *ne na* proude wedis, / *Ne* sauand bot to sustene with oure owen sary craftis.

23 "E ʒour manars fra all othire mens so mekill ere deffirrid" (*Wars of Alexander*, 4223).

24 Ibid., 4267–75, my transliteration and emphases: "Hald we no hors for na harow ne na horned stottis, / Ne nauthire sondire we þe soile ne na sede sawis, / Seke we neuire no sustinance to saue with oure lyuys. / Set we na saynes in þe see ne sese we na fischis, / Ne nouthire hunt we ne hauke ne hent we na foules, / Bot sike as growis on þe gronde with-outen gomes werke. / And þat we fede vs with in-fere & fillis full oure tables, / A dayntefull diete þat damage vs neuire. / Haue we no cures of courte ne na cointe sewes."

25 Ibid., 4360–4, my translation and emphases: "Ne rede we neuire na retorik ne rial to speke; / Bot certis in all simpilnes sett we oure wordis, / Đat latis neuire lesing in oure lippis spring. / Ne foloʒe we na ficesyens ne philisophour scolis, / As sophistri & slik thing to sott with þe pepill."

26 Pseudo-Calisthenes, *Romance of Alexander*, para. 223, 123.

27 *Wars of Alexander*, 4614–17, my translation: "All þis condicions I call bot comon of bestis, / Đat has no sent in þaire saule ne sauour in na gude. / Bot we þat fourmed is & fast & has fre will / Differris as in oure fraunches fere fra ʒoure kynde."

28 Ibid., 4624–35.

29 Ibid., 4711–14, my translation: "I, Philip son þe fell kyng þe fondere of grece, / Sire Alexander þe athill þat aʒe all þe barbres / Eftir þe day & þe dethe of Dary & Porrus, / Đus fere I foloʒed haue my faes."

30 Ibid., 5431–9, my translation: "Đan pas þai thethen till a place of perlious bestis, / With clouen clees, sais þe clause as kynd of þe hoggs. / Đai ware thike & threuen wele thre foote o brede, / Quare-with þai faʒt with in-fere & fellid of his kniʒtis, / Đai ware so brefe at a blisch borely & grym. / On ilka best a bares hede full of breme tuskis, / Đus ware þai fourmed all be-fore & farand be-hynde / Like as it ware lepards & lions with tailis. / ʒit was þar gedird out of gripis & griffons emange."

31 Ibid., 5475–80, my translation: "ʒit was wonand in þis watir as women it semed, / Đat ferly faire ware of face with haare to þaire heelis. / Ouire-stride þar any

strange man or be þir strandes sailed, / Ðai droȝe þam doun in-to þe depe & drowned þaim for euire, / Or els þai tillid þaim to þe trees as þe buke tellis, / And gert þaim laike with þaim so lange till þaim þe life wantis."

32 Ibid., 5524–5, my translation: "So hiȝe to heuen þai hem hale in a hand-quile, / Midel-erth bot as a mylnestane na mare to him semed."

33 Ibid., 5527–8, my translation: "Ðe vertu of þe verray god envirounis him swythe, / And þan þai fell on a fild as ferre fra his ost."

34 Ibid., 5531.

35 Ibid., 5535–8, my translation: "Ðan gert he gomes for to gang & grayth him a tonn / Of grene glitterand glas with gerrethis of iren, / Ðat he miȝt sitt in him-selfe E with his seȝt þersee / Ane E othire E all þing at outwith it lengid."

36 Ibid., 5547–52, my translation: "Ðare saȝe he figours of fischis & fourmes di-uerse, / Ðat kend he neuir so many kindis ne of so qwaynt hewis. / Sum ferd all on foure feete & farand as bestis, / Bot quen þai blischt on þis berne þan bade þai na langir. / And oþir sellis he saȝe at sai wald he neuir, / Ðat ware unlikly to leue to any man wittis."

37 Abel, *Roman d'Alexandre*, 109, my translation: "Nous avons montré combien l'esprit du Roman, depuis les origines judéo-byzantines jusqu'à la forme que lui avaient donnée les Arabes, est constamment dominé par la peur de la divinité, par l'aversion pour tout ce qui est au delà de la mesure humaine. Et cet esprit se ma-nifestait, particulièrement, dans le traitement qui avait été constamment apporté aux deux épisodes de la descente sous la mer et de la montée au ciel."

38 Ibid., 110, my translation: "Curiosité satisfaite de l'homme courageux, sans plus, que son plaisir paie de son effort. On est loin ici, de la témérité impie de l'Alexan-dre byzantin, qui reprend trois fois, en solitaire, son audacieuse entreprise, jusqu'à ce que Léviathan lui-même le prenne dans sa gueule effroyable pour le re-jeter sur le rivage. L'esprit du XIIIe siècle éprouve déjà les picotements de l'avi-dité à connaître de la Renaissance, que la peur de transgresser les interdictions n'empêchera jamais de cueillir les fruits délicieux de la science."

39 See *Wars of Alexander*, 5656–77.

40 Pseudo-Callisthenes, *Romance of Alexander*, para. 259, p 147.

41 Ibid., para. 259, 148–9.

42 The text alerts us to the polyvalent readings of the monster by having the lesser magi, in the absence of the most able of them all, provide an interpretation antici-pating further martial glory for Alexander. The chief magus returns to provide a second, negative reading, the true one.

43 Pseudo-Callisthenes, *Romance of Alexander*, para. 259, 148.

44 Ibid., para. 260, 149.

45 Abel, *Roman d'Alexandre*, 11, my translation: "Elle a introduit d'un coup, mas-sivement, dans la conscience et la pensée du monde grec, puis a légué aux souve-nirs du monde civilisé tout entier, une quantité énorme de notions … En tout premier lieu, le monde élargi atteignit une ampleur et en même temps une co-hérence nouvelles."

46 Kunz, *Precious Stones*, 125.

47 *Pseudo-Callisthenes, The Romance of Alexander*, 14.

48 The seminal work on the versions of the Oedipus legend is that of Robert, *Oidipus*.

49 Although other mediaeval cities were symbolic within the same tradition, these three were the seats of the three Christian members of the nine "worthies": Godfrey of Bologna, Charlemagne, and Arthur. There is a parallel tradition of Scriptural cities that are built up only to be destroyed, beginning with Eden and continuing to Enoch, built by Cain, and Babylon, built by Nimrod.

50 Delehaye, *Les Légendes hagiographiques*, 71–2.

51 While a guest at the court of Pelops, where he had been given refuge as an exile, Laius conceived a passion for the king's son and abducted him. Laius' rape of Chryssipus is taken in mythology as the first occurrence of unnatural sex. Unable to escape and free himself from the degrading practice, the youth commits suicide.

52 All versions of the riddle are more or less alike; I summarize here Lydgate's.

53 Delcourt, *Oedipe*, 143, my translation: "Dès qu'Apollonius de Tyane a nommé l'Empuse, le sortilège dont elle menace Ménippe s'évanouit."

54 Ibid., 144, my translation: "La Sphinx demande à Oedipe quel animal a quatre pieds le matin, deux à midi, trois le soir. Ce qu'il doit répondre, ce n'est point son nom à elle, comme c'est le cas si souvent, c'est son nom à lui, l'Homme."

55 *Oedipus*, trans. and intro. Hadas, 26–7.

56 Delcourt, *Oedipe*, 24.

57 See ibid., chap. 1, passim.

58 Ibid., 23, my translation: "Ils sont conduits à la mer dans un coffre et déposés sur l'eau loin des côtes, sans avoir touché le sol. Si leur difformité est telle qu'elle efface en eux le caractère humain, ils sont brûlés et la cendre jetée à la mer, ce qui était le sort réservé aux animaux monstrueux."

59 Ibid., 35, my translation: "De même, peu a peu, en Grèce, à l'époque classique, on a cessé d'exposer les nouveau-nés contrefaits. À Rome, Tite-Live parle d'anormaux grandis, ce qui prouve qu'on en épargnait à leur naissance, nous ignorons du reste dans quelles conditions: les parents les gardaient-ils ou les exposaient-ils de manière à leur sauver la vie? Je crois que ce n'est pas seulement par pitié que l'on donnait un maximum de chances de salut et aux émissaires et aux anormaux … Celui qui a été consacré et que les dieux ont choisi de sauver devient bénéfique. Les forces dont il était chargé sont restées aussi lourdes, mais elles ont changé de signe."

60 Ibid., 35, citing and commenting on Hubert and Mauss, "Essai sur la nature et les fonctions du sacrifice," *Mélange d'histoire des religions*, 83f., my translation: " 'On s'explique ainsi comment le même mécanisme sacrificiel peut satisfaire à des besoins religieux dont la différence est extrême. Il porte la même ambiguïté que les forces religieuses elles-mêmes; la victime représente aussi bien la mort que la vie, la maladie que la santé, le péché que le mérite … Elle est le moyen de

concentration du religieux; elle l'exprime, elle l'incarne, elle le porte. C'est en agissant sur elle qu'on agit sur lui, qu'on le dirige, soit qu'on l'attire et l'absorbe, soit qu'on l'expulse et l'élimine.' Cette complexité existe, non seulement dans le rituel, mais aussi dans la légende, par exemple dans celle d'Oedipe, d'abord chassé de la communauté comme un 'esprit' maléfique, puis élu par les dieux et devenant d'autant plus puissant qu'il a été plus misérable."

61 An echo of the prohibition of contact between monster and earth?

62 See Constans, *La Légende d'Oedipe*, 173.

63 Delcourt, *Oedipe*, 30–1.

64 Constans, *La Légende d'Oedipe*, 27, my translation: "Selon Euripide et Hygin, il a le pied écrasé par une roue du char [du père]. Irrité, il arrache Laïus de son siège et le tue."

65 Ibid., 31, my translation: "Le Sphinx nous déchire par son énigme, personne ne peut détruire l'énigme."

66 Delcourt, *Oedipe*, 110–11, my translation: "Les Sirènes, comme les Keres, les Erinyes, les Harpyies, les Oiseaux de Stymphale, sont les esprits des morts ... Tous ces êtres ont un trait commun: ils sont avides de sang et de plaisir érotique."

67 Lydgate, *Siege of Thebes*, ed. Axel Erdmann, 757–69, my translation: "Weren destitut / of a gouernour, / Azeynst her foon / hauyng no socour / Hem to defende / but the quene allon; / ... / For which the lordes all be on assent / with-Inne the toun / set a parlement, / ... / To condescende / be way of Mariage, / She to be Ioyned to this manly knyght."

68 Delcourt, Oedipe, 130–3.

69 Ibid., 75.

70 Ibid., 202.

71 Ibid., 213.

72 Major versions which, however, will not be discussed here include the legend of Pope Gregory the Great, which makes him doubly incestuous, being the progeny of brother and sister and husband of his own mother. See *Gesta Romanorum,* ed. Sidney H.S. Herrtage. See also the legend of St Julian, in Jacobus De Voragine, *The Golden Legend*, trans. G. Ryan and H. Ripperger, 128–33.

73 Lydgate, *Seige of Thebes*, 194–209, my translation: "But how the wallys / weren on heghte reised, // It is wonder / and merveil forto here. // ... // How this kyng / thys prudent Amphyoun, // With the swetnesse / and melodious soun // And ar-monye / of his swete song // The Cyte bylt / that whilom was so strong, // Be ver-tue only / of the werbles sharpe, // That he made / in Mercuries harpe, // Of which the strenges / were not touched softe, // Whereby the walles / reised weren lofte, / / With-oute craft / of eny mannys hond."

74 Compare, for example, the terrain between Camelot and Haut Desert in *Sir Gawain and the Green Knight*.

75 Lydgate, *Siege of Thebes*, 620–5, my translation: "Body and feet / of a fers lyoun; // And lik a mayde in soth was hede and face, // Fel of his look / and cruel to man-ace // ... Wors than Tygre / dragon / or serpent".

76 Ibid., 694–7, my translation: "Thy false fraude / shal anon be qwyt. / Me lyst not nowe whisper neither rowne. / But thy problem / I shal anon expowne so opynly / thou shalt not go ther-fro."

77 Ibid., my translation: "And forth they gon / to a forest large, // Adiacent / unto this contre, // Percen his feet / and honge him on a tre" (930–2). "Vnto the queene / and gan a processe make // First how he was / in the forest take, // wounded the feet / and so forþ euery thyng" (971–3).

78 Lydgate, *Fall of Princes*, 3262–5, my translation: "Afftir his hurtis Edippus dede hym call. / For Edippus is no more to seyne, / Who that conceyueth th'exposicioun, / But feet ipershid throuhout bothe tweyne."

79 Ibid., 3459–65, my translation: "This seid problem concludith in this cas, / Which the serpent gan sleihtili purpose, / That whan a child is first born, allas, / Kynde to his dethward anon doth hym dispose; / Ech day a iourne; ther is noon other glose; / Experience can teche in eueri age, / How this world heer is but a pilgrymage."

80 The story was enormously popular and existed in numerous languages. It is certainly curious that in one of the Greek versions, the narrator of the story is identified as Dionysius the Areopagite! See Baum, "Judas Iscariot," 523f.

81 Ibid., 483–4.

82 De Voragine, *The Golden Legend*, 174.

83 *Sir Gawain and the Green Knight*, ed. Tolkien and Gordon, line 360. All references to the poem are from this edition. All transliterations are my own: "And if I carp not comely, let all þis cort rych / bout blame."

84 Ibid., 917–19: "þe teccheles termes of talkyng noble / þat fyne fader of nurture."

85 Ibid., 1–2: "Siþen þe sege and þe assaut watȝ sesed at Troye, / þe borȝ brittened and brent to brondeȝ and askeȝ."

86 Shichtman, "Sir Gawain," 3.

87 *Sir Gawain*, 14–19: "On mony bonkkes ful brode Bretayn he setteȝ / wyth wynne, / Where werre and wrake and wonder / Bi syþeȝ hatȝ wont þerinne, / And oft boþe blysse and blunder / Ful skete hatȝ skyfted synne."

88 Ibid., 93–5: "Of sum auenturus þyng an vncuope tale, / Of sum mayn meruayle, þat he myȝt trawe, / Of alderes, of armes, of oþer auenturus."

89 Blanch and Wasserman, "The Medieval Court," 181–3.

90 *Sir Gawain*, 240–4: Forþi fantoum and þe fayryȝe þe folk þere hit demed. / Þerfore to answare watȝ arȝe mony aþel freke, / And al stouned at his steuen and stonstil seten / In a swoghe sylence purȝ þe sale riche; / As al were slypped vpon slepe so slaked hor loteȝ."

91 For a more detailed discussion of the "eoten" and the Cain tradition see Williams, *Cain and Beowulf*.

92 For instance, Chambers, *The Medieval Stage*. 1:186.

93 For instance, Robertson, "Why the Devil Wears Green" and Randall, "Was the Green Knight a Fiend?"

94 For instance, Leighton "Christian and Pagan Symbolism.".

95 See Puhvel, "Art and the Supernatural."

96 *Sir Gawain*, 199–202: "He loked as layt so lyȝt, / So sayd al þat hym syȝe; Hit semed as no mon myht / Vnder his dyntteȝ dryȝe."

97 Besserman, "Green Knight," 227.

98 *Sir Gawain*, 444–9: "For þe hede in his honde he haldeȝ vp euen, / Toward þe derrest on þe dece he dresseȝ þe face, / And hit lyfte vp þe yȝe-lyddeȝ and loked ful brode, / And meled þus much with his muthe, as ȝe may now here: / 'Loke, Gawan, þou be grayþe to go as ȝou hetteȝ, / And layte as lelly til þou me, lude, fynde.' "

99 Ibid., 354–7: "I am þe wakkest, I wot, and of wyt feblest, / And lest lur of my lyf, quo laytes þe soþe / Bot for as much as ȝe ar myn em I am only to prayse, / No bounte bot your blod I in my bode knowe."

100 Ibid., 309–12: "What, is þis Arþurez hous, quoþ þe haþel þenne, / Þat al þe rous rennes of þurz ryalmes so mony? / Where is now your sourquydrye and your conquestes, / Your gryndellayk and your greme, and your grete wordes?"

101 Ibid., 658–60: "And fyched vpon fyue poynteȝ, þat fayld neuer, / ne samned neuer in no syde, ne sundred nouþer, / Withouten ende at any noke aiquere, I fynde."

102 From the Anglo-Saxon *beld*, boldness, rashness; equivalent to the Latin *audacia*.

103 Shichtman, "Sir Gawain," 11.

104 *Sir Gawain*, 691–3: "Now rideȝ þis renk þurȝ þe ryalme of Logres, / Sir Gauan, on Godeȝ halue, þaȝ hym no gomen þoȝt. / Oft leudleȝ alone he lengeȝ on nyȝteȝ."

105 Ibid., 713–17: "Mony klyf he ouerclambe in contrayeȝ straunge, / Fer floten fro his frendeȝ fremedly he rydeȝ. / Ay vche warþe oþer water þer wyȝe passed / He fonde a foo hym byfore, bot ferly hit were, / And þat so foule and so felle þat feȝt hym byhode."

106 Ibid., 947–53: "An oþer lady hir lad bi þe lyft honde, / Þat watȝ alder þen ho, an auncian hit semed, / And heȝly honowred with haþeleȝ aboute. / Bot vnlyke on to loke þo ladyes were, / For if þe ȝonge watȝ ȝep, ȝolȝe watȝ þat oþer; / Riche red on þat on rayled ayquere, / Rugh ronkled chekeȝ þat oþer on rolled."

107 Puhvel, "Art and the Supernatural," 31.

108 Loomis, *Wales and the Arthurian Legend*, 124.

109 Ibid., 124f.

110 *Sir Gawain*, 1330–6: "Syþen þay slyt þe slot, sesed þe erber, / Schaued wyth a scharp knyf, and þe schyre knitten; / Syþen rytte þay þe foure lymmes, and rent of þe hyde, / Þen breke þay þe bale, þe boweleȝ out token / Lystily forlancyng þe lere of þe knot; / Þay gryped to þe gargulun, and grayþely departed / Þe wesaunt fro þe wynt-hole, and walt out þe gutteȝ."

111 Ibid., 1597–1611: "A hundreth houndeȝ hym hent, / Þat bremely con hym bite, / Burneȝ him broȝt to bent, / And doggeȝ to dethe endite … Fyrst he hewes of his hed and on hiȝe setteȝ / And syþen rendeȝ him al roghe bi þe rygge after /

Braydeʒ out þe boweles, brenneʒ hom on glede, / With bred blent þerwith
his braches rewardeʒ. / Sypen he britneʒ out þe brawen in bryʒt brode
cheldeʒ."

112 Whereas the description of the deer hunt and the hunt of the boar each consists
     of four stanzas, balanced by four stanzas of description of the bedroom scenes,
     the hunt of the fox is presented in three stanzas, and the last temptation is ex-
     tended to five.

113 *Sir Gawain*, 1770–2: For þat prynces of þris depresed hym so þikke, / Nurned
     hym so neʒe þe þred, þat nede hym bihoued / Oþer lach þer hir luf, oþer lodly
     refuse.

114 Ibid., 1777–8: "With luf-laʒyng a lyt he layd hym bysyde / Alle þe specheʒ of
     specialté þat sprange of her mouthe."

115 The connotation of circular shapes in the Middle Ages, preeminently including
     rings, is commonly one of female sexuality (viz., Chaucer's use of the figure of
     the ruby-in-the-ring/ruby-out-of-the-ring in, for example, *Troilus and Criseyde*);
     the psychological force of the girdle, belt, or other intimate female garment is
     best seen, perhaps, in the saga of Saint George, who binds the savage dragon he
     defeats with the cincture of the maiden he will wed.

116 *Sir Gawain*, 1846–50: " 'Now forsake ʒe þis silke,' sayde þe burde þenne, / 'For
     hit is symple in hitself? And so hit wel semeʒ. / Lo! so hit is littel, and lasse hit
     is worþy; But who-so knew þe costes þat knit ar þerinne, / He wolde hit prayse
     at more prys, parauenture.' "

117 Haines, *Fall of Sir Gawain*.

118 Newman, *Idea of a University*, 175–6.

119 Besserman, "Gawain's Green Girdle."

120 P. Saintyves, "Ceintures magiques."

121 *Sir Gawain*, 2309–14: "He lyftes lyʒtly his lome, and let hit doun fayre, / With
     þe barbe of þe bitte bi þe bare nek; / þaz he homered heterly, hurt hym no more
     / Bot snyrt hym on þat on syde, þat seuered þe hyde. / Þe scharp schrank to þe
     flesche þurʒ pe schyre grece, / Þat pe schene blod ouer his schulderes schot to
     þe erþe."

122 Shoaf. *The Poem as Green Girdle*, 29–30.

123 Ibid., 30.

124 See Arthur, *Medieval Sign Theory*, 106ff.

125 See, for example, Ryan, "Sir Gawain and St Winifred."

126 *Sir Gawain*, 2498–2502: "Þe nirt in þe nek he naked hem schewed / Þat he laʒt
     for his vnleute at þe leudes hondes / for blame. / He tened quen he shulde telle, /
     He groned for gref and grame."

127 Ibid., 2513–17: "Þe kyng comforteʒ þe knyʒt, and alle þe court als / Laʒen
     loude þerat, and luflyly acorden / Þat lordes and ladis þat longed to þe Table, /
     Vche burne of þe broþerhede, a bauderyk schulde haue, / A bende abelef hym
     aboute of a bryʒt grene."

128 Ibid., 2522–5: "Þus in Arthrus day þis aunter bitidde, / Þe Brutus bokeȝ þerof beres wyttenesse; / Syþen Brutus, þe bolde burne, boȝed hider fyrst, / After þe segge and þe asaute watȝ sesed at Troye."

129 Ibid., 2525–9: "After þe segge and þe asaute watȝ sesed at Troye, / iwysse / Mony auentereȝ here-biforne / Haf fallen suche er þis. / Now þat bere þe croun of þorne, / He bryng vus to his blysse! AMEN."

CHAPTER SEVEN

1 *Commentary on the Republic*, translation from Coulter, *Literary Microcosm*, 50.
2 See, for instance, Saintyves, "Les Saints cephalophores," 158–231.
3 De Voragine, *The Golden Legend*. All references to the *Life* of Saint Christopher are to this edition unless otherwise indicated.
4 Ibid., 379.
5 See, for instance, Gaidoz, "Saint Christophe."
6 See Reinach, *Pierres gravées*, xlv, 94, 98.
7 Saintyves, "Les Saints céphalophores," 34–5.
8 Ibid., 27–8.
9 Ibid., 36–7, my translation: "En Allemagne, le 25 juillet, on sacrifiait les coqs que l'on avait fait danser les jours précédents en l'honneur de Thor ou de saint Christophe."
10 *Contendings of the Apostles*, ed. and trans. Budge, 201–14.
11 See *MT*, 3.1033B; see also *Letter Nine,* 1105B.
12 *Contendings of the Apostles*, 208.
13 *Golden Legend*, 380.
14 Saintyves, "Les Saints céphalophores," 31.
15 It should be pointed out, however, that *The Golden Legend* anticipates this illogical description by having the child instruct Christopher to plant the staff "when thou *shalt have returned* to the other side of the river" (379, my emphasis).
16 *Contendings*, 213.
17 *Passion of St Christopher*, trans. Fraser, 307–25.
18 *Golden Legend*, 381.
19 *Passion of St Christopher*, 309.
20 *Golden Legend*, 381, emphasis added.
21 *Contendings*, 209.
22 See Saintyves, "Les Saints céphalophores," 36.
23 Saintyves, "Les Saints céphalophores," 158.
24 Ibid., 158 passim.
25 Ibid., 174.
26 For a discussion of the various versions, see Lacaze, "*Vie de Saint Denis*."
27 *Geu Saint Denis,* ed. Seubert.
28 Grimal, *Dictionnaire de la mythologie*, 333, my translation: "C'est autour de ce mythe que se forma la théologie orphique. De sa descente aux Enfers, à la pour-

suite d'Eurydice, Orphée était censé avoir rapporté des renseignements sur la façon de parvenir au pays des Bienheureux et d'éviter tous les obstacles et les pièges qui attendent l'âme après la mort."

29 See Graves, *The Greek Myths*. 1:28.d.

30 Ibid., 28.2.

31 Baring-Gould, *Lives of the Saints*, 1:195–7.

32 Lacaze, *Vie de Saint Denis*, 91.

33 Moreover, Eleutherius and Rusticus speak these few lines simultaneously, unlike even the most minor characters who, though minor, are at least given individual lines.

34 Baring-Gould, *Lives of the Saints*, 1:196.

35 The vintage festival was held in France on the 8th and 9th of October, corresponding to the harvest, well into the nineteenth century.

36 Occasional debunking began as early as Hilduin's invention of the legend and reached a high point in the twelfth century with Peter Abelard.

37 *Golden Legend*, 616–17.

38 *Geu Saint Denis*, lines 111–36, my translation: "Le second parisien: 'Beau maistre, ce Dieu qui est vostre, / Est il ore nouvel ou vieulx?' / Saint Denis: 'Amy, nostre Dieu est vray Diex / Et vray homs et vieulx et nouvel.' / Le second: 'Nouvel est donc et non nouvel. C'est pure contradiction.' / S. Denis: Vraiement et sans fiction: / Nouvel est il et non nouvel.' / Le second: 'C'est donc liart et fauvel / Qui vont ensemble a la charue.' / Le tiers: 'Non pas, mez quant il va la rue, / Il a de vielx drap, robe neuve. / Et par cela ce veillart preuve / Qu'il est nouvel et ancïen.' / Le premier: 'Il est donc maez logicïen. / … Lisbie *le plus noble bourgeois*: 'Toute vostre sophistrie / Sy ne fait nulle chose au fait.' "

39 Ibid., 144–7, my translation: "Nostre Dieu est vielx sans viellesce / Et sy est jeune sans jeunesce, / Commencement et finement, / Sans fin et sans commencement."

40 Ibid., 184–6, my trans.: " 'Comment pourroient estre ensemble / tout puissans? Que vous en semble?' / Lisbie: 'Sire, il ne peuvent estre deulz.' "

41 Ibid., 201–4, my translation: "Puis qu'a ce point m'avez mené / Qu'il n'est Dieu fors le Dieu dez cielx / Dont viennent doncques tant de Dieux / Comme en aoure par le monde?"

42 Ibid., 305–6, my translation: "A Diex tant sont cez raisons bonnes, / Soutilles, profondes et haultes."

43 Ibid., 321: "destruit, confont, anichile."

44 Ibid., 388–97, my translation: "Le premier: 'Sire, il presche .i. Dieu a Paris / Qui fait tous les monls et les vauls. / Il va a cheval sans chevauls. / Il fait; il defait tout ensemble. / Il vit, il meurt; il sue, il tremble. / Il pleure, il rit; il vueille et dort. / Il est jeune et viex; foible et fort. / Il fait d'un coq une poulete. / Il jeue des ars de Toulete. / Ou je ne scay que puet estre."

45 Ibid., 956–8, my translation: "De cuer, de bouche et d'euvre ensemble / Nous troiz la sainte Trinité / Confessons une déité."

46 Caens, "Nouvelles recherches," 9–31.

47 Ibid., 15, n. 1.

48 *Geu Saint Denis*, 1011–22, my translation, my emphasis:

> Doultz Jhesucrist qui m'as fourmé,
> Qui par grace m'as refourmé,
> Qui estoie tout deformé,
>
> ....
> Recoif m'ame par ta bonté

49 J. Gessler reports having received a letter in 1935 from the parish priest of Rinxent in northern France describing a lively devotion to Saint Wilgeforte that included petitions for aid in keeping toddlers on their feet while learning to walk and to assist deformed children. See Gessler, *La Vierge barbue.*

50 Cahier, *Caractéristiques des saints*, 1:122.

51 Reau, *L'Iconographie de l'art Chrétien*, 3:1342–5.

52 *Commentarii in Psalmos*, 561, my translation: "Cithara habet lignum crucis, habet chordas ex interioribus ovium, habet ex Evangeliis plectrum."

53 *Appendix*, 626, my translation: "Chorda est corpus, quod tenditur, et maceratur inter poenam carnis, et dolorem cordis."

54 See *Opera Omnia*, ed. Frette, 31:638.

55 Giesel, *Studien zur Symbolik*, 173 my translation: "Das wort chorda, für das im Lateinischen bisweilen auch nervus oder fides steht."

56 See Demons, "La Statue de sainte Wilgeforte."

57 See Roheim, "Aphrodite, or the Woman with a Penis," in *The Panic of the Gods*, 169–205; Delcourt, *"Hermaphroditea."*

58 Bynum, *Jesus as Mother*, 139.

59 Gaskell, *Sacred Language*, 404.

60 Bynum, *Jesus as Mother*, 111–12.

61 Julian of Norwich, *Revelations of Divine Love*, chap. 58, 159.

62 Ibid., 159–60.

63 *Golden Legend*, 352–3.

64 *Golden Legend*, 353.

65 Saintyves, *Les saints successeurs des dieux*, 366, my translation: "Aucune légende fut plus populaire pendant tout le Moyen Âge. Dès la fin du XIIIeme siecle, on en connaît huit versions en rimes françaises dont l'une est l'oeuvre d'un poète illustre, Robert Wace ... Bien plus, c'est la seule légende à laquelle était attachée, dans la foire populaire, une vertu surnaturelle propre, non pas à l'invocation de la sainte mais au voisinage du récit de sa vie et de son martyre. Les femmes en couche se la faisaient lire et l'on posait sur elles le livre lui-même pour soulager leurs douleurs et en hâter la fin."

66 For a recent discussion of these saints, see Bullough, "Transvestites," 1381–94.

67 Burchard of Worms, "Apologia de Barbis."

68 *Enchiridion Sarisburnensis*, as cited in Baron Sloet, *De Heilige Ontkommer of Wilgeforthis*, 14, my translation (emphasis added).

CHAPTER EIGHT

1 *City of God*, 16.7.

2 *Dialogue Concerning Heresies*, 235. In defending the cult of the saints against Tyndale and other dissenters, St Thomas seems at a loss when confronted with the grotesque saints. He attempts to rationalize the cult of Uncumber; perhaps, he suggests, petitioners wish, not to be uncumbered of their husbands, but of the cumbersome habits of their husbands, or even of difficulties in general, or, perhaps, of their own "cumberous" tongues (which, he muses, may be the origin of their marital problems).

3 Wittkower, "Marvels of the East," 185.

4 Martin Heidegger, *Chemins qui ne mènent nulle part*, 80, my translation: "This word [World] is not reducible to Cosmos or Nature; History is also part of the World ... This designation indicates especially and above all the World in its constitution regardless of how the relationship of the World to its constitution is conceived."

5 Ibid., my translation: "This word [*subjectum*] designates that which is made present-before (*das Vor-Liegende*), which as grounding (*Grund*) gathers everything to itself. This metaphysical definition of the notion of the subject had originally no special relation to man, and even less so to the 'ego.' "

6 Ibid., my translation, 81–2.

7 Ibid., my translation, 81.

8 And as she lay upon the durtie ground

> Her huge long taile her den all overspred,
> Yet was in knots and many boughtes upwound,
> Pointed with mortall sting. Of her there bred
> A thousand yong ones, which she dayly fed,
> Sucking upon her poisonous dugs, eachone
> Of sundry shapes, yet all ill favorèd:
> Soone as that uncouth light upon them shone,
> Into her mouth they crept, and suddain all were gone.
>
> (Spenser, *The Faerie Queene*, book 1, canto 1, 127–35)

> The one seemed woman to the waist, and fair,
> But ended foul in many a scaly fold
> Voluminous and vast, a serpent armed
> With mortal sting. About her middle round
> A cry of Hellhounds never ceasing barked

With wide Cerberean mouths full loud, and rung
A hideous peal; yet when they list, would creep,
If aught disturbed their noise, into her womb.

(Milton, Paradise Lost, book 2, 650–7)

Both citations are taken from *The Norton Anthology of English Literature*.

9 See the introduction by Jean Céard to Paré, *Des monstres et prodiges*, xxxii. All references to this work are from this edition.

10 Ibid., xxxix, my translation: "en quoy sont comprises les perfections de ce Tout, qui représente le grand corps de l'univers."

11 Ibid., xv.

12 Le Paulmier, *Ambroise Paré*, 89.

13 Paré, *Des monstres et prodiges*, xv-xvi, my translation: "Et quant a cest advertissement que vous faictes touchant les Monstres, je les ay recueillis de Rondelet, Gesnerus, Cardan, Boiastuau, lequel pour le jourdhuy est ordinairement entre les mains des Dames et Demoiselles. Davantage n'est-il permis de les voir en chair et en os tous les jours en ceste ville de Paris et ailleurs?"

14 Le Paulmier, *Ambroise Paré*, 90.

15 Park and Dalston, "Unnatural Conceptions," 24.

16 Ibid., 23.

17 Paré, *Des monstres et prodiges*, 4.

18 Park and Dalston, "Unnatural Conceptions," 43.

19 "There is no art delivered to mankind that hath not the works of nature for his principle object, without which they could not exist, and on which they so depend." *The Defence of Poesy*, in *The Norton Anthology of English Literature*, vol. 1, 506.

20 Park and Dalston, "Unnatural Conceptions", 43.

21 Browne, *Religio Medici*, in *The Norton Anthology*, 1:1722.

22 Bacon, *Novum Organum*, ii, 29.

23 Lascault, *Le Monstre*, 195, my translation: "De même que la forme monstrueuse montre l'ordre biologique à la fois comme menace et comme essentiel, elle paraît inséparable d'un modèle linguistique qui permet de la penser et elle conteste ce modèle: elle ne se compare qu'aux anomalies qui peuvent se rencontrer dans *l'ordre* du discours. Obéissant à une grammaire propre, le monstre *transgresse* les lois grammaticales habituelles et établit un rapport polémique, mais nécessaire avec elle."

24 Heidegger, *Chemins*, 84, my translation: En effet, plus complètement le monde semble disponible comme monde, plus objectivement l'objet apparaît, plus subjectivement, c'est-à-dire plus péremptoirement, se dresse le sujet, et plus irrésistiblement la considération du monde, la théorie du monde se change-t-elle en une théorie de l'homme – l'anthropologie.

25 Ibid., 75, my translation: Ce qui dans le passé est constant, c'est-à-dire ce au compte de quoi l'explication historique peut porter l'unique et le multiple de

l'histoire, c'est ce qui a toujours déjà été (das Immer-schön-einmal-Dagewesene), l'ensemble du comparable. À partir de la constante comparaison de tout avec tout se fait alors le compte du compréhensible, lequel est alors confirmé et consolidé comme le plan de l'histoire. Le secteur de la recherche historique ne s'étend qu'aussi loin que porte l'explication historique. L'unique, le rare, le simple, bref ce qui, dans l'histoire, est grand, ne va jamais de soi; il reste toujours inexplicable. La recherche historique ne nie pas la grandeur, elle l'explique comme exception.

26 Ibid., 82, my translation: Par rapport à l'entente grecque, la représentation moderne signifie tout autre chose. Cette signification s'exprime le plus clairement dans le mot *repraesentatio*. Re-présenter signifie ici: faire venir devant soi, en tant qu'obstant (Entgegenstehendes) le simple existant, le rapporter à soi, qui le représente, et le ré-fléchir dans ce rapport à soi en tant que région d'où échoit toute mesure.

Bibliography

Abel, Armand. *Le Roman d'Alexandre: Légendaire médiéval.* Brussels: S.A. Édi-
teurs, 1955.

Ailly, Pierre d'. *Ymago mundi.* Trans. Edmond Buron. 3 vols. Paris: Maisonneuve
Frères, 1930–31.

Alanus de Insulis. "De Incarnatione Christi" (Rythmus Alter), in Migne, *Patrologia
latina* 210, col. 579B–580C.

– "De Incarnatione Dei: Rhythmus Perelegans," in Migne, *Patrologia latina* 210,
col. 577A–580A.

Albertus Magnus. *Quaestionibus super de animalibus* and *De natura et origine animae,* in vol. 12 of *Opera Omnia.* Ed. Bernard Geyer. Westfal: In Aedibiis Aschen-
dorff, 1951.

Aldrovandi, Ulysses. *Monstrorum Historia.* In *Collected Works.* Vol. 6. Bononiae,
1642.

Allen, Prudence. *The Concept of Woman: The Aristotelian Revolution, 750 BC – 1250
AD* Montreal: Eden Press, 1985.

Amelli, Ambrogio. *Miniature sacree profane dell'anno 1023 illustranti l'enciclope-
dia medioevale di Rabano Mauro.* Montecassino, 1896.

Anderson, James F. *Reflections on the Analogy of Being.* The Hague: Martinus
Nijhoff, 1967.

Anselm of Canterbury [Saint]. "On Truth," in *Anselm of Canterbury: Selections.* Eds.
Jasper Hopkins and Henry Richardson. Toronto: Edward Mellen Press, 1974–76.

Anson, John. "The Female Transvestite in Early Monasticism: The Origin and Development of a Motif." *Viator* 5 (1974): 1–32.

Appollodorus. *Gods and Heroes of the Greeks.* The Library of Appollodorus. Trans.
Michael Simpson. Amherst, MA: University of Massachusetts Press, 1976.

Aquinas, Thomas [Saint]. *Opera Omnia*. Ed. S.E. Frette. 34 vols. Paris: L. Vives (1871–80).

– *The Soul*. Trans. John Patrick Rowan. St Louis: B. Herder Books, 1951.

– *Summa Theologica: Latin and English*. Cambridge: Blackfriars; New York: McGraw Hill, 1964–67.

Aristotle. *On Sophistical Refutations; On Coming to Be and Passing Away; On the Cosmos*. Trans. E.S. Foster and D.J. Furley. Cambridge: Harvard University Press, Loeb Classical Library, 1955.

– *The Generation of Animals* and *Metaphysics*. Ed. and trans. W.D. Ross. Oxford: Clarendon Press, 1924.

Armstrong, Hilary. "Negative Theology." *Downside Review* 95 (1977): 176–89.

– "Pagan Eros and Christian Agape." *Downside Review* 79 (1961): 105–21.

Arnobius. *Commentarii in Psalmos: Psal.CXLV*, in *Patrologia latina* 53, col. 561.

Arthur, Ross G. *Medieval Sign Theory and Sir Gawain and the Green Knight*. Toronto: University of Toronto Press, 1987.

Attridge, Derek. "The Wake's Confounded Language," in *Coping with Joyce: Essays from the Copenhagen Symposium*, edited by Morris Beja and Shari Benstock, 262–8. Columbus, OH: Ohio State UP, 1989.

Augustine [Saint]. *On Christian Doctrine*. Trans. D.W. Robertson Jr. Indianapolis: Bobbs-Merrill, 1958.

Babylonian Talmud. Trans. and ed. I. Epstein. London: Soncino Press, 1961.

Bachelard, Gaston. *La Terre et les rêveries du repos*. 1948. Paris: Librairie Jose Corti, 1979.

Bacon, Francis [Sir]. *The New Organon*. Ed. Fulton J. Anderson. New York: Liberal Arts Press, 1960.

Bakhtin, Mikhail. *Rabelais and His World*. Trans. Helene Iswolsky. Bloomington IN: Indiana University Press, 1984.

Baltrusaitis, Jurgis. *Le Moye. âge fantastique: Antiquités et exotismes dans l'art gothique*. Paris: Armand Colin, 1955.

– *Aberrations: Quatre essais sur la légende des formes* Paris: O. Perrin, 1957.

– *Réveils et prodiges: Le gothique fantastique*. Paris: Armand Colin, 1960.

Barasch, Frances. *The Grotesque: A Study in Meanings*. Paris and The Hague: Mouton, 1971.

Baring-Gould, S. *The Lives of the Saints*. London: John Hodges, 1877.

Barkan, Leonard. *Nature's Work of Art: The Human Body As Image of the World*. New Haven: Yale University Press, 1975.

– *The Gods Made Flesh: Metamorphosis and the Pursuit of Paganism*. New Haven and London: Yale University Press, 1986.

Bartholomeus Anglicus. *Bartholomaeus Anglicus on the Property of Things*. Ed. R. James Long. Toronto: Pontifical Institute of Mediaeval Studies, 1979.

Bauhinus, G. *De hermaphroditorum monstrorumque partuum*. Oppenheim, 1614.

Baum, Paull F. "The Medieval Legend of Judas Iscariot." *PMLA* 31 (1916): 481–632.

Berger de Xivray, J. *Traditions tératologiques*. Paris: L'Imprimerie Royale, 1836.

Besserman, Lawrence. "Gawain's Green Girdle." *Annuale Medievale* 22 (1982): 84–101.

– "The Idea of the Green Knight." *ELH* 53 (1986): 219–39.

Blanch, Robert, and Julian Wasserman. "The Medieval Court and the Gawain Manuscript." In *The Medieval Court in Europe*, edited by Edward E. Haynes, 176–88. Munich: Houston German Studies, 1986.

Boccaccio, Giovanni. *Genealogie*. In *The Renaissance of the Gods*. Intro. Stephen Orgel. New York and London: Garland Publishing, 1976.

– *Decameron*. Ed. Vittore Branca. Milan, 1985.

Boethius. *De Institutione Arithmetica*. In *Boethian Number Theory*, ed. and trans. Michael Masi. Amsterdam: Rodolphi, 1983.

Boffito, Giuseppe. "La leggenda degli antipodi." In *Miscellanea di studi critici edita in onore di Arturo Graf*, ed. A. Della Torre. Bergamo: Galileiana 1903.

Boiastuau, P. *Histoires prodigieuses qui ayent esté observées dupuis la nativité de Jésus Christ jusqu'à notre siècle*. Paris, 1560.

Brehaut, Ernest. *An Encyclopedist of the Dark Ages: Isidore of Seville*. New York: Burt Franklin, 1964.

Bridaham, L.B., and R.A. Cram. *Gargoyles, Chimeres, and the Grotesque in French Gothic Sculpture*. New York, 1930.

Browne, Thomas [Sir]. *Religio Medici*. In *The Norton Anthology of English Literature*, 5th ed., vol. 1. New York, 1986.

Budge, E.A. Wallis, ed. and trans. *The Contendings of the Apostles*. 2 vols. London: Henry Frowde, 1901.

Buhler, W. *Kupferstichalphabet de Meister E.S.* Neueste illustrierte Welt-Chronik für 1499. Strassburg: J.E.H. Heitz, 1934.

Bullough, Vern L. "Transvestites in the Middle Ages." *American Journal of Sociology* 79 (1974): 1381–94.

Burchard of Worms. "Apologia de barbis," in *Corpus Christianorum* LXII. Turnholti, Belgium: Brepols, 1985.

Burrell, David. *Analogy and Philosophical Language*. New Haven and London: Yale University Press, 1973.

Buschinger, Danielle, and André Crépin, eds. *Les Quatre éléments dans la culture médiévale*. Goppingen: Kummerle Verlag, 1983.

Butturff, Douglas. "The Monsters and the Scholar: An Edition and Critical Study of the Liber Monstrorum." Ph.D. diss., University of Illinois, 1968.

Bynum, Caroline Walker. *Jesus as Mother*. Berkeley: University of California Press, 1982.

Caens, Maurice. "Nouvelles recherches sur une thème hagiographique: La céphalophorie." *Recueil d'Études Bollandistes: Subsidia Hagiographica* 37, 9–31.

Cahier, Charles. *Caractéristiques des saints dans l'art populaire*. 2 vols. Paris: Poussielgue Frères, 1867.

Caillois, Roger. *Babel: Orgueil, confusion et ruine de la littérature*. 3rd. ed. Paris: Gallimard, 1948.

– *Au coeur du fantastique*. Paris: Gallimard, 1965.

Canguilhem, Georges. "La Monstruosité et le monstrueux," *Diogène* 40 (1962): 29–43.

– *La Connaissance de la vie*. Paris: J. Vrin, 1969.

– *On the Normal and the Pathological*. Trans. Carolyn R. Fawcett, with the editorial collaboration of Robert S. Cohen. Studies in the History of Modern Science. Dordrecht: D. Reidel, 1978.

Cantimpré, Thomas de. *De naturis rerum*. In A. Hilka, ed., *Festschrift zur Jahrhundertfeier der Universität Breslau*. Breslau, 1911.

Caprotti, E. *Mostri, draghi e serpenti nelle silografie dell'opera di Ulisse Aldrovandi e dei suoi contemporanei*. Milan, 1980.

Cary, George. *The Medieval Alexander*. 1956. Reprint, Cambridge: Cambridge University Press, 1967.

Cassirer, Ernst. *The Philosophy of Symbolic Forms*. Trans. Ralph Manheim, 1955. 3 vols. New Haven: Yale University Press Press, 1975.

Catherine of Siena [Saint]. *The Cell of Knowledge: Early English Mystical Treatises by Margery Kempe and Others*. New York: Crossroads, 1981.

Céard, Jean. *La Nature et les prodiges*. Geneva: Librairie Droz, 1977.

Chambers, E.K. *The Medieval Stage*. London: Oxford University Press, 1925.

Chenu, Marie-Dominique. *Toward Understanding St Thomas*. Trans. A.M. Landry and D. Hughes. Chicago: Henry Regnery Co., 1964.

Cicero, Marcus Tullius. *Academic Questions*. In *Selections: Opera Philosophica*. Trans. C.D. Yonge. London: H.G. Bohn, 1853.

Clayborough, Arthur. *The Grotesque in Art and Literature*. Oxford: Clarendon Press, 1965.

Clébert, Jean-Paul. *Dictionnaire du symbolisme animal: Bestiaire fabuleux*. Paris: Édition Albin Michel, 1971.

Clement [Saint]. *Clementine Homilies*. Trans. Rev. Thomas Smith. T. & T. Clark: Edinburgh, 1870.

Colie, Rosalie L. *Paradoxia Epidemica: The Renaissance Tradition of Paradox*. Princeton: Princeton University Press, 1966.

Colish, Marcia. *The Mirror of Language: A Study in the Medieval Theory of Knowledge*. Rev. ed. London and Lincoln, NE: Nebraska University Press, 1983.

Constans, Léopold. *La Légende d'Oedipe: Étudiée dans l'antiquité, au moyen âge et dans les temps modernes en particulier dans le roman de Thèbes, texte français du XIIème siècle*. Geneva: Slatkine Reprints, 1974.

Cordier, H. *Les Monstres dans la légende et dans la nature: Les cynocéphales*. Paris, 1890.

Coulter, James. *The Literary Microcosm: Theories of Interpretation of the Later Neoplatonists*. Leiden: E.J. Brill, 1976.

Curtius, E.R. *European Literature and the Latin Middle Ages*. Trans. Willard R. Trask. Bolingen Series, 36. Princeton: Princeton University Press, 1953.

D'Andrea, Antonio. "L'Allegoria dei poeti." In *Dante e la forma dell'allegoresi*. Ed. M. Picone, 71–8. Ravenna: Longo Editore, 1987.

D'Ayzac, F. "Iconographie du Dragon". *Revue de l'Art Chrétien* (1864): 75–95; 169–94; 333–61.

Dacos, Nicole. *La Découverte de la Domus Aurea et la formation des grotesques à la renaissance.* London: Warburg Institute, 1969.

Daniel, Howard. *Devils, Monsters, and Nightmares: An Introduction to the Grotesque and Fantastic in Art.* London: Abelard-Shuman, 1964.

Davidson, G. *A Dictionary of Angels.* New York and London: Free Press, 1977.

De Bruyne, Edgar. *The Esthetics of the Middle Ages.* Trans. Eileen B. Hennessy. New York: F. Ungar, 1969.

de Laborde, A. *Les Manuscrits de la Cité de Dieu de Saint Augustin.* 3 vols. Paris, 1909.

De Voragine, Jacobus. *The Golden Legend.* Trans. Granger Ryan and Helmut Ripperger. 1941. Reprint, Salem, NH: Ayer Co., 1991.

Debidour, V.H. *Le Bestiaire sculpté du moyen âge en France.* Paris: Arthaud, 1961.

Delcourt, Marie. "Le Complexe de Diane dans l'hagiographie chrétienne." *Revue de l'histoire des religions* 153 (1958): 1–33.

– *Hermaphrodite: Myths and Rites of the Bisexual Figure in Classical Antiquity.* Trans. Jennifer Nicholson. London: Studio Books, 1961.

– *Hermaphroditea: Recherches sur l'être double promoteur de virilité dans le monde classique.* Paris: Collection Latomus, 1966.

– *Oedipe ou la légende du conquérant.* 2nd ed. Paris: Les Belles Lettres, 1981.

– *Stérilités mystérieuses et naissances maléfiques dans l'antiquité classique.* Paris: Les Belles Lettres, 1986.

Delehaye, Hippolyte. *Les Légendes hagiographiques.* 4th. ed. Brussels: Société des Bollandistes, 1955.

Deleuze, Gilles. *Logique du sens.* Paris: Éditions de Minuit, 1969.

Demons, F., "La Statue de Sainte Wilgeforte à estampuis." *Annales de la Société Historique et Archéologique de Tournai* 13(1908): 52–3.

Denis, F. *Le Monde enchanté, cosmographie et histoire naturelle fantastique du moyen âge.* Paris, 1843.

Denzinger, Henricus. *Enchiridion symbolorum.* Barcinone: Herder, 1963.

Didron, Adolphe Napoleon. *Christian Iconography.* London: H.G. Bohn, 1851–91.

Douglas, Mary. *Purity and Danger: An Analysis of Concepts of Pollution and Taboo.* London: Routledge and Kegan Paul, 1966.

Dumezil, Georges. *Le Problème des centaures.* Paris: P. Geuthner, 1929.

Durand, Gilbert. *L'Imagination symbolique.* Paris: Presses Universitaires de France, 1964.

– *Les Structures anthropologiques de l'imaginaire: Introduction à l'archétypologie générale.* Paris: Bordas, Collection Études Supérieures, 1969.

Duret, Claude. *Histoire admirable des plantes et herbes esmerveillables.* Paris, 1605.

Eckhardt, Caroline, ed. *Essays in the Numerical Criticism of Medieval Literature.* Lewisburg, PA: Bucknell University Press, 1980.

Einhorn, J.W. *Spiritalis Unicornis*. Munich: W. Fink, 1976.

Eliade, Mircea. *The Forge and the Crucible*. Trans. Stephen Corrin. London: Rider & Co., 1962.

– *Shamanism, Archaic Techniques of Ecstasy*. Trans. Willard R. Trask. London: Kegan Paul, 1964.

– *Rites and Symbols of Initiation: The Mysteries of Birth and Rebirth*. Trans. Willard R. Trask. New York: Harper and Row, 1965.

– *The Two and the One*. Trans. J.M. Cohen. Chicago: University of Chicago Press, 1965.

– *Zalmoxis, the Vanishing God*. Trans. Willard R. Trask. Chicago and London: The University of Chicago Press, 1970.

Encyclopedia of Religion. Ed. James Hastings. 12 vols. New York: Scribner, 1951.

Eriugena, John Scotus. *Homélie sur le prologue de Jean*. Trans. Édouard Jeauneau. Sources Chrétiennes 151. Paris: Éditions du Cerf, 1969.

– *Commentaire sur l'Évangile de Jean*. Trans. and intro. Édouard Jeauneau. Paris: du Cerf, 1972.

– *Expositiones in ierarchiam coelestem*. Ed. J. Barbet. Corpus Christianorum XXXI. Turnholt, 1975.

– *Periphyseon: The Divine Nature*. Trans. I.P. Sheldon; revised by John J. O'Meara. Montreal: Bellarmin, 1987.

Evans, Joan, and Mary S. Serjeanston, eds. *English Medieval Lapidaries*. EETS, 190. London: Oxford University Press, 1960.

Evola, J. *The Metaphysics of Sex*. Translation of *Metafisica del Sesso*. New York: Inner Traditions International, 1983.

Faggin, Giuseppe. *Diabolicità del Rospo*. Vicenza: Neri pozza Editore, 1973.

Feibleman, James K. "Disorder." In *The Concept of Order*, ed. Paul G. Kuntz, 3–13. Seattle: University of Washington Press, 1968.

Flaubert, Gustave. *The Temptation of Saint Anthony*. Trans. Kitty Mrosovsky. Ithaca, NY: Cornell University Press, 1981.

Foucault, Michel. *The Order of Things: An Archaeology of the Human Sciences*. Trans. R.D. Laing. New York: Vintage Books, 1973.

Foussard, Jean-Claude. "Apparence et apparition: La Notion de 'phantasia' chez Jean Scot." In *Jean Scot et l'histoire de la philosophie*, ed. René Roques, 337–48. Colloques Internationaux du CNRS, no. 561. Laon, 1975.

Fraser, J., trans. "The Passion of Saint Christopher." *Revue Celtique* 34 (1913): 307–25.

Friedman, John Block. *The Monstrous Races in Medieval Art and Thought*. Cambridge, MA: Harvard University Press, 1981.

Gaidoz, M.H. "Saint Christophe a tête de chien en Irlande et en Russie." *Mémoires de la Société Nationale des Antiquaires de France*. 76 (1924): 192–201.

Gaskell, George Arthur. *A Dictionary of the Sacred Language of all Scriptures and Myths*. New York: Lucis Publishing Co., 1930.

Geisberg, M. *Der deutsche Einblatt-Holzschnitt in der ersten Haefte des XVI. Jahrh.* Munich, 1927.

Gellrich, Jesse M. *The Idea of the Book in the Middle Ages: Language Theory, Mythology, and Fiction.* Ithaca, NY and London: Cornell University Press, 1985.

Gersh, Stephen. *From Iamblicus to Eriugena: An Investigation of the Prehistory and Evolution of the Pseudo-Dionysian Tradition.* Leiden: E.J. Brill, 1978.

Gesner, Konrad. *Icones animalium quadrupedum viviparorum et oviparorum ...* Tiguri, 1560.

– *Icones animalium aquatilium ...* Tiguri, 1560.

– *Historiae animalium.* Frankfurt: Henrici Laurentii, 1617–21.

Gessler, Jean. *La Vierge barbue: La légende de sainte Wilgeforte ou Ontcommer.* Brussels: Folklore Brabançon, 15, 1938.

Giesel, Helmut. *Studien zur Symbolik der Musikinstrumente im Schriftum der Alten und Mittelalterlichen Kirche.* Regensburg: G. Bosse, 1978.

Girard, René. *Violence and the Sacred.* Trans. Patrick Gregory. Baltimore, MD and London: Johns Hopkins University Press, 1979.

Grant, Robert M. *The Secret Sayings of Jesus.* London: Collins, 1960.

Graves, Robert. *The Greek Myths.* 2 vols. 1955. Baltimore, MD: Penguin Books, 1964.

Graves, Robert, and Raphael Patai. *Hebrew Myths: The Book of Genesis.* London: Cassel & Co., 1964.

Griffiths, John, ed. *The Cell of Self-Knowledge: Early English Mystical Treatises by Margery Kempe and Others.* New York: Crossroad, 1981.

Grimal, Pierre. *Dictionnaire de la mythologie greque et romaine.* Paris: Presses Universitaires de France, 1982.

Hadas, Moses, trans. *Oedipus.* New York: Liberal Arts Press, 1955.

Haines, Victor Yelverton. *The Fortunate Fall of Sir Gawain: The Typology of Sir Gawain and the Green Knight.* Washington, DC: University Press of America, 1982.

Halleux, Robert and Jacques Schamp, trans. and eds. *Les Lapidaires grecs.* Paris: Les Belles Lettres, 1985.

Hamilton, Edith, and Huntington Cairns, eds. *The Collected Dialogues of Plato, Including the Letters.* 1961. Princeton, NJ: Princeton University Press, 1989.

Hardy, Edward R. ed., *Christology of the Later Fathers.* Philadelphia: Westminster Press, 1954.

Haren, Michael. *Medieval Thought: The Western Intellectual Tradition from Antiquity to the Thirteenth Century.* Houndmills, Basingstoke, England: Macmillan, 1992.

Harf-Lancner, Laurence. *Les Fées au moyen âge: Morgan et Mélusine.* Paris: Champion, 1984.

– *Métamorphose et bestiaire fantastique du moyen âge.* Paris: École Normale Supérieure des Jeunes Filles, 1985.

Harpham, Geoffrey Galt. *On the Grotesque: Strategies of Contradiction in Art and Literature.* Princeton, NJ: Princeton University Press, 1982.

– *The Ascetic Imperative in Culture and Criticism.* Chicago and London: University of Chicago Press, 1987.

Hart, Kevin. *The Trespass of the Sign: Deconstruction, Theology, and Philosophy.* Cambridge and New York: Cambridge University Press, 1989.

Hedelin. *Des satyres, brutes, monstres, et démons.* Paris, 1627.

Hegel, Georg Wilhelm Freidrich. *Hegel's Phenomenology of Spirit.* Trans. Howard P. Kainz. University Park, PA: Penn State University Press, 1994.

Heidegger, Martin. *Existence and Being.* Chicago: Henry Regnery Co., 1949.

– *Chemins qui ne mènent nulle part.* Paris: Gallimard, 1962.

Hermann, H.J. *Die Illuminierten Handschriften im Tirol.* Leipzig: K.W. Hiersemann, 1905.

Herodotus. *The Histories.* Trans. Aubrey de Selincourt. London: Harmondsworth, England, 1972.

Herrtage, Sidney J.H., ed. *The Early English Version of the Gesta Romanorum.* London: Early English Text, Society, Oxford University Press, 1962.

Hesiod. *Theogeny; and Works and Days.* Trans. and intro. M.L. West. Oxford and New York: Oxford University Press, 1988.

Hildegard of Bingen. *De Operatione*, in *Welt und Mensch*, ed. Heinrich Schipperges. Salzburg: Otto Muller Verlag, 1965.

– *Scivias.* Ed. Aldegundis Fuhrkotter with Angela Carlevaris. *Corpus Christianorum continuatio mediaevalis* 52 A. Turnholt, 1978.

Hopkins, Jasper. *Nicholas of Cusa on Learned Ignorance: A Translation and an Appraisal of De Doctrina Ignorantia.* Minneapolis: Arthur J. Banning Press, 1981.

Hopkins, Jasper, and Henry Richardson, eds. and trans. *Anselm of Canterbury.* 4 vols. Toronto: The Edward Mellen Press, 1974–76.

Hortus Sanitatis. Strassburg: Johann Pruss, 1497.

Hubert, Henri and Marcel Mauss. *Sacrifice: Its Nature and Function.* Trans. W.D. Hall. London: Cohen and West, 1964.

Hugh of St Victor. *Appendix ad Hugonis opera dogmatica*, in *Patrologia latina* 177, col. 626.

– *Didascalicon.* Trans. and ed. Jerome Taylor. New York: Columbia University Press 1961.

Huizinga, J. *The Waning of the Middle Ages.* Trans. F. Hopman. London: Penguin Books, 1987.

Iamblichus. *The Exhortation to Philosophy.* Trans. Thomas M. Johnson, ed. Stephen Neuville. Grand Rapids MI: Phanes Press, 1988.

– *The Theology of Arithmetic.* Trans. Robin Waterfield. Grand Rapids MI: Phanes Press, 1988.

Isidore of Seville. *Etymologiarum Sive Originum Liber XI.* Trans. with an introduction by William D. Sharpe. In *Isidore of Seville: The Medical Writings.* Transactions of the American Philosophical Society. n.s., 54, pt. 2, 1963.

Izzi, Massimo *I Mostri e l'Immaginario.* Rome: Manilo Basaia, 1982.

Jacobus of Liege. *Speculum musicale.* Ed. Roger Bragard. Rome: American Institute of Musicology, 1955.

Jacobus de Voragine. *The Golden Legend of Jacobus de Voragine.* Trans. Granger Ryan and Helmut Rippergen. London: Arno Press, 1969.

James, M.R. "Pictor in Carmine." *Archaeologia* 94: 141–66.

Janson, H.W. *Apes and Ape Lore in the Middle Ages and the Renaissance.* London: Warburg Institute, 1952.

Jennings, Lee Byron. *The Ludicrous Demon.* Berkeley and Los Angeles: University of California Press, 1965.

Jones-Davies, Marie-Thérèse, ed. *Le Paradoxe au temps de la renaissance.* Paris: Touzot, 1982.

Julian of Norwich, *The Revelations of Divine Love.* London: Burns and Oates, 1961.

Jung, C.G. *Métamorphoses et symboles de la libido.* Paris: Montaigne, 1932.

Kappler, Claude. *Monstres, démons, et merveilles à la fin du moyen âge.* Paris: Payot, 1980.

– *Le Monstre: Pouvoir de l'imposture.* Paris: PUF, 1980.

Kavanaugh, Kieran, ed. and trans. *John of the Cross: Selected Writings.* New York: Paulist Press, 1987.

Kayser, Wolfgang. *The Grotesque in Art and Literature.* Trans. Ulrich Weisstein Gloucester, MA: P. Smith, 1968.

Kircher, Athanasius. *Turris Babel.* Amsterdam: Waesberg, 1679.

Kirchmaier, George. *On the Unicorn.* In Edmund Goldsmid, *Un-Natural History.* Collectanea Adamantaea, 15, Edinburgh 1886.

Klaeber, F., ed. *Beowulf.* Boston: D.C. Heath, 1950.

Klibansky, Raymond. *Plato's Parmenides in the Middle Ages and the Rennaissance.* London: The Warburg Institute, 1953.

– *Saturn and Melancholy.* London: Nelson, 1964.

– *Continuity of the Platonic Tradition during the Middle Ages.* 1939 Reprint, Munich: Kraus, 1981.

Klingender, F. *Animals in Art and Thought to the End of the Middle Ages.* Cambridge, MA: MIT Press, 1971.

Knight, Richard Payne. *Discourse on the Worship of Priapus.* London, 1865.

Kuntz, Paul G., ed. *The Concept of Order.* Seattle, WA and London: University of Washington Press, 1968.

Kunz, George Frederick. *The Curious Lore of Precious Stones.* Philadelphia, PA: J.B. Lippincott, 1913.

Lacan, Jacques. *Speech and Language in Psychoanalysis.* Trans. with notes by Anthony Wilden. Baltimore, MD: Johns Hopkins University Press, 1981.

Lacaze, Charlotte. *The "Vie de Saint Denis" Manuscript.* New York and London: Garland Publishing Inc., 1979.

L'Ancre, Pierre. *Tableau de l'inconstance des mauvaises anges.* Paris: A. L'Angelier, 1607.

Lascault, Gilbert. *Le Monstre dans l'art occidental: Un problème esthétique.* Paris: Klincksieck, 1973.

Lawler, Justus George. *Celestial Pantomime: Poetic Structures of Transcendence.* New Haven and London: Yale University Press, 1979.

Le Paumier, Claude Stephen. *Ambroise Paré d'après de nouveaux documents découverts aux archives nationales.* Paris: Charavay Frères, 1884.

Leclercq, Jean. "Influence and Noninfluence of Dionysius in the Western Middle Ages." In *Pseudo-Dionysius: The Complete Works.* Trans. Colm Luibheid. New York: The Paulist Press, 1987.

– ed. *S. Bernardi Opera.* Rome: Editiones Cistercienes, 1963.

Lee, H. *The Vegetable Lamb of Tartary.* London: Sampson and Law, 1887.

Leighton, John M. "Christian and Pagan Symbolism and Ritual in *Sir Gawain and the Green Knight.*" *Theoria* 43 (1974): 49–62.

Leroquais, V. *Les Sacramentaires et les missels.* Paris, 1924.

Liebman, C. *Étude sur la vie en prose de St Denis* New York: W.J. Humphrey Press, 1942.

Livingston, Paisley, ed. *Disorder and Order: Proceedings of the Stanford International Symposium.* Anma Libri. Saratoga, CA, 1984.

Livre des merveilles (Marco Polo, Odoric de Pordonone, Mandeville, Hayton, etc.). Paris: Berthaud, 1907.

Loomis, Roger Sherman. *Wales and the Arthurian Legend.* Cardiff: University of Wales Press, 1956.

Lycosthenes, Conrad. *Prodigiorum ac ostentorum chronicon ...* Basel, 1557.

Lydgate, John. *Siege of Thebes.* Ed. Axel Erdmann. EETS, Extra Series, 108. Oxford: Oxford University Press, 1960.

– *Fall of Princes.* Ed. Henry Bergen. EETS, Extra Series, 121. Oxford: Oxford University Press, 1967.

MacCormac, Earl R. *A Cognitive Theory of Metaphor.* Cambridge, MA: MIT Press, 1985.

MacFarlane, "Isidore of Seville on the Pagan Gods." *Transactions of the American Philological Society* 70 (1980).

Macrobius. *The Saturnalia.* Ed. Percival Vaughn Davies. New York: Columbia University Press, 1969.

– *De Nuptiis Philologiae et Mercurii.* Ed. Fr. Eyssenhardt. Lipsiae: Teubneri, 1893.

Maeterlinck, L. *Le Genre satirique dans la peinture flamande.* Paris: G. van Oest, 1907.

Mandeville, John [Sir]. *Travels.* Ed. C.W.R.D. Moseley. Harmondsworth, England: Penguin Books, 1987.

Manzalaoui, M.A., ed. *Secretum Secretorum: Nine English Versions.* EETS, 276. Oxford: Oxford University Press, 1977.

Marenbon, John. *Early Medieval Philosophy (480–1150).* London and New York: Routledge, 1988.

Martin, Ernst. *Histoire des monstres de l'Antiquité jusqu'à nos jours.* Paris, 1880.

Marvell, Andrew. "To His Coy Mistress." In Norton Anthology of English Literature, 5th ed. Vol. 1. Ed. M.H. Adams. New York: W.W. Norton, 1986.

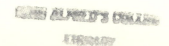

Mazzeo, Joseph. *Renaissance and Seventeenth Century Studies*. New York: Columbia University Press, 1964.

McCulloch, Florence. *Mediaeval Latin and French Bestiaries*. Chapel Hill NC: University of North Carolina Press, 1962.

McKeon, Richard, ed. *The Basic Works of Aristotle*. New York: Random House, 1971.

Megasthenes. *Ancient India as Described by Megasthenes and Arrian*. Ed. and intro. J.W. McCrindle. Calcutta: Chuckervertty, Chatterjee, 1960.

Mely, Fernand de. *Les lapidaires de l'antiquité et du moyen âge*. Paris: E. Leroux, 1898–1902.

Michel, Alain. "Rhétorique, philosophie, christianisme: Le Paradoxe de la renaissance devant les grands courants de la pensée antique." In *Paradoxe au temps de la renaissance*, ed. Marie-Thérèse Jones-Davies, 47–58. Paris: J. Touzot, 1982.

Middle English Physiologus. Ed. Hanneke Wirtjes. Oxford: EETS, Oxford University Press, 1991.

Milton, John. *Paradise Lost*. In *The Norton Anthology of English Literature*. 5th ed., vol. 1. New York, 1986.

Molanus. *De historia ss. imaginum et picturam*. 4 vols. Ed. Joannes Paquot. Louvain, 1771.

More, St Thomas. *A Dialogue Concerning Heresies*, ed. Thomas Lawler. In *The Complete Works*. Vol. 6 New Haven, CT: Yale University Press, 1981.

Newman, Barbara. *Sister of Wisdom: St Hildegard's Theology of the Feminine*. Berkeley: University of California Press, 1987.

Newman, John Henry [Cardinal]. *The Idea of a University*. Ed. I.T. Ker. Oxford: The Clarendon Press, 1976.

O'Meara, John J., introduction to *Periphyseon: The Division of Nature*. Montreal: Bellarmin, 1987.

O'Rourke, Fran. *Pseudo-Dionysius and the Metaphysics of Aquinas*. Leiden: E.J. Brill, 1992.

Obsequens, Julius. *Prodigiorum Liber*. Bale, 1552.

Odoric de Pordenone. *Relatio*. In *Recueil de voyages et de documents pour servir à l'histoire de la géographie*, ed. Henri Cordier. Vol 10. Paris, 1891.

Old English Physiologus. Trans. Albert S. Cook and James H. Pitman. New Haven: Yale University Press, 1921.

Palladius, *On the People of India and the Brahmins: The Brahmin Episode*. Ed. and trans. S.V. Yankowski. Ansback: E. Kottmeier & E.G. Kostetzky, 1962.

Paré, Ambroise. *Des monstres et prodiges*. Ed. Jean Céard. Geneva: Droz, 1971.

Park, Katherine, and Lorraine J. Dalston. "Unnatural Conceptions: The Study of Monsters in Sixteenth and Seventeenth-Century France and England." *Past and Present* 92 (1981): 21–54.

Payne, Ann. *Medieval Beasts*. London: British Library, 1990.

Peck, Russell A. "Number as Cosmic Language." In *Essays in the Numerical Criticism of Medieval Literature*, ed. Caroline Eckhardt, 15–64. Lewisburg, PA: Bucknell University Press, 1980.

Pettazzoni, R. "The Pagan Origins of the Three-Headed Representations of the Christian Trinity." *Journal of the Warburg and Courtauld Institutes* 9 (1946): 135–51.

– *The All Knowing God.* Trans. H.J. Rose. London: Methuen & Co., 1956.

– *L'essere supremo nelle religioni primitive.* Turin: Einaudi, 1957.

Philo. "On the Creation" and "Allegorical Interpretation." In *Philo.* Trans. F.H. Colson and Rev. G.H. Whitaker. 10 vols. London and Cambridge, MA: Loeb Classical Library, Harvard University Press, 1929.

Plato. *Sophist and Timaeus.* In *The Collected Dialogues of Plato, including the Letters,* ed. Edith Hamilton and Huntington Cairns. Princeton: Princeton University Press, 1961.

Pliny. *Natural history.* 10 vols. Trans. H. Rackham. Cambridge, MA: Harvard University Press, 1938.

Plotinus. *Enneads.* In *Works.* Trans. A.H. Armstrong. Cambridge, MA: Harvard University, 1966.

Porphory the Phoenician. *Isagoge.* Trans. and intro. Edward W. Warren. Toronto: Pontifical Institute of Mediaeval Studies, 1975.

Proclus. *In platonis rem publicam commentarii.* Ed. G. Kroll. Lipsiae: Teubneri, 1899–1901.

Pseudo-Callisthenes. *The Romance of Alexander the Great.* Trans. from the Armenian version with an introduction by Albert Mugrdich Wolohojian. New York and London: Columbia University Press, 1969.

Pseudo-Dionysius. *The Complete Works.* Trans. Colm Luibheid. New York: Paulist Press, 1987.

Puhvel, Martin. "Art and the Supernatural in *Sir Gawain and the Green Knight.*" *Arthurian Literature* 5 (1955): 1–69.

Rabanus Maurus. *De universo: Excerpts (De Avibus).* N.p., n.d.

Ramusio, Giambattista. *Navigazione e viaggi.* Venice, 1550–59.

Randall, Dale. "Was the Green Knight a Fiend?" *Studia Philologica* 57 (1960): 479–91.

Randall, Lillian M.C. *Images in the Margins of Gothic Manuscripts.* Berkeley and Los Angeles: University of California Press, 1966.

Réau, Louis. *L'iconographie de l'art chrétien.* 6 vols. Paris: Presses Universitaires de France, 1955–59.

Reinach, S. *Pierres gravés.* Paris: Firmin Didot, 1895.

Renouvin, J. *Histoire de l'origine et des progrès de la gravure dans les Pays Bas et l'Allemagne.* Brussels: M. Hayez, 1860.

Rist, J.M. *Plotinus: The Road to Reality.* Cambridge: Cambridge University Press, 1967.

Ritter, G., and J. Lafond. *Manuscrits peints de l'école de Rouen.* Rouen: A. Lestringant, 1913.

Robert, Carl. *Oidipus: Geschichte eines poetischen Stoffes im grieschen Alterum.* 2 vols. Berlin, 1915.

Robertson, D.W., Jr. "Why the Devil Wears Green." *MLN* 69 (1954): 470–2.

Rodkinson, Michael L., ed. The Babylonian Talmud. Boston: The Talmud Society, 1918.

Roheim, Geza. *Panic of the Gods*. New York: Harper and Row, 1972.

Romance of William of Palerne. Ed. Walter W. Skeat. London: EETS, Extra Series 1, 1867.

Rondelet, G. *Histoire entière des poissons*. Lyon: M. Bonhome, 1558.

Roques, René. "Symbolisme et théologie négative chez le Pseudo-Deny." *Bulletin de l'Association Guillaume Budé* 4th series (March 1957): 97–112.

– *Libres sentiers vers l'érigénisme*. Rome: Ateneo, 1975.

– *L'Univers dionysien: Structure hiérarchique du monde selon le pseudo-denys*. Paris: Éditions du Cerf, 1983.

– Preface to *Pseudo-Dionysius: The Complete Works*. Trans. Colm Luibheid. New York: Paulist Press, 1987.

Rorem, Paul. "Biblical and Liturgical Symbols within the Pseudo-Dionysian Synthesis." *Studies and Texts* 71. Toronto: Pontifical Institute of Medieval Studies, 1984.

– "Introduction" to *Pseudo-Dionysius: The Complete Works*. Trans. Colm Luibheid. New York: Paulist Press, 1987.

Rosan, L.J. *The Philosophy of Proclus*. New York: Cosmos, 1949.

Rowland, Beryl. *Birds with Human Souls: A Guide to Bird Symbolism*. Knoxville TN: The University of Tennessee Press, 1978.

– *Animals with Human Faces: A Guide to Animal Symbolism*. Knoxville TN: The University of Tennessee Press, 1973.

Ryan, J.S. "Sir Gawain and St. Winifred: Hagiography and Miracle in West Mercia." *Parergon*, n.s. 4, 1986.

Saintyves, P., *Les Saints successeurs des dieux*. Paris: E. Nourry, 1907.

– "Ceintures magiques et processions enveloppantes." *Revue des traditions populaires*. 25 (1910): 113–23.

– "Les Saints céphalophores: Étude de folklore hagiographique." *Revue de l'histoire des religions* 99 (1929): 158–231.

Saluti, Coluccio. *Epistolario*. 4 vols. Ed. Francesco Novati. Rome: E.C. Forzani, 1891–1911.

Santarcangeli, Paolo. *Il Libro dei Labirinti*. Florence: Vallechi Editore, 1965.

Saward, John. "Towards an Apophatic Anthropology." *Irish Theological Quarterly* 41, 3 (1974): 222–34.

Schedel, Hartmann. *Chronica Mundi*. Nuremberg, 1493.

– *Buch der Chronicon*.

Schramm, A. *Der Bilderschmuck der Frühdrucke*. 8 vols. Leipzig: Deutsches Museum für Buch und Schrift, 1920–24.

Secretum Secretorum: Nine English Versions. Ed. M.A. Manzalaoui. EETS, Original Series 276. Oxford: Oxford University Press, 1977.

Serres, Michel. *Hermès ou la communication*. Paris: Éditions de Minuit, 1968.

Seubert, Bernard James, ed. *Geu Saint Denis*. Geneva: Librairie Droz, 1974.

Seznec, Jean. *Les Sources de l'épisode des dieux dans la Tentation de Saint Antoine*. Paris: J. Vrin 1940.

– *La survivance des dieux antiques*. London: Warburg Institute, 1940.

– *Nouvelles études sur la tentation de saint Antoine*. London: The Warburg Institute, 1949.

Shichtman, Martin B. "Sir Gawain and the Green Knight: A Lesson in the Terror of History." *Papers on Language and Literature* 22 (1986): 3–15.

Shoaf, R. A. *The Poem as Green Girdle: Commercium in Sir Gawain and the Green Knight*. Gainesville, FL: University of Florida Press, 1984.

Sidney, Philip [Sir]. *Defence of Poesy*. In *The Norton Anthology of English Literature*. 5th ed., vol. 1. New York, 1986.

Skeat, Walter W. *Wars of Alexander: An Alliterative Romance*. Ed. and Trans. chiefly from the *Historia Alexandri Magni de Preliis* by W.W. Skeat. EETS, Extra Series 47. London: Trubner, 1886.

– ed. *The Romance of William of Palerne*. EETS, Extra Series 1. New York, 1981.

Sloet van de Beele, L.A.J.W. [Baron]. *De Heilige Ontkommer of Wilgeforthis*. 'S-Gravenhagen: M. Nijhoff, 1884.

Solinus. *The excellent and pleasant worke, Collectanea rerum memorabilium of Caius Julius Solinus*. Trans. Arthur Golding. Gainsville, FL: Scholars' Facsimiles and Reprints, 1955.

Spenser, Edmund. *Faerie Queene*. In *The Norton Anthology of English Literature*. 5th ed., vol. 1. New York, 1986.

Strabo. *The Geography of Strabo*. Trans. and ed. Horace Leonard Jones. London: William Heinemann, 1939.

Syrianus. *In Metaph*. Ed. W. Kroll. Berlin, 1902.

Tannahill, Reay. *Flesh and Blood: A History of the Cannibal Complex*. London: Hamilton, 1975.

Tertullian. *Liber adv. Valentinianos: contre les valentiniens*. Paris: Cerf, Sources Chrétiennes 280–1, 1980–81.

Texelius, P. *Phoenix visus et auditus*. Roterdam, 1703.

Thevet, A. *La Cosmographie universelle*. Paris, 1575.

Thomas de Cantimpré. *Liber de monstruosis homenilius Orientis*. In *Festschrift zur Jahrhundertfeier der Universität Breslau*, ed. Alfons Hilka. Breslau, 1911.

Thompson, C.J.S. *The Mystic Mandrake*. London: Rider & Co., 1934.

Thorndike, Lynn. *A History of Magic and Experimental Science*. 6 vols. New York: Columbia University Press, 1941.

Todorov, Tzvetan. *Introduction à la littérature fantastique*. Paris: Éditions du Seuil, 1970.

Tolkien, J.R.R., and E.V. Gordon, eds. *Sir Gawain and the Green Knight*. Oxford: The Clarendon Press, 1960.

Trouillard, Jean. *La Mystagogie de Proclus*. Paris: Société d'Édition Les Belles Lettres, 1982.

Tuzin, Donald. "Cannibalism and Arapesh Cosmology." In *The Ethnography of Cannibalism*, edited by Paula Brown and Donald Tuzin, 67–71. Washington: Society for Psychological Anthropology, 1983.

Uhlfelder, Myra, ed. *Periphyseon*. Indianapolis: Bobbs-Merrill, 1976.

Van Den Broek, R. *The Myth of the Phoenix*. Leiden: E. J. Brill, 1972.

Villeneuve, Roland. *Histoire du cannibalisme*. Mesnil sur l'Estree: Le Livre Club du Libraire, 1965.

Von Megenberg, Konrad. *Buch der Natur*. Augsberg: Johannes Bamler, 1478.

– *Buch der Natur*. In A. Schramm, *Der Bilderschmuck der Frühdrucke*. 8 vols. Leipzig: Deutsches Museum für Buch und Schrift, 1920–24.

Von Simson, Otto. *The Gothic Cathedral: Origins of Gothic Architecture and the Medieval Concept of Order*. Princeton, NJ: Princeton University Press, 1974.

Wakeman, Mary. *God's Battle with the Monsters: A Study in Biblical Imagery*. Leiden: E. J. Brill, 1973.

Wars of Alexander: An Alliterative Romance. Ed. and trans. chiefly from the *Historia Alexandri Magni de Preliis* by W.W. Skeat. EETS Extra Series 47. London: Trubner, 1886.

Weisheipl, James. *Friar Thomas d'Aquino: His Life, Thought and Work*. New York: Doubleday, 1974.

Whaite, H.C. *Saint Christopher in English Mediaeval Wallpainting*. London: E. Benn Ltd., 1929.

Wildridge, T. Tindall. *The Grotesque in Church Art*. London: William Andrews & Co., 1899. Reprint, Detroit, MI: Gale Research Co., 1969.

Williams, David. "Radical Therapy in the Miller's Tale." *Chaucer Review* 15 (1981): 227–35.

– *Cain and Beowulf*. Toronto: University of Toronto Press, 1982.

Wilson, Peter Lamborn. *Angels*. New York, 1980.

Wittgenstein, L. *Tractatus Logico-Philosophicus*. Trans. C.K. Ogden. 1922. New York and London: Routledge and Kegan Paul, 1986.

Wittkower, Rudolf. "Marvels of the East: A Study in the History of Monsters." *Journal of the Warburg and Courtauld Institutes* 5 (1942): 159–97.

– *Allegory and the Migration of Symbols*. Boulder, CO: Westview Press, 1977.

Wolters, Clifton, trans. *The Cloud of Unknowing and Other Works*. Harmondsworth, England: Penguin, 1973.

Wood, Charles T. "The Doctor's Dilemma." *Speculum* 56 (1981): 710–27.

Wright, Thomas. *Histoire de la caricature et du grotesque dans la littérature et dans l'art*. Paris, 1875.

Yannaras, Christos. *De l'absence et de l'inconnaisance de dieu d'après les écrits aréopagitiques et Martin Heidegger*. Trans. Jacques Touraille. Paris: Cerf, 1971.

Index

Page numbers in italics refer to illustrations.